THE
SOURCES OF
SHAKESPEARE'S PLAYS

To Geoffrey Bullough

THE
SOURCES OF
SHAKESPEARE'S PLAYS

by

KENNETH MUIR

NEW HAVEN
YALE UNIVERSITY PRESS
1978

Published in the United Kingdom and Commonwealth
by Methuen & Co. Ltd.
First published in the United States of America
by Yale University Press in 1978

Library of Congress catalog card number: 77–10295
International Standard Book Number: 0–300–02212–3

Printed in Great Britain.

CONTENTS

PREFACE

WHEN *Shakespeare's Sources I* appeared in 1957 I had hoped to complete the second volume by 1960. For various reasons this proved to be impossible and I have had many enquiries, and a few reproaches, during the past fifteen years. Meanwhile Professor Geoffrey Bullough had completed in eight volumes his *Narrative and Dramatic Sources of Shakespeare* and this splendid work has necessitated a change of plan in mine. As my first volume has been out of print, and as I have changed my mind on a number of points, I have revised this volume and added a discussion of the Histories. The other part of the original plan – a detailed discussion of Shakespeare's reading – will, I hope, be published in a series of separate essays.

It will be noticed that the revision of the previous work has been substantial and that the publication of *Shakespeare as Collaborator*, *Shakespeare's Tragic Sequence*, and *Shakespeare the Professional*, together with a forthcoming book on the Comedies, has enabled me to save a good deal of space in the present volume.

In my original preface I acknowledged the generous help of many scholars. Six of them, John Dover Wilson, Kenneth Allott, Ernest Schanzer, James Maxwell, Frederick May and Arnold Davenport are now dead. Many of them have been appointed to chairs, including G. K. Hunter, Harold Brooks, Ernst Honigmann, Inga-Stina Ewbank and R. A. Foakes. I have incurred renewed indebtedness to them all. I also mentioned two theses written under my supervision: I must now add those of Dr S. Carr, Mr P. Akhtar, Pauline Dalton, and Dorothy Earnshaw. My greatest debt, however, is to Geoffrey Bullough.

I was awarded a Visiting fellowship at the Folger Shakespeare Library in 1957; and in 1975 the Leverhulme Trust awarded me an Emeritus Fellowship which has enabled me to expedite the work with the expert assistance of Mrs Jane Sherman. To both these bodies and to her I wish to express my gratitude.

University of Liverpool   KENNETH MUIR

ABBREVIATIONS

I

INTRODUCTION

THE PURPOSE of this book is, first, to ascertain where possible what sources Shakespeare used for the plots of his plays and to discuss the use he made of them; and, secondly, to give illustrations, necessarily selective, of the way in which his general reading is woven into the texture of his work. Since Anders wrote *Shakespeare's Books* in 1904 several bibliographies and many annotated editions of his plays have appeared. These have increased our knowledge of Shakespeare's reading[1] and have shown that it was more extensive than was thought at the beginning of the century.

It is necessary at the outset to say something of Shakespeare's knowledge of foreign languages. T. W. Baldwin in his monumental volumes[2] has given us a clear idea of the kind of education Shakespeare would have followed at a petty school and a grammar school. As he somewhere acquired the equivalent knowledge, there is no reason to doubt that he attended both; but it is possible that the crisis in his father's fortunes may have meant that he did not complete the full curriculum. He acquired a reasonable knowledge of Latin, and perhaps a smattering of Greek.

The extent of Shakespeare's classical learning is nevertheless still a matter of dispute. Some believe that Jonson's 'small Latin and less Greek' should be taken to mean 'hardly any Latin and no Greek'.[3] Others think that although Shakespeare had little or no Greek, he understood Latin 'pretty well' (to use the phrase of an early biographer[4]), and that his knowledge of the language was small only in comparison with Jonson's or Chapman's. Those who adhere to the former point of view show that many of the parallels with Latin literature, collected by generations of critics, may well be fortuitous, or may be borrowed from some intermediate source; that Golding's translation of the *Metamorphoses* is so bad that a good Latin scholar would not have tolerated it;[5] that Shakespeare's actual quotations from Latin authors are mostly in early plays – *Henry VI* and *Titus Andronicus* – in which he may have had collaborators, or of passages so familiar that they prove nothing about his competence as a latinist; that he makes a number of blunders about classical mythology;[6] that his spelling 'triumpherate' shows that he was ignorant of the derivation of the word;[7] and that he is guilty of shocking anachronisms. None of these arguments has much substance. It is true that many of the alleged parallels between Shakespeare's works and Latin literature are unconvincing. Percy Simpson's list of parallels does not contain a single one which is beyond dispute.[8] He does not distinguish between works which were available in translation and those which were not. In some cases he has ignored sources more easily accessible than those he suggests: Shakespeare did not have to go to Latin comedy for the plot of *Pericles* when he had more obvious sources, which he certainly used, by Gower and Twine. Some ideas and images which may be traced ultimately to Latin writers had become commonplaces by the sixteenth century. There is no reason to believe that Helena, at the end of the first scene of *A Midsummer-Night's Dream*, is echoing Propertius in her complaints about Cupid.[9] Laertes' words about the dead Ophelia –

> from her fair and unpolluted flesh
> May violets spring –   (v. i. 233–4)

fit in with the flower-imagery associated with the girl and are not necessarily based on lines by Persius which, we are told, Shakespeare could have read in the notes to Mantuan:[10]

> nunc non e tumulo fortunataque favilla
> nascentur violae?

On the other hand, since Shakespeare alludes to two of Horace's poems in the storm-scenes of *King Lear*, critics have been unduly sceptical about two Horatian echoes in earlier plays.[11] Horace instructs a girl:[12]

> prima nocte domum claude neque in vias
> sub cantu querulae despice tibiae.

Shylock similarly instructs Jessica:

> When you hear the drum,
> And the vile squealing of the wry-neck'd fife,
> Clamber not you up to the casements then,
> Nor thrust your head into the public street.
>
> (II. v. 28–31)

The other parallel is even more striking. The line in one of Horace's *Satires* (II. 5) –

> Furius hibernas cana nive conspuet Alpes –

must surely be the origin of the address by the French King to his nobles in *Henry V*:

> Rush on his host as doth the melted snow
> Upon the valleys, whose low vassal seat
> The Alps doth spit, and void his rheum upon.
>
> (III. v. 50–2)

Golding's translation of Ovid's *Metamorphoses* is read today largely because it is known to have been a favourite of Shakespeare's, but we cannot deduce from its clumsiness that he could read Latin only with difficulty. He doubtless read some Ovid at school, and a copy of the *Metamorphoses*, bearing his possibly forged signature, is still in existence. Even at the end of his career, thirty years after he left school, he still remembered enough Latin to improve on the accuracy of Golding's translation. Prospero's farewell to his art is based on Medea's invocation in Book VII, and the phrasing is influenced by Golding's. In the opening words,

> Ye elves of hills, brooks, standing lakes,

Shakespeare borrows Golding's precise phrasing. But it is equally clear that he also used the original Latin. Ovid uses the words 'ventos abigoque vocoque'; Golding translates 'I rayse and lay the windes'; Shakespeare, more accurately, has 'call'd forth the mutinous winds'. A more striking proof that Shakespeare was not merely relying on Golding can be seen from their versions of the lines:

> vivaque saxa, sua convulsaque robora terra,
> et silvas moveo. (VII. 204–5)

Golding translates:

> And from the bowels of the Earth both stones and trees doe drawe.
> Whole woods and Forestes I remoue: (VII. 272–3)

Prospero boasts that he has

> rifted Jove's stout oak
> With his own bolt . . .
>   and by the spurs pluck'd up
> The pine and cedar.

It has been pointed out[13] that 'pluck'd up' conveys, more faithfully than Golding's version, the sense of 'convulsa'; that Shakespeare specifies the particular kind of tree, as Golding does not; and that by the epithet 'stout' he alludes to the alternative meaning of 'robora'.

Shakespeare, then, used translations when they were available; but he did not use them slavishly, and there is plenty of evidence that he read Latin works of which there was no translation – two plays by Plautus, Buchanan's and Leslie's works on Scottish history, and (if the last two Sonnets were indeed his) a Latin version of poems in the Greek Anthology. He knew some Virgil in the original, though he may also have read four translations by Douglas, Surrey, Phaer, and Stanyhurst. He knew some of Erasmus' *Colloquia*;[14] he consulted his *Adagia*;[15] he probably read *The Praise of Folly*, either in the original or in Challoner's translation;[16] and apparently he knew *De Conscribendis Epistolis*. Erasmus, writing of banishment, uses images of armour and milk:

animum armare solet. Hujus ut ita dicam, lacte cum ab ipsis sis incunabulis enutritus.

He was echoing Boethius, who was writing of adversity in general, not of banishment; so that Friar Lawrence's words to Romeo are more likely to come from Erasmus than from Boethius in Chaucer's translation:[17]

> I'll give thee armour to keep off that word;
> Adversity's sweet milk, philosophy,
> To comfort thee, though thou art banished.
>
> (III. iii. 54–6)

There is also some evidence that Shakespeare had read some of Seneca's plays in the original, as well as the Tudor translation of the *Ten Tragedies*.[18]

The absence of Latin quotations in the later plays may merely indicate that Shakespeare had come to recognize that, as part of his audience would not understand them, they were of dubious dramatic value, and they were therefore an indulgence he could not afford.

The mistakes made by him with regard to classical mythology prove very little. He makes Antony speak of Dido and Aeneas together in the underworld, though Virgil's Dido scorns her lover when she encounters him there. It would be dangerous to assume that Shakespeare had not read, or had forgotten, the sixth book of the *Aeneid*. His treatment of mythology here and elsewhere was creative. It may even be suggested, not altogether frivolously, that he was aware that in the year of Antony's death, Virgil's epic was not yet written. He often fused medieval with classical sources: when he gives Dido a willow in *The Merchant of Venice* (v. i. 10) he drew on Chaucer's tales of Dido and Ariadne in *The Legend of Good Women*. He has been blamed for his conflation of Arachne and Ariadne to form the name of Ariachne; but as he was perfectly familiar with the stories of both ladies, this cannot be taken as a proof of ignorance. He may have varied the name to suit the metre, or have wished to recall Ariadne's thread as well as Arachne's, or have even used the name to characterize the turmoil in Troilus' mind.[19]

Shakespeare frequently takes liberties with the spelling of classical proper names, but similar liberties were taken by Elizabethans whose latinity is not in dispute. Spellings like 'triumpherate' do not necessarily prove Shakespeare's ignorance: they may be due to compositors, and in this particular case a quibble may have been intended. Most Elizabethans, including the learned, allowed themselves considerable licence with regard to spelling. Shakespeare himself spelt 'silence' as 'scilens',[20] although he must have known its derivation: and Marston, who could compose in Latin, has the same odd spelling.

A similar defence may be made of the anachronisms. Some may be due to ignorance or carelessness. Shakespeare may have forgotten that Aristotle lived after the fall of Troy; but he must have known that the famous Cato lived after Coriolanus.[21] Most of the anachronisms, however, can be justified on dramatic grounds, as most critics now recognize.[22]

Perhaps the strongest argument in favour of Shakespeare's having had a fluent knowledge of Latin is afforded by his coinages. Occasionally he blunders, as when he uses 'orifex' for 'orifice'; but generally speaking, his coinages, or those reputed to be his, compare favourably with those of Marston and Chapman. Indeed, it may be argued that the excessive latinisms in *Troilus and Cressida* may be due to Shakespeare's attempt to emulate the style of Chapman's Homer.

Of modern languages Shakespeare acquired some knowledge of

French, Italian, and perhaps a smattering of Spanish. He could certainly read French; and he could write it sufficiently well for his purposes in *Henry V*. He had read Eliot's *Ortho-Epia Gallica*, a conversation manual, and he had lodged with a French family.[23] There is evidence, too, that he had read Florio's *First Fruites* and *Second Frutes*, presumably because he had started to learn Italian.[24] Some of his plots were not available, so far as is known, in any other language. He could have read Boccaccio in a French translation; but he appears to have read Giraldi Cinthio's *Hecatommithi*, Ariosto's *Orlando Furioso*, and one or two plays in the original Italian.[25]

Shakespeare is known to have made use of translations, including Florio's Montaigne,[26] Holland's Pliny,[27] and Chapman's Homer.[28] It is less certain that he knew Holland's translation of Plutarch's *Moralia* and of Livy, or Googe's Palingenius.[29] The doubt in these and other cases is due to the widespread dissemination of their ideas. Palingenius, for example, speaks of men whom 'dreadful dreams doe cause to shake', as Macbeth speaks of 'terrible dreams/That shake us nightly' (III. ii. 18–19); he says that

> *Beastes* consist of brutish minde,
>   To sleepe and foode, addicted all,   (p. 114)

and asks 'What is Man? a foolishe beast' (p. 114) as Hamlet asks

> What is a man
> If the chief good and market of his time
> Be but to sleep and feed? A beast, no more!
>
> (IV. iv. 33–5)

and he says that ambition is

> Much like a spurre, and many brings to toppes of Vertue hye
> With prickes . . .   (p. 98)

resembling Macbeth's comparison of ambition to a spur to prick the sides of his intent (I. vii. 25–8). But interesting as these parallels are, Palingenius is notoriously unoriginal, and so we cannot be certain that Shakespeare derived his imagery from this source.

There were a number of collections similar to Erasmus's *Adagia* which were designed to assist writers in their compositions. Dekker, it is thought, echoed the Fathers by a discreet use of *Flores Doctorum*. Shakespeare, too, took at least one idea from Lactantius, either from the *Flores*, or, more likely, from Ponet's *Treatise on Politic Power*.[30]

This example may serve to illustrate the impossibility of determining to which of two or more sources Shakespeare was indebted, especially when we remember that many books of the period have not survived.

It is possible that Shakespeare read hundreds of books which have left no trace on his writings; but the most unlikely books did leave their traces. It is difficult to believe that he was conscious of echoing Henry Swinburne's *Brief Treatise of Testaments and Last Willes* in the third scene of *Hamlet*,[31] Lewkenor in the third scene of *Othello*,[32] or Rich in the third scene of *Twelfth Night*;[33] and we may suppose that, like Coleridge, he created much of his poetry from forgotten reading.[34]

The influence of certain books on Shakespeare's work has been examined in detail. The Bible left its mark on every play in the canon and, as Richmond Noble showed,[35] the earlier echoes are mostly from the Bishops' Bible, which was read in church, and the later ones mostly from the Geneva version. There are only one or two doubtful echoes from the Catholic versions. We may suspect that neither Noble nor Carter[36] has exhausted the subject, for an earlier critic, Walter Whiter, demonstrated[37] that the story in St Mark's Gospel of the woman with an issue of blood influenced the phrasing of the Duke's words in the first scene of *Measure for Measure*. St Mark tells how

> a certaine woman, which was diseased with an *issue* of blood . . . when shee had heard of Iesus, shee came in the presse behind, and *touched* his garment . . . when Iesus did know in himselfe *the vertue that went out of him*, he turned him round about in the prease, and said, Who hath *touched* my clothes?   (v. 25–30)

The Duke tells Angelo:

> Heaven doth with us as we with torches do,
> Not light them for themselves; for if our virtues
> Did not go forth of us, 'twere all alike
> As if we had them not. Spirits are not finely touch'd
> But to fine issues.   (I. i. 33–7)

The subject of the Duke's discourse is taken from the previous chapter in the gospel: 'Commeth the candle in, to bee put vnder a bushell, or vnder the bed, and not to be put on a candlesticke?' There are some echoes from the Prayer Book, and a great many from the *Homilies* appointed to be read in church.[38]

The Ovidian influence was pervasive, especially in the earlier plays,[39] and the *Metamorphoses* was probably Shakespeare's main source for information about classical mythology. *A Mirror for Magistrates*, a popular but dreary collection of poems, redeemed only by Sackville's splendid contribution, left its mark on several of the Histories, and on the pseudo-histories, *King Lear* and *Cymbeline*.[40] Florio's translation of Montaigne affected both the thought and vocabulary of later plays, although there are only two extended borrowings, both in *The Tempest*.[41] There are echoes of Samuel Harsnett's *Declaration of Egregious Popishe Impostures*, not only in *King Lear*, but also in *The Tempest*. David Kaula has recently argued[42] that Shakespeare echoed a whole series of pamphlets in the arch-priest controversy – this I find hard to believe.

It is certain that as an actor Shakespeare was acquainted with a large number of plays in which he took part.[43] Most of these are doubtless lost. Although he did not act in Marlowe's plays, he echoed *Tamburlaine*, *Dido*, and *Edward II*; he quoted from *Doctor Faustus* in *Troilus and Cressida*; he quoted a line from *Hero and Leander* in *As You Like It*, and referred there to Marlowe as 'dead shepherd'. But, as everyone recognizes, his debt to Marlowe was more profound. His own blank verse was developed from Marlowe's 'mighty line' and his own conception of tragedy was evolved from Marlowe's.

Shakespeare learnt a good deal from the other University Wits, and their pioneering work reduced the period of his apprenticeship. He had read several of Greene's works, including his two best novels, *Menaphon* and *Pandosto*, and two of the coney-catching pamphlets.[44] He had read the attack on himself in *A Groatsworth of Wit* – if Greene wrote that death-bed diatribe.[45] Although it used to be argued by enthusiastic editors[46] that Greene's heroines served as models for Shakespeare's, it is only in *Cymbeline* and *The Winter's Tale* that there seems to be much resemblance, and this is more to do with situation than characterization. The wronged wives, Imogen and Hermione (Greene's Bellaria), forgive their husbands, as Greene's heroines in novels and plays invariably do, but there the resemblance ends. From Greene's practice Shakespeare may have seen the advantages of interweaving several plots, but this is something he could equally well have learnt from Lyly, whose comedies were of seminal importance. Many characteristics of Shakespearian comedy can be traced to Lyly's – wit combats, the disguising of girls as boys, mischievous pages, interspersed songs, and many other things. Furthermore, as I argued long ago,[47]

Shakespeare learned from Lyly how to write prose, and though in

1 Henry IV he poked fun at the excesses of Euphuism, he remained
to the end of his career profoundly affected by it. . . The civilized
prose of the great comedies owes much in its constructions, its
rhythms, its balance and its poise to the example of Lyly. It sharp-
ened the edges of [Shakespeare's] wit and gave his dialogue more
bite and sparkle.

To this may be added the fact that even as late as *King Lear* Shakespeare
bore unconscious witness to his familiarity with *Euphues*. Ferardo in
that novel complains of his daughter's ingratitude, declaring as Lear
did of Cordelia, that he had hoped to find comfort from her care in
his old age.[48] He asks:

> Is this the comfort that the parent reapeth for all his care? Is obstinacy
> payed for obedyence, stubbernnesse, rendred for duetie, malycious
> desperatnesse, for filiall feare?

In this context Lyly uses words which seem to be echoed by Shakespeare:

> But why cast I the effects of this vnnaturalnesse in thy teeth, seeing I
> my selfe was the cause? I made thee a *wanton*, and thou hast made me
> a *foole*: I brought thee vp like a *cockney*, and thou hast handled me
> like a *cockescombe*.

Lear blames his flesh for begetting unnatural daughters; and the Fool
tells him:

> Cry to it, Nuncle, as the *cockney* did to the eels when she put 'em
> i'th'paste alive; she knapp'd 'em o'th'*Coxcombs* with a stick, and
> cried 'Down, *wantons*, down!'   (II. iv. 119–23)

There is some evidence that Shakespeare had read some of the Nashe–
Harvey controversy, as it left its traces on *Love's Labour's Lost*;[49] but
one of Nashe's pamphlets, *Pierce Penilesse*, seems to have left its mark
on *Hamlet*,[50] and to a lesser extent on *Othello*.[51] Shakespeare alludes to
Soliman and Perseda;[52] he was clearly influenced by Thomas Kyd's
more famous play, *The Spanish Tragedy*, the revenge play that provided
a model for the original *Hamlet* and Shakespeare's variations on the
same theme. Thomas Lodge gave him the plot of *As You Like It* and a
few phrases in *Richard II*, but he had less influence on Shakespeare than
the other University Wits.[53]

Shakespeare knew most of Sidney's work, including *Astrophel and*

Stella, The Defence of Poesy,[54] and *Arcadia,*[55] and most of Daniel's – *Delia, Rosamond,*[56] *A Letter from Octavia,*[57] *Cleopatra,*[58] *The Civil Wars,*[59] and *The Queens Arcadia.*[60] He had, of course, read *The Faerie Queene,* but Spenser seems to have influenced him less than many minor writers.[61]

So many books and plays have perished that even if we had read all the extant English books published before 1616, we could still assume that we had not read all the books known to Shakespeare; and some ideas and phrases apparently echoed from books we know may in fact come from books which are now lost. Even apart from this, some resemblances may be quite fortuitous; or Shakespeare may have derived the word, the phrase, the image, or the idea from casual conversation, from overhearing in a tavern, from the playhouse, from dictionaries, or from letters. An interesting example of the kind of pitfall into which the source-hunter is liable to fall is afforded by the death of Cleopatra, and her referring to the fatal asp as 'baby'.

> Dost thou not see my baby at my breast
> That sucks the nurse asleep?   (v. ii. 307–8)

One critic pointed out a parallel with Peele's *Edward I,* in which an asp is addressed with the words 'Suck on, sweet babe'.[62] But this striking comparison was a commonplace. Nashe, in *Christ's Tears,* says,[63] 'At thy breasts . . . aspisses should be put out to nurse'; and Cooper, writing of Cleopatra in his *Thesaurus* (1587), speaks of 'two serpents sucking at hir pappes'. Yet we cannot be sure that Shakespeare derived the idea from any, or all, of these sources, for it is possible that the sucking image was suggested by Charmian's apostrophe 'O eastern star!' This may have recalled the star in the east, which led the Magi to Bethlehem, where they found the infant Jesus in his mother's arms.[64] It must therefore be borne in mind that apparently close parallels may be deceptive, and that even when Shakespeare is known to have read the work in question, his actual source may be different. In other cases, as we shall see, a single line in one of his plays may combine echoes of more than one source. When, for example, the Clown tells Autolyous, 'We are but plain fellows, sir', and he replies, 'A lie: you are rough and hairy' (IV. iv. 710–11), he is thinking of the story of Jacob and Esau. In the Geneva version Jacob is 'plain' (i.e. clean-shaven) and Esau is 'rough'; but in the Bishops' Bible Esau is described as 'hairy'.[65] There is a similar conflation in *The Merry Wives of Windsor,* this time of two versions of Psalm xlix.[66] Pistol tells Ford:

He woos both high and low, both rich and poor,
Both young and old, one with another, Ford.

(ii. i. 101–2)

This is partly based on the prayer-book version: 'High and low, rich and poor; one with another'; but it also echoes the metrical version:

Both hie and low, both rich and poore
that in the world doe dwell.

Pistol alludes to the same verse in an earlier scene: (i. iii. 83)

And high and low beguiles the rich and poor.

He proceeds to extemporize in doggerel verse: (92–5)

And I to Ford shall eke unfold
How Falstaff, varlet vile,
His dove will prove, his gold will hold,
And his soft couch defile.

The same rhymes and references to illicit gain and adultery are to be found in the metrical version of the next psalm:

When thou a theefe dost see,
by theft to liue in wealth,
With him thou runst and dost agree,
likewise to thriue by stealth.
When thou dost them behold,
that wiues and maids defile,
Thou lik'st it well, and waxest bold
to vse that life most vile.

Shakespeare thus combined a variety of different sources in the texture of his verse, and the process, in most cases, was apparently unconscious. Just as J. Livingston Lowes was able to demonstrate that 'The Ancient Mariner' and 'Kubla Khan' were a complex tissue of words and phrases borrowed from Coleridge's multifarious, and probably forgotten, reading, so it would be possible, if we had a complete knowledge of Shakespeare's reading, to show that words, phrases, and images coalesced in his poetry. Nor is there reason to doubt that the conditions of such coalescence were the same as with Coleridge: two or more passages became linked in his mind if they had a common factor, although the resulting phrase might not include that factor. T. W.

Baldwin has provided us with many illustrations of the process. One stanza in *Lucrece* may serve as an example:[67]

> The aged man that coffers up his gold
> Is plagu'd with cramps and gouts and painful fits,
> And scarce hath eyes his treasure to behold,
> But like still-pining Tantalus he sits,
> And useless barns the harvest of his wits,
>   Having no other pleasure of his gain,
>   But torment that it cannot cure his pain.   (855–61)

Ovid briefly refers to the story of Tantalus in the *Metamorphoses* (IV. 458–9) and in a note on this passage Regius says: 'hac autem poena avari omnes affici videntur, qui patris pecuniis per avaritiam uti non possunt'. The connection between the story of Tantalus and avarice is brought out in Horace's first satire, a passage quoted by Erasmus in his *Adagia*, where Shakespeare may have seen it:

> Tantalus a labris sitiens fugientia captat
> flumina. quid rides? mutato nomine de te
> fabula narratur: congestis undique saccis
> indormis inhians, et tamquam parcere sacris
> cogeris aut pictis tamquam gaudere tabellis.
>
> (I. i. 68–72)

Erasmus goes on to quote (under the same heading) a passage from one of the Odes (III. 16):

> Contemptae dominus splendidior rei,
> quam si, quicquid arat impiger Apulus
> occultare meis dicerer horreis,
>   magnas inter opes inops.

This reference to the hoarding of wheat links up with the parable of the covetous man (Luke, xii. 15–21) who proposed building greater barns, only to be told (in the Geneva version): 'O foole, this night will they fetch away thy soule from thee'. On this parable the Geneva version has the following note:

Christ condemneth the arrogancie of the rich worldlings, who as though they had God locked vp in their coffers and barnes, set their whole felicitie in their goods, not considering that God gaue them life and also can take it away when he will.

Shakespeare seized on the coffers and barns of this note and turned them into verbs. Thus in a poem derived mainly from Livy and an annotated edition of Ovid, we have in one stanza echoes from two poems of Horace, a Biblical parable and the marginal note on it, and possibly (if we are to believe Professor Baldwin) from Juvenal's description of the miseries of old age. It is probable that Shakespeare, here and elsewhere, consulted the *Adagia* of Erasmus.[68]

We cannot hope to track down more than a small fraction of the passages which Shakespeare made use of, for reasons stated above. Caroline Spurgeon believed that the famous triple image of flatterers–dogs–sweets, first analysed by Walter Whiter, was peculiar to Shakespeare, exhibiting a personal phobia; but it may well have been a literary commonplace.[69]

We are on surer ground when we attempt to trace the sources of his plots, though even here there are obstacles in the way. In a number of cases – e.g. *Hamlet, The Two Gentlemen of Verona, The Merry Wives of Windsor* – there was probably a lost source-play – and not much can be deduced about the changes made by Shakespeare. The Histories present a special problem, since there is so much disagreement about the material on which the poet worked. It used to be generally accepted that *King John* was based on *The Troublesome Raigne*, but Professor Honigmann has argued that Shakespeare's play came first. There may have been a lost play behind *Richard II*; both *Henry IV* and *Henry V* were derived in part from *The Famous Victories*, a play which exists in such a mangled text that we can only guess how much Shakespeare owed to it.[70] The authenticity of *1 Henry VI* and *Titus Andronicus* is still a matter of dispute and until we know how much, if at all, Peele contributed to these plays, any discussion of their sources must be tentative. There is a similar problem with *Henry VIII* which some critics still regard as partly Fletcher's.

Shakespeare's method of composition differed from play to play. For some of his plots he seems to have used only one source, but generally speaking he combined two or more. In the remainder of this book the plays will be discussed in approximately chronological order. The narrative poems have been excluded from consideration and so, too, have the apocryphal plays – *Edward III* and *The Two Noble Kinsmen*. I have given my views on these plays in *Shakespeare as Collaborator*.

II

EARLY PLAYS

THE COMEDY OF ERRORS

IT IS convenient to begin with *The Comedy of Errors*, although it may not have been Shakespeare's very first play, because it shows him, even so early, challenging the most admired writers of comedy, Plautus and Terence, on their own ground, and overgoing them both in complexity and ingenuity of plot and in subtlety of characterization. The two Plautine comedies which provided the basis for Shakespeare's plot – the *Menaechmi* and the *Amphitruo* – were frequently included in grammar school curricula.[1] There is no reason to think that Shakespeare knew any of the Italian adaptations of the *Menaechmi*, and William Warner's English translation did not appear until 1595. The fact that in this translation the wife refers to herself as a stale,[2] as Adriana does, may be fortuitous; for if Shakespeare had seen the manuscript of the translation one would have expected more verbal echoes, and not this solitary one.

The main plot is taken from the *Menaechmi*, in which one of the twins, Menaechmus Surreptus, arranges to have dinner with a courtezan named Erotium. Menaechmus Sosicles is taken for his brother and gets the meal instead. Peniculus, a parasite, who was to have shared the meal, exposes Menaechmus to his wife. Eventually all is explained. Shakespeare begins his play with a scene, taken from the story of Apollonius of Tyre (in either Gower's version or Twine's)[3] in which Ægeon explains how he lost his wife and sons. His name is probably derived from Aegeus, who was drowned in the Aegean sea, which provides the geographical background of the play. Ægeon is condemned to death because of a trade war between Ephesus and Syracuse, suggested by another play of errors, *Supposes*, which was to serve as the main source of *The Taming of the Shrew*. Antipholus of Ephesus says he was brought to the town by Duke Menaphon; and in Greene's *Menaphon*[4] there is a shipwreck which parts the husband from the wife and their infant son, and pirates who separate wife and baby. In *Apollonius of Tyre* and its derivatives, including *Pericles*, the wife is supposed to die in childbirth, the father leaves his daughter in the care of others, and she is stolen by pirates. In *The Comedy of Errors* there is a shipwreck which severs the husband and one of the twins from the wife and the other, and rude Corinthian fishermen afterwards rob the wife of her son. Shakespeare greatly complicates matters by adding twin servants, separated like their masters, the name Dromio being taken, perhaps, from Lyly's *Mother Bombie*.[5] The possibilities of error are thereby multiplied. Antipholus of Ephesus can be mistaken by his father, and by Dromio of Syracuse; Antipholus of Syracuse can be mistaken by Adriana, Luciana, the Courtezan, Dromio of Ephesus, the Goldsmith, and the Merchant.

Shakespeare may have studied Golding's translation of the geographer Solinus (1582) for details of the journeys of his characters, for this is the name given his Duke; but he seems also to have taken hints from the missionary journeys of St Paul.[6] Certain details are taken from Acts, xix, describing his visit to Ephesus: Antipholus of Syracuse complains of sorcerers and witches, as well as of the cheats mentioned by Plautus, and we are told in this chapter of exorcists, evil spirits, and people who 'used curious arts'. The change of setting from Epidamnum to Ephesus may have been suggested by the *Miles Gloriosus*, another play of errors, which immediately follows the *Menaechmi* in editions of Plautus. But Apollonius had been reunited to his wife in the same city, as Ægeon is reunited to Æmelia, the temple of Diana being changed to a Christian priory.

Shakespeare does not directly use the substance of Act I of the *Menaechmi*; but he incorporates much of the material of Act II in his second scene, and develops the whole of his second act from *Menaechmi*, II. 3. For the first scene of the third act, in which Antipholus of Ephesus is kept out of his own house while his twin is within, Shakespeare took a hint from the fourth act of *Menaechmi* where the husband is told by the wife when he promises to return the cloak: 'Otherwise thinke not to roost within these doors againe'; and Erotium shuts him out, so that he exclaims:[7]

Now I am euerie way shut out for a very bench-whistler; neither shall I haue entertainment heere nor at home.

Shakespeare amplified this hint by memories of the famous scene in the *Amphitruo* (IV), in which the hero is shut out of his own house while Jupiter is with his wife. The business of the chain was suggested by a 'spinther' which had formerly belonged to the wife and which the Courtezan's maid gives to the wrong Menaechmus to have repaired. Shakespeare's chain is intended by Antipholus of Ephesus as a present for his wife; when he is shut out he decides to give it to the Courtezan, although afterwards he apparently promises it in exchange for a diamond ring. When the Courtezan is refused the promised chain by the wrong Antipholus, she decides to tell Adriana that her husband had taken the ring; and Antipholus of Ephesus is arrested at the suit of the Goldsmith for refusing to pay for the chain. Adriana, convinced that her husband is mad, goes with Dr Pinch to secure him and exorcize him; and when they afterwards meet Antipholus of Syracuse, they assume that he has escaped. He and Dromio take refuge in the priory. The arrival of the other Antipholus and the Abbess's recognition of Ægeon, now being led to execution, lead to the resolution of the plot.

It will be seen that Shakespeare's play is much more complex than Plautus'. The invention of the two Dromios leads to many additional 'errors'; the invention of Luciana provides a bride for Antipholus of Syracuse and a confidante for Adriana; and the wife becomes the central figure of the play, instead of a peripheral one, while the Court-ezan becomes a minor figure, her relationship with Antipholus being comparatively innocent, and surprisingly unmercenary. The invitation to dinner is given by the wife, not by the Courtezan, to the wrong Antipholus. The change to a Christian setting enables Adriana to plead for the sanctity of marriage. Although Shakespeare adds more farcical elements – Dromio's wife and Dr Pinch, for example – he also added elements that are not farcical at all. The doomed Ægeon opens the play on a serious note and his discovery of his wife provides a moving scene, looking forward to *Pericles*. The study of Adriana's jealous love, the lyrical proposal of Antipholus of Syracuse to Luciana, and his sense of bewilderment and horror, lift the play above the farcical. There is some good verse – both blank and rhymed – and Shakespeare's immaturity is most apparent in the rhymed doggerel which takes us back to *Ralph Roister Doister* and *Gammer Gurton's Needle*.[8]

T. W. Baldwin has given a detailed account of the way in which Shakespeare constructed *The Comedy of Errors* from heterogeneous materials, as we have shown from the above summary. He summed up his conclusions in the following passage:[9]

> His grammar-school training had been insistent that he must gather into notebook and mind materials out of which later to compile by imitation his own work. So here he assembles in his mind all accessible plays on mistaken identity; *Amphitruo, Menaechmi,* possibly *Miles,* and probably Gascoigne's . . . *Supposes. . . The Comedy* is not merely constructed principally from two plays of Plautus; it also analyses and reconstructs those plays into the *Andria* formula of Terentian structure.

Not all scholars have agreed with Baldwin about Shakespeare's Five-Act Structure,[10] and not all have agreed with him that the play was written as early as 1589, or that there is a valid parallel between the sentence of death on Ægeon and the execution of a seminary priest in October 1588;[11] but Baldwin has given us by far the most comprehensive examination of Shakespeare's use of his source-material in this play.

2

THE TWO GENTLEMEN OF VERONA

THE ULTIMATE SOURCE of the play was *Diana* by J. de Montemayor, which Shakespeare could have read in a French translation (1578), or possibly in B. Yonge's English version, not published until 1598, but made some sixteen years previously.[1] The central situation is similar to that of *The Two Gentlemen*: Felismena dresses as a man, finds that her lover Felix is wooing Celia, becomes his page, and is sent with a letter to Celia, who falls in love with the messenger. Celia dies and Felix and Felismena eventually marry. Here we have the germ of the Julia–Silvia–Proteus triangle; but there is no equivalent of Valentine, no conflict between love and friendship, and Silvia does not fall in love with the messenger, as Olivia in *Twelfth Night* was later to do. A play was performed in 1585 entitled, no doubt inaccurately, *Felix and Philiomena*,[2] and this may well have been Shakespeare's model, although there is nothing to suggest that it contained the sex-rivalry of two friends. There are numerous analogues of the conflict between love and friendship. In one of the most famous, the story of Titus and Gisippus in *The Governour* of Sir Thomas Elyot (1531), friendship triumphs over love, Gisippus relinquishing Sophronia to his friend: 'Here I renounce to you clerely all my title and interest that I nowe haue or mought haue in that faire mayden'. The lady is not consulted, Titus taking his friend's place on the wedding night, without her knowing it. Elyot has to predicate a close resemblance between the two friends. Titus does not act treacherously as Proteus does and he is not guilty of attempted rape, so that Gisippus' conduct is not as absurd as that of Valentine when he offers to relinquish Sylvia. Sophronia does not seem to mind which man she has; but both Julia and Sylvia have reason to be outraged by Valentine's offer. Presumably Shakespeare was aware of the absurdity, despite parallels in the *Sonnets* – which may have been written afterwards. There the Dark Lady seduces the poet's friend, and the poet in any case condemns his own enslavement to a woman he despises. There is another analogy in Lyly's *Euphues*, where the hero betrays his friendship for Philautus by wooing Lucilla, who is quite willing to respond for a while, afterwards jilting Euphues and marrying another man 'of little wealth and lesse wit' (Bullough, I. 221 ff.).

Whether Shakespeare derived his variations on Montemayor's tale from an unknown source, dramatic or otherwise,[3] or invented them himself does not greatly matter. It is clear, not merely from the last scene of the play, but also from the portrait of the knight-errant, Eglamour, and from the comments of Speed and Launce, that Shakespeare was satirizing romantic ideas of love and friendship. Moreover, his two heroines are very unlike their reputed models. Julia is not Amazonian like Felismena, Silvia is not the sort of woman to die of an unrequited passion like Celia – or like Viola's imaginary sister – nor could she change partners like Lucilla, or meekly accept a substitution in bed like Sophronia. By giving his women identities, minds of their own, morals, and common sense, Shakespeare torpedoes the pseudo-romantic attitudes of his heroes. Yet Julia's tearing of Proteus' letter, which she afterwards pieces together, was obviously suggested by the devious behaviour of Felismena on receiving a letter from Felix.

3

THE TAMING OF THE SHREW

THERE ARE three theories about the relationship of Shakespeare's play to *The Taming of a Shrew*: (1) that *A Shrew* was the main source of Shakespeare's play; (2) that it was piratically derived from it; (3) that both *A Shrew* and *The Shrew* were derived from a lost play, the *Ur-Shrew*. Not many critics cling to the first of these views. The third view, of the lost play, has the advantage of evading the awkward differences between most bad quartos and *A Shrew*. There are hardly any verbal echoes of Shakespeare's play in *A Shrew*; and although there is some plagiarism from Marlowe, most of the verse is at least respectable, beyond the scope of the normal pirate. Richard Hosley, in what is the most convincing contribution to a continuing debate,[1] has argued that *A Shrew* postdates *The Shrew*, that it is a piratical version of it, and that the author responsible deliberately deviated from Shakespeare's play, altering the names of most of the characters, giving the Shrew a third sister, and adding an epilogue to round off the Sly story.

If we accept Hosley's arguments, as I have gradually come to do, Shakespeare must have based his play on a number of different sources. The Sly Induction is derived ultimately from a story in *The Arabian Nights*, a variant of which Shakespeare could have read in *De rebus burgundicis* of Heuterus (1584), or in a lost collection of stories by Richard Edwardes (1570). (Translations of Heuterus by Goulart into French (1600) and English (1607) were, of course, too late for Shakespeare to have used them.) The drunk artisan tricked by the Duke of Burgundy in Goulart's version is entertained with a pleasant comedy.[2] Shakespeare, unless an epilogue dropped out during the thirty years that elapsed before his play appeared in print, avoided a scene in which the tricked drunkard awakens to his normal existence.

The second strand in the play was provided by Gascoigne's *Supposes* (1566), a lively version of Ariosto's *I Suppositi*. As the prologue explains, the word 'Suppose', as used in the play, 'is nothing else but a mystaking or imagination of one thing for an other'. Gascoigne calls attention to twenty-five supposes in marginal notes. Most of these are caused by the numerous disguises, master as servant, servant as master, stranger for friend, and friend for stranger. Polynesta, the heroine, is pregnant by Erostrato, but Shakespeare's Bianca is a virgin. Erostrato's servant, posing as his master, persuades a Siennese merchant to pretend to be his rich father whose coming with a dowry he had promised, by warning him that Ferrara was dangerous to people from Sienna. (From this incident Shakespeare derived Ægeon's plight in *The Comedy of Errors*.) When Erostrato's father arrives there follow complications similar to those in Shakespeare's play. Cleander, the aged suitor corresponding to Gremio, turns out to be the father of Dulipo, the bogus Erostrato. Shakespeare does not make use of this twist in the plot. He gives Bianca three suitors and adds the business of the Latin and music teachers. It has been suggested[3] that the Latin lesson is based on a scene in *The Three Lords and Three Ladies of London* (1590), but the debt may be the other way round. Hortensio's marriage to a widow and Lucentio's to Bianca provide two apparently docile wives to contrast with the genuinely obedient Katherine.

The main plot, of the taming, seems to have no identifiable source. The taming of a shrew is a popular theme and there may well have been something closer to Shakespeare's plot than *A Shrewde and Curste Wyfe*, a ballad in which the shrew is chastened with birch rods. Hosley points out a number of parallels[4] – the contrast of the shrew with her sister, the description of the shrew as mad, a fiend, as angry as a wasp, and the mention of the rout at the wedding – but the only one that makes it fairly certain that Shakespeare did know the ballad is 'He that can charme a shrewde wyfe,/ Better then thus', which is close to Shakespeare's 'He that knows better how to tame a shrew'; but Menaechmus, in W.W.'s translation, exclaims similarly: 'Would euery man could tame his shrewe as well as I doo mine' (i. iii).

Details of the taming plot may be derived from various sources. The scolding of the tailor is similar to an anecdote about Sir Philip Caulthrop in Legh's *Accedens of Armoury* (1562).[5] The scene of the wager is reminiscent of *The Book of the Knight of La Tour-Landry*, which Caxton translated in 1484.[6] Three merchants wager on their wives' obedience. There is an analogue of the scene in which Katherine agrees with statements she knows are absurd in *El Conde Lucanor* but Shakespeare is unlikely to have known this.

There are some curious parallels[7] with one of Erasmus' *Colloquies*, translated as *A Mery Dialogue, Declaringe the Propertyes of Shrowde Shrewes and Honest Wyves* (1557), in which a young wife, who has become shrewish through her husband's misbehaviour, like Adriana in

The Comedy of Errors, is advised to be patient so that she may gradually reform her husband. Two passages in the first scene of the play seem to echo passages in the colloquy:

> But if it were, doubt not her care should be
> To comb your noddle with a three-legg'd stool. . .
> A pretty peat! it is best
> Put finger in the eye, an she knew why.
>
> (I. i. 63–4, 78–9)

Compare the following:

> I gat me a thre foted stole in hand, and he had but ones layd his littell finger on me, he shulde not haue founde me lame. . . (Sig. A3ᵛ)

> She withdrew her good mynde and dylygence and when her husband called vpon her, she put the finger in the eye, and wepte. (Sig. A9)

Shakespeare seems to have echoed another of the *Colloquies* – one that had not been translated – in Katherine's sermon to the disobedient wives:[8]

> our Condition is much preferable to theirs: For they, endeavouring to get a Maintenance for their Families, scamper thro all the Parts of the Earth by Land and Sea. In Times of War they are call'd up by the Sound of the Trumpet, stand in Armour in the Front of the Battle; while we sit at home in Safety.

So Katherine tells the other wives that the husband is

> one that cares for thee,
> And for thy maintenance commits his body
> To painful labour both by sea and land,
> To watch the night in storms, the day in cold,
> Whilst thou liest warm at home, secure and safe.
>
> (v. ii. 147–51)

There were, of course, countless sermons on the subordination of women to their husbands. The same doctrine had been preached by Luciana in *The Comedy of Errors*. Hosley quotes an interesting passage from *A Very Frutefull and Pleasant Boke Called the Instruction of a Christen Woman* by Juan Vives, translated by Richard Hyrde (*c.* 1529). Although there is no reason to believe that Shakespeare had read this book, one sentence suggests that Katherine's tactical submission may be interpreted as a strategic victory: 'A good woman by lowely obeysaunce ruleth hir husbande'.[9]

The names of Tranio and Grumio, but nothing else, were taken from the *Mostellaria* of Plautus.

The three plots are brilliantly linked structurally (as the attempts by Garrick and others to play the Taming on its own inadvertently proved) but they are also linked thematically.[10] In all three plots there are characters who are rôle-playing. Sly, for a few hours, is made to play the part of a lord; characters in the Bianca plot pretend to be servant or master, music tutor or Latin tutor, father or son; Petruchio pretends to be a male shrew in order to cure Katherine; and she enters into the game of pretending. The play is not, therefore, the crude and degrading farce it has been thought to be by some critics; but, it must be confessed, some of the verse, particularly in the first scene, is flat and feeble. This is not merely a device, as used later in *Much Ado about Nothing*, to throw into relief the more vital pair of lovers, but a positive lack of poetry; it compares unfavourably in this respect with all the other early plays.

4

TITUS ANDRONICUS

Titus andronicus presents us with a number of problems. In the first place, it may not be wholly Shakespeare's. On the one hand there is H. T. Price's conviction that there was no other dramatist of the period who was capable of displaying the powers of construction apparent in this play;[1] on the other hand, two recent editors have thought to detect traces of Peele's style in the early part of the play.[2] The second problem is the question of date, which is not relevant to the question of sources. Thirdly, there is the difficulty of knowing whether *The History of Titus Andronicus*, published in the eighteenth century, was derived from, and was substantially the same as, Shakespeare's main source. Fourthly, there is the question of the date of the ballad on the subject, whether it was based on the play, or one of its sources. My own view, for which I would not go to the stake, is that the play was substantially Shakespeare's. The traces of Peele's style may be no more significant than the Marlovian style of scenes of unquestioned Shakespearian authorship; but I suspect, nevertheless, from stylistic differences between the early scenes and the later ones, that Shakespeare was rewriting a play by another dramatist. We do not know whether the play described by Henslowe as new on 24 January 1594 was really new, or a revision of an earlier play. Critics have seen links between *Titus Andronicus* and *A Midsummer-Night's Dream*, but this does not necessarily mean a proximity of date.

There is no trace of Elizabethan phraseology in the chapbook tale. It purports, indeed, to be 'Newly Translated from the Italian Copy' and there may well have been an Elizabethan version which served as Shakespeare's source. But we cannot know whether the chapbook was contaminated by memories of Shakespeare's play, or to what extent the Elizabethan version differed from its eighteenth-century successor.[3] The ballad appears to contain verbal echoes from the play.[4]

Where there are so many unsolved problems, a discussion of the use Shakespeare made of his sources is nugatory. The historical background is an absurd hotch-potch, unlike that of Shakespeare's other Roman plays,[5] although he seems to have been reading Plutarch's *Lives* and to have taken some of the names of his characters from the life of Scipio[6] – Marcus, Lucius, Martius, Aemilius, Publius Mutius, and Sempronius.

The chapbook does not mention the stories of Philomel and Thyestes, but Shakespeare must have been reminded of both by the accounts of Lavinia's rape and Titus' revenge. Although there are no specific verbal echoes of Golding's translation of Ovid's *Metamorphoses* or of Jasper Heywood's translation of *Thyestes*, there are misquotations in Latin from Seneca's *Hippolytus*,[7] and it has been suggested that Titus' petition to Pluto (IV. iii. 13–17) may be influenced by the first act of *Thyestes*.[8] In any case, as Eugene Waith has cogently argued,[9] the curiously decorative style in which the mutilated Lavinia is described is essentially Ovidian.

In the past critics sought to deprive Shakespeare of the responsibility for this horrific tragedy. Now, in the days of the theatre of cruelty, and following the splendid Olivier production, there has been a tendency to overvalue it. It is a nice irony that Shakespeare's most shocking play should be closest in spirit to the classics.[10]

❊

❊ 5–7 ❊
HENRY VI : PARTS 1–3

THE GENERAL ATTITUDE to the three parts of *Henry VI* underwent a
change when Peter Alexander demonstrated[1] that *The Contention* and
The True Tragedy were not sources, written by a group of dramatists,
of the Second and Third Parts of *Henry VI*, but piratical versions of
those plays. Critics began to speak more kindly of the dramatic
qualities of the plays, and even to find in them a typically Shakespearian
philosophy of history.[2] The plays, moreover, to everyone's surprise,
proved to be stage-worthy, not merely in the Barton adaptation at the
Royal Shakespeare Theatre, but also in the comparatively straight
versions of the trilogy used at the Old Vic and the Birmingham Rep-
ertory Theatre, as well as in the television adaptation, *The Age of Kings*.

The demonstration that *The Contention* and *The True Tragedy* were
not sources did not in itself prove that Shakespeare was the sole author
of the trilogy or that he did not base it on the work of others. The most
natural interpretation of Greene's attack on Shakespeare in *A Groatsworth of Wit* – if indeed Greene wrote that pamphlet –[3] was that it was
an accusation of plagiarism;[4] although it could mean simply that an
actor without a university education was presuming to imitate and
rival the University Wits. John Dover Wilson in his edition of the
plays argued that Greene wrote them with the help of Nashe, and
that they were revised by Shakespeare. A. S. Cairncross, the editor of
the other chief modern edition, believes that Shakespeare wrote all
three plays and that they were not revisions of the work of others.
The difficulty of Wilson's theory is that scholars disagree on the identity
of the authors involved and on their respective shares. If one examines
the extraordinary divergencies with regard to Part I, for example, one
will be impressed again by the vanity of dogmatizing. Tucker Brooke
thought the play was by Peele and Shakespeare, a view shared by A. W.
Pollard. Allison Gaw believed that six authors were involved in the
composition of the play. Hart detected traces of Greene, Peele, Nashe,
and Shakespeare. E. K. Chambers discerned Peele and Shakespeare,
and traces of Greene in two scenes of Act V. Dover Wilson ascribed
the whole of Act I to Nashe, and most of the rest of the play to Greene,

with many scenes revised by Shakespeare. There are indeed only three scenes in the whole play which Dover Wilson, Chambers, and Hart agree to ascribe to Shakespeare:[5] II. iv, v, and IV. ii.

There is an obvious danger of crediting to Shakespeare those scenes or passages we happen to like, and of handing over to Nashe, Greene, or Peele (or Marlowe, or Lodge) what we regard as inferior. Shakespeare by including the scenes of others in his revision made himself responsible for them.[6] The parallels with Nashe's work, accumulated by Dover Wilson, are less impressive when we consider that he found many echoes of Nashe in *1 Henry IV* and had to postulate his hand in the source of that play; and one has to remember that there are parallels between Nashe's works and other Shakespearian plays. No one has suggested that Nashe wrote the *Ur-Hamlet* or that he collaborated in *Love's Labour's Lost*.[7]

As Dover Wilson admits,[8] parallels are not necessarily a proof of common authorship. The young Shakespeare, being an actor as well as a poet, naturally absorbed the stylistic tricks of the plays in which he had performed; and when he began to write, especially if a script was urgently required, he would drop into the mannerisms of the University Wits.[9] It is seldom possible to distinguish between Greene's authentic work, Shakespeare's revision of it, and Shakespeare's original writing in the manner of Greene.

There is a further complication. We do not know whether Henslowe's entry about 'harey the vi', which attracted crowds to the Rose Theatre early in 1592, and is marked 'ne' by him on 3 March, is a reference to *1 Henry VI* or to some other play; and we do not know to which play, if there were two, Nashe refers in *Pierce Penilesse*, before 8 August of the same year, where he praises scenes concerned with Talbot.[10] Those who believe that the three parts of *Henry VI* were written in chronological sequence must assume that the Henslowe reference is not to 'Shakespeare's' play, while those who believe that the Henslowe play was the one we know, and that it was indeed new, are driven to assume that *1 Henry VI* was written after the other two parts. The rival views are stated effectively and at length by Dover Wilson and Cairncross in their editions of the plays, and there is no need for us to cover the same ground. My own views may be summarized: (1) I accept the views of Alexander and Cairncross that the second and third parts were wholly Shakespeare's, and that he was not rewriting plays by Greene or Peele; (2) I accept Dover Wilson's view that *1 Henry VI* was written after the other two parts; and that (3)

Part I is not wholly Shakespeare's. Dover Wilson advances what seem to be strong arguments to show that the author (or authors) of Parts 2 and 3 were ignorant of Part I.[11] It is true that these are links between Part I and the others – notably Suffolk's final speech[12] – but this can be explained by the fact that the author knew what was coming in Part 2, since that play had already been performed.

The strongest arguments against Shakespeare's sole authorship of Part I are neither the appearance of Greene's favourite turns of phrase nor the alleged echoes of Nashe, but rather the inconsistency of characterization, the alternation of competence and incompetence, and the weakness of construction. Hereward Price in his valuable essay, *Construction in Shakespeare*, argued that Shakespeare was greatly superior to all the University Wits in his power of dramatic construction, a verdict with which we may agree. It is even applicable to the Second and Third Parts of *Henry VI*. It is manifestly not applicable to Part I.[13] Geoffrey Bullough, who believes that Shakespeare wrote it all, has to admit:

> The play does not follow the sequence in the chronicles but darts about the period in a bewildering way . . . until it seems that *1 Henry VI* is not so much a Chronicle play as a fantasia on historical themes. (III. 25)

Although playing fast and loose with historical fact, it might still be an excellently constructed play. What is more significant is the way in which its authors seem ignorant of each other's contributions. In the first scene Rouen and Orleans are lost to the French; but the English still occupy Orleans in Act II and Rouen in Act III.

An obvious case of lack of co-ordination concerns Falstaff. In the first scene we are told of his cowardice at the battle of Patay. In I. iv Talbot complains of it, and much later, in IV. i, he strips him of the order of the Garter because of his conduct at Patay. But in between these scenes, in III. ii, Falstaff runs away out of cowardice, and this duplicates the Patay incident. It is incredible that the same author could be responsible for this scene as for the others.

One other preliminary point has to be made. Thirty years elapsed between the first performances of the three parts of *Henry VI* and their inclusion in the First Folio. How often they were performed in the interval we do not know, but when *Henry V* was written, Shakespeare referred in the epilogue to the popularity of the earlier plays. It is very unlikely that no changes were made in the text when the plays were

revived. There are, in fact, two passages in the last two scenes of Part 2,
which stand out from their contexts. One is Young Clifford's discovery
of his father's body during the battle of St Albans:

> Shame and confusion! All is on the rout;
> Fear frames disorder, and disorder wounds
> Where it should guard. O war, thou son of hell,
> Whom angry heavens do make their minister,
> Throw in the frozen bosoms of our part
> Hot coals of vengeance! Let no soldier fly.
> He that is truly dedicate to war
> Hath no self-love; nor he that loves himself
> Hath not essentially, but by circumstance
> The name of valour.   [*Sees his father's body.*
>   O, let the vile world end
> And the premised flames of the last day
> Knit earth and heaven together!
> Now let the general trumpet blow his blast,
> Particularities and petty sounds
> To cease! Wast thou ordain'd, dear father,
> To lose thy youth in peace and to achieve
> The silver livery of advised age,
> And in thy reverence and thy chair-days thus
> To die in ruffian battle? Even at the sight
> My heart is turn'd to stone; and while 'tis mine
> It shall be stony. York not our old men spares;
> No more will I their babes. Tears virginal
> Shall be to me even as the dew to fire;
> And beauty, that the tyrant oft reclaims,
> Shall to my flaming wrath be oil and flax.
> Henceforth I will not have to do with pity.[14]
>
> (v. ii. 31–56)

The style of these lines surely belongs to a period at least five years
after the composition of the rest of the play. Gloucester's soliloquies in
Part 3, splendid as they are, belong to an earlier stratum and they are
reported fairly accurately in the piratical text of the play. Young
Clifford's lines have left no trace, although the more conventional lines
which follow have.

As Holinshed and Grafton often copied Hall, it is sometimes impossible to tell which of the three was being used; but it is certain that all

three *were* used. In addition, it can be shown that the authors used Fabyan's *Chronicle* in Part I and that Shakespeare used Foxe's *Acts and Monuments* in the other two parts. The consultation of several different works for a single play is in accordance with Shakespeare's usual practice, as already exhibited in *The Taming of the Shrew* and *The Comedy of Errors*, so that this fact cannot be used as evidence of multiple authorship. But in view of the doubts expressed above about the authorship of Part I, it would be hazardous to draw any conclusions from that play about Shakespeare's use of his sources. It so happens that the Temple-Gardens scene – one of the three ascribed by nearly all critics to Shakespeare – has no known source and was presumably invented by him to symbolize the beginnings of the Wars of the Roses, as the entry of the son who has killed his father and the father who has killed his son in Part 3 symbolizes its results in human misery. The next scene generally ascribed to Shakespeare (II. v) could be based on Hall or on Holinshed. There are no verbal echoes of either, but Shakespeare's indebtedness to the *Chronicles* is shown by the way he follows them in their confusion of one Edmund Mortimer, who was never imprisoned, with another Edmund, his uncle, who was imprisoned by Glendower and afterwards married his captor's daughter, as we know from *1 Henry IV*. This scene, too, was dramatically necessary to link the *Henry VI* trilogy with the ultimate cause of the Wars of the Roses in the deposition of Richard II. If Part I was written after the other two parts, there was an obvious need to introduce the theme of civil war, which is the sole theme of the plays already written. If, on the other hand, Part I was written first, Shakespeare's revision of it may have been to forge the links with the other two plays.

The third 'Shakespearian' scene is IV. ii, although it is not different in kind, perhaps, from other Talbot scenes in Act IV. These scenes are historically out of sequence since Talbot was killed in 1453, more than twenty-two years after the burning of Joan, whereas in the play Joan's capture occurs after Talbot's death. The Talbots, moreover, were killed at Castillon, not at Bordeaux which had been recaptured by the English in 1451. In IV. ii, on the other hand, Bordeaux is relieved by the approach of the Dauphin's army. These changes were made to enhance the stature of Talbot, the virtual hero of Part I, and to suggest indirectly that his defeat was due to witchcraft. Joan's insults over his body and that of his son, Talbot's attempt to persuade his son to flee (Scene v,) and his son's refusal are based on Hall, though without verbal echoes. Although Chambers thought the scene was by Peele, it seems to look forward to the scene in which Aumerle is pardoned in *Richard II*, another scene where an alien hand used to be suspected.[15]

> *John.* The world will say he is not Talbot's blood
> That basely fled when noble Talbot stood.
> *Tal.* Fly to revenge my death, if I be slain.
> *John.* He that flies so will ne'er return again.
> *Tal.* If we both stay, we both are sure to die.
> *John.* Then let me stay; and, father, do you fly.
> Your loss is great, so your regard should be;
> My worth unknown, no loss is known in me;
> Upon my death the French can little boast;
> In yours they will, in you all hopes are lost.
> Flight cannot stain the honour you have won;
> But mine it will, that no exploit have done;
> You fled for vantage, every one will swear;
> But if I bow, they'll say it was for fear.
> There is no hope that ever I will stay
> If the first hour I shrink and run away.
> Here, on my knee, I beg mortality,
> Rather than life preserv'd with infamy.
> *Tal.* Shall all thy mother's hopes lie in one tomb?
> *John.* Ay, rather than I'll shame my mother's womb.
> *Tal.* Upon my blessing I command thee go.
> *John.* To fight I will, but not to fly the foe.
> *Tal.* Part of thy father may be sav'd in thee.
> *John.* No part of him but will be shame in me.
>
> (IV. v. 16–39)

Part 2, as we have seen, is based almost wholly on Hall's *Chronicle*, except for the scene of the bogus miracle which derives ultimately from More's *Dialogue of the Veneration and Worship of Images*, but immediately from Foxe's *Acts and Monuments*. Shakespeare disposes his material in a masterly way, with Duke Humphrey as the central figure, the patriot whose criticism of the marriage settlement arranged by Suffolk makes enemies of Suffolk and the Queen; whose ambitious wife makes him vulnerable; and whose murder is followed by the banishment and killing of Suffolk, and the horrifying death of the Cardinal, his third enemy. The misgovernment of the realm by self-seeking nobles and saintly King enables York to obtain support from the Nevilles in his claim to the throne.

Shakespeare makes a number of changes, although his general account conforms to that of Hall, the loss of France having been dealt with in Part 1. He makes York's acceptance of the Irish appointment a deliberate plan to obtain an army; he conflates York's two attempts to seize power, historically separated by several years, and omits his imprisonment on the failure of the first attempt. The structure of the play is tightened up by the working out of the prophecies of the spirit raised by Margery Jourdain and Bolingbroke – Suffolk being killed by Walter (pronounced Water) Whitmore, and Somerset slain at the battle of St Albans, under an ale-house sign of a castle.

The first mention of Cade by York in III. i as stubborn and brave does not fully conform with Hall's portrait of the rebel as 'of a goodly stature, and pregnaunt wit', a good general, 'sober in communicacion, wyse in disputyng, arrogant in hart, and styfe in his opinion';[16] but in Act IV Shakespeare departs still further from his source, depicting a sinister buffoon. Whether the denigration of Cade was caused, as some believe, by Shakespeare's innate conservatism, or by the fear of the censorship which afterwards prevented the performance of *Sir Thomas More*, the black comedy of these scenes is brilliantly designed to bring out the chaos caused by the feuding nobles.

One other alteration may be mentioned. Hall makes no suggestion that Suffolk and Margaret were lovers. Shakespeare shows them mutually attracted when they first meet, but Suffolk decides to conceal his love; but when they finally part their expressions of love cast a retrospective light on their whole relationship.

Here, no doubt, as with Cade, the characters developed in the course of composition. An even more striking example is that of Richard, Duke of Gloucester, who in Part 2 is comparatively colourless, but who is developed in Part 3 into the dynamic figure of evil who was to achieve the throne as Richard III. Although Shakespeare must have known in general terms how the character was to be developed, he did not wish it to be too prominent at this stage, where York's ambitions were his main concern.

The weakness of the play is neither in construction nor in characterization, but in the verse. Admirable as much of it is, Shakespeare had not yet learnt how to vary his style to suit the characters. They speak with eloquence, but they speak alike, and seem not so much men talking to men, as actors declaiming. Only with Cade and his followers does Shakespeare provide individual voices, and they speak in prose. Young Clifford, as we have seen, suddenly acquires an individual voice in the penultimate scene of the play; but this passage reads like a later revision.

Part 3 covers the period from the battle of St Albans in 1455 to the murder of Henry VI some sixteen years later; but we are not conscious of any great lapse of time. Shakespeare achieves this compactness by omission and telescoping. In Act I he jumps from the last event of Part 2, the battle of St Albans, to York's death five years later; in Act II he dramatizes only the battle of Towton, others being reported, and one being omitted altogether. Act III begins with Henry's capture on his return to England, and ends with Edward IV's marriage in 1464. In Act IV two defeats of Edward's forces, which took place in 1469 and 1470, are reduced to one. In Act V Shakespeare dramatizes the battles of Barnet and Tewkesbury, which took place in 1471, and concludes with Richard's murder of Henry in the Tower.

The most remarkable alteration, however, concerns Part 2 as well as Part 3. York's son, Richard, the future Richard III, was born in 1452 and was only three years old at the time of the battle of St Albans: he had been sent abroad with his brother, George. Yet in the play he is already fully adult and taking an active part in the battle. In the first act of Part 3, he persuades York to break his oath, but is not (as far as we are shown) ambitious for the crown. In Act II, when he vows to avenge his father's death, he is a loyal and loving son rather than a conscienceless Machiavel. It is not until III. ii that Richard's villainy is revealed, and his determination to achieve the crown by murdering his rivals. Up to that point in the play – at least if we are ignorant of the sequel – we think of Richard as one who is moved by family loyalty, concerned with avenging his father's murder, as ruthless with the Lancastrians as they had been with the Yorkists, and perhaps illustrating the inevitable deterioration of morals, the stifling of humanity and compassion, during a prolonged war.[17]

RICHARD III

SHAKESPEARE'S conception of his villain-hero, Richard III, came ultimately from Sir Thomas More's *History of Richard III*, which was afterwards embodied in the *Chronicles* of Hall and Holinshed. It is difficult to be absolutely certain which of the two was Shakespeare's main source – in some other plays he used both, and Holinshed incorporates much of Hall's actual phrasing. It can, however, be shown that a number of details used by Shakespeare are to be found in Holinshed, but not in Hall;[1] and there are a few in Hall (or in Grafton's *Chronicle at Large* in which Hall is often incorporated), but absent from Holinshed.[2] Of the details peculiar to Holinshed, the following have been noted. The line in the first scene about Edward IV's illness –

> And his physicians fear him mightily –   (137)

is based on 'there was little hope of recouerie in the cunning of his physicians'.[3] The bleeding of Henry VI's corpse in the presence of his murderer –

> dead Henry's wounds
> Open their congeal'd mouths and bleed afresh! –
> (I. i. 55–6)

is based on Holinshed's account:[4]

> The dead corps . . . laid on a beire or coffen bare faced, the same in presence of the beholders did bleed; where it rested the space of one whole daie. From thense he was carried to the Blackfriers, and bled there likewise.

In II. iii, the lines of the citizens (38–44) –

> Truly, the hearts of men are full of fear.
> You cannot reason almost with a man
> That looks not heavily and full of dread. . .
> Before the days of change, still is it so;
> By a divine instinct men's minds mistrust
> Ensuing danger; as by proof we see

The water swell before a boist'rous storm –

are used by J. Dover Wilson to show[5] that Shakespeare here used Holinshed rather than Hall:

> Then began here & there some maner of mutteryng emongest the people, as though all thyng shoulde not longe be well, though they wyste not what they feared nor wherfore: were it, that before suche greate thynges, mennes hertes (of a secrete instinct of nature) mis-geueth theim, as the south wynde somtyme swelleth of hym selfe before a tempest.   (Hall, f. xiii)

> Yet began there here and there abouts, some maner of muttering among the people, as though all should not long be well, though they neither wist what they feared, nor wherefore: were it, that *before* such great things, *mens hearts* of a secret *instinct* of nature misgiue them; as the sea without wind *swelleth* of himselfe sometime *before* a tempest.   (Holinshed, 721/2/57)

The words italicized by Boswell-Stone were not intended by him to suggest that they were peculiar to Holinshed's account. In fact they are common to both chroniclers. The account, however, of Richard's visit to Exeter in 1483, and his disturbance at the resemblance between Rugemont and Richmond, is apparently peculiar to Holinshed.[6] Then again, as Boswell-Stone pointed out,[7] the mistake of 'mother's' for 'brother's' (v. iii. 324) is a proof that Shakespeare used the 1587 edition of Holinshed, which has the same mistake.

Yet it has been shown that Shakespeare must have taken some details from Hall. A misunderstanding of Hall accounts for his erroneous assumption that Antony Woodeville, Lord Rivers, and Lord Scales were three persons, rather than one. Holinshed omits Scales. Another certain borrowing from Hall is the expansion of Holinshed's bare mention of Burdet's execution, 'that was for a word spoken in hast cruellie beheaded'. Hall explains:[8]

> This Burdet was a marchaunt dwellyng in Chepesyde at the signe of the croune, which now is the signe of the floure de luse ouer agaynst soper lane. This man merely in rufflyng time of king Edward the iiij his raign, sayd to his owne sonne that he would make him inheritor of the croune, meaning his owne house.

Shakespeare makes use of this passage in Richard's lines:

Tell them how Edward put to death a citizen

> Only for saying he would make his son
> Heir to the crown – meaning indeed his house.
>
> (III. v. 76–8)

How closely on occasion Shakespeare followed one or other chronicle can be seen from the orations of Richard and Richmond in the last act of the play. In the former,

> A sort of vagabonds, rascals, and runaways,
> A scum of Bretons . . .   (v. iii. 316–17)

is derived from 'traitors, theeues, outlawes and runnagates of our owne nation' and 'a number of beggerlie Britans'. Richmond in both is called a milksop; in both the soldiers are bidden to advance their standards; and in both St George is invoked.[9]

It is unlikely that Shakespeare had read Thomas Legge's play, *Richardus Tertius*. Some parallels, however, have been pointed out with two scenes in Shakespeare's plays – three with the wooing of Anne, and one with the wooing of Elizabeth.[10] The former are called forth, probably independently, by the facts of the situation and the latter – 'factum prius nequit infici' and 'What is done cannot be now amended' (IV. iv. 292) – is a commonplace.

Another play, which survives only in a debased text, *The True Tragedie of Richard III* (1594), was certainly known to Shakespeare when he wrote *Hamlet*, since a line in the play-scene –

> The croaking raven doth bellow for revenge –
>
> (III. ii. 248–9)

telescopes two lines in *The True Tragedie*:

> The screeking Rauen sits croking for reuenge,
> Whole heads of beasts comes bellowing for reuenge.
>
> (1892–3)

The speech from which these lines are taken[11] is spoken by Richard before the battle of Bosworth. Although the scene in Shakespeare's play differs a good deal – the ghosts of Richard's victims appear to him in a dream, and the speech which follows was probably suggested by Holinshed's reference to 'a dreadfull and terrible dreame', a 'strange vision' which 'stuffed his head and troubled his mind with manie busie and dreadfull imaginations' – it looks nevertheless as though the

ghosts and the terrified self-questioning were suggested by these lines
in the old play:

> [The] horror of my bloodie practise past,
> Strikes such a terror to my wounded conscience,
> That sleepe I, wake I, or whatsoeuer I do,
> Meethinkes their ghoasts comes gaping for reuenge,
> Whom I haue slaine in reaching for a Crowne.
> Clarence complaines, and crieth for reuenge.
> My Nephues bloods, Reuenge, reuenge, doth crie.
> The headlesse Peeres comes preasing for reuenge.
> And euery one cries, let the Tyrant die. . .   (1877–85)

> Being alone, I dread the secret foe:
> I doubt my foode, least poyson lurke therein. . .
> Then such a life I count far worse to be,
> Then thousand deaths vnto a damned death:
> How wast death I said? who dare attempt my death?
> Nay who dare so much as once to thinke my death?
>   (1898 ff.)

Richard's calling for a horse, and his refusal to fly –

> *King.* A horse, a horse, a fresh horse.
> *Page.* A[12] flie my Lord, and saue your life.
> *King.* Flie villaine, looke I as tho I would flie, no –
>   (1985–7)

doubtless suggested the corresponding passage[13] in Shakespeare's play.
G. B. Churchill, J. Dover Wilson, and Geoffrey Bullough list other
parallels.[14] Of these the most substantial is that in both plays Rivers
uses the phrase 'but green' about the reconciliation between the parties
in a context which includes the words 'traine' and 'malice'. Other
parallels (e.g. the meeting between Stanley and Richmond before the
battle and the gloominess of the weather) seem much less significant.
Nor is it likely that Shakespeare deliberately avoided dramatizing the
same events as the anonymous dramatist because he was sensitive about
the charge of plagiarism levelled against him by Robert Greene in
A Groatsworth of Wit.

   The historical period of the play covers the years between the death
of Henry VI in May 1471 and the battle of Bosworth in August 1585,
but the events are telescoped, and they are linked more closely to the
previous trilogy. Clarence was not sent to the Tower until 1477, five

years after Richard's marriage to Anne, and Edward IV did not die
until 1483. The first three acts of the play therefore comprise the events
of some dozen years, and the last two acts the two years of Richard's
reign. Shakespeare omits, for example, Gloucester's successful campaign against the Scots in 1482, the death – indeed, the very existence –
of Richard's son, and Henry Tudor's abortive attempt to invade
England in 1483; but he adds the theatrical wooing of Anne beside
the corpse of her father-in-law, and although he follows the chroniclers
in having Richard persuade Queen Elizabeth to let him marry her
daughter, he alters the chronological position of the episode, making it
follow, and not precede, the death of Anne, and he apparently means
us to suppose that Queen Elizabeth only pretends to consent.

The two most important changes, however, remain to be mentioned.
Queen Margaret had returned to France in 1476, ransomed by Louis
XI; but Shakespeare, in order to strengthen the links with the previous
plays in which Margaret is a dominant figure, has her remain in
England to await the decline and fall of her enemies. The other change
relates to the character of Richard himself, who is not merely the
villain depicted by More, by the chroniclers who copied him, and by
the author of *The True Tragedie*. Nor is he simply the sinister and
dynamic figure who had emerged in *Henry VI*, Part 3. His gusto, his
delight in his own cleverness, what Lamb called 'his habitual jocularity',
owe most perhaps to the influence of Marlowe; but Shakespeare went
beyond his model.

There are two parallels with the 'Complaint' of Clarence, written by
Baldwin in *A Mirror for Magistrates*. As Dover Wilson pointed out,[15]
the prophecy that a G would destroy Edward's children is not ascribed
by Holinshed to the invention of 'wicked heades' as it is by Baldwin;
and Shakespeare's Richard admits that he has invented the prophecy,
following Baldwin's phraseology very closely. Later on, Clarence describes how the murderers, having tried unsuccessfully to strangle him,

> bound me whether I would or no,
> And in a butte of Malmesey standing by,
> Newe Christned me, because I should not crie.

> (369–71)

So Richard, referring to the reason why Clarence is being imprisoned,
that his name begins with G, adapts Baldwin's jest:

> Alack, my lord, that fault is none of yours;
> He should, for that, commit your godfathers.

O, belike his majesty hath some intent
That you should be new christ'ned in the Tower.

(I. i. 47–50)

Harold Brooks has pointed out[16] a number of interesting parallels with
Seneca's plays. He suggests, first, that the place given to the Duchess
of York corresponds to that of Hecuba in the *Troades*, both women
being mothers of sons who were fatal to their countries. Hecuba,
Andromache, Polyxena, and Helen resemble the Shakespearian quartet
of the Duchess, Elizabeth, Anne, and Margaret. Margaret, the hated
Lancastrian among a trio of Yorkists, resembles Helen, the hated
Greek among Trojans. Elizabeth, like Andromache, has lost her son
and heir. Anne, like Polyxena, marrying an enemy, knows that she is
to be sacrificed. There are a number of minor parallels which reinforce
the resemblance between the situations of the two groups of women.
Bullough has printed[17] a scene from Jasper Heywood's translation of
Hercules Furens (1561), in which Lycus, during the absence of Hercules,
having invaded his country, tries to seduce Megara, whose father and
brothers he has slain. Brooks gives a detailed comparison of the scene
with the one in which Richard woos Anne. Lycus and Richard are
motivated not by the love they pretend but by ambition; both are
responsible for the deaths of the relatives of the women they wish to
marry; and both women are in mourning.

Whether Shakespeare was directly influenced by *Hercules Furens* –
or by *Octavia*, *Medea*, and *Hippolytus*, as Brooks argues – or whether
the influence was indirect, there can be little doubt that *Richard III* is
the most Senecan of Shakespeare's plays. The chorus of wailing women,
the ghosts of victims vowing vengeance, the stichomythia, and the
general atmosphere, all reveal that Shakespeare had learned from
Seneca, as he had learned from Plautus and Terence. The construction
of the play, with the rise and fall of the hero, may owe something to
A Mirror for Magistrates; but it could be regarded as more promising
in some ways than any of Shakespeare's previous plays. Structurally it
is clearly an advance on *Henry VI*; and although, as we have seen,
The Comedy of Errors was more complex than its Plautine original, it
was enormously indebted to it. With *Richard III* Shakespeare had to
construct his own plot, selecting some historical events and rejecting
others for dramatic effect, and emphasizing the pattern by continual
reminders of the past and ironical foreshadowings of the future.[18]

✳
✳ 9 ✳

ROMEO AND JULIET

Of the various versions of the Romeo and Juliet story by Luigi da
Porto, Matteo Bandello, Luigi Groto, Boaistuau, William Painter, and
Arthur Brooke, there are some slight indications that Shakespeare may
have read besides Brooke, Painter, da Porto, and Groto; but as Brooke
asserts that he saw 'the same argument lately set foorth on stage', some
of the indebtedness to Italian sources may be illusory. It will be
necessary, however, to detail the more significant of the alleged
borrowings.[1]

Luigi da Porto's tale is set in Verona, the feuding families are the
Montecchi and the Cappelletti, and Romeo goes in disguise to the
Cappelletti house in the hope of seeing a woman who has scorned
him. He and Giulietta fall in love. Romeo frequently climbs her
balcony to listen to her discourse; on one occasion she happens to see
him and exclaims:[2]

> Che fate quì a quest'ora così solo?
>
> (ed. E. Cochin, p. 46)

So Juliet in the play asks:

> What man art thou that thus bescreened in night
> So stumblest on my counsel?   (II. ii. 52–3)

Giulietta, like Juliet, goes alone to the Friar's cell for her wedding. In
the versions of Bandello and Brooke, Romeo is attacked by Tybalt
and forced to defend himself; in da Porto he attacks Tebaldo only
when he has seen many of his kin wounded. So in Shakespeare Romeo
attacks Tybalt only after the death of Mercutio. In the tomb Giulietta
awakens just before Romeo dies of the poison; she dies, somewhat
improbably, by holding her breath.

Some fifty years after Luigi da Porto's version, Luigi Groto dramatized it in *Hadriana* (1578). There are two possible links with Shakespeare. In the scene of parting at dawn, there is a reference, as in Romeo
and Juliet, to the nightingale:[3]

> S'io non erro, è presso il far del giorno.
> Udite il rossignuol, che con noi desto,
> Con noi geme fra spini, e la rugiada
> Col pianto nostro bagna l'herbe.   (II. iii. 237–40)

But, of course, nightingales make frequent appearances in aubades. The other parallel concerns the consolation offered to Juliet's father:

> Non perde il suo colui, che l'altrui rende.
> A la terra doveansi i corpi; l'alme
> A Dio, tutto 'l composto a la Natura.
> Non biasmate colui che ve li toglie
> Si tosto.   (IV. iii. 2–6)

So Friar Lawrence declares:

> Heaven and yourself
> Had part in this fair maid; now heaven hath all,
> And all the better is it for the maid.
> Your part in her you could not keep from death,
> But heaven keeps his part in eternal life. (IV. v. 66–70)

Here again this is stock consolation to be expected from a friar; and Shakespeare may well have arrived at the idea quite independently.

This play was preceded by Bandello's tale (1554), by Pierre Boaistuau's French version (1559), and by Painter's English translation in his *Palace of Pleasure* (1567). Of these Shakespeare probably knew Painter, although the one sign that he did so is the resemblance between '40 houres at the least' (Painter) and the 'two and forty hours' during which Juliet would be under the influence of the drug. Brooke does not mention the duration. It should be mentioned, however, that Shakespeare agrees with Boaistuau, and not with Bandello, Painter, or Brooke, in making Romeo go to the Capulet's ball in the hope of meeting his cruel mistress.

The main source, perhaps – as Professor Bullough thinks – the only source, of the play was undoubtedly *The Tragicall Historye of Romeus and Juliet* by Arthur Brooke (1562), a poem based on Bandello. Brooke describes the feud between the Montagews and Capulets, and the attempt by Prince Escalus to effect a peace. Romeus, after months of unrequited love for a wise and virtuous maid, is persuaded by a friend to frequent balls and banquets, so as to discover a kinder mistress. At Christmas-tide he and his friends go to a masked ball at the Capulets' house; he and Juliet fall in love and afterwards discover each other's identity. Romeus passes by her window week after week and gazes at her until one night she sees him and insists that, unless he intends marriage, he must cease his suit. Romeus thereupon goes to consult Friar Lawrence, who eventually consents to the marriage, hoping thereby to effect a reconciliation between the two families. Juliet, using her Nurse as a messenger, is told to go to confession, where she is married to Romeus. A month or two after the marriage a fight breaks out, in the course of which Romeus kills Tibalt in self-defence. Romeus is banished and, after a last night together, the lovers are parted. Juliet's mother, seeing her grief but unaware of the cause, gets Capulet to find her a husband. Juliet refuses to marry Paris and, on the advice of Friar Lawrence, she takes the sleeping-potion. In due course she is placed in the family vault. Meanwhile the messenger sent by the Friar to Romeus fails to reach him; Romeus hears from his servant of Juliet's death, buys poison of an apothecary, returns to Verona, and takes the poison in the vault. Friar Lawrence arrives just as Romeus dies; Juliet awakens and asks for her husband; seeing him dead, she takes his dagger and kills herself. The Watch arrive together with the Prince, and the Friar gives a lengthy account of the whole story. The Nurse is banished, the Apothecary hanged, the Friar pardoned, and the families reconciled.

Shakespeare disposes his material in accordance with the requirements of Five-Act Structure. He begins his play with a brawl between the two families; the climax of the third act is the fight between Romeo and Tybalt, representing the warring families, which results in the hero's banishment; and the conclusion of the play is the reconciliation of the two families. Within this structure, the personal tragedy of the lovers is played out. In the first act the lovers meet; in the second act they are married; in the third act the marriage is consummated and the lovers are separated; in the fourth act Juliet has her mimic death; and in the last act the lovers severally commit suicide. The action is condensed from the months of Brooke's poem into a few days. This not only increases the speed and intensity of the action: it also shows the passionate impulsiveness of the lovers, and they consummate their marriage in the knowledge that they must separate on the morrow. In some ways, of course, especially when considered in relation to the later tragedies, the play is 'immature'. Shakespeare was writing a tragedy of fortune, the only kind his story allowed, and too much depends on accident: the quarantine which delays the messenger, and

the awakening of Juliet one minute too late. But already Shakespeare
was manipulating his source-material with a masterly sense of dramatic
possibilities.

Brooke purported to describe

> a coople of vnfortunate louers, thralling themselues to vnhonest
> desire, neglecting the authoritie and aduise of parents and frendes,
> conferring their principall counsels with dronken gossyppes, and
> superstitious friers (the naturally fitte instrumentes of vnchastitie)
> attemptyng all aduentures of peryll, for thattaynyng of their wished
> lust, vsyng auriculer confession (the kay of whoredome, and treason)
> for furtheraunce of theyr purpose, abusyng the honorable name of
> lawefull mariage, to cloke the shame of stolne contractes, finallye,
> by all meanes of vnhonest lyfe, hastyng to most vnhappye deathe.

Luckily for his poem, however, Brooke does not carry out this didactic
programme. Sympathy for the lovers keeps breaking in; and Shakespeare goes much further in enlisting the sympathies of his audience.
Old Capulet's abominable treatment of Juliet has the effect of retrospectively justifying her secret marriage. Although the Friar, if judged
by standards of realism, behaves very foolishly, Shakespeare nowhere
explicitly condemns him, but even uses him as *raisonneur*. We are
never in danger of supposing that the love of Romeo and Juliet is
merely a lust of the blood, partly because Shakespeare juxtaposes it
with the bawdy comments of Mercutio and the Nurse. Few English
critics have agreed with Masefield's strange description of Juliet as 'a
deceitful, scheming liar' and of Romeo as 'a frantic madman'.[4] On the
contrary, Shakespeare shows us Romeo 'behaving with exemplary
composure and forbearance, though insulted by a quarrelsome bully
in the presence of his friends'.[5] We are convinced of Juliet's integrity
and essential purity by her delicate avowal of love in the balcony
scene, by her soliloquy when awaiting the arrival of her husband on
their wedding night, by her repudiation of the Nurse as 'ancient
damnation', and by her courage when she drinks the potion.

The character of Mercutio is developed from a single reference by
Brooke to

> one calde *Mercutio*.
> A courtier that ech where, was highly had in price:
> For hee was courteous of his speeche, and pleasaunt of deuise.[6]
>
> (254–6)

The character in the play, in life as in death, exemplifies the futility of
the blood-feud; he acts as a foil to Romeo and as a critic of romantic
love; and his death involves Romeo in the act that leads to his banishment. Tybalt, likewise, appears only once in Brooke's poem as a
young man 'exercisde in feats of armes,/And noblest of the rowte'
(964). In the play he is not noble. He is introduced into several scenes
as the most violent of the Capulets – so irrational that even without
Mercutio's death all our sympathies would be with Romeo. The
development of the character enabled Shakespeare to emphasize again
the futility of the feud, and to give every provocation to Romeo.
This was the more necessary, as he had altered the time of the fight, so
that it takes place on the day of the wedding, Romeo challenging
Tybalt instead of killing him in self-defence.

The other characters are developed from hints given by Brooke.
Paris, Capulet, Montague, and the Nurse are not essentially different
from the characters in the poem, but they are made much more real
and effective. Juliet is younger than in the source; and Romeo's passion
for Rosaline becomes the typical romantic love of the sonneteers for a
cruel beauty, instead of the sexual pursuit of a virtuous maid. It makes a
more effective contrast with Romeo's love for Juliet.

It has been shown[7] that there are many verbal echoes of Brooke's
poem in Shakespeare's play. On three occasions the phrasing of the
poem is repeated almost word for word.[8] Friar Lawrence's words to
Romeo, after he has been sentenced to banishment, for example:

> Art thou a man? thy form cries out thou art. . .
>
> (III. iii. 109)

are close to Brooke's line:

> Art thou (quoth he) a man: thy shape saith so thou art.
>
> (1353)

Sometimes two phrases in the poem are fused together.[9] When
Romeus first sees Juliet 'he swalloweth downe loues sweete impoy-
sonde baite' (219); and Juliet after the feast exclaims:

> What if with friendly speach the traytor lie in wayte?
> As oft the poysonde hooke is hid wrapt in the pleasaunt bayte?
>
> (387–8)

The two passages are linked by 'poison' and 'bait'; and the Chorus at
the beginning of Act II says that Romeo

> to his foe suppos'd he must complain,
> And she steal love's sweet bait from fearful hooks. (7–8)

Benvolio's description of the fight 'To't they go like lightning' was possibly suggested by Brooke's comparison of the two combatants to 'thunderboltes, throwne downe out of the skie' (1031). The scene in which Juliet drinks the potion is closely based on Brooke's account – her fear of being stifled, her fear of waking too soon, her fear of Tybalt's corpse. Romeo asks the Apothecary for 'such soon-speeding gear', and Brooke's Apothecary hands Romeus the poison with the words 'This is the speeding gere' (2585).

There are many other examples of verbal indebtedness, some of them being in a different context. Brooke's lovers, on their wedding night, lament its brevity and the 'hastiness of Phoebus steeds' (920). Shakespeare's Juliet, longing for the consummation of her marriage, cries:

> Gallop apace, you fiery-footed steeds
> Towards Phoebus' lodging; such a waggoner
> As Phaethon would whip you to the west,
> And bring in cloudy night immediately. (III. ii. 1–4)

Golding used the epithet 'fiery-footed' and speaks of Phaethon as a waggoner; and Shakespeare was apparently reminded of the passage in Ovid, as well as of the lines in Marlowe's *Edward II*:[10]

> Gallop apace bright *Phoebus* through the skie,
> And duskie night, in rustie iron carre:
> Between you both, shorten the time I pray.

Some of the imagery of the play, particularly that relating to voyages, seems to have been suggested by Brooke, who has many images derived from his experience of seafaring. He speaks of the lodestars,[11]

> the wery pilates marke,
> In stormes to gyde to hauen the tossed barke;

an image used by Shakespeare in one of the grandest of his sonnets:

> an ever-fixed mark,
> That looks on tempests and is never shaken;
> It is the star to every wand'ring bark,
> Whose worth's unknown, although his higth be taken.

Brooke, like Shakespeare, speaks of Juliet's bed as the 'long desired port' towards which Romeus's 'stearless ship' (800), his 'Sea-beaten barke' is driven. Another long simile describes the efforts made to reach harbour:[12]

> As when the winter flawes with dredfull noyse arise,
> And heaue the fomy swelling waues vp to the starry skies,
> So that the broosed barke in cruell seas betost,
> Despayreth of the happie hau'n, in daunger to be lost:
> The pylate bold at helme, cries Mates strike now your sayle:
> And turnes her stemme into the waues, that strongly her assayle,
> Then driuen harde vpon the bare and wrackfull shore,
> In greater daunger to be wract, than he hath been before:
> He seeth his ship full right against the rocke to runne,
> But yet he doth what ly'th in him the perilous rocke to shunne:
> Some times the beaten boate, by cunning gouernment,
> The anchors lost, the cables broke, and all the tackle spent:
> The roder smitten off, and ouerboord the maste,
> Doth win the long desired porte, the stormy daunger past.
>
> (1361–74)

Whiter, with his customary acuteness, pointed out the images relating to voyages in Shakespeare's play.[13] He referred to the scene where the Nurse is hailed by Mercutio as a sail, and Peter as a convoy, and Romeo's two speeches, just before he meets Juliet for the first time, and just before his suicide. The first of these runs:

> I fear, too early; for my mind misgives
> Some consequence, yet hanging in the stars,
> Shall bitterly begin his fearful date
> With this night's revels and expire the term
> Of a despised life clos'd in my breast,
> By some vile forfeit of untimely death.
> But He that hath the steerage of my course
> Direct my sail!   (I. iv. 106–13)

Here the sequence of words and images is close to that of the later speech. In both we have stars, bitter(ly), date(less), and death; sail and steerage correspond to pilot and bark; and the legal expressions of term and forfeit correspond to seal and bargain:

> Death, that hath suck'd the honey of thy breath,
> Hath had no power yet upon thy beauty. . .
>   O, here

Will I set up my everlasting rest
And shake the yoke of inauspicious stars
From this world-wearied flesh. Eyes, look your last.
Arms, take your last embrace. And lips, O you
The doors of breath, seal with a righteous kiss
A dateless bargain to engrossing death!
Come, bitter conduct, come, unsavoury guide.
Thou desperate pilot, now at once run on
The dashing rocks thy sea-sick weary bark.
(v. iii. 92–3, 109–18)

This speech, however, is linked not merely to the earlier one quoted, but also to a sonnet in Sidney's *Astrophel and Stella*, No. 85:

I see the house, my heart thy selfe containe,
    Beware full sailes drowne not thy tottring barge:
    Least joy, by Nature apt sprites to enlarge,
Thee to thy wracke beyond thy limits straine. . .
But giue apt seruants their due place, let eyes
See Beautie's totall summe summ'd in her face:
Let eares heare speech, which wit to wonder ties,
Let breath sucke vp those sweetes, let armes embrace
    The globe of weale, lips *Loue's* indentures make:
    Thou but of all the kingly Tribute take.

In Romeo's speech and in Sidney's sonnet we have the same injunctions to eyes, arms, and lips, and in the same order. Shakespeare's 'suck'd', 'honey', and 'breath' may be compared with Sidney's 'breath suck vp those sweetes'; the legal image of sealing a bargain with a kiss is echoed from Sidney's 'indentures'; and the image of the weary bark shipwrecked on the rocks is echoed from Sidney's 'tottring barge' and 'wracke'.[14]

The same speech was also influenced by the concluding stanzas of Daniel's *Complaint of Rosamond*, as editors have recognized:

When naught respecting death, the last of paines,
Plac'd his pale collours, th'ensigne of his might,
Vpon his new-got spoyle before his right. . .

Pittifull mouth (quoth he) that liuing gauest
The sweetest comfort that my soule could wish:
O be it lawful now, that dead thou hauest,
Thys sorrowing farewell of a dying kiss.

> Ah how me thinks I see death dallying seekes
> To entertaine it selfe in loues sweet place:
> Decayed Roses of discoloured cheekes,
> Doe yet retaine deere notes of former grace:
> And ougly death sits faire within her face.

Here we have the idea of the beauty unmarred by death, a reference to
Death as a lover, the mention of a farewell kiss to a dead woman, and
the mention of the ensign of death, to suggest Romeo's lines:

> Thou art not conquer'd; beauty's ensign yet
> Is crimson in thy lips and in thy cheeks,
> And Death's pale flag is not advanced there. . .
>   Shall I believe
> That unsubstantial Death is amorous,
> And that the lean abhorred monster keeps
> Thee here in dark to be his paramour?

(v. iii. 94–6, 102–5)

Brooke could give Shakespeare little beyond the story and a number of
phrases and images; but into his play Shakespeare infused the quintessence of Elizabethan love-poetry. In the last scenes he wrote the
finest poetry which had yet been heard on the English stage; it was the
first play in which he went beyond Marlowe; and in the characters of
Mercutio and the Nurse he displayed for the first time his unequalled
power for the dramatic presentation of character.[15]

❊ 10 ❊

RICHARD II

THE EXACT SOURCES of *Richard II* are still a matter of controversy.
It has been argued[1] that Shakespeare used, in addition to Holinshed's
Chronicles, Hall, Berners' Froissart, *Woodstock*, *A Mirror for Magistrates*,
Daniel's *Civile Wars*, and three French manuscripts: *Chronicque de la
Traïson et Mort de Richart Deux Roy Dengleterre*, Le Beau's version of
this (*Chronique de Richard II depuis l'an 1399*), and Créton's chronicle,

mostly, but not altogether, in verse. To attribute such erudition to
Shakespeare was altogether too much for J. Dover Wilson and,
believing as he did in the validity of the parallels collected by himself
and previous critics, he was driven to postulate a lost play. Shakespeare,
he supposed, did not even have to consult Holinshed: he made use of
Woodstock, the other play, and Daniel's *Civil Wars*:[2]

> I can see no reason for believing that he took the trouble to read
> Holinshed or any other chronicle for his *Richard II*, any more than
> he had done for his *King John*. Daniel's poem, an actor's knowledge
> of *Thomas of Woodstock*, and our hypothetical play-book by the
> author of *The Troublesome Reign of King John* are together sufficient
> to account for all the facts.

They might account for all the facts if there were any direct evidence
for the existence of the lost play. The indirect evidence advanced by
Dover Wilson has not met with general acceptance – the 'strange
mixture of historical erudition and inaccuracy' displayed by the
dramatist, several points which are unintelligible in the play as it
stands, the survival of passages from the old play in v. iii, and the
presence of fossil-rhymes in i. iii and iii. iii. The mixture of historical
erudition and inaccuracy is to be found also in *Macbeth*; and if Shakespeare consulted recondite sources it would not be for the sake of
historical accuracy, but rather as a stimulus to his imagination, and as a
means of amplification. The alleged unintelligibility of certain passages
can be explained by imperfections in the text, or by revision, or by
sheer carelessness. The fossil-rhymes may be explained by the fact that
some of Shakespeare's *Sonnets* were written about this time, or else by
Shakespeare's rewriting in blank verse of scenes originally written in
rhyme. But the strongest argument against Dover Wilson's theory is
that it presupposes an unknown dramatist – the author, too, of *The
Troublesome Raigne* – who possessed the erudition denied to Shakespeare. It is obvious that the author of *The Troublesome Raigne* did not
have such erudition; and it is known, on the other hand, that Shakespeare did use a number of different sources in other plays (e.g. *Macbeth*,
King Lear, *The Merchant of Venice*) and it is easier to believe that he
followed the same practice in *Richard II* than that the author of *The
Troublesome Raigne* went to this trouble.

Peter Ure tried to redeem Shakespeare from the aspersion of 'aca-
demic' by showing that he had no need to consult the French sources,
or even Froissart, or Hall.[3] He could have taken the main outlines of

his play from Holinshed, and taken hints here and there from *Woodstock*, Daniel, and *A Mirror for Magistrates*. Apparent resemblances between the play and the French chronicles are fortuitous, Shakespeare inventing for dramatic reasons incidents which, unknown to him, he could have found in Créton or *Traïson*. It is not possible to prove that Shakespeare read the French chronicles; but they were not quite inaccessible. Holinshed, Hall, and Daniel all used *Traïson*, and Holinshed used Créton's poem. Holinshed, indeed, refers three times to Créton's poem as 'Master Dees French booke',[4] and four times to *Traïson* as 'an old French pamphlet belonging to Iohn Stow'.[5] Ure asserted[6] that Stow's copy contained only the first fifth of *Traïson* in translation; but it is possible, of course, that he also possessed the whole of the original, as Hall apparently did. Ure showed, however, that Holinshed is unlikely to have used more than the translation. But if Shakespeare had wanted to follow up Holinshed's references he could probably have done so, for he is thought to have been acquainted with Holinshed, Camden, and Lambarde, and through them he could have met Dee and Stow.

The evidence that he actually did so is not overwhelming. Créton mentions more than once that Richard's face grew pale with anger.[7]

> La face en ot de mal-talent pâlie,
>   Ce me sembla. . .
> Le roy en ot de maltalent le vis
> Descoulouré. . .
> Là fut le roy, qui ot souvent la face
> Descoulourée. . .

But, even apart from similar passages in Froissart, there is no reason to suppose that Shakespeare required a source for such a commonplace.

A messenger in Créton's poem describes the way people of all ages flock to support Bolingbroke:[8]

> Lors véissiez jeune, viel, feble et fort
> Murmure faire, et par commun accord,
> Sans regarder ni le droit ni le tort,
>   Eulx esmouvoir. . .
> A lui soubsmet, jeunes et anciens. . .

This is paralleled by Scroope's speech (III. ii. 113 ff.) which, after describing the white-beards and boys who have joined Bolingbroke, adds that 'both young and old rebel'. The passage from Holinshed

(501/2/55), quoted by Ure, about Bolingbroke's journey to London, is much less close:

> For in euerie towne and village where he passed, children reioised, women clapped their hands, and men cried out for ioy.

But Scroope's speech could have been amplified from the information supplied by Holinshed on Bolingbroke's initial successes:

> he found means ... forthwith to assemble a great number of people...
> And thus, what for loue, and what for feare of losse, they came
> flocking vnto him from euerie part.   (498/2/54)

The appeals to heaven made by Richard in III. ii, the use of Salisbury to bring evil tidings, and the account of successive disasters in the same scene, may all be paralleled in Créton's account, as in the stanza:[9]

> Et quant le roy lui ot tout laissié dire
> Sachiez de vray qu'il n'ot pas fain de rire;
> Car de tous lez lui venoient, tire à tire,
>   Meschief et paine.

Here again there is no proof that Shakespeare was indebted to Créton. A monarch threatened by rebellion in an Elizabethan play would inevitably assume that God was on his side; Salisbury was a convenient character to use in this scene; and the other parallel is a commonplace. The idea that

> had not God, for some strong purpose, steel'd
> The hearts of men, they must perforce have melted,
> And barbarism itself have pitied him. . .   (v. ii. 34–6)

is an obvious means of arousing the sympathies of the audience for the tragic hero; but it could have been suggested by Créton's lines, which however, related to an earlier episode:[10]

> Plus de cent fois en getay mainte larme;
> N'il n'est vivant si dur cuer ne si ferme,
> Qui n'en éust pleuré, veu le diffame
>   C'on lui faisoit.

It may be mentioned that in both Créton's account and in *Traïson*, Richard in the scene of his surrender to Bolingbroke, addresses him as 'Beau cousin de Lancastre';[11] in the play Richard addresses him as 'Fair cousin'. The same epithet, however, is used by Stow in his account of the interview: 'Fair Cousin of Lancaster'; and Froissart makes Richard call Bolingbroke 'Fair cousin' in the abdication scene.

The most striking parallel, however, is the comparison of Richard's betrayal and suffering to Christ's, to be found in both Créton and *Traïson*. In the prose section of his chronicle, Créton compares the rejection of Richard by the people to Christ's:[12]

> Lors dist le duc Henry moult hault aux communes de ladicte ville: 'Beaux seigneurs, ve-cy votre roy, or regardez que vous en ferez ne volez faire'. Et ilz respondirent à haute-voix: 'Nous voulons qu'ill soit mené à Westmoustier'. Et ainsi il leur délivra. A celle heure il me souvint-il de Pilate, le quel fist batre notre Seigneur Jhésu-Crist a l'estache, et apres le fist mener devant le turbe des Juifs disant: 'Beaux seigneurs, ve-cy votre roy'. Lesquelz respondirent: 'Nous voulons qu'il soit crucifié'. Alors Pilate en lava ses mains disant: 'Je suis innocent du sancjuste'. Est ainsi leur délivra notre Seigneur. Assez semblablement fist le duc Henry quant son droit seigneur livra au turbe de Londres, à fin telle que s'ilz le faisoient mourir, qu'll peust dire: 'Je suis innocent de ce fait icy'.

In *Traïson* there are several similar passages.[13] On the betrayal of the King by Northumberland, the author compares the traitor to Judas and Ganelon. A few pages later Richard compares himself to Christ:

> Adonc regarda ses compaignons qui plouroyent et leur dist en souspirant, Ha mes bons loyaulx amis nous sommes tous trahiz et mis entre les mains de nos ennemis sanz cause pour Dieu auez pascience et vous souuiengne de nostre Saulueur qui fu vendu et mis entre la main de ses ennemis sanz ce quil leust deseruy.   (52)

A third passage refers to Christ's passion:

> et se a mourir fault prenons la mort en gre et ayons memoire de la passion de notre Saulueur et des sains martirs qui sont en Paradiz.
>
> (56)

Although Holinshed refers to a prelate as a Pilate, and although Shakespeare often associates treachery with Judas, it is worth noting that the betrayal into the hands of Bolingbroke is omitted by him. The emphasis on the Christ-parallel is to be found in Créton, *Traïson*, and Shakespeare, but not elsewhere.

There are a number of minor parallels with *Traïson*. The word 'hardie' in the phrase 'si hardie de mectre la main sur les lices'[14] is used in precisely the same context by Shakespeare (I. iii. 46) and both writers use the expression 'base court' to describe the place where Richard meets Bolingbroke.[15] On the whole there seems to be a slight balance of probability that Shakespeare was acquainted, directly or indirectly, with Créton's poem and *Traïson*.

The evidence that Shakespeare had read, seen, or acted in *Woodstock* is less in doubt, for there are a number of substantial, if unimportant, echoes. It has been shown by Harold Brooks and others that he was well acquainted with *A Mirror for Magistrates*.[16] There are no certain echoes of Stow and Froissart, but Tillyard was surely right when he said[17] that

> quite apart from any tangible signs of imitation it is scarcely conceivable that Shakespeare should not have read so famous a book as Berners's Froissart, or that having read it he should not have been impressed by the bright pictures of chivalric life in those pages.

Paul Reyher argued[18] that Shakespeare was indebted to Froissart for his characterization of John of Gaunt and Dover Wilson suggested[19] that Gaunt's death-scene was based on Froissart's chapter entitled 'Howe the duke of Lancastre dyed', his death being due to his son's banishment and his grief at the King's misgovernment:

> for he sawe well that if he longe perceyuered and were suffred to contynewe, the realme was lykely to be utterly loste. with these ymagynacyons and other, the duke fell sycke wheron he dyed.
>
> (Cap. 230)

Froissart mentions that on Gaunt's death Richard 'in maner of joye wrote therof to the Frenche kyng'. Dover Wilson has further suggested[20] that Gaunt's admonitions to his nephew were based on an earlier passage in Froissart's Chronicle:

> He consydred the tyme to come lyke a sage prince, and somtyme sayd to suche as he trusted best. Our nephue the kynge of Englande wyll shame all or he cease: he beleueth to lyghtly yuell counsayle who shall distroy hym; and symply (if he lyue longe) he wyll lese his realme, and that hath been goten with moche coste and trauayle by our predecessours and by us: he suffreth to engendre in this realme bytwene the noble men hate and dyscorde, by whom he shulde be serued and honoured, and this lande kepte and douted.
>
> (Cap. 224)

A. P. Rossiter, however, claimed[21] that it was not necessary to go beyond Woodstock, plus Stow and Hall, for the model of Shakespeare's Gaunt, since he is merely 'the type of virtuous Englishry variously represented by Duke Humphrey, by Woodstock', and by the Bastard in *King John*. Ure was also inclined to doubt[22] whether Shakespeare owed anything to Froissart, and he pointed out that the patriotic Gaunt is to be found in several Elizabethan works. Nevertheless, even though Shakespeare had to have an outspoken critic of the King, and even though he certainly took hints from *Woodstock*, it seems unlikely that Froissart did not contribute to his idea of Gaunt.

About seventy echoes have been listed from Daniel's *Civile Wars*,[23] and although many of these are dubious and others not peculiar to Daniel's poem, enough remain to convince all recent editors that Shakespeare was influenced by it, especially in II. i, IV. i, and Act v. Both poets altered the age of the Queen, making her a woman instead of a child; Shakespeare was clearly indebted to Daniel for the account of the entry into London by Richard and Bolingbroke; he blended Daniel with the *Homilies* for the Bishop of Carlisle's speech; and the meditation in prison by Daniel's Richard appears to have influenced a passage in the scene of the King's parting from the Queen. Richard compares his situation with that of a herdsman he sees through the grating of his cell:[24]

> Thou sit'st at home safe by thy quiet fire
> And hear'st of others harmes, but feelest none;
> And there thou telst of kinges and who aspire,
> Who fall, who rise, who triumphs, who doe mone:
> Perhappes thou talkst of mee, and dost inquire
> Of my restraint, why here I liue alone,
> O know tis others sin not my desart,
> And I could wish I were but as thou art.   (III. 65)

So in the play Richard tells the Queen:

> In Winter's tedious nights sit by the fire
> With good old folks, and let them tell thee tales
> Of woeful ages, long ago betid:
> And ere thou bid good-night, to quit their grief,
> Tell thou the lamentable tale of me,
> And send the hearers weeping to their beds. (v. i. 40–5)

It is difficult to be certain that Shakespeare had read Hall's account of Richard II because Holinshed borrowed so much from it. The verbal

parallels, as Ure insisted,[25] may be fortuitous; and we are left with the
fact that Shakespeare begins his second tetralogy, as Hall begins his
massive chronicle, at precisely the same point – the quarrel between
Mowbray and Bolingbroke. The theme of Hall's book is the over-
throw of the legitimate monarch and the evils that ensued therefrom.
At the critical point of the story, just before Bolingbroke's landing,
Hall says[26] that Richard

> sawe his title iust, trewe, and vnfallible, and beside that he had no
> small truste in the Welshemen, hys conscience to be cleane, pure,
> immaculate wythout spot or enuye.

He pities Richard in prison, and after the murder he comments:[27]

> What trust is in this worlde, that suretie may hath of his life, &
> what constancie is in the mutable comonaltie, all men maie appar-
> antly perceyue by the ruyne of this noble prince, which beeyng an
> vndubitate kyng, crouned and anoynted by the spiritualtie, honored
> and exalted by the nobilitee, obeyed and worshipped of the comon
> people, was sodainly disceyued by theim whiche he moste trusted,
> betrayed by them whom he had preferred, & slayn by theim whom
> he had brought vp and norished: so that all menne maye perceyue
> and see, that fortune wayeth princes and pore men all in one balance.

It is often said that the published accounts of the reign of Richard II
showed a Lancastrian bias, and it is implied that for dramatic reasons
Shakespeare was compelled to give a more sympathetic portrait of his
hero. Yet it is obvious from Elizabeth I's identification of herself with
Richard at the time of the Essex rebellion, the censoring of the depo-
sition-scene in the early editions of the play, the difficulties which beset
Hayward for his history of Henry IV (which begins with the deposition
of Richard), and the unambiguous teaching of the *Homilies* that it
would have been impossible for a dramatist to approve openly of
Richard's deposition, even if he had wanted to do so – which Shakespeare did not. In fact, all the sources of the play exhibited considerable
sympathy for Richard. Holinshed, after discussing Richard's virtues
and vices, is outspoken in condemning the way he was treated:[28]

> But if I may boldlie saie what I thinke: he was a prince the most
> vnthankfullie vsed of his subiects, of any one of whom ye shall
> lightlie read. . . . Yet in no kings daies were the commons in greater
> wealth, if they could haue perceiued their happie state: neither in
> any other time were the nobles and gentlemen more cherished, nor

churchmen lesse wronged. But such was their ingratitude towards their bountifull and louing souereigne, that those whom he had cheeflie aduanced, were readiest to controll him.

Bolingbroke's want of moderation and loyalty led to the scourging of himself and his descendants, for he was guilty of

> tigerlike crueltie . . . wooluishlie to lie in wait for the distressed creatures life, and rauenouslie to thirst after his bloud, the spilling whereof should haue touched his conscience.   (508/2/11)

Daniel's portrait of Richard was more sympathetic than that of the chronicler; and Froissart, who was personally acquainted with the King, gives a moving expression of his grief:[29]

> And when I departed fro hym it was at Wynsore; and at my departynge the kyng sent me by a knight of his . . . a goblet of syluer and gylte, weyeng two marke of siluer, and within it a C. nobles, by the which I am as yet the better, and shal be as long as I lyve; wherfore I am bounde to praye to God for his soule, and with moche sorowe I write of his dethe.   (Cap. 245)

Even if he had not read Créton and *Traïson*, Shakespeare had plenty of precedent for his sympathetic portrayal of Richard in the last three acts of the play, just as he had ample material for depicting Richard's misgovernment in the first two acts. Indeed, the impression one gets of Richard in the early part of the play is a good deal worse than that derived from Hall, Holinshed, or Daniel, partly because of the influence of *Woodstock* and partly because of the patriotic sentiments put into the mouth of Gaunt.

A more detailed consideration of two passages in the play will show the way in which a number of different sources coalesced in these set pieces.[30] The first is Gaunt's attempt to console his son on his banishment, and Bolingbroke's reply. After his banishment, Bolingbroke tells the King:

> Your will be done. This must my comfort be –
> That sun that warms you here shall shine on me,
> And those his golden beams to you here lent
> Shall point on me, and gild my banishment.
>   (i. iii. 144–7)

When the King has left the stage, Gaunt tries to comfort his son by telling him to call his exile 'travel that thou tak'st for pleasure':

All places that the eye of heaven visits
Are to a wise man ports and happy havens.
Teach thy necessity to reason thus:
There is no virtue like necessity.
Think not the King did banish thee,
But thou the King . . .
Go, say I send thee forth to purchase honour,
And not the King exiled thee; . . .
Suppose the singing birds musicians,
The grass whereon thou tread'st, the presence strew'd,
The flowers fair ladies, and thy steps no more
Than a delightful measure or a dance
For gnarling sorrow hath less power to bite
The man that mocks at it and sets it light.   (273 ff.)

Bolingbroke replies bitterly:

O who can hold a fire in his hand
By thinking on the frosty Caucasus?
Or cloy the hungry edge of appetite,
By bare imagination of a feast?
Or wallow naked in December snow
By thinking on fantastic summer's heat?
O no! the apprehension of the good
Gives but the greater feeling to the worse.
Fell sorrow's tooth does never rankle more
Than when he bites, but lanceth not the sore. . . .
Where'er I wander, boast of this I can,
Though banish'd, yet a trueborn Englishman.

T. W. Baldwin pointed out[31] that when Gaunt begins to console his
son, 'he takes his departure from a stock quotation which occurs under
patria in the quotation books', namely Ovid's[32]

Omne solum forti patria est, vt piscibus aequor,
Ut volucri vacuo quicquid in orbe patet.

This sentiment is rendered by Brooke in his poem about Romeo and
Juliet:[33]

Vnto a valiant hart there is no banishment,
All countreys are his natiue soyle beneath the firmament.

As to his fishe the sea, as to the fowle the ayre,
So is like pleasant to the wise eche place of his repayre.

(1443–6)

Shakespeare must have read this passage when he was writing *Romeo and Juliet*, though he does not give his own Friar Lawrence this particular argument. To console a friend who has been sent into exile was, in fact, a favourite exercise. Erasmus, for example, in his *De Conscribendis Epistolis* provided a letter on this very subject; and Shakespeare was acquainted with this book and made use of it for Friar Lawrence's speech of consolation to Romeo.[34] There does not seem, however, to be anything in Erasmus' epistle very close to the passage in *Richard II*.

Baldwin showed that Shakespeare must have used the original Latin when he wrote this scene. 'Omne solum' becomes 'All places'; and 'solum', by a pun, suggested 'sol', the sun, which appears as 'the eye of heaven' (another Ovidian phrase); and 'patria' is expanded to 'ports and happy havens'.

Another book certainly known to Shakespeare was Lyly's *Euphues*, and towards the end of the book Lyly prints a letter offering consolation to a banished friend:[35]

I thincke thee happy to be so well rydde of the courte and bee so voyde of crime. Thou sayest banishment is bitter to the free borne –

a sentence which may have suggested Bolingbroke's last line –

Though banish'd, yet a trueborn Englishman.

Lyly continues:

I speake this to this ende, that though thy exile seeme grieuous to thee, yet guiding thy selfe with the rules of Philosophye it shall bee more tollerable. . . . *Plato* would neuer accompt him banished that had The Sunne, Fire, Aire, Water, and Earth, that he had before, where he felt the Winters blast and the Summers blaze, where the same Sunne, and the same Moone shined. . . .

So Bolingbroke comforts himself with the reflection that the same sun will shine on him. Lyly continues with Plato's view:

whereby he noted that euery place was a Countrey to a wise man, and all partes a pallace to a quiet minde.

Gaunt tells Bolingbroke that

all *places* that the eye of heaven visits
Are to a *wise man* ports and happy havens.

Lyly proceeds to tell an anecdote about Diogenes:

When it was cast in *Diogenes* teeth that the *Synoponetes* had banished
hym *Pontus*, yea, sayde hee, I them of *Diogenes*.

So Gaunt urges Bolingbroke:

Think not the King did banish thee,
But thou the King.

Lyly's later remark that 'the Nightingale singeth as sweetly in the
desarts as in the woodes of *Crete*' may have suggested Gaunt's mention
of the singing birds. The certainty that Shakespeare knew his *Euphues*,
together with the four or five echoes from this passage, are substantial
evidence that he was echoing Lyly. But it is fairly certain that he was
also echoing Cicero's *Tusculan Disputations* (either in the original or in
Dolman's translation). In the fifth book there is a long discussion of
exile as one of the worst of evils:[36]

What is there, that a man should feare? Exile perhaps, which is
counted one of the greatest euels. . . But if you counte it a misery,
to be from your contrey: then trulye is euery prouince ful of
wretched men, of whom very fewe retourne home againe into theyr
countrey. . .

And truly, exyle and banishment, if we weygh the nature of the
things, and not the shame of the name, how much differeth it from
that continuall wanderinge, in the whyche these most notable
philosophers . . . haue spent their whole age, and the course of their
life? . . . For in what soeuer place we haue such thynges, there we
may liue well and happelye. And therfore, hereunto, that saying of
Teucer may well be applyed. My countrey (quod he) is, wheresoeuer
I liue well.

There is no direct evidence that Shakespeare read this passage, but in
the same book is another passage which Steevens believed to lie behind
Bolingbroke's speech:[37]

But he sayeth, he is contented only with the remembraunce of his
former pleasures. As if, a man well nye parched with heate, so that,
he is no longer able to abide the sonne should comfort him selfe

with the remembraunce, that once heretofore, he had bathed him selfe in the cold ryuers of Arpynas. For truly, I see not, howe the pleasures that are past, may ease the gryeues that are present.

That Shakespeare did indeed know Cicero's book appears to be clinched by a fact pointed out by J. C. Maxwell.[38] Shortly after the above passage, Cicero asks:

What parte of Barbary is there, more wylde or rude, then India? Yet neuerthelesse, emonges theim those which are counted wyse men, are fyrst bred vp, bare and naked. And yet suffer both the colde of the hil Caucasus, and also, the sharpenes of the winter, without any paine. And when they come to the fyer, they are able to abide the heate, well nie, till they rost.

Here there are a number of parallels: 'wyse men'/'wise man'; 'bare and naked'/'bare' imagination '. . . naked'; 'colde . . . Caucasus . . . sharpenes . . . winter'/'Caucasi nives hiemalem: frosty Caucasus . . . hungry edge . . . December snow'; and 'fyer'/'fire'. It must be admitted however that there is a very similar passage in Valerius Maximus (III. 3), a popular school author, under the heading of *patience*.

Apud Indos vero patientiae meditatio tam obstinate usurpari creditur, ut sint qui omne vitae tempus nudi exigant modo Caucasi montis gelido rigore corpora sua durantes: modo flammis sine ullo gemitu obiicientes: atque haud parva his gloria contemptu doloris acquiritur; titulusque sapientiae datur.

Here again we have the frosty Caucasus, the mention of fire and wise men, and the use of the adjective 'nudi'. In one respect, indeed, it might be argued that Shakespeare is nearer to Valerius Maximus than he is to Cicero: Bolingbroke's repetition of 'thinking' may be compared with 'patientiae meditatio'. But it is the juxtaposition of the three passages in Cicero that makes it certain that Shakespeare had read the *Tusculan Disputations*, and the passage about the Caucasus might well link up with the parallel passage in Valerius Maximus he had translated at school.

The other passage to be considered is the speech spoken by John of Gaunt on his death-bed. In Daniel's *Civile Wars* there is a description of Flint Castle; but Shakespeare echoed this not in the scene which takes place before the castle, but in Gaunt's description of England:

> A place there is, where proudly raisd there stands
> A huge aspiring rocke neighb'ring the skies;
> Whose surly brow imperiously commands
> The sea his bounds that at his proud feet lies;
> And spurnes the waues that in rebellious bands
> Assault his Empire and against him rise:
> Vnder whose craggy gouernment there was
> A niggard narrow way for men to passe.   (II. 49)

In another passage Daniel asks:

> With what contagion, *France*, didst thou infect
> The land by thee made proud, to disagree?   (IV. 43)

In a third passage Daniel refers to the advantages of being cut off from the manners and morals of the continent. He complains of 'the deedes hye forraine wittes inuent' (IV. 88) and of their 'vile cunning'. He admits that there may be fairer cities, and goodlier soils, but argues that we are spared

> Such detestable vile impietie.   (IV. 89)

He therefore exhorts Neptune:

> *Neptune* keepe out, from thy imbraced Ile
> This foul contagion of iniquitie;
> Drowne all corruptions comming to defile
> Our faire proceedings ordred formally;
> Keepe vs meere *English*, let not craft beguile
> Honor and Iustice with strang subtiltie.   (IV. 90)

In the next stanza he again uses the image of conflict between sea and shore:

> And now that current with maine fury ran . . .
> Vnto the full of mischiefe that began
> T'a vniuersall ruine to extend
> That *Isthmus* failing which the land did keepe,
> From the intire possession of the deepe.

In *Richard II* (II. i), York complains of the influence of Italian fashions, and Gaunt describes the advantages of being cut off from other countries:

> This royal throne of kings, this scept'red isle,
> This earth of majesty, this seat of Mars,

This other Eden, demi-paradise,
This fortress built by Nature for herself,
Against infection and the hand of war,
This happy breed of men, this little world,
This precious stone set in the silver sea,
Which serves it in the office of a wall,
Or as a moat defensive to a house,
Against the envy of less happier lands;
This blessed plot, this earth, this realm, this England,
This nurse, this teeming womb of royal kings,
Fear'd by their breed, and famous by their birth,
Renowned for their deeds as far from home,
For Christian service and true chivalry,
As is the sepulchre in stubborn Jewry
Of the world's ransom, blessed Mary's Son;
This land of such dear souls, this dear dear land,
Dear for her reputation through the world,
Is now leas'd out – I die pronouncing it –
Like to a tenement or pelting farm.
England, bound in with the triumphant sea,
Whose rocky shore beats back the envious siege
Of wat'ry Neptune, is now bound in with shame,
With inky blots and rotten parchment bonds.

(II. i. 40–64)

There is a similar passage in *King John* (II. i):

that white-fac'd shore,
Whose foot spurns back the ocean's roaring tides,
And coops from other lands her islanders –
Even till that England, hedg'd in with the main,
That water-walled bulwark, still secure
And confident from foreign purposes. . .   (23–8)

There are too many links between the Daniel and Shakespeare passages
for them to be accidental. Rock, sea, bounds, spurns, Neptune, isle,
main, and infect are all common words, but their juxtaposition, the
certainty that Shakespeare knew Daniel's poem, and the use of the
same image would appear to be conclusive proof of Shakespeare's
indebtedness.

The germ of the whole scene may have been the passage from

Froissart's *Chronicles* already quoted.[39] But in *Woodstock* Shakespeare
would have found a passage about fashions which may have coloured
York's lines at the beginning of the scene. In *Woodstock*, too, he would
have found the phrase 'pelting farm' and the word 'landlord' in a
speech by Richard himself:[40]

> Our great father toiled his royal person
> Spending his blood to purchase towns in France;
> And we his son, to ease our wanton youth
> Become a landlord to this warlike realm,
> Rent out our kingdom like a pelting farm
> That erst was held as fair as Babylon.   (IV. i. 143–8)

The end of Gaunt's speech may have been suggested by two separate
passages in *Woodstock* in which Gloucester says:[41]

> I would my death might end the misery
> My fear presageth to my wretched country.

> Send thy sad doom, King Richard: take my life.
> I wish my death might ease my country's grief.

Then J. W. Lever has argued[42] that Shakespeare was also indebted to
John Eliot's translation of some lines by Du Bartas in praise of France.
As Shakespeare had certainly read *Ortho-Epia Gallica* (1593) – he
echoed it in *Love's Labour's Lost* – he had presumably read these verses:

> O Fruitfull *France*! most happie Land, happie and happie thrice!
> O pearle of rich *European* bounds! O earthly Paradice!
> All haile sweet soile! O *France* the mother of many conquering
> knights,
> Who planted once their glorious standards like triumphing wights,
> Upon the banckes of *Euphrates* where *Titan* Day-torch bright
> Riseth, and bloodie swords unsheathd where *Phoebus* drounds his
> light,
> The mother of many Artist-hands whose workemanship most rare
> Dimmes *Natures* workes, and with her fairest flowers doth
> compare.
> The Nurse of many learned wits who fetch their skill diuine
> From *Rome*, from *Greece*, from *Aegypt* farre, and ore the learnedst
> shine,
> As doth the glymmering-Crimsin-dye ouer the darkest gray:
> *Titan* ore starres, or Phoebus flowers ore marigolds in May.

Thy flouds are Ocean Seas, thy townes to Prouinces arise,
Whose ciuill gouernement their walles hath raisd to loftie skies.
Thy soile is fertill-temperate-sweete, no plague thine aire doth
trouble,
Bastillyons fower borne in thy bounds: two Seas and mountaines
double.

The stress on the happiness of France 'most happie Land' etc., the comparison to a pearl and to an earthly paradise, the reference to the crusades, the mention of the country as mother and nurse (as Shakespeare calls England 'teeming womb' and 'Nurse'), the reference to walls, and the statement that 'no plague thine aire doth trouble' all find parallels in Shakespeare's lines.

Peter Ure, however, called attention[43] to the resemblances between Sylvester's version of the same lines and Gaunt's speech. He, like Shakespeare, applies what Du Bartas says of France to England:[44]

> All-haile (deere ALBION) *Europes* Pearle of price,
> The Worlds rich Garden, Earths rare Paradice:
> Thrice-happy Mother, who aye bringest-forth
> Such Chiualry as daunteth all the Earth. . .
> Sweet is thine Aire, thy soile exceeding Fat,
> *Fenc'd from the World* (as better-worth then That)
> With triple Wall (of Water, Wood, and Brasse)
> Which neuer Stranger yet had power to passe. . .

Ure pointed out that 'The Worlds rich Garden' may be compared with 'This other Eden' and that Sylvester and Shakespeare, but not Eliot or Du Bartas, both speak of chivalry. (It might be said, however, that Eden is implied by Paradise as much as by garden, and that chivalry is implied by the reference to the crusades.) As Sylvester's version was not published until 1605, as there is no evidence that it existed ten years previously, and as Shakespeare and Eliot, but not Du Bartas and Sylvester, both use the word 'nurse', it seems reasonable to assume that Shakespeare was echoing Eliot, and that Sylvester, in translating Du Bartas, blended the original with memories of Shakespeare's lines which he might have heard on the stage, or read in one of the first three quartos, or in *England's Parnassus*.

The idea of England as an island-fortress was, of course, familiar, and it dated at least from the Armada year. Shakespeare combined it not merely with the material he found in Eliot's translation, but also with some stanzas by Thomas Lodge entitled 'Truth's Complaint over England'. To Dorothy Earnshaw belongs the credit of this discovery.[45] Lodge links the idea of England as an island-fortress with a comparison of England to Eden:[46]

> Within an Iland compast with the waue,
> A safe defence a forren foe to quell,
> Once *Albion* cald, next *Britaine Brutus* gaue,
> Now *England* hight, a plot of beautie braue,
> Which onely soyle, should seeme the seate to bee,
> Of Paradise, if it from sinne were free.
>
> Within this place, within this sacred plot,
> I first did frame, my first contented bower,
> There found I peace and plentie. . . .

Here the sequence of ideas is very close to that of Gaunt's speech: Iland (Isle) – defence (defensive) – England – seate – Paradise (demi paradise) – sacred plot (blessed plot) – peace (war).

Truth is the spokesman in Lodge's poem and John of Gaunt, speaking as a prophet, makes a similar pronouncement. There are several other links between Lodge's poem and this scene of the play.[47] Lodge speaks of the import of fashions:

> Then flew not fashions euerie day from *Fraunce*.

York, in the play, complains of the aping of Italian fashions. Lodge uses the images of the unbroken colt:

> For as the horse well mand abides the bit,
> And learnes his stop by raine in riders hand,
> Where mountaine colt, that was not sadled yet,
> Runnes headlong on amidst the fallowed land,
> Whose fierce resist scarce bends with anie band:
> So men reclaimde by vertue, tread aright,
> Where led by follies, mischiefes on them light.

So York urges Gaunt to deal mildly with the young King:

> For young hot Coltes being rag'd do rage the more.
>
> (II. i. 70)

A few lines later Lodge mentions that

> the great commaunder of the tides,
> God *Neptune* can allay the swelling seas.

In between these two passages there is an image of an unweeded garden:[48]

> Yet as great store of Darnell marres the seed,
> Which else would spring within a fertile field:
> And as the fruitfull bud is choakt by weede:
> Which otherwise a gladsome grape would yeeld,
> So sometimes wicked men doe ouerweeld,
> And keepe in couert those who would direct,
> The common state, which error doth infect.

This stanza may have suggested the garden imagery in *Richard II*, particularly the speeches of the gardeners (III. iv):

> I will go root away
> The noisome weeds which without profit suck
> The soil's fertility from wholesome flowers. . .
> When our sea-walled garden, the whole land,
> Is full of weeds; her fairest flowers chok'd up,
> Her fruit-trees all unprun'd. (37 ff.)

Lodge shows that the happiness of England depends on the conduct of the prince. Once upon a time

> Their Prince content with plainnesse loued Truth,
> And pride by abstinence was kept from youth.

But he seems to imply that times have changed:

> For common state can neuer sway amisse
> When Princes liues doo levell all a right,
> Be it for Prince that *England* happie is,
> Yet haplesse *England* if the fortune light;
> That with the Prince, the subiects seeke not right,
> Vnhappie state, vnluckie times they bee,
> When Princes liues and subiects disagree.

Lodge speaks of the bramble growing at Court, and he complains of flatterers and rack-rents:

> And who giues most, hath now most store of farmes,
> Rackt rents, the Lord with golden fuell warmes.

So Gaunt blames Richard for England's woes, warns him of flatterers, and complains that England

> Is now leas'd out . . .
> Like to a tenement or pelting farm. (II. i. 59–60)

These lines are, in fact, closer to the passage already quoted from *Woodstock*; but, as we have seen, passages were more likely to coalesce in Shakespeare's mind if they had words or phrases in common.

Lodge's poem was published in a volume entitled *An Alarum against Usurers* (1584), and in the opening treatise there are a number of words and phrases which might have influenced *Richard II*. On two pages a reference to 'farmes' is followed by the use of the word 'glose' in connection with youth, and also the phrase 'not yet stayed' (p. 14). (Cf. II. i. 10, 2, 60: 'youth', 'glose' 'unstaid youth' 'Farme'. But Holinshed uses the word 'vnstaid' in connection with Gloucester.) On the same pages Lodge has the words 'riotous', 'lasciuious', and 'giues the willing Iade the spure' (p. 16). York uses 'lascivious' (p. 19), and Gaunt 'riot' (p. 33) and 'spurs' (p. 36). There is another allusion to the proverbial 'the spur to a willing horse, or the raine to an unwildie colt'. There are frequent references to bonds (p. 64), and there is one sentence (p. 53) which Shakespeare used with little change:

> They bee the Caterpillers of a Common weale. . . .   (p. 24)

So Bushy, Bagot, and their accomplices are described as

> The caterpillers of the commonwealth. (II. iii. 166)

Sir Edmund Chambers, however, cited William Harrison's words about sturdy beggars in his *Description of England* as 'thieues and caterpillers in the commonwealth'; and doubtless the phrase was something of a cliché.

These two passages are exceptional in their fusion of many different sources, although other speeches were apparently composed with equal care. The Bishop of Carlisle's speech against Bolingbroke's usurption (IV. i. 114 ff.) is a blend of the *Homilies* with the chronicles, whilst Richard's lament on the fate of kings (III. ii. 145 ff.) reads like the quintessence of *A Mirror for Magistrates*. Yet, as in the plays written about the same time, there are scenes of great dramatic power alongside others which are, for whatever reason, much less effective. There is likewise a disturbing contrast between the masterly presentation of the major characters and the conventional and even fumbling portrayal of some of the others. We cannot be certain, to give a notorious example, whether the scene in which Aumerle is pardoned was meant to be funny. The most curious point about the dramaturgy, however, is that in the opening scene we are not informed that the King himself was ultimately responsible for the death of Woodstock – this is revealed only in the second scene. Shakespeare may have been relying on the audience's knowledge of *Woodstock*, or he may have felt that the first scene would be more effective if neither Bolingbroke nor Mowbray was obviously in the wrong. As it turns out, Mowbray keeps the King's secret and dies as a crusader while Bolingbroke rebels, and is as guilty of Richard's death as Richard had been of Woodstock's.

❊ II ❊

A MIDSUMMER-NIGHT'S DREAM

THERE WAS probably no comprehensive source of *A Midsummer-Night's Dream*, although Thomas Nashe mentioned in 1589 a play about the King of the Fairies.[1] The Theseus matter came from North's translation of Plutarch's *Lives* and *The Knight's Tale* of Chaucer. Oberon's list of Theseus' conquests –

> Perigouna, whom he ravished?
> And make him with fair Ægles break his faith,
> With Ariadne and Antiopa –   (II. i. 78–80)

appear on nearly adjacent pages of North; and Plutarch, in comparing Theseus with Romulus, deplores the Greek's faults 'touching women and ravishements'.[2] From *The Knight's Tale* Shakespeare took a number of details – the celebration of the wedding of Theseus and Hippolyta, the observance of May Day – though here there may also be a memory of Wyatt's sonnet[3] – and the name Philostrate, who is Emily's page, not the Master of the Revels. It may be added that the rivalry between Lysander and Demetrius for Hermia's love recalls at moments the rivalry of Palamon and Arcite.

Chaucer, too, provides a link between Quince's play and the Oberon–Titania plot. In *The Merchant's Tale* there is a reference to Pyramus and Thisbe:

> By Pyramus and Thisbe, may men lere
> Though they were kept ful long streit ouer all
> They ben accorded, rowning through a wall
> Ther nis no wight couth finde such a sleight.
>
> (2128-31)

These lines occur between two references to Pluto and Proserpina as the King and Queen of the fairies:

> Ful ofte tyme king Pluto and his quene,
> Proserpina, and al hir fayry
> Disporten hem, and maken melody.   (2038-40)

In the other passage (2227 ff.) Pluto and Proserpina have a long argument about female treachery, Proserpina defending her own sex. Pluto gives January his sight again at the moment when Damian is making love to May. So in *A Midsummer-Night's Dream* we have a quarrel between the King and Queen of the fairies and the recovery of the sight of the enchanted lovers by supernatural agency. As Bullough remarks (I. 370):

> The idea of fairy monarchs commenting on human life and taking sides for and against mortals while quarrelling between themselves probably came to Shakespeare from Chaucer.

Oberon himself, however, probably owes most to *Huon of Bourdeaux* in which a wood is described as 'full of the Fayryes and strang things' (like the wood near Athens) and 'in that wood abideth a King of the Fayryes named *Oberon*, he is of height but of three foote, and crooked shouldered, but yet he hath an Angell-like visage'. Huon is anxious to meet with Oberon but is terrified when he does.[4] Shakespeare also knew Greene's *James IV* in the Induction of which Oberon is a character. Titania is mentioned three times in Ovid's *Metamorphoses*, once as a name for Diana (III. 173) and twice as a name for Circe (XIV. 382, 438).[5] Fairies were thought by some to be survivals of Diana's train; and that the Indian Boy's mother was a votaress of Titania's order does not disprove this identification, for Diana, as Lucina, was the goddess of childbirth. Some information about Robin Goodfellow Shakespeare could have acquired from Reginald Scot's *Discoverie of Witchcraft* (1584). Scot declares that not many people believe in Robin Goodfellow's existence; he stresses the fact that since Robin is reputedly a spirit he could not have sexual intercourse with women; and he refers in one sentence to spirits, elves, fairies, changelings, Robin Goodfellow, the puckle 'and such other bugs'. But it seems likely that Shakespeare's character is derived from folk-lore rather than from books, and that Robin is fused with the puckle. There are fairies in Lyly's *Endymion*; but the diminutive fairies had apparently been invented by Shakespeare himself when he wrote the Queen Mab speech for Mercutio. Oberon and Titania are more like the conventional fairies in size, but Cobweb and Mustardseed seem to vary in size from that of Mercutio's fairies to that of Titania herself.[6] The magic juice probably came from Montemayor's *Diana*.[7] Some dubious parallels have been pointed out with Marlowe's *Dido*.[8]

Scot mentions the case of a man turned into an ass (v. 3), but a more likely source of Bottom's transformation, in view of Titania's infatuation, is *The Golden Asse* as translated by William Adlington (1566) in which a matron consummates her love with the metamorphosed narrator.

Shakespeare, then, appears to have taken hints from a number of different sources – Plutarch, Chaucer, Montemayor, Apuleius, Scot, and possibly Marlowe and Lyly – but only with the interlude of Pyramus and Thisbe can we examine in detail the sources he employed. It has been conjectured that the story of *Romeo and Juliet*, taken by Shakespeare from Brooke's poem and Painter's tale, was derived ultimately from the story of Pyramus and Thisbe; for in both tales the lovers, because of their parents' opposition, meet in secret, in both the hero commits suicide in the mistaken belief that the heroine is dead, and in both the man's suicide is followed by that of the woman. The resemblance between the two stories had, indeed, been pointed out by George Pettie, who remarked[9] at the end of one of his stories (Icilius and Virginia) 'that sutch presinesse of parentes brought *Pyramus and Thisbe* to a wofull end, *Romeo* and *Julietta* to untimely death'. Parental opposition is also important in the main plot of *A Midsummer-Night's Dream*. Shakespeare may have turned to the Pyramus story while he was writing *Romeo and Juliet*, for in the last scene of the play Juliet calls Romeo a churl, and Golding uses 'churles' in his version of Ovid's story.[10] There is no doubt that Shakespeare knew the original Latin as well as the translation, and that he had read Chaucer's version in *The Legend of Good Women*. He probably knew Gower's version in *Confessio Amantis*.[11] There is no evidence that he had read Lydgate's version in *Reson and Sensualyte*[12] but it can be shown that he had perused several Elizabethan versions.

Even Ovid's original account is a trifle absurd. The whispering through a hole in the wall, the lovers' alacrity in suicide, the way Pyramus' blood spurts out to stain the mulberry leaves, like water from a burst pipe, are more likely to evoke a smile than the admiration for his cleverness Ovid intended to arouse.

Before Golding's translation appeared, there was a strip-cartoon version of the story, which appeared as a border on the title-page of several books published by Tottel. One of these is More's *Dialogue of comfort against tribulacion* (1553). The upper part of the picture shows a lion, with Thisbe keeping a discreet distance. To the left is a crude piece of masonry which may represent Ninus' tomb, but seems more likely to be the wall that parted the two lovers, for it contains a slit, which Shakespeare was to call a chink or cranny. The lower part of the picture shows Thisbe bending over Pyramus' body. The picture is very crudely drawn; nor does it seem to have any connection with More's *Dialoge*, unless we assume that the lovers might have been less hasty if they had had the benefit of More's comfort against tribulation.[13]

Golding is the one pre-Shakespearian version to use the word 'cranny':

> The wall that parted house from house had riuen therein a crany
> Which shronke at making of the wall. (IV. 83-4)

'Cranny' was also Bottom's word for it (III. i. 62) and it was incorporated in Wall's speech:

> And this the cranny is, right and sinister,
> Through which the fearful lovers are to whisper.
> (V. i. 162-3)

Both Golding and Shakespeare say[14] that Thisbe left her mantle behind. In other versions the Ovidian 'velamina' becomes a 'wimpel' (Chaucer and Gower), a 'kerchief,'[15] and a 'scarf.'[16] In Ovid the lovers tell the wall that they are not ungrateful to it for enabling them to converse. In Golding this becomes:

> And yet thou shalt not finde vs churles: we thinke our selues in det
> For the same piece of courtesie, in vouching safe to let
> Our sayings to our friendly eares thus freely come and goe.
> (IV. 95-7)

This absurd politeness to the wall becomes in Quince's version:

> Thanks, courteous wall. Jove shield thee well for this!
>
> (v. i. 176)

One characteristic of Golding's translation is the desperate prevalence of the auxiliary *did*, as in these lines:

> This neighbrod bred acquaintance first, this neyghbrod first did
> stirre
> The secret sparkes, this neighbrod first an entrance in did showe,
> For loue to come to that to which it afterward did growe.
>
> (IV. 74–6)

So in Quince's Prologue we get four *dids* in three lines:

> This grisly beast, which Lion hight by name,
> The trusty Thisby, coming first by night,
> Did scare away, or rather did affright;
> And as she fled, her mantle she did fall;
> Which Lion vile with bloody mouth did stain.
>
> (v. i. 138–42)

Shakespeare, however, does not make direct use of two of Golding's most ludicrous passages. One of them describes Thisbe's discovery of Pyramus' body:

> Alas what chaunce my *Pyramus* hath parted thee and mee?
> Make aunswere O my *Pyramus*: It is thy *Thisb*, euen shee[17]
> Whome thou doste loue most heartely that speaketh vnto thee.
> Giue eare and rayse thy heauie heade.   (IV. 172–5)

The other describes Thisbe's suicide:

> This said, she tooke the sword yet warme with slaughter of hir
> loue –
> And setting it beneath hir brest, did to hir heart it shoue.[18]
>
> (IV. 196–7)

Shakespeare seems to have echoed a poem on the language of flowers in Robinson's *A Handful of Pleasant Delites* in Ophelia's mad-scene; and he uses the stanza form of Thomson's Pyramus poem in the same anthology in the laments of the lovers:

> In *Babilon*
> not long agone,
> a noble Prince did dwell:

> whose daughter bright
> dimd ech ones sight,
> so farre she did excel.
>
> Now am I dead,
> Now am I fled;
> My soul is in the sky.
> Tongue, lose thy light;
> Moon, take thy flight.
> Now die, die, die, die, die.   (v. i. 293–8)

Like Thomson, Shakespeare refers to Pyramus as a knight (v. i. 269), and the joke is pointed by Flute's earlier question: 'What is Thisby? a wand'ring knight?' (I. ii. 38). Thomson likewise refers to the fatal thread of the Fates:

> Oh Gods aboue, my faithfull loue
> shal neuer faile this need:
> For this my breath by fatall death,
> shal weaue *Atropos* threed.   (ed. Arber, p. 32)

Douglas Bush suggested that these lines 'may have been in Shakespeare's mind when, in providing a tragic vehicle for Bottom, he burlesqued the theatrical heroics of an earlier age'.[19] Certainly the mixed metaphor – a breath weaving a thread – makes the passage memorable; and both Pyramus and Thisbe refer to the Fates in similar terms:

> O Fates! come, come;
> Cut thread and thrum;
> Quail, crush, conclude, and quell.
>   (v. i. 277–9)
>
> O Sisters Three,
> Come, come to me,
> With hands as pale as milk;
> Lay them in gore,
> Since you have shore
> With shears his thread of silk.[20]   (v. i. 327–32)

Thomson uses an archaic pronunciation for the sake of a rhyme:

> For why he thought the Lion had,
> faire *Thisbie* slaine.

> And then the beast with his bright blade,
>   he slew certaine.

Peter Quince does the same thing with the same word:

> This beauteous lady Thisby is certain.   (v. i. 129)

Both Thomson and Shakespeare use the expression 'make moan'.[21]

Shakespeare owed less to the version of the story given in another miscellany, *A Gorgious Gallery of Gallant Inventions*, for that is merely dull, rather than ridiculous; but his reading of it was not entirely barren. He noticed, we may suppose, the lines describing Thisbe's first glimpse of the cranny:

> And scarcely then her pearcing looke, one blinke therof had got,
> But that firme hope of good successe, within her fancy shot.

This seems to have suggested Pyramus' line:

> Show me thy chink, to blink through with mine eyne.
>
>   (v. i. 175)

The anonymous author uses the elegant variation 'name' and 'hight' in successive lines; and Quince goes one better when he speaks of 'Lion hight by name'. Pyramus is described as 'more fresh than flower in May'; and Shakespeare's is described as

>   most lily-white of hue,
> Of colour like the red rose on triumphant brier.
>
>   (III. i. 83-4)

Pyramus, reviving a moment before he dies, is called 'The Gentilman'; and Quince assures Bottom that the character is 'a most lovely gentleman-like man' (I. ii. 77). The last parallel is to be found in the lines describing Thisbe's suicide:

> Then *Thisbie* efte, with shrike so shrill as dynned in the skye,
> Swaps down in swoone, she eft reuiues, & hents the sword
>
>   hereby.
> Wherwith beneath her pap (alas) into her brest shee strake,
> Saying thus will I die for him, that thus dyed for my sake.

Shakespeare borrows 'pap' and makes it funnier by giving it to Pyramus.[22]

Shakespeare took very little from Chaucer's version of the story, the only one which was not in some way ludicrous. But we may suppose that the lines, as they were then printed[23]

> Thus wolde they sayne, alas thou wicked wal
> Through thyn enuye, thou vs lettest al –

suggested the exclamation:

> O wicked wall, through whom I see no bliss![24]
>
> (v. i. 178)

There remains to be considered the version from which Shakespeare appears to have taken most – that contained in Thomas Mouffet's poem, *Of the Silkewormes, and their Flies*. He is best known for his *Theatre of Insects*, written in Latin and finished in 1589. The poem on silkworms was not published until 1599, four years after *A Midsummer-Night's Dream* was first staged, but it is likely to have been written some years earlier, perhaps as early as 1589. Shakespeare, we must suppose, read it in manuscript.[25] The poem was written to advocate the cultivation of the silkworm in England, and the tale of Pyramus and Thisbe was relevant because silkworms feed on mulberry leaves and, according to Ovid, the fruit, white before the tragedy, was stained for ever with the blood of the lovers:

> For when the frute is throughly ripe, the Berrie is bespect
> With colour tending to a blacke.

Mouffet, who was 'a godly and learned phisitian and skilful mathematician', a distinguished naturalist, a future M.P., a member of the Countess of Pembroke's circle, had little talent as a poet. Some of his lapses are caused by his blissful unconsciousness of ambiguities. The word *bottom*, for example, is the technical term for the silkworm's cocoon, and Mouffet tells us that the 'little creepers' leave 'their ouall bottoms there behind' (p. 18). Shakespeare christened the leading actor in Quince's company Bottom; and as the silkworm was a notable spinner, Bottom was appropriately made a weaver. Two of the fairies were linked with Mouffet's topic by the names of Moth and Cobweb. The orange-tawny beard that Bottom offers to wear (I. ii. 83) and the orange-tawny bill of the ousel-cock in the song with which he awakens Titania (III. i. 114) recall Mouffet's lines which describe the white moths by a process of *lucus a non lucendo*:[26]

> No yellow, where there is no Iealousie . . .
> No orenge colour, where there wants despight,
> No tawny sadde, where none forsaken be.

Shakespeare did not confine his attention to the story of Pyramus and Thisbe:[27] but casual echoes of other parts of the poem are less significant than the many echoes of the stanzas in which the story is told. Mouffet continually used the words 'eke' and 'whereat', and Shakespeare seems to parody this in the lines:

> Whereat, with blade, with bloody blameful blade . . .
>
> (v. i. 145)

> Most brisky juvenal, and eke most lovely Jew.
>
> (III. i. 85)

Mouffet uses 'chinck' in a later part of the poem, and 'chinckt' in the Pyramus part:

> When night approacht, they ech bad ech adew,
> Kissing their wal apart where it was chinckt,
> Whence louely blasts and breathings mainly flew:
> But kisses staide on eithers side fast linckt,
> Seal'd to the wal with lips and Louers glue:
>   For though they were both thick and many eake,
>   Yet thicker was the wal that did them breake.
>
> (p. 11)

Shakespeare uses 'chink' several times, as in the line –

> I see a voice; now will I to the chink – (v. i. 190)

and Mouffet's stanza perhaps suggested the line:

> I kiss the wall's hole, not your lips at all. (v. i. 200)

Mouffet and Shakespeare both speak of the lion as 'grisly' and use 'fell' in the same context. It may even be suggested that Mouffet's curious method of stating that the beast was a lioness ('grisly wife'), together with the fact that the other versions of the story are divided about its sex, led to Snug's comprehensive denial:

> Then know that I as Snug the joiner am
> A lion fell, nor else no lion's dam.   (v. i. 220–1)

Mouffet, like Shakespeare, uses the Fates and 'quell' in the same context; he, like Shakespeare, refers to Thisbe as 'poor soul' and to Pyramus as a paragon; and it may have been his description of the lovers as

Each of their sex the floure and paragon   (p. 9)

which suggested Thisbe's comparison of Pyramus to flowers and
vegetables:

> These lily lips,
> This cherry nose,
> These yellow cowslip cheeks,
> Are gone, are gone;
> Lovers, make moan;
> His eyes were green as leeks.   (v. i. 321–6)

But the lines also echoed Mouffet's account of Thisbe's reactions on
encountering the body of her lover:

> Her lippes grew then more pale than palest Boxe,
> Her cheekes resembled Ashwood newly feld,
> Graynesse surpriz'd her yellow amber locks,
> Not any part their liuely lustre held.   (p. 16)

Shakespeare makes matters worse by transferring 'yellow' from hair to
cheeks, and he adds the comparison of eyes to leeks.

The words addressed by Thisbe to the dead Pyramus –

> Speake loue, O speake, how hapned this to thee?
> Part, halfe, yea all of this my soule and mee.
> Sweete loue, reply, it is thy *Thisbe* deare,
> She cries, O heare, she speakes, O answere make:
> Rowse vp thy sprights: these heavie lookers cheere –
>
> > (p. 16)

are parodied by Shakespeare in 'O Pyramus, arise,/Speak, speak'
(v. i. 317–18) and in Bottom's words when he wants to play the part of
Thisbe:

> Ah Pyramus, my lover dear! Thy Thisby dear, and lady dear!
>
> > (I. ii. 45–6)

and the absurd Mouffet phrase 'those heauie lookers cheere' contributed
to Bottom's lines:

> That liv'd, that lov'd, that lik'd, that look'd with cheer.
>
> > (v. i. 286)

In Golding's version of Pyramus' suicide, the pipe is cracked accidentally:

> The bloud did spin on hie
> As when a Conduite pipe is crackt, the water bursting out
> Doth shote itself a great way off and pierce the Ayre about.
>
> (IV. 147–9)

But in Mouffet's account the pipes are deliberately pierced:

> Then falling backward from the crimsin floud,
> Which spowted forth with such a noyse and straine,
> As water doth, when pipes of lead or wood,
> Are goog'd with punch, or cheesill slit in twaine,
>   Whistling in th'ayre, and breaking it with blowes,
>   Whilst heauie moysture vpward forced flowes. (p. 14)

This is closer to Quince's line, with the significant word 'broached':

> He bravely broach'd his boiling bloody breast.
>
> (V. i. 146)

Finally it may be suggested that the idea of Bottom's transformation may have come from Mouffet's lines:

> Transforme thy selfe into a Courser braue,
> (What cannot loue transforme it selfe into?)
> Feede in her walkes. . . .   (p. 7)

This is distantly echoed in Titania's instructions to her attendant fairies: 'Hop in his walks'.[28]

Even this does not exhaust the probable sources of the Pyramus interlude. It is described as

> A tedious brief scene of young Pyramus
> And his love Thisby; very tragical mirth.
>
> (V. i. 56–7)

It looks as though Shakespeare was referring to *Cambises* which is described on the title-page as 'A lamentable tragedy mixed full of pleasant mirth'; and, sure enough, if we examine Preston's play, we find that Shakespeare may have delved there too. In the prologue we hear of the fate of Cyrus: 'But he, when sisters three had wrought, to shere his vitall thred'. A mother laments her son in words that have been compared with Thisbe's lament; and the boy's lips, 'silk soft and pleasant white' may have suggested the lily lips of Pyramus.[29] A study of the tragical mirth of Quince's interlude throws considerable light on the way many different sources fused in Shakespeare's mind.

It is possible, of course, that all the versions of the Pyramus and

Thisbe story, which Shakespeare had read over the years, coalesced in his mind without his being aware of the contributing factors; but it seems more likely that he consulted them all during the actual composition of *A Midsummer-Night's Dream*. One purpose, no doubt, of the performance of Quince's company was to show that lovers cannot rely on the intervention of Oberon or Puck to save them from the consequences of their irrationality. A second purpose was to arouse hearty laughter by exhibiting the absurdities of amateur actors. A third purpose was to show intelligent members of the audience that *Romeo and Juliet*, written about the same time, was an unsatisfactory tragedy because it depended too much on a series of accidents. A fourth purpose, akin to that of Nashe in his retelling of Marlowe's *Hero and Leander* in comic style, was to amuse a sophisticated audience by the contrast between the burlesque and the original. A fifth purpose, for which almost any play would have served, was to provide an occasion for various reflections on the relation of life to art, actors being shadows and life a dream.[30] Lastly, Shakespeare had compiled a kind of anthology of bad poetry as a vehicle of criticism. Quince's play serves to satirize not merely the crude mingling of tragedy and comedy still prevalent in 1595 in the lower levels of popular drama – and in Quince's defence it could be argued that his comedy is unintentional – but also many of the absurd faults of style into which the poetasters of the age were liable to fall. By a beautiful piece of artistic economy, Shakespeare was able to cull his choice blooms of absurdity, not from the vast stores of bad poetry available to him, but from all the best-known versions of the Pyramus and Thisbe story. In this respect, as well as in its celebration of married love, the play must have delighted the private audience of wedding guests before whom it was first performed.[31]

LOVE'S LABOUR'S LOST

THE MAIN PLOT of *Love's Labour's Lost*, concerned with the vow of Navarre and his lords to study for three years and to see no woman, may perhaps have been suggested, however faintly, by Pierre de la

Primaudaye's *L'Academie francaise* which Bowes translated in 1586: but in this book women were not specifically banned. The characters of the underplot have affinities with the *Commedia dell'Arte*. Some, rather vague, historical parallels have been offered connecting Ferdinand of Navarre with Henri of Navarre, and others for the Princess's embassy. Certainly the names of Berowne, Longaville, and Dumain were connected with Henri's fight for the French crown, Biron and Longueville being his supporters, and the Duc de Mayenne his opponent.[1]

The researches of Professor M. C. Bradbrook, Dr F. A. Yates, and others have shown that the play contains a good deal of topical satire, although there is no general agreement about the identification of the different characters. Holofernes, for example has been thought to be a satirical portrait of Chapman (Acheson), of Thomas Harriot (Dover Wilson), of Florio (Warburton), of Richard Lloyd (Lefranc) and of Gabriel Harvey. Armado has been identified with Ralegh, Harvey and Antonio Perez.[2] One agrees with Dr Anne Barton that[3]

> contemporary references of this kind if and where they exist, are ultimately less important than the nature of the play as a complex and quite autonomous work of art.

It is best to consider Holofernes as a pedant and Armado as a *miles gloriosus*. Their contemporary identifications are obscure and shifting, partly no doubt because the play underwent revision and updating.

The plot, meagre as it is, was probably Shakespeare's invention, whatever hints he picked up from fiction or contemporary history.

KING JOHN

DISCUSSION of the sources of *King John* is complicated by questions of date and of possible revision. If the play was written before 1591, as some have supposed, Shakespeare could not have made use of the anonymous play, *The Troublesome Raigne of King John*, published in that year, nor could he have echoed Daniel's *Civil Wars*, and we should be driven to assume that both the anonymous dramatist and Daniel were echoing Shakespeare's play, even though Shakespeare elsewhere echoed Daniel. On the other hand, some of the verse of *King John* appears to be more 'mature' than that of Shakespeare's earliest plays and its general characteristics would suggest a date in the middle 'nineties. It would be natural to suppose that it was written between the first and second tetralogies – one dealing with the Wars of the Roses and the other with their cause – but, despite the obvious links between *Richard II* and *Henry IV*, which make it certain that Shakespeare intended a sequel, most critics fancy that *King John* came after *Richard II*. It could, of course, be a revision of an earlier play, as some editors have suspected *Richard II* to be.

The most persuasive arguments for an early date for *King John* have been advanced by Ernst Honigmann in the New Arden edition; but I agree with the consensus of later critics that *The Troublesome Raigne* was written before, not after, Shakespeare's play.[1] *The Troublesome Raigne* is unlike a piratical text in most respects: apart from anything else it is considerably longer than the play from which it was supposedly derived. It could theoretically be an imitation rather than a piracy, a rival company cashing in on the success of Shakespeare's play, just as (it has been suggested) *The Merchant of Venice* was written to emulate *The Jew of Malta*. Only two lines in the two plays are identical. There are, indeed, a number of echoes which show that one author must have read the other (e.g. 'mounting spirit'/'mounting minde'; 'landless knight'/'landles boy'; 'A woman's will; a cank'red grandam's will!'/'A Will indeede, a crabbed Woman's will'). But these echoes are less significant than the close structural resemblance which could have resulted only from an intimate knowledge of the earlier play. We may even allow the faint possibility that Shakespeare had access to medieval Latin manuscripts. What makes the Honigmann theory impossible, however, is that there are some obscurities in Shakespeare's play which can be elucidated by reference to *The Troublesome Raigne*. This is not because the anonymous author made plain what Shakespeare had left obscure, but because Shakespeare cut out some connecting links.

This can be shown by several stock examples.[2] One obscurity surrounds the Duke of Austria's possession of Richard I's lion-skin. Shakespeare, like the authors of *The Troublesome Raigne* and *Kynge*

Rycharde Cuer de Lyon, confuses the Duke of Austria, who had imprisoned Richard and died before him, with Limoges, whose castle
Richard was besieging when he died of wounds. Some of Shakespeare's
audience would know the story about the lion-skin, but could they be
expected to know why the Bastard was annoyed at the betrothal of
Blanche to the Dauphin? In *The Troublesome Raigne* the Bastard is
given a long speech when he sees his 'Father's foe clad in [his] Father's
spoyle'; (i. 557) Blanche hints that she will love him if he wins back the
lion-skin; and the Bastard later reproaches the Queen because she had
half-promised that he would marry Blanche. Surely the only probable
explanation of Shakespeare's obscurity here is that he was condensing
the earlier play.

Another example is afforded by the second coronation. Shakespeare's
John merely remarks:

> Some reasons of this double coronation
> I have possess'd you with, and think them strong;
> And more, more strong, when lesser is my fear,
> I shall indue you with. (iv. ii. 40–3)

His lords complain at some length about gilding refined gold and
painting the lily, but this is all the answer they get. In *The Troublesome
Raigne* John is given more than twenty lines (i. 1538–60) of somewhat
evasive explanation, but it is apparent, though not in Shakespeare's
play, that the King thinks that Arthur, who had the stronger claim to
the throne, has been murdered.

The anti-papal and anti-monastic bias of *The Troublesome Raigne*
makes the motives of the Monk who poisons John easy to understand. Shakespeare eliminates much of the anti-monastic propa-
ganda, including the Decameronian scandal of i. 1181–288 (which
he presumably found distasteful) and thereby obscures the Monk's
motive.[3]

There can surely be little doubt that in each of these cases Shakespeare's version postdates that of *The Troublesome Raigne*. If this be
admitted, very little remains of the theory that Shakespeare consulted
the *Historia Maior* (1571) of Matthew Paris, the Wakefield (or Waver-
ley) Chronicle, and the Chronicle of Radulph of Coggeshall. Even the
strongest resemblances between Shakespeare's play and these three
chronicles prove to be less than convincing when they are examined.
For example, the loss of John's baggage in the Wash is thought by
Honigmann to derive from Matthew Paris:[4]

Whilst crossing the river known as Wellstrem, by an unexpected
event (*inopinato eventu*) he lost his waggons, his carriages, his pack-
horses with his treasures, his precious vases and all his regalia which
he loved with his own peculiar individual care. For the ground
opened in the midst of the waves and formed a deep whirlpool
which swallowed up everything together with men and horses, so
that not one man escaped to inform the King of the disaster; but the
King, escaping with difficulty with his army, passed the following
night (*vix elapsus, nocte sequenti pernoctavit*) at Swinehead Abbey.
Here, it was believed, he became so deeply depressed through
having his possessions swallowed by the waves (*rebus a fluctibus
devoratis*) that, falling a prey to violent fears, he began to be seriously
ill.

Honigmann believes that two speeches in *King John*, both spoken by
the Bastard, were influenced by this passage, especially by the words
for which the original Latin has been given:

> I'll tell thee, Hubert, half my power this night,
> Passing these flats, are taken by the tide –
> These Lincoln Washes have devoured them;
> Myself, well-mounted, hardly have escap'd.
>
> > (v. vi. 39–42)

> For in a night the best part of my pow'r,
> As I upon advantage did remove,
> Were in the Washes all unwarily
> Devoured by the unexpected flood.   (v. vii. 61–4)

Neither passage, however, refers to the loss of John's treasure, which
Shakespeare does not mention; the fact that he uses the words 'hardly
have escap'd' is not as significant as Honigmann implies, since the
narrowness of the escape is implied both by Holinshed's words ('yet
the king himselfe, and a few other, escaped the violence of the waters,
by following a good guide') (92/1/53) as well as by the Bastard's
words in *The Troublesome Raigne*:

> When in the morning our troupes did gather head,
> Passing the Washes with our carriages,
> The impartiall tyde deadly and inexorable,
> Came raging in the billowes threatning death,
> And swallowed vp the most of all our men.

My selfe vpon a Galloway right free, well pacde,
Out stript the flouds that followed waue by waue,
I so escapt to tell this tragick tale.   (II. 831–8)

Nor can it be said that there is any significance in the fact that Matthew
Paris and Shakespeare refer to the disasters – different in the two authors
– as unexpected, while in *The Troublesome Raigne*, it is the *news* of the
disaster which is unexpected. Honigmann also argues that the floods
came at night in Matthew Paris and Shakespeare, during the day in
The Troublesome Raigne; but the statement that John passed the
following night at Swineshead Abbey does not at all imply that the
floods took place at night. The parallels with Matthew Paris would be
significant only if it could be proved that Shakespeare's play preceded
The Troublesome Raigne.

The evidence that Shakespeare knew the Wakefield Chronicle is
even flimsier. It consists of Shakespeare's statement that Queen Elinor
died on 1 April. But, as Boswell-Stone suggested, Shakespeare may
have chosen this date because Holinshed, on the same page as his
reference to Elinor's death, mentions a bright fire in the skies on that
day. We know from *Julius Caesar* that 'The heavens themselves blaze
forth the death of princes' (II. ii. 31).

The third Latin Chronicle, Radulph of Coggeshall's *Chronicon
Anglicanum*, was condensed by Holinshed in his account of the attempted
blinding of Arthur, and Honigmann believes that Shakespeare knew
it too. This opinion he bases on a number of points, of which the three
most substantial are:

(1)   That in both Coggeshall and *King John*, but not in Holinshed,
Arthur is informed of his fate, and laments it before the arrival of the
executioners. This is not strictly true since Shakespeare's Hubert, who
informs Arthur of his fate, is in charge of the blinding.

(2)   That in both accounts Arthur pleads for delay; but Shakespeare's
'Let me not be bound' is not a request for delay.

(3)   That in both accounts 'Arthur is consoled by the compassion of
the executioners or attending soldiers'. This, too, is misleading.
Coggeshall states that Arthur was consoled after the expulsion of the
executioner from the room. Shakespeare gives one line to one of the
attendants when he is sent from the room: 'I am best pleas'd to be
from such a deed' (IV. i. 86). Arthur is not consoled.

On the other hand, there are three points in the blinding-scene in
both plays, but not in Coggeshall. Arthur is not bound; the attendants

are Hubert's assistants; and Hubert gives Arthur the warrant to peruse. It may be noted, too, that neither dramatist makes use of the fact that Arthur was to be castrated as well as blinded.

Shakespeare's main sources, we may conclude, consisted of *The Troublesome Raigne* and Holinshed's *Chronicles*. He begins his play at line 23 of *The Troublesome Raigne*, and thereafter follows it scene by scene, although he makes many alterations in the process. He reduces the first scene from 421 lines to 276, but enlarges the next four scenes from 618 to 945. He does not allow Faulconbridge's mother to be present during the establishment of his parentage. Although the outlines of the Bastard's character are in *The Troublesome Raigne*, Shakespeare makes it much more interesting by giving him the superb speech on commodity (in which a Kent-figure poses as an Edmund) and by the addition of the scene where Hubert is made to prove his innocence by carrying Arthur's body in his arms.

Shakespeare also amplifies Constance's part. In *The Troublesome Raigne*, Philip says to her:

> Out with it Ladie, that our Act may end
> A full Catastrophe of sad laments.   (I. 1156–7)

Constance is brief:

> My tongue is tunde to storie forth mishap:
> When did I breath to tell a pleasing tale?
> Must *Constance* speake? let teares preuent her talke:
> Must I discourse? let *Dido* sigh and say,
> She weepes againe to heare the wrack of *Troy*:
> Two words will serue, and then my tale is done:
> *Elnors* proud brat hath robd me of my Sonne.
>   (I. 1158–64)

Shakespeare, on the other hand, gives her some 140 lines, an impressive vehicle for great actresses, no doubt, although in my experience most audiences feel that the lady doth protest too much.

A last example of Shakespeare's alterations may be given – John's temptation of Hubert. In *The Troublesome Raigne*, John is given only six lines:

> *Hubert de Burgh* take *Arthur* here to thee,
> Be he thy prisoner: *Hubert* keepe him safe,
> For on his life doth hang thy Soueraignes crowne,

> But in his death consists thy Soueraignes blisse:
> Then *Hubert*, as thou shortly hearst from me,
> So vse the prisoner I haue giuen in charge. (1118–23)

Hubert makes no reply to the King; but he says to Arthur:

> Frolick yong Prince, though I your keeper bee,
> Yet shall your keeper liue at your commaund.

In Shakespeare's play there is a scene of some fifty lines in which John, by confessing his love of Hubert, obtains a promise from Hubert to do anything for him. The scene culminates in the lines:

> Good Hubert, Hubert, Hubert, throw thine eye
> On yon young boy. I'll tell thee what, my friend,
> He is a very serpent in my way;
> And wheresoe'er this foot of mine doth tread,
> He lies before me. Dost thou understand me?
> Thou art his keeper.
> *Hub.*   And I'll keep him so
> That he shall not offend your Majesty.
> *K. John.*   Death.
> *Hub.*   My lord?
> *K. John.*   A grave.
> *Hub.*   He shall not live.
> (III. iii. 59–66)

This scene is an enormous improvement on that in *The Troublesome Raigne* where we are left in the dark about both John's intentions and Hubert's attitude. Nevertheless, by making a definite commitment to murder, Shakespeare arouses expectations which he does not fulfil, since it turns out that John has changed his mind and substituted blinding for death.

Despite some excellent scenes and some well-drawn characters, *King John* is not a success. Shakespeare avoids depicting John as the patriot who defied the Pope, and he equally avoids depicting him as a villain. Our attitude to him – and presumably Shakespeare's too – is ambivalent. Attempts have been made to show that the play is unified by the themes of betrayal or 'commodity' or by the imagery of fire and fever.[5] Perhaps James L. Calderwood and R. L. Smallwood have been most successful in discerning an overall pattern in the play.[6]

Shakespeare explores the motives and behaviour of men in a conflict for power. . . . The struggle exposes the hypocrisy of political

grandiloquence; it leads to the destruction of innocent victims. . . .
But . . . the play reveals the gradual movement from cynicism and
detachment to self-possession and integrity in Hubert and the
Bastard.

III

COMEDIES AND HISTORIES

14

THE MERCHANT OF VENICE

STEPHEN GOSSON in his *Schoole of Abuse* (1589) speaks approvingly of a play called *The Jew* 'showne at the Bull . . . representing the greedinesse of worldly chusers, and bloody mindes of usurers'. It has been argued that the worldly choosers were those who chose the gold and silver caskets, and that the bond story exhibits the bloody minds of usurers. On the other hand, it is pointed out that dramatists before 1579 did not, so far as we know, have the technical skill to combine two plots in this way, that both Gosson's phrases may refer to a single plot, and that 'bloody', a common epithet for both usurers and Jews, does not necessarily imply the use of the pound-of-flesh story.[1]

Two other lost plays, *The Venesyon Comodye* (acted 1594) and Dekker's *The Jew of Venice* (of unknown date, but probably not before 1596) have been mentioned as possible sources of *The Merchant of Venice*,[2] but nothing is known about them. Although, therefore, there may have been a dramatic source for Shakespeare's play, it is just as likely that he dramatized the story given in Ser Giovanni Fiorentino's *Il Pecorone*.[3] In this tale (IV. 1) Ansaldo is a wealthy merchant of Venice whose godson, Giannetto, tries on two occasions to win the lady of Belmonte, a rich widow who agrees to marry the first man who enjoys her, on condition that should he fail he should forfeit all his wealth. On both occasions Giannetto is given drugged wine and he falls asleep without enjoying the lady. He is so ashamed that he tells Ansaldo that he has twice been shipwrecked. Ansaldo borrows 10,000 ducats from a Jew, to enable him to equip a third ship for Giannetto, the condition of the loan being that if the money is not repaid on St John's Day, he will forfeit a pound of his flesh. Giannetto, being warned by a maid not to drink the wine, pretends to be asleep, enjoys the lady, marries her, and is proclaimed sovereign. Until St John's Day, he forgets about Ansaldo's bargain with the Jew; and when she hears why he is so sad, his wife sends him to Venice with 100,000 ducats, following him disguised as a lawyer. The Jew refuses the ducats 'so that he could say he had killed the greatest of the Christian merchants'. The 'lawyer' proclaims that she will settle any dispute and Giannetto persuades the Jew to appear before her. She advises him to accept the 100,000 ducats, but he refuses. She tells him to take the pound of flesh and then, at the last moment, warns him that if he takes more than a pound, or sheds a drop of blood, he will be executed. The Jew then asks for the money instead, which is refused him, and he finally tears up the bond. Giannetto offers the 100,000 ducats to the lawyer, but she demands his ring. On his return to Belmonte with Ansaldo, the Lady accuses Giannetto of giving the ring to one of his former mistresses. He bursts into tears and the Lady explains. Ansaldo, somewhat oddly, is married to the girl who warned Giannetto not to drink the drugged wine. Shakespeare retained the main outlines of the story, but made considerable alterations, as we shall see.

The pound-of-flesh story was known to Shakespeare in two or three other versions. In Alexander Silvayn's *The Orator*, translated by L. Piot (1596), there are speeches by the Jew and the Christian which clearly influenced Shakespeare's trial-scene.[4] The Jew begins by saying: 'Impossible is it to breake the credite of trafficke amongst men without great detriment vnto the Commonwealth'. This idea is used three times in the course of the play. The Jew refers to those who 'bind al the bodie . . . vnto an intollerable slauerie', as Shylock refers to the treatment of slaves in Venice. The Jew says: 'A man may aske why I would not rather take siluer of this man, then his flesh'. Shylock similarly remarks:

> You'll ask me why I rather choose to have
> A weight of carrion flesh than to receive
> Three thousand ducats.   (IV. i. 40–2)

These points are not made in *Il Pecorone*; but it should be mentioned that the Jew's speech is made after he has been warned that if he cuts more or less than a pound, he will be beheaded, and that there is no mention made of a drop of blood.

Another version of the pound-of-flesh story is to be found in
Anthony Munday's *Zelauto* (1580);[5] but in this case the usurer is not a
Jew, and he demands not a pound of flesh, but the right eyes of two
victims. The motive is jealousy: one of the men had married Cornelia,
a girl the usurer had himself wished to marry, and the other has married
the usurer's daughter. The two brides disguise themselves as scholars
and attend the trial. The judge appeals in vain for mercy, contrasting
Christian duty with Turkish practice. The disguised women intervene
and the usurer is defeated by Cornelia:

> If in pulling foorth their eyes, you diminishe the least quantitie of
> blood out of their heads, ouer and besides their only eyes, or spyll
> one drop in taking them out: before you styrre your foote, you
> shall stand to the losse of bothe your owne eyes.
>
> (Bullough, I. 489)

John Russell Brown lists a number of parallels with *The Merchant of
Venice*.[6] The usurer, for example, is made to leave all of which he
dies possessed to his son-in-law. Perhaps the most striking parallel,
however, is the following:

> In fayth, then fare well frost, more such haue we lost. . . . A colde
> sute, and a harde penniworth haue all they that traffique for such
> merchandize. . . . I should haue but a colde sute with my wooing.
> But belyke you are betrothed already: and that makes you so dayntie,
> if you be tell me, that I may loose no more labour.

It would seem certain that these lines are echoed in one of the casket-
scenes (II. vii. 73–5):

> Fare you well, your suit is cold. . .
> Cold indeed, and labour lost,
> Then farewell, heat, and welcome, frost.

Another pound-of-flesh story, a ballad about a Jewish usurer, Gernutus,
is, in Professor Bullough's opinion, probably pre-Shakespearian;[7]
but I incline to the view that it may be influenced by Shakespeare's
play, and also by Robert Wilson's play, *The Three Ladies of London*, in
which the Jewish usurer is called Gerontus. The ballad describes the
Jew at the trial 'with whetted blade in hand', and there are a few other,
fainter, parallels with Shakespeare's version.

For the Jessica–Lorenzo plot Shakespeare took some hints from
Zelauto in which, as we have seen, the usurer's daughter becomes his

heir. He was also influenced by *The Jew of Malta*, in which Abigail,
Barabas's daughter, falls in love with a Christian, turns nun, and
betrays her father. When she first goes to the nunnery it is in order to
secure for her father the treasure he has hidden there. She throws
down the money-bags, as Jessica throws down a casket to Lorenzo.
Barabas, hugging the bags, exclaims:[8]

> Oh my girle,
> My gold, my fortune, my felicity. . .
> Oh girle, oh gold, oh beauty, oh my blisse!

Shylock has the same ludicrous juxtapositions when he hears of his
daughter's flight. It was, perhaps, the revival of *The Jew of Malta* at
the time of the Lopez case, or the later revival in 1596, that led Shakespeare to write of a villainous Jew, perhaps because it was Essex,
Southampton's friend, who had denounced Lopez as a traitor.[9]

A third source may have contributed to the Jessica plot, a tale by
Masuccio di Salerno about a young gentleman of Messina, who falls in
love with the daughter of a miser from whom he borrows money, and
with the help of a slave-girl, given as security, he robs the miser and
elopes with the daughter.[10]

The casket story was even more popular than that of the pound of
flesh. Both were included in the *Gesta Romanorum*, but only the former
in the translations of Wynkyn de Worde (*c.* 1512) and Richard
Robinson (1577, 1595). As the word 'insculpt' is used in the latter with
regard to the posy on the leaden vessel, and by Morocco in the first of
the casket-scenes – and used nowhere else by Shakespeare – it is fairly
certain that this is the version he used:[11] but the inscription on the
leaden casket is quite different from Shakespeare's, and the other two
are interchanged.

The fusion of the casket story with the pound-of-flesh story, whether
done by the author of *The Jew* or by Shakespeare, has several advantages.
The heroine of the tale in *Il Pecorone*, who cheats her lovers by drugging
them, and is herself cheated by her maid, would not do as a heroine, in
spite of her adventure at the trial. Furthermore Giannetto lies to his
generous godfather and shows a callous forgetfulness of his danger.
Shakespeare removed both blemishes by substituting the casket story
for the Lady of Belmonte's method of choosing a husband. Instead of
being a predatory widow, Portia is a rich heiress, bound by the terms
of her father's will. Bassanio is Antonio's bosom friend, not his godson; he confesses the reason for his journey to Belmont, and it is

Antonio's ill-fortune, not Bassanio's forgetfulness, that puts Antonio in Shylock's power.

The theme of friendship plays a significant part in the play; and the nature of true love is a theme which could be naturally developed from the casket story. This may also have suggested the contrast between the values represented by Bassanio and Antonio on the one hand and Shylock on the other; between the world of Belmont and the commercial world of Venice; while the fact that Shylock was a Jew as well as a usurer enabled Shakespeare to bring out a contrast between the Old and New Testaments, as commonly and misleadingly understood. Indeed, Portia appeals to the common element in the religion of Jew and Christian.

The invention of Shylock's daughter, suggested by Marlowe or Masuccio, or both, gives the Jew a stronger motive for revenge than the one given in *Il Pecorone*. It has even been argued, despite Shylock's initial expression of hatred for Antonio, that he has no intention, at the beginning, of enforcing the bond. Shakespeare adds three further motives: hatred of Antonio as a Christian, hatred of him as an opponent of usury, and hatred of him for his ill-usage – spitting on Shylock's gaberdine, calling him misbeliever and cut-throat dog. Shylock is not the simple villain of the sources, Shakespeare alone stressing the faith and race of the usurer. It has been suggested that the lenient treatment of Shylock after his defeat would not have satisfied an audience whose anti-semitism had been reactivated by the Lopez trial.[12]

Shakespeare made many other changes. Nerissa is provided with a more suitable husband than Ansaldo had been, and more suitable than Antonio would have been. Nerissa, despite some speculation to the contrary, does not reveal the secret of the caskets to Bassanio; and she is disguised as a lawyer's clerk to enable Shakespeare to duplicate the business of the rings. Bassanio gives his ring only at Antonio's request, a request he could not honourably refuse. The trial, moreover, takes place before the Duke; and Shakespeare dispenses with the constitutional peculiarity of *Il Pecorone* in which the visiting lawyer is allowed to settle disputes. It may be mentioned that Jessica disguises herself as a boy for her elopement, and that she and Lorenzo recover the audience's sympathy – if they were in danger of losing it – by Portia's trust and by their dialogue at the beginning of Act v.

✤

✤ 15–16 ✤

HENRY IV : PARTS 1–2

THE FAMOUS VICTORIES OF HENRY THE FIFTH (1598), an anonymous play dating from an earlier period, survives only in a debased,
piratical, and abbreviated version. It may be assumed that the original
provided the basic structure for Shakespeare's trilogy on the hero of
Agincourt; but how closely he followed the original must remain a
matter of conjecture. Apparently it contained nothing about the
rebellions against Henry IV,[1] which comprise more than half the
scenes of Shakespeare's two plays, and for this material Shakespeare
went to Holinshed's *Chronicles*. Some have supposed that Shakespeare
also made use of Hall's *Chronicle*,[2] but as Holinshed borrowed a great
deal from Hall, including his phrasing, it is difficult to be certain either
way. Shakespeare's reference to 'the dreamer Merlin and his prophecies'
could be derived from Hall's 'deuinacion of that mawmet Merlyn';[3]
but it could just as easily come from Thomas Phaer's account of
Glendower in *A Myrroure for Magistrates* (1559).[4] Indeed, if one
examines Hotspur's words about Glendower it becomes apparent that
Shakespeare fused one of Holinshed's sentences with some lines in *A
Myrroure for Magistrates*:

>   he angers me
> With telling me of the moldwarp and the ant,
> Of the dreamer Merlin and his prophecies,
> And of a dragon and a finless fish,
> A clip-wing'd griffin and a moulten raven,
> A couching lion and a ramping cat,
> And such a deal of skimble-skamble stuff
> As puts me from my faith.   (I, III. i. 148–55)

Holinshed speaks of

> a foolish credit giuen to a vaine prophesie, as though king Henrie
> was the moldwarpe, curssed of Gods owne mouth, and they three
> were the dragon, the lion, and the woolfe, which should diuide this
> realme betweene them.   (Bullough, IV. 185)

Phaer describes how Glendower, enticed by false prophecies, aspired to be Prince of Wales:

> And for to set us hereon more agog,
> A prophet came (a vengeaunce take them all)
> Affirming Henry to be Gogmagog
> Whom Merlyn doth a Mouldwarp euer call,
> Accurst of god, that must be brought in thrall
> By a wulf, a Dragon, and a Lyon strong,
> Which should deuide his kingdome them among.
> This crafty dreamer made us thre such beastes
> To thinke we were these foresayd beastes in deede.
>
> (Bullough, IV. 201)

Shakespeare picked up moldwarp, dragon, and lion from Holinshed, and added references to Merlin from *A Myrroure*. He did not identify the moldwarp with Henry, nor dragon, lion, and wolf with the rebels. He added, too, ant, fish, raven, griffin, and cat.

Another passage in *1 Henry IV* –

> You swore to us,
> And you did swear that oath at Doncaster –
> That you did nothing purpose 'gainst the state,
> Nor claim no further than your new-fall'n right,
> The seat of Gaunt, Dukedom of Lancaster –
>
> (v. i. 41–5)

could derive from Hall's statement:[5]

> Thou madest an othe to vs vpon the holy Gospelles bodely touched and kissed by thee at Dancastre that thou wouldst neuer claime the croune, kyngdome or state royall but onely thyne awne propre inheritaunce.

But it may equally well be based on Holinshed – on a passage already used by Shakespeare in *Richard II*:[6]

> At his comming vnto Doncaster . . . he sware vnto those lords, that he would demand no more, but the lands that were to him descended by inheritance from his father.

The letter from an unknown lord, read by Hotspur at the beginning of II. iii, has also been thought to be based on Hall, but it seems likely to be an amalgam of Holinshed and Daniel. One passage in particular –

Our plot is a good plot as ever was laid; our friends true and constant
– a good plot, good friends and full of expectation – (II. iii. 20)

seems to echo Daniel's lines:

> strong was their plot,
> Their parties great, meanes good, th'occasion fit:
> Their practise close, their faith suspected not.   (III. 88)

A fourth example of reputed borrowing from Hall relates to the scene
at Windsor (I. iii). Hall, speaking of Hotspur's refusal to give up his
prisoners, uses the phrase 'to deliuer theym vtterly denayed' (f. xix^v).
This seems to link up with Hotspur's statement in the play, 'I did deny
no prisoners' (I. iii. 29) and the King's later remark, 'Why, yet he doth
deny his prisoners'. But as the whole point of the scene is the denial by
the Percys, it is not surprising that Shakespeare should use the word
'deny'. There is therefore no certainty that Shakespeare consulted Hall
for Part 1; and the evidence that he made use of Hall for Part 2, is even
weaker.

Daniel's account of the reign concentrates on the Percy's rebellion,
on the battle of Shrewsbury, on the King's illness, and his final interview with Hal. He stresses the King's guilt in attaining the crown; like
Shakespeare, he has the King advise Hal to 'busy giddy minds with
foreign quarrels':

> But some great actions entertaine thou still
> To hold their mindes who else will practise ill.
>
> (III. 127)

The description of Prince Hal before the battle (1, IV. i. 97 ff.) seems to
be a fusion of Daniel's lines –

> that new-appearing glorious starre
> Wonder of Armes, the terror of the field
> Young *Henrie* –   (III. 110)

with hints from *The Faerie Queene* (I. xi. 33–4), from the description of
the Earl of Surrey in *The Unfortunate Traveller* (in which mention is
made of the plumed estrich, Pegasus, and eagles), and even perhaps
from *De Guiana Carmen Epicum* in which Chapman uses the words
'baiting' and 'Estridge'.[7] Hal saves the King's life and fights with
Hotspur in single combat, two points in which Daniel and Shakespeare improve on the chroniclers, although the dramatist might well
have decided, without Daniel's example, to end the rivalry between

Hal and Hotspur, foreshadowed in *Richard II*, with such a combat. The historical Hotspur was thirty-nine at the time of his death; Daniel and Shakespeare make him the same age as the prince. It has also been argued,[8] less cogently, that Hotspur's pursuit of honour may owe something to Daniel's feeble lines:

> And ô that this great spirit, this courage bold,
> Had in some good cause bene rightly showne!
> So had not we thus violently then
> Haue termd that rage, which valor should haue ben.
>
> (III. 114)

Daniel and Shakespeare agree against Holinshed that the Welsh contingent was not present at the battle of Shrewsbury.

The influence of Daniel on Part 2 is less apparent. The one certain echo is of a stanza describing the illness of the King:[9]

> Whose harald sicknes, being sent before
> With full commission to denounce his end,
> And paine, and griefe, enforcing more and more,
> Beseigd the hold that could not long defend,
> And so consum'd all that imboldning store
> Of hote gaine-striuing bloud that did contend
> Wearing the wall so thin that now the mind
> Might well looke thorow, and his frailty find. (III. 116)

So Clarence says:

> No, no; he cannot long hold out these pangs.
> Th'incessant care and labour of his mind
> Hath wrought the mure that should confine it in
> So thin that life looks through, and will break out.

Shakespeare had also read Stow's account of the reign in *The Annales of England* (1592). This is shown by the list of Hotspur's prisoners. Holinshed mentions (520) 'Mordacke earle of Fife, son to the gouernous Archembald earle Dowglas'. The absence of a comma after 'gouernour' made Shakespeare suppose Mordake to be Douglas's son.[10] But from Stow he would have learnt that Mordake was 'the eldest sonne'. Hence the lines:

> Mordake, Earl of Fife and eldest son
> To beaten Douglas. (1, I. i. 71–2)

From Stow's account of the Prince's highway robberies, Shakespeare would have learnt that Hal not merely paid back the money, but also gave the victims 'great rewards for their trouble and vexation'. So in the play Hal insists that 'the money shall be paid back again with advantage' (II. iv. 527–8). In *The Famous Victories* there is no suggestion that the money will be repaid; but Shakespeare would doubtless have introduced this touch independently of Stow, in accordance with his policy of white-washing Hal and of minimizing the gravity of his early behaviour. The incident of Hal's committal to prison by the Lord Chief Justice, and the King's comment thereon quoted by Hal after his accession (v. ii. 108 ff.) could be derived from Stow; but the account in Elyot's *Boke named the Gouernour* is very similar, and Shakespeare certainly knew that. Shakespeare follows Stow in the error of referring to Prince John as Duke of Lancaster.[11]

A number of echoes have been pointed out from several of Nashe's works, most of them in the prose scenes of Part 1.[12] The two most convincing are from *Summers Last Will and Testament*, not printed until 1600, but written in 1592. Will asks:

> What haue we to doe with scales and hower-glasses, except we were Bakers or Clock-keepers? I cannot tell how other men are addicted, but it is against my profession to vse any scales but such as we play at with a boule, or keepe any howers but dinner or supper. It is a pedanticall thing to respect times and seasons.
>
> (ed. McKerrow, III. 247)

So the Prince asks Falstaff:

> What a devil hast thou to do with the time of the day? Unless hours were sups of sack, and minutes capons, and clocks the tongues of bawds, and dials the signs of leaping-houses, and the blessed sun himself a fair hot wench in flame-coloured taffeta, I see no reason why thou shouldst be so superfluous to demand the time of the day.
>
> (I, I. ii. 7 ff.)

The other parallel is with two speeches by Bacchus:

> So, I tell thee, giue a soldier wine before he goes to battaile . . . it makes him forget all scarres and wounds, and fight in the thickest of his enemies, as though hee were but at foyles amongst his fellows. Giue a scholler wine, going to his booke, or being about to inuent, it sets a new poynt on his wit, it glazeth it, it scowres it, it giues him *acumen*.
>
> (III. 265)

I beseech the gods of good fellowship, thou maist fall into a con-
sumption with drinking smal beere. Euery day maist thou eat fish.

(III. 268)

So Falstaff complains of Prince John of Lancaster:

Good faith, this same young sober-blooded boy doth not love me;
nor a man cannot make him laugh – but that's no marvel; he drinks
no wine. There's never none of these demure boys come to any proof;
for thin drink doth so over-cool their blood, and making many
fish-meals, that they fall into a kind of male green-sickness; and
then, when they marry, they get wenches.

Falstaff proceeds to sing the praises of sherris-sack, which engenders
wit and bravery (IV. iii. 85 ff.).

These parallels, along with slighter ones, persuaded John Dover
Wilson that Nashe had a hand in *The Famous Victories*. It is certainly
curious that the supposed echoes are from several of Nashe's works –
not from a single one as in *Hamlet* – and his praise of a play about
Henry V might be taken as evidence of his part-authorship of *The
Famous Victories*, since he was not above puffing his own works. Yet
there is no trace of these Nashe echoes in the corrupt text of *The
Famous Victories* and perhaps a more likely explanation is that Shakespeare had been steeping himself in the works of an avowed Bohemian
and 'villanist' to obtain a suitable atmosphere for his scenes concerning
the unregenerate Prince.

In any case, it is important to bear in mind that we have only a very
rough idea of the contents of the play (or plays) which formed the
basis of *The Famous Victories*, and we know nothing at all of the other
play about Henry V. The Nashe influence may be indirect; and our
ignorance should make us chary of attributing to Daniel, Phaer, or
Stow what may have come through a dramatic source.

One minor dramatic source there probably was. *Richard II*, as we
have seen, was considerably influenced by *Woodstock* and the continuing
influence of that play has been suspected in *1 Henry IV*.[13] In *Woodstock*
(III. iii) Crossby, Fleming, and Nimble are distributing blank charters.
Crossby speaks of 'rich chuffs', and Nimble of 'bacon-fed pudding
eaters' and 'caterpillars'. Other characters speak of 'whoresons' and
say 'we can be but undone'. In the Gadshill robbery scene the same
words are used:

Fal. Strike; down with them; cut the villains' throats. Ah, whoreson caterpillars! bacon-fed knaves! They hate us youth. Down with them; fleece them.

Trav. O, we are undone, both we and ours for ever!

Fal. Hang ye, gorbellied knaves, are ye undone? No, ye fat chuffs.   (1, II. ii. 80 ff.)

Shakespeare may unconsciously have recalled the *Woodstock* scene; but it should be mentioned that the words are spread over some 140 lines and that 'bacon-fed' is the only expression not otherwise used by Shakespeare.

It will be realized, therefore, that because of our lack of information about one Henry V play and the debased text of the other, we cannot be certain of the extent of Shakespeare's originality. But it is fairly safe to assume that he relied mainly on Holinshed for the historical material and on *The Famous Victories* for the rest. As one would expect, he is careful to give only a selection of historical events, and he frequently alters facts for the sake of dramatic effect.

Shakespeare, as we have seen, makes Hotspur the same age as Hal, although he was older than Henry IV. On the other hand, he makes Hal older than the twelve years he was when his father came to the throne, and only sixteen at the battle of Shrewsbury. There was an obvious advantage in having Hal and Hotspur of an age, in making Henry wish his son were like Hotspur, in inventing the rivalry which runs all through the play, and in having Hal kill his rival and so acquire his honours. The King, too, is much older than he was historically, sick in mind and body, and suffering from a guilty conscience. This Shakespeare reveals by the King's confession to Hal, by his insomnia, and by transferring his proposed crusade from the end of his reign to the beginning. It is first mentioned in the final scene of *Richard II*.

A large number of historical facts are passed over in silence – Henry's marriage, an attempt on his life, the rise of the Lollards, the rebels' inducements to Douglas, a French invasion of the Isle of Wight, and three Welsh expeditions. Glendower, however, apparently refers to these in his boast:

> Three times hath Henry Bolingbroke made head
> Against my power; thrice from the banks of Wye
> And sandy-bottom'd Severn have I sent him
> Bootless home and weather-beaten back. (1, III. i. 64–7)

Shakespeare invents the affected courtier who annoys Hotspur on the battlefield; he associates the portents of March 1402 with Glendower's birth; he invents the battle beside the Severn between Glendower and Mortimer; and he changes in several ways the scene in which the rebels divide up the kingdom. According to Holinshed the division was carried out by deputies, not by the rebel leaders; Shakespeare adds Hotspur's temperamental irritation with Glendower, the quarrel about the division, and the language barrier between Mortimer and his wife.

The meeting of the King with Hal in III. ii is based on one which took place nine years later. Instead of being sent for by the King, Hal seeks an interview and arrives with friends. The King has with him 'three or foure persons, in whome he had most confidence'. Hal offers his father a dagger with which to kill him.

Sir Walter Blunt in Holinshed is merely mentioned as the King's standard-bearer, who is killed at the battle of Shrewsbury. Shakespeare, taking a hint from his name, makes him a man of renowned integrity and plain-dealing, respected by the rebels. He is made to convey the 'liberal kind offer of the King', instead of the Abbot of Shrewsbury; and in the battle he is killed by Douglas. Two other changes may be mentioned. Hal is made to save his father's life and so complete their reconciliation – a point borrowed from Daniel:

> Hadst thou not there lent present speedy ayd
> To thy indaungerde father nerely tyrde,
> Whom fierce incountring *Dowglas* ouerlaid,
> That day had there his troublous life expirde. (III. iii)

The other change relates to the freeing of Douglas without a ransom. According to Holinshed, this is done by the King. Shakespeare makes Hal ask the King if he may dispose of him; and when the latter consents, the Prince turns to his brother:

> Then, brother John of Lancaster, to you
> This honourable bounty shall belong:
> Go to the Douglas, and deliver him
> Up to his pleasure, ransomless and free;
> His valours show upon our crests today
> Have taught us how to cherish such high deeds
> Even in the bosom of our adversaries.   (v. iv. 25–31)

This adds to Hal a final touch of knightly magnanimity, already apparent in his epitaph on Hotspur.[14]

The historical material for the remainder of Henry IV's reign was less interesting and Shakespeare telescoped some events and omitted others. The period between the battles of Shrewsbury and Bramham Moore was five years: Shakespeare condenses it into a few weeks, omitting the visit of Northumberland to the King and the restoration of his lands: thereby he made the danger to the state seem greater. The period between the suppression of Scrope's rebellion and the King's death was nearly eight years: Shakespeare appears to date the commencement of Henry's fatal illness from the day he received the news that the rebellion had been quelled. The dramatist eliminated the comparatively peaceful years – as he was later to omit the good years of Macbeth's reign – so as to emphasize the sickness of the state caused by Bolingbroke's usurpation of the throne. The main political interest is not in the rebellion but in the relationship between Hal and his father, carried over from Part 1. One would never suspect from the play that Hal was actively engaged in political intrigue, that he tried to bring about his father's abdication, and that he was dismissed from the Council.[15] These things were not mentioned by the sources Shakespeare used; and even if he had come across them, he would probably not have introduced them into the play. It is arguable, indeed, that Shakespeare went too far in white-washing the Prince. We never see him committing any of the seven deadly sins; he does not seem interested in sex; and, if he steals, he quickly recompenses his victims. His first soliloquy in Part 1, in which he promises to reform, was presumably inserted to alert the original audience to what is going to happen; but it leaves a modern audience with the impression, whether right or wrong, that he is hypocritically pretending to be a prodigal.

Shakespeare introduces Rumour at the beginning of Part 2 – based, it is thought,[16] on Virgil's Fama in the fourth book of the *Aeneid* – to introduce the false account of victory, which is in none of the known sources. Northumberland is not, as Holinshed reports, genuinely sick, but crafty-sick. He is persuaded by his wife and Lady Percy to discontinue the war; in Holinshed there is no mention of their persuasions, nor any suggestion of cowardice.

John of Lancaster's rôle is enlarged. He is substituted for Waterton in the army sent to fight with Northumberland; and he, rather than Westmorland, is responsible for tricking the rebels at Gaultree forest. Scrope's motives in rebelling are more altruistic in the *Chronicles* than they are in the play; and Shakespeare omits altogether the idea of martyrdom:

The archbishop suffered death verie constantlie, insomuch as the common people tooke it, he died a martyr, affirming that certaine miracles were wrought as well in the field where he was executed, as also in the place where he was buried: and immediatlie vpon such bruits, both men and women began to worship his dead carcasse, whom they loued so much when he was aliue.

(Holinshed 530/2/7; Bullough, IV. 274)

Many events recorded in the *Chronicles* were not relevant to the theme of the play – the rumour spread by the Countess of Oxford that King Richard was alive, a controversy about taxation between the lords spiritual and temporal, the kidnapping of the Earl of March's children, some further Welsh atrocities, some details about Anglo–French relations, and some affairs relating to the Lollards. The only incidents dramatized by Shakespeare from the last twelve pages of Holinshed devoted to the reign are the reconciliation of the King with the Prince after he has taken away the crown from the pillow, and the King's death, although this takes place off stage.

In both parts of *Henry IV* Shakespeare roughly alternates historical material with the comic scenes from *The Famous Victories*. Some critics think that Shakespeare's debt to this play was confined to his taking a hint or two from it; others have argued that he owed more to it than to Holinshed. C. A. Greer compiled a list of 34 resemblances between *Henry IV* and *The Famous Victories*, and argued[17] that only 6 of these could have come from the *Chronicles*. In fact at least 14 of Greer's points could be derived from other sources. Yet there is no doubt that Shakespeare owed a good deal to the play of which *The Famous Victories* is a truncated version. The comic scenes of *Henry IV* begin with the plotting of the Gadshill robbery, *The Famous Victories* with the sharing of the loot. By devoting a whole scene to the planning of the robbery, Shakespeare was able to introduce the complication of making the Prince and Poins agree to rob the robbers, and so to white-wash the Prince's character. The Prince of *The Famous Victories* does not return the money, wishes his father were dead, and batters on the door with a 'very disordered' company. Shakespeare's Hal is much more amiable; his striking of the Lord Chief Justice is merely reported; and he is never in danger of overthrowing the rule of law. In *The Famous Victories*, he tells Ned:

Hen. 5. But *Ned*, so soone as I am King, the first thing I wil do, shal

be to put my Lord chief Justice out of office, and thou shalt be
my Lord chiefe Justice of England.

Ned.   Shall I be Lord chiefe Justice? By gogs wounds, ile be the
brauest Lord chiefe Justice that euer was in England.

Hen. 5. Then *Ned*, ile turne all these prisons into fence Schooles,
and I will endue thee with them, with landes to maintaine them
withall.   (Bullough, IV. 312)

The corresponding passage in *1 Henry IV* is significantly different:

Fals.   But, I prithee, sweet wag, shall there be gallows standing
in England when thou are king. . . . Do not thou, when thou are
king, hang a thief.

Prince. No; thou shalt.

Fals.   Shall I? O rare! By the Lord, I'll be a brave judge!

Prince. Thou judgest false already: I mean thou shalt have the
hanging of the thieves, and so become a rare hangman.

                              (I. ii. 56 ff.)

Sir John Oldcastle in *The Famous Victories*, who provided a name for
the companion of the Prince in Shakespeare's play, before he was
rechristened as Sir John Falstaff, is neither old, nor fat, nor a sot, nor
witty, nor even a coward; nor, apparently, is he a Lollard, though
Falstaff's occasional lapses into bogus religiosity may be a residue of an
Oldcastle who was depicted as a hypocrite.

In the second scene of *The Famous Victories*, a boy describes a tavern
brawl which led to the summoning of the Mayor and Sheriff – a
brawl mentioned also by Stow. This may have suggested the scene in
1 Henry IV in which the Sheriff arrives in search of Falstaff (II. iv) and
also the scene in Part 2 where Pistol is ejected from the tavern. But in
neither scene is the Prince taken to prison, as in the boy's account.

In the Agincourt scenes of *The Famous Victories*, Dericke describes
how he would thrust a straw into his nose to make it bleed. Bardolph
similarly tells how Falstaff urged him and his companion 'to tickle our
noses with spear-grass to make them bleed, and then to beslubber our
garments with it, and swear it was the blood of true men' (1, II. iv. 300).

A more significant parallel is the passage in which Dericke and John
Cobler re-enact the scene in which Hal boxed the Lord Chief Justice's
ear. So in *1 Henry IV* there is a pre-enactment of the scene between Hal
and his father, Falstaff first playing the King and afterwards the Prince.
It is probable that in the original version of *The Famous Victories* the

rôles of Dericke and John Cobler were interchanged and the scene repeated,[18] and that this gave Shakespeare the idea of the replication of his playlet. It should be noted that the parody of Hal's interview with the King comes before what it parodies, and that during the actual interview an audience cannot help remembering the bogus ones.

The recruiting-scene in *2 Henry IV* (III. ii) seems to owe something to Scene x in *The Famous Victories* where John Cobler is recruited; but the misuse of impressment is mentioned by Holinshed, by Barnabe Riche, and by Dudley Digges, whose brother wrote two poems in praise of Shakespeare.

The basic structure of the scene in *The Famous Victories* in which the King dies is the same as Shakespeare's. The King enters with two lords, and in both plays asks for music; the Prince, on being left by the others, thinks his father is dead and goes out with the crown. Shakespeare, however, gives Hal a soliloquy about the cares of kingship before he thinks his father is dead. In both plays the King awakes, finds the crown gone, calls his lords who bring back the Prince and, after being reproached by the King, Hal explains his mistake, and they are reconciled. In *The Famous Victories*, the King confesses:

> God knowes my sonne, how hardly I came by it,
> And how hardly I haue maintained it.
>
> (Bullough, IV. 318)

This is expanded by Shakespeare to a long speech of advice, including the lines:

> God knows, my son,
> By what by-paths and indirect crook'd ways
> I met this crown. (IV. v. 184–6)

Finally, in the last scene of *2 Henry IV*, and in the ninth scene of *The Famous Victories*, Hal banishes his former associates:

> Ah *Tom*, your former life greeues me,
> And makes me to abandon and abolish your company for euer.
> And therfore not upon pain of death to approch my presence
> By ten miles space, then if I heare wel of you,
> It may be I will do somewhat for you.   (Bullough, IV. 321)

So in Shakespeare's play, Hal banishes Falstaff, setting a ten-mile limit, promising 'competence of life', and advancement if he reforms.

There are sufficient resemblances between the two parts of *Henry IV* and *The Famous Victories* to make it certain that this was one of Shake-speare's sources. But it must be remembered that there was another play about Henry V, mentioned by Henslowe as new on 18 November 1595, eighteen months after *The Famous Victories* was entered in the Stationers' Register. This too may have influenced Shakespeare, for a speech has accidentally survived, apparently spoken by Hal to his brother over the dead body of Hotspur and another rebel:[19]

> Brother, they were two members of our state
> Yet both infected with a strong disease
> And mortal sickness, proud ambition;
> Which being rank and villainously near,
> Had they not been prevented might have proved
> Fatal and dangerous. Then, since scornful death
> Hath like a skillful artist cured that fear
> Which might have proved so hurtful to ourselves,
> Let us commit in sad and mournful sound
> Their worths to fame, their bodies to the ground,
> For the dead Percy bore a gallant mind,
> England has my prayers left behind.

If this comes from Henslowe's 'new' play, it is difficult to explain what have been regarded as references to a play about Oldcastle and Hotspur in Gabriel Harvey's *Foure Letters* (1592), in which he speaks of 'clownes; gowty Diuels, and buckram Giants . . . hypocritical hoat spurres' and 'some old lads of the Castell'.[20] Was there a play as early as 1592 in which Oldcastle talked of men in buckram? And was this the play which has come down to us as *The Famous Victories*? Or is it a third pre-Shakespearian play about Hal and is this the explanation of the absence of all the Nashe parallels in *The Famous Victories*?[21]

THE MERRY WIVES OF WINDSOR

IF there is any truth in the legend that Elizabeth I asked Shakespeare to write a play to show Falstaff in love, *The Merry Wives of Windsor* was presumably written in haste, certainly before *Henry V*, and possibly before Shakespeare had finished *2 Henry IV*.[1] But the legend may have been invented to explain why the dramatist took Falstaff out of his proper setting, just as the poaching at Charlecote was invented to explain some of the jokes in the first scene of the play.[2]

Many critics, regarding the play as a rushed job, have argued that Shakespeare was adapting an earlier play. Henry Porter was commissioned by Henslowe in 1599 to write a sequel to his *Two Angry Women of Abingdon*.[3] This play has not survived and may never have been finished; its date makes it impossible for Shakespeare to have made use of it; and it was written for a rival company. A more plausible suggestion is that of *The Jealous Comedy*, a lost anonymous play, acted in 1593 by Shakespeare's company.[4] As nothing whatever is known about this play there is no point in discussing its influence on *The Merry Wives of Windsor*.

There are several tales which have some affinity with the main plot of *The Merry Wives of Windsor*. Ser Giovanni Fiorentino's *Il Pecorone*, as we have seen, had been used for *The Merchant of Venice*; so it is reasonable to assume that Shakespeare had read the second story in the book, in which a student asks the advice of his professor on the seduction of a woman who, unknown to them both, is the professor's wife. When the husband returns home, after his suspicions have been aroused, the student hides under the newly-washed laundry – not the dirty clothes of Shakespeare's play – and he duly reports his narrow escape and his subsequent amorous success to the husband. Although the seducer makes a confidant of the cuckolded husband, as Falstaff does of the disguised Ford, in other ways the situations are different. Mistress Ford is chaste; she and Mistress Page plot to trick Falstaff; Falstaff is not young, and not successful; he pursues both women at the same time; and he is more interested in financial than in sexual advantage.

Shakespeare also knew *Riche his Farewell to Militarie Profession* (1581), at least when he wrote *Twelfth Night*; and the fifth story in the book is about an adulterous wife who tricks a former lover, a doctor, into carrying out of the house a bag containing another of her lovers. The doctor thinks he is conveying the woman, but 'seyng a face to appeare with a long beard, was in such a maze, that he could not tell in the worlde what he might saie'. The wife, in fact, is in love with a third man, a soldier. Perhaps the doctor's surprise on seeing the beard may have suggested Evans's remark (IV. ii. 170): 'I like not when a 'oman has a great peard; I spy a great peard under his muffler'.[5]

A third story, in *Tarltons Newes Out of Purgatorie* (1590), another book with which Shakespeare was acquainted, is about a young wife, married to an old doctor, and in love with a young man named Lionello. Lionello consults the doctor about his love-affair, ignorant that he is speaking to his mistress's husband. The wife conceals her lover. This tale had little or no influence on the play.[6]

A fourth story in Painter's *Palace of Pleasure* (I. 49) is about a student named Filenio who sends almost identical letters to three women; they compare notes and determine to punish him, though Filenio afterwards gets his revenge.[7]

The story of Anne Page and her three suitors, the unsuccessful ones each backed by one of her parents and opposed by the other, is analogous to Plautus' *Casina*, in which Lysidamus wants to marry his slave-girl to his bailiff, so that he can afterwards have her as his mistress, and Euthynicus, his son, who also desires the girl, proposes to marry her to his armour-bearer. The mother, anxious to foil her husband's plan, supports the son's. There is no third suitor, however, and Casina, who turns out to be free-born, is able to marry Euthymicus.[8] No translation of *Casina* had then been published but Shakespeare could, of course, have read the original, or some unknown derivative from it.

The pinching of Falstaff by fairies was doubtless suggested by Lyly's *Endimion*, in which fairies pinch Corsites: 'Pinch him, pinch him, blacke and blue'.[9]

Even if Shakespeare was transforming an earlier play to accommodate Falstaff, it would have been in accordance with his usual practice to conflate it with other source-material. It is certain that he introduced some topical material relating to a Garter installation, presumably that of Lord Hunsdon, the Lord Chamberlain, whose servants Shakespeare's company officially were. This took place in April 1597. At the same time the Duke of Württemberg was elected *in absentia* to the same order, five years after he had first visited England, when he had expressed a wish to be so honoured.[10] There are also some obscure topical allusions to post-horses,[11] and, if Leslie Hotson is right, satire of Justice Gardiner.[12]

It would, I think, have been perfectly possible for Shakespeare to have composed *The Merry Wives of Windsor* from the source-materials we have outlined, without having recourse to a lost play. By combining stories of jealous and cuckolded husbands and of lovers who unknowingly confide in their victims, stories in which the lover has several narrow escapes, with a story about a man who sends the same love-letter to more than one woman, and a play (or tale) in which parents back rival suitors of their daughter, Shakespeare would have had the skeleton of his play. The material was, of course, transformed by having Falstaff as the would-be seducer; and the Garter celebrations doubtless suggested Windsor as a suitable setting. In spite of a few loose ends, *The Merry Wives of Windsor* remains a brilliant feat of dramaturgy.

HENRY V

WE ARE FACED at the outset with the same problems that confronted us with *Henry IV*: to what extent the text of *The Famous Victories* gives a fair idea of the play, or plays, it purports to represent, and to what extent Shakespeare was influenced by this play and by *Harey the V*, performed by the Admiral's men in 1595 and 1596.

Shakespeare's main source was Holinshed's *Chronicles*, but he also used Hall and *The Famous Victories*, probably used Grenewey's translation of *The Annales of Cornelius Tacitus* (1598), possibly used Daniel's *Civile Wars*, and, though this is much less likely, *The Batayll of Egynge-courte* (c. 1530).[1]

The evidence that Shakespeare consulted Hall consists of a large number of small details in which the play is closer to Hall than to Holinshed. J. H. Walter, indeed, goes so far as to say that 'Shakespeare's debt to Holinshed is in effect superficial, Hall is the source of his inspiration'.[2] It is true that Hall's attitude to historical events is more thoughtful and coherent than Holinshed's and that Shakespeare absorbed his attitude to a considerable extent; but it seems likely nevertheless that the facts of Henry V's reign derive from Holinshed, and a good deal of his actual phrasing. The echoes from Hall come mostly in patches: there are hardly any in Acts II, III, and V, and there are a number in I. ii and IV. ii. But even the clustering echoes are not particularly striking, and the remainder may well be accidental. The Archbishop of Canterbury may refer to Henry IV's reign as an 'unquiet time' (I. i. 4) because that is the title of Hall's chapter; and Exeter may warn the French king of the inevitable sufferings which would result from a war –

> the widows' tears, the orphans' cries,
> The dead men's blood, the prived maidens' groans,
> For husbands, fathers, and betrothed lovers –
>   (II. iv. 106–8)

because Hall had spoken in similar terms of the French mourning after Agincourt:

> And yet the dolor was not onely hys, for the ladies swouned for the deathes of theyr housebandes, the Orphalines wept, and rent their heares for the losse of their parentes, the fayre damoselles defied that day in the whiche they had lost their paramors.   (f. xxᵛ)

But, after all, any poet writing on the subject would have come up with the same, fairly obvious, list of mourners.

One famous remark in the play is derived from Holinshed – it is not in Hall:

> It is said, that as he heard one of the host vtter his wish to another thus: I would to God there were with vs now so manie good soldiers as are at this houre within England! the king answered: I would not wish a man more here than I haue, we are indeed in comparison to the enimies but a few, but if God of his clemencie doo fauour vs, and our iust cause (as I trust he will) we shall speed well inough.
>   (553; Bullough, IV. 394)

So Westmoreland exclaims:

> O that we now had here
> But one ten thousand of those men in England
> That do not work to-day!   (IV. iii. 16–18)

This provides the cue for one of the King's most rousing speeches. It should be mentioned, however, that a Latin biography, the *Vita et Gesta Henrici Quinti*, ascribes the remark to Walter Hungerford and mentions the figure of 10,000 – 'decem milia de melioribus sagitariis Angliae' – so Shakespeare may have been acquainted, directly or indirectly, with this *Life*.[3]

Shakespeare is at his worst when he is slavishly following Holinshed's narrative. The one passage in all his plays where he fell below the level of a score of his contemporaries is in the Archbishop of Canterbury's exposition of the Salic Law:

> Herein did he much inueie against the surmised and false fained law Salike, which the Frenchmen alledge euer against the kings of England in barre of their iust title to the crowne of France. The verie words of that supposed law are these, *In terram Salicam mulieres ne succedant*, that is to saie, Into the Salike land let not women succeed. Which the French glossers expound to be the realme of France, and that this law was made by king Pharamond; whereas yet their owne authors affirme, that the land Salike is in Germanie, betweene the riuers of Elbe and Sala; and that when Charles the great had ouercome the Saxons, he placed there certeine Frenchmen, which hauing in disdeine the dishonest maners of the Germane women, made a law, that the females should not succeed to any inheritance within that land, which at this daie is called Meisen, so that if this be true, this law was not made for the realme of France, nor the Frenchmen possessed the land Salike, till foure hundred and one and twentie yeares after the death of Pharamond, the supposed maker of this Salike law, for this Pharamond deceassed in the yeare 426, and Charles the great subdued the Saxons, and placed the Frenchmen in those parts beyond the riuer of Sala, in the yeare 805.
>
> (Holinshed, 545; Bullough, IV. 378)

The first part of the Archbishop's paraphrase runs as follows:

> There is no bar
> To make against your Highness' claim to France
> But this, which they produce from Pharamond:
> *In terram Salicam mulieres ne succedant* –
> "No woman shall succeed in Salique land";
> Which Salique land the French unjustly gloze
> To be the realm of France, and Pharamond
> The founder of this law and female bar.
> Yet their own authors faithfully affirm
> That the land Salique is in Germany,
> Between the floods of Sala and of Elbe;
> Where Charles the Great, having subdu'd the Saxons,
> There left behind and settled certain French;
> Who, holding in disdain the German women
> For some dishonest manners of their life,

Establish'd then this law; to wit, no female
Should be inheritrix in Salique land;
Which Salique, as I said, 'twixt Elbe and Sala,
Is at this day in Germany called Meisen.
Then doth it well appear the Salique law
Was not devised for the realm of France;
Nor did the French possess the Salique land
Until four hundred one-and-twenty years
After defunction of King Pharamond,
Idly suppos'd the founder of this law;
Who died within the year of our redemption
Four hundred twenty-six; and Charles the Great
Subdu'd the Saxons, and did seat the French
Beyond the river Sala, in the year
Eight hundred five.   (I. i. 35–64)

The feebleness of this speech suggests that Shakespeare's imagination
was not engaged; and he may have doubted the righteousness of the
King's cause. There was bound to be a suspicion that the King was
following his father's advice to 'busy giddy minds with foreign
quarrels'; and the *realpolitik* of the two churchmen who open the play
makes it clear that they are backing the war against France in return
for the King's agreement not to confiscate church property. As
Holinshed puts it:

they determined to assaie all waies to put by and ouerthrow this
bill: wherein they thought best to trie if they might mooue the
kings mood with some sharpe innuention, that he should not regard
the importunate petitions of the commons.

(Holinshed, 545; Bullough, IV. 377)

Hall, a supporter of Henry VIII's policy with regard to the monasteries,
is satirical at the expense of the clergy in the earlier reign:

the fat Abbotes swet, the proude Priors frouned, the poore Friers
curssed, the sely Nonnes wept, and al together wer nothyng pleased
nor yet content. Now to finde a remedy for a mischief and a tent to
stop a wounde, the Clergy myndyng rather to bowe then breake,
agreed to offre to the kyng a greate some of money to staye this
newe moued demaund. The cause of this offre semed to some of the
wise prelates nether decente nor conuenient, for they will forsawe
and perfightly knewe that yf the commons perceiued that they by

reward or offre of money would resist their request and peticion,
that thei stirred and moued with a fury would not onely rayle and
despise theim as corruptours of Princes and enemyes of the publique
wealthe, but would so crye and call on the kyng and his temporall
lordes that they were lyke to lese bothe worke and oyle, cost and
liuying: Wherefore they determined to cast all chaunces whiche
mighte serue their purpose, and in especiall to replenishe the kynges
brayne with some pleasante study that he should nether phantasy
nor regard the serious peticion of the importunate commons.

(f. iii^v)

It seems likely that Shakespeare's own attitude was as ambivalent as
Hall's, admiration for the victor of Agincourt and patriotic feeling
being counter-balanced by a dislike of ecclesiastical chicanery and of
dubious moral claims.

Shakespeare omits the trial of Sir John Oldcastle for heresy and his
escape from the Tower of London. His Oldcastle had deviated from
his namesake and by this time had been rechristened. In any case the
heresy issue would have been irrelevant in a play devoted to what Hall
called 'the victorious acts' of Henry V.

The conspiracy by Cambridge, Scroop, and Grey was apparently
not mentioned in *The Famous Victories*. Shakespeare provides his hero
with an eloquent speech on Scroop's hypocrisy, but he conceals the
fact that the plot was on behalf of the Earl of March, whose title to the
throne was stronger than Henry's own. Hall, Holinshed, and Daniel
all suggest that Cambridge wrongly confessed to being bribed by the
French, a suggestion that was followed in *A Mirror for Magistrates*:[4]

> We sayd for hier of the French kinges coyne, we did
> Behight to kil the king: and thus with shame
> We stayned our selues, to saue our frend fro blame.
>
> (Bullough, IV. 419)

Henry's speech at Harfleur, warning its inhabitants of what will
happen if the town is sacked, is apparently based on a speech made
four years later at the siege of Rouen. In spite of this horrific speech,
Shakespeare makes Henry instruct his soldiers to show mercy after the
surrender: according to Hall and Holinshed, Harfleur was nevertheless
sacked.

It was probably Shakespeare's idea to have representatives of
Scotland, Wales, and Ireland in Henry's army – despite the danger of a

Scottish invasion of England mentioned in Act I – in order to reflect
the policy of multi-national unity advocated in Elizabeth's reign, the
pride of the Tudors in their Welsh ancestry, and the prospect of the
accession of the Stuarts.

The King's tour of the English camp on the eve of the battle may
have been suggested by *The First English Life of King Henry the Fifth*, in
which there is an account of Henry's practice at the siege of Harfleur.[5]
Others think the episode owes something to the account given by
Tacitus of how Germanicus went among his troops in disguise to
estimate their morale: an English translation of the *Annals* had recently
been published (1598).[6] The plight of the English army is described
briefly by Holinshed, and at greater length by Hall, especially in the
French King's oration before the battle:

> And on the otherside is a smal handfull of pore Englishemen which
> are entred into thys regon in hope of some gain or desire of proffite,
> whyche by reson that their vitaill is consumed and spent, are by
> daily famyn sore wekened, consumed and almost without spirites:
> for their force is clerly abated and their strength vtterly decaied, so
> that or the battailes shall ioyne they shalbe for very feblenes van-
> quished and ouercom, and in stede of men ye shall fight with
> shadowes.   (f. xv*v*)

This passage probably formed the basis of the Constable's oration in
IV. ii; but Shakespeare also drew on memories of an earlier campaign
in France when the Black Prince's forces were similarly outnumbered,
and he was familiar with *Edward III*, in which the episode was dramatized. There are also some interesting resemblances between the plight
of the English army and that described in Xenophon's *Anabasis*, as
Mary Renault has recently pointed out.[7]

Shakespeare says nothing whatever about the instructions to the
archers by which the battle was won. He could have found them in
Holinshed, or in *The Famous Victories*:

> Then I will, that every archer prouide him a stake of
> A tree, and sharpe it at both endes,
> And at the first encounter of the horsemen,
> To pitch their stakes downe into the ground before them,
> That they may gore themselues upon them,
> And then to recoyle backe, and shoote wholly altogither,
> And so discomfit them.   (Bullough, IV. 333)

Shakespeare omitted these facts, presumably because he wished to stress the miraculous and providential nature of the victory.

It has been argued[8] that as originally written, Falstaff appeared in the French scenes; and that it was Falstaff, not Pistol, who was made to eat the leek by Fluellen. The main evidence for this is the soliloquy in v. i in which Pistol says 'my Doll is dead' and 'Old I do wax'. Pistol's wife is Nell, and he is not, so far as we know, old. It is more likely, however, that 'Doll' is a misprint, or a slip by Shakespeare himself; for the tone of the soliloquy, in verse, is quite unlike any of Falstaff's speeches in *Henry IV*. It is surely out of character for Falstaff to say: 'from my weary limbs/Honour is cudgell'd' (78–9).

Shakespeare's play owes most to *The Famous Victories* in the scene where Pistol captures M. de Fer (IV. iv), which is based on a scene between Dericke and a French soldier, and in Henry's wooing of Princess Katherine. It could be argued that here he was following the old play too closely, as the scene gives the impression that the King is putting on an act as a plain, blunt, unimaginative Englishman.

The differing critical opinions about the play, and about the character of Hal both here and in *Henry IV*, are not wholly due to changing attitudes to war and patriotism, nor even to changing stage conventions. Shakespeare himself provides the material for regarding Henry as a great and heroic figure, even as an ideal king; but he also was the first to put forward the kind of reservations some modern critics have expressed. It is impossible to believe that Shakespeare took the Archbishop's justification of the war as anything but a pretext; and some members of any audience would notice that in his conversation with the soldiers on the eve of Agincourt, the King evades the question of whether it is a just war. The choruses, splendid as they are, exhibit Shakespeare's anxiety about the limitations of his theatre, and this may conceal an unresolved conflict between his public and private feelings about his hero.[9]

✻

✻ 19 ✻

MUCH ADO ABOUT NOTHING

THERE IS LITTLE that need be added to Charles T. Prouty's comprehensive book[1] on the sources of *Much Ado About Nothing*. He discusses eight plays, two of them lost, and the same number of non-dramatic versions of the Hero–Claudio story. Pasqualigo's *Il Fedele* (1579), Fraunce's *Victoria* (c. 1581) and Munday's *Fedele and Fortunio* (1585) – versions in Latin and English of the Italian play – 'all deal with the vengeance of a rejected lover who is denied his former pleasures'. There is no evidence that Shakespeare knew any of these plays.[2] There is some resemblance[3] between G. B. Della Porta's *Gli duoi fratelli rivali* and Shakespeare's play; but as it was not yet published when *Much Ado* was performed the resemblance is probably fortuitous. A more likely source is a lost play, entitled *Ariodante and Genevra*, which was performed at Court in February 1583 by the boys of Merchant Taylors school, and which, from its title, may have been a dramatization of Peter Beverley's *Ariodanto and Jenevra* (1566), a tedious poem based on Ariosto's *Orlando Furioso*. Another lost play, also presented at Court, described as 'the matter of Panecia' was probably based on Bandello's tale in which the heroine's name is Fenicia. This play, performed on 1 January 1575, has been suggested as Shakespeare's main source; but as we know nothing about its actual contents, as it was never published, and as Shakespeare was still at school, when it was performed, it seems unlikely that he was acquainted with it.

In any case, even if Shakespeare based his comedy on one of the two lost plays, he was also familiar with two or three other versions of the story: *The Faerie Queene* (II. iv); *Orlando Furioso*, probably in the original as well as in Harington's translation (1591); Bandello's *Novelle* (1554), and Belleforest's *Histoires Tragiques* (1574) based on them. *Much Ado About Nothing* is based on both Bandello and Ariosto, or on versions deriving ultimately from those two writers, or else on a lost version, narrative or dramatic, combining both strains. In all versions of the story the hero is tricked into believing that the heroine is unchaste by a rival who wishes to prevent their marriage. In Ariosto's account, and its derivatives, Genevra's maid, an unwitting accomplice, dresses up as her mistress and (as in Shakespeare's play) a challenge to a duel is mentioned. In Bandello's version and its derivatives, on the other hand, more is made of the friendship of the rivals; the trick does not involve the dressing up of the maid; Fenicia swoons on being accused of unchastity and does not recover until 'the news of her death had been spread abroad'; her father arranges for an empty coffin to be entombed; and the repentant slanderer confesses to Fenicia's betrothed, who promises her father that he will marry none but a wife chosen by him. Here Shakespeare would have found the name of Hero's father, Lionato. From Whetstone's version in *The Rocke of Regard* (1576) he may have got the idea of Claudio's rejection of Hero in church: Frizaldo explains to Rosina, the maid whom he had promised to wed, that he has arranged a wedding with Giletta only to revenge himself by rejecting her and marrying Rosina instead.

By analysing all the extant versions Prouty attempts to show what changes Shakespeare made. In all the extant versions, except Whetstone's, the 'rival's friendship with the hero is important in varying degrees'. Shakespeare played down the love-versus-friendship theme, perhaps because he had used it in *The Two Gentlemen of Verona*, or because it had by this time become stale, or (as Bullough suggests[4]) because ' "natural" villainy was becoming . . . more popular . . . than the errant gentlemen of euphuistic fiction'. There are two points where the love-versus-friendship theme is broached, as Prouty points out, but in neither case is it developed. Claudio soon learns that Don Pedro has not betrayed him; and although Benedick, at Beatrice's insistence, challenges Claudio to a duel, it never takes place. The theme was always somewhat artificial. Although we can accept readily enough Shakespeare's own resignation of mistress to friend, there is an element of absurdity in the final scene of *The Two Gentlemen of Verona*. By the time he wrote *Much Ado About Nothing*, Shakespeare could not make the slanderer of Hero other than a villain: hence the invention of Don John. As the play was to be a comedy, Shakespeare had to inform the audience before the church-scene that Don John's villainy would come to light; and for this purpose he created Dogberry whose character was nicely designed to postpone the unmasking of the villain. If he had been more intelligent and less loquacious Hero would never have been accused before the altar; and if he had been even more stupid Hero's name might never have been cleared. Bullough mentions[5] that the police in Pasqualigo's play 'make amusing malapropisms', but this was probably a coincidence.

There is no evidence, beyond the titles, about the contents of the two lost plays; but at the date when they were performed, sub-plots seem to have been exceptional. It is probable, therefore, that Shakespeare himself was responsible for combining the Hero–Claudio plot with that of Benedick and Beatrice. He may have derived a hint from *The Courtier* of Castiglione, in which Lord Gaspare and the Lady Emilia carry on a similar kind of merry war.[6] Mirabella in *The Faerie Queene* (VI. vii) has been suggested as another source for the character of Beatrice.[7] On the journey to Cupid's court, Mirabella is guarded by Disdain and Scorn; and Hero, doubtlessly exaggerating because she is being overheard by Beatrice, says that 'Disdain and scorn ride sparkling in her eyes'. But Shakespeare did not have to read Spenser in order to find out that some women were disdainful and scornful; nor did he have to read Castiglione to find prototypes of quarrelling lovers – although he had certainly read both these authors. There may have been some unidentified source of the stratagem by which Beatrice and Benedick are made to avow their love for each other; but it could just as easily have been suggested by the main plot. There Claudio is deceived into falling out of love with Hero by overhearing Borachio; in the other plot Beatrice and Benedick are tricked by a similar device into falling in love, or to put it more accurately, into a realization that they love each other. Prouty suggested that Shakespeare obtained a unity of tone by the recurrent device of overhearing, used throughout the play; and Masefield earlier had stated that the theme of the play was the power of report to alter human destiny[8]. It may be added that the unity is achieved partly by means of the imagery – disguise and counterfeiting are expressed in images as well as in the actual plot[9] – and also by the prevalence of antithesis.

Beatrice and Benedick, by an effective stroke of irony, have been in love all the time, as every audience knows. They despise the conventional behaviour of romantic lovers, and both of them confuse this behaviour with love itself. They are contrasted with Hero and Claudio; but this does not mean that we need accept Prouty's view that that couple is equally 'unromantic', and that their marriage is one of convenience. Such an alteration in the stories of Ariosto and Bandello would, it is true, give Claudio more excuse for his public repudiation of Hero, in that if she is unchaste both she and her father have been guilty of cheating. Yet Claudio, on the evidence of his speeches, is

genuinely in love, even when he repudiates Hero; and although it is a
convenient alliance for both parties, it cannot be regarded merely as a
marriage of convenience.

There are a number of loose ends in the play – Margaret's behaviour
is given only a muddled explanation, there is some confusion about
Don Pedro's wooing of Hero for Claudio; but audiences accept these
without difficulty. They are more worried by the contrast between the
lively prose and vivid characterization of the Beatrice–Benedick scenes
and the rather conventional verse of the Hero–Claudio scenes. This
contrast, however, was clearly intended as an exercise in perspective.
Shakespeare had done almost the same thing in *The Taming of the Shrew*.

20

JULIUS CAESAR

SHAKESPEARE'S use of North's translation of Plutarch's *Lives* has
been studied by a large number of critics and editors.[1] He had read
some of the *Lives* as early as 1595, for there is a verbal echo of the
first of them in his account of the amours of Theseus.[2] He had read the
Life of Caesar, and may even have been considering a play on the
subject by the time he wrote *Henry V*.[3] Then in 1599 he utilized the
Lives of Caesar, Antonius, and Brutus for the main incidents in *Julius
Caesar*; but it is possible that its structure owes something to a lost
play.[4] In the bad quarto of *3 Henry VI* the words 'Et tu, Brute' read
like an interpolation from a play about the assassination of Caesar;
and in the *The Massacre at Paris*, also a bad quarto, there is apparently
an allusion to Caesar's words on the morning of his assassination: 'Yet
Caesar shall goe forth./Let mean conceits and baser men feare death'
(996–7). There are, nevertheless, enough verbal echoes of Plutarch's
three Lives to make it reasonably certain that North was Shakespeare's
main source. The first three acts draw upon all three Lives, and the
remaining acts are based mainly on the Life of Brutus. Shakespeare
follows North even in his mistakes, as one might expect – *Decius*
Brutus, *Caius* Ligarius – but he omits, amplifies, and alters. It has often

been pointed out that he takes considerable liberties with historical facts. There was a gap of four months between the triumph mentioned in the first scene and the feast of the Lupercal; and the disrobing of Caesar's images by the Tribunes took place later at the time of the projected coronation. In the play, for obvious dramatic economy, these widely separated events take place on the same day. To take another example, Brutus made two speeches after the assassination, one in the Capitol and one in the market-place, and Antony did not make his speech until the following day, after the reading of the will. Shakespeare telescopes Brutus' speeches into one, and makes it successful with the mob, so as to have a dramatic reversal, and to magnify Antony's triumphant manipulation of the citizens. Antony's speech is delivered immediately after Brutus', and the reading of the will becomes part of the speech. Octavius did not, in fact, arrive in Rome until some weeks later; and Shakespeare omits his quarrels with Antony before the setting up of the triumvirate.

The quarrel scene between Brutus and Cassius is a typical example of Shakespeare's method of altering the facts to increase the dramatic effectiveness of the scene. According to Plutarch, Brutus did 'condemne and noted *Lucius Pella*' on the day after the quarrel with Cassius; and Cassius was annoyed, not because he knew the man, or had pleaded for him, but because he had let off with a caution two of his own friends attainted and convicted of similar offences, that is, of 'robbery and pilfery'. Shakespeare makes the offence bribery and opens the scene with a reference to it. The interference of Phaonius, the counterfeit cynic philosopher, which brings the first quarrel to an end, is utilized by Shakespeare; but whereas Phaonius merely quotes Homer –

> My Lords, I pray you harken both to mee,
> For I haue seene moe yeares than suchye three –

Shakespeare has no reference to Homer, but North's doggerel verse may have suggested to him the idea of making the intruder a poet who rhymes vilely:[5]

> Love, and be friends, as two such men should be;
> For I have seen more years, I'm sure, than ye.
>   (IV. iii. 129–30)

But the quarrel is over by the time he appears on the scene. A little later, Shakespeare twice mentions Portia's death – although the first account may have been meant to supersede the second – and the revelation of the bereavement makes the audience regard Brutus more sympathetically, despite his self-righteous attitude. At the end of the scene Shakespeare introduces the ghost, transferring its appearance from Abydos to Sardis, and making it Caesar's ghost, and not merely Brutus' evil spirit.[6] Plutarch's Brutus is 'thinking of weighty matters', not listening to a song. The two battles in which Cassius and Brutus lose their lives are run together.

Equally significant are the changes made by Shakespeare in the characters. He emphasizes Caesar's physical weaknesses and his *hubris*, but at the same time he makes him nobler than he is in Plutarch's portrait. For example, Caesar's reason for refusing to read Artemidorus' warning – 'What touches us ourself shall be last serv'd' – is apparently Shakespeare's invention. According to Plutarch, '*Caesar* tooke it of him, but coulde neuer reade it, though he many times attempted it, for the number of people that did salute him'. Sir Thomas Elyot says that Caesar, 'beinge radicate in pride', neglected to read the scroll, 'not esteminge the persone that deliuered it'.[7]

Brutus is given some humanizing touches – his care for Lucius, for example – and Shakespeare closely follows Plutarch's report of Portia's speech to her husband; but he is made self-righteous, self-deluded, and overbearing, substituting ideas for realities. Casca's character, on which depends much of the effectiveness of the report of the scene where Caesar refuses the crown, is largely Shakespeare's invention. (The historical Casca was not ignorant of Greek.)

Although Shakespeare borrows numerous phrases from North's prose – from all three Lives – he follows it less closely than he was to do in the other Roman plays.

It is probable that Shakespeare had also read a translation of Appian's *Auncient Historie and exquisite Chronicle of the Romanes Warres, both Civile and Foren* (1578) as there are several details apparently derived from this source. There is a reference to Caesar's falling sickness immediately after his refusal of the crown.[8] There is the same ambiguity as in Shakespeare about the motives of the conspirators, who killed Caesar 'eyther for enuie . . . or as they said, for the loue of their countryes libertie'. Brutus acted 'either as an ingrate man . . . or very desirous of his countrys libertie, preferring it before all other things, or that he was descended of the auntient *Brutus*'.[9] Plutarch, however, suggests that the conspirators other than Brutus were motivated by 'some priuate malice or enuy'. Appian uses the phrase that on the day of his assassination '*Caesar* came forth', and Shakespeare uses it five times in the corresponding scenes.[10] Antony's speech at Caesar's funeral is unlike the one given in the play but, as Professor Schanzer pointed out,[11] Shakespeare may have derived hints from Appian's account of Antony's theatrical delivery of his oration. Indeed, Shakespeare's character, in *this* play, has little relation to Plutarch's 'plaine man, without subtilty' and considerable resemblance to the complex character depicted by Appian – loyal, histrionic, emotional, ruthless, and cunning. Appian describes Antony's uncovering of Caesar's body:[12]

> Then falling into moste vehement affections, vncouered *Caesars* body, holding vp his vesture with a speare, cut with the woundes, and redde with the bloude of the chiefe Ruler.

Shakespeare likewise speaks of 'Our Caesar's vesture wounded'. Plutarch describes the same incident but without the verbal parallel. Antony took

> *Caesars* gowne all bloudy in his hand . . . shewing what a number of cuts and holes it had vpon it. – He vnfolded before the whole assembly the bloudy garments of the dead, thrust through in many places with their swords.

According to Appian, the people carried the litter 'as an holye thing, to be buried in an holy place' and there 'they buryed the body, and abode al night about the fyre'.[13] Plutarch mentions that the mob burnt Caesar's body 'in the middest of the most holy places'. Shakespeare fuses the two sources in the line:

> We'll burn his body in the holy place.
>
> (III. iii. 255)

Appian and Shakespeare agree on the spelling of Calphurnia's name, North usually spelling it 'Calpurnia'. Finally, Antony's prophecy of civil strife may be based on Appian's account of an earlier occasion, when Antony prophesied:[14]

> By inspiration, forespeaking warres, murders, attendures, banishments, spoyles, and all other mischiefe to come vppon them, protesting great execrations to them that were the cause of it.

But Shakespeare probably knew Kyd's *Cornelia*, translated from Garnier's Senecan tragedy.[15] Here, too, he would have found descriptions of the horrors of civil war, with particular emphasis on unburied bodies. Kyd[16] tells us that

> in the flowred Meades dead men were found;
> Falling as thick (through warlike crueltie)
> As eares of Corne for want of husbandry.   (I. 198–200)

The wars of Marius and Sulla

> spilt such store of blood in euery street,
> As there were none but dead-men to be seene.
> (II. 142–3)

Cassius complains of Rome that

> o're our bodies (tumbled vp on heapes,
> Lyke cocks of Hay when Iuly shares the field)
> Thou build'st thy kingdom.   (IV. 8–10)

Italy and other countries

> Are full of dead mens bones by *Caesar* slayne.
> (IV. 110)

Discord and Bellona urge on the slaughter. There is a stench of blood, dismembered bodies, 'wretched heapes' of wounded men crying in vain for mercy. This description uses the words 'ranging' and 'confines', as Antony does.[17]

Antony's prophecy has an analogue at the end of the anonymous play, *Caesar's Revenge*, when Discord, come from Hell, accompanied by Caesar's ghost, expresses their satisfaction at the slaughter:

> I, now my longing hopes haue their desire,
> The world is nothing but a massie heape
> Of bodys slayne, the Sea a lake of blood.

So Antony refers to

> Caesar's spirit, ranging for revenge,
> With Até by his side come hot from hell.
> (III. i. 271–2)

Professor Schanzer points out[18] that this play, like *Julius Caesar*, contains three tragedies – the tragedy of Caesar's *hubris*, ending with his assassination, an Elizabethan revenge tragedy, and the tragedy of Brutus. In *Caesar's Revenge* the revenge tragedy predominates; in *Julius Caesar* that of Brutus. The hubristic tragedy of Caesar's fall is itself an inheritance from the plays of Muret, Grévin, and Garnier, through the author of *Caesar's Revenge* and Shakespeare himself may have been influenced by one or other of plays now lost. At least we can say[19] that the treatment of Brutus' tragedy in *Caesar's Revenge* resembles Shakespeare's

> in being psychological, consisting in Brutus' mental torments which the memories of his ingratitude to Caesar make him suffer. Just before the first appearance to him of Caesar's ghost Brutus exclaims in soliloquy:

> > Caesar upbraues my sad ingratitude.
> > He saued my life in sad Pharsalian fields,
> > That I in Senate house might work his death.
> > O this remembrance now doth wound my soul
> > More than my poniard did his bleeding heart.

> And upon the ghost's appearance Brutus expresses his longing for death... Caesar's ghost... foretells Brutus: 'Thine own right hand shall work my wish'd revenge', which may have suggested the words that Shakespeare puts into the mouth of his Brutus at the discovery of Cassius' suicide:

> > O Julius Caesar, thou art mighty yet!
> > Thy spirit walks abroad, and turns our swords
> > In our own proper entrails.

> At the end of the play Brutus appears, still pursued by the ghost, and kills himself in despair.

Brutus' remorse, the identification of the evil spirit with Caesar's ghost, the linking of the suicide of the conspirators with the ghost's presence on the battlefield, and Brutus' melancholy may have influenced Shakespeare's treatment – though all these points were natural ways of developing the tragedy of Brutus.[20]

Another minor source was first pointed out by Professor Harold Brooks.[21] The warning schedule of Artemidorus and Caesar's remark to the Soothsayer are both influenced by Caesar's 'complaint' in *A Mirror for Magistrates*. According to Plutarch, Caesar said to the Soothsayer:

> The Ides of Marche be come: So be they, softly aunswered the Soothsayer, but yet are they not past.

The version in Appian, 'but they be not yet gone' is closer to Shakespeare's; but that in *A Mirror* is closer still:

(Quod I) the Ides of Marche bee come, yet harme is none.
(Quod hee) the Ides of Marche be come, yet th'ar not gone.

(374–5)

Shakespeare certainly drew on a number of different sources for his account of the portents preceding Caesar's assassination, some of which he used again in *Hamlet*:

> The graves stood tenantless, and the sheeted dead
> Did squeak and gibber in the Roman streets;
> As stars with trains of fire, and dews of blood,
> Disasters in the sun; and the moist star
> Upon whose influence Neptune's empire stands
> Was sick almost to doomsday with eclipse.

(I. i. 115–20)

Here we have five portents mentioned – ghosts in the streets of Rome, stars with trains of fire, dews of blood, disasters in the sun, and an eclipse of the moon. In *Julius Caesar* itself we have thunder and lightning, an earthquake, a tempest dropping fire, a slave with a burning brand, a lion in the Capitol, 'Men, all in fire' walking the streets, an owl hooting at noonday in the market-place, 'exhalations, whizzing in the air', Calphurnia's dream, a lioness whelping in the streets, ghosts, a war in the heavens, 'Which drizzled blood upon the Capitol', comets, and a beast without a heart. It is interesting to compare Plutarch's account:

> For, touching the fires in the element, and spirites running vp and downe in the night, and also the solitarie birdes to be seene at noone dayes sitting in the great market place; are not all these signes perhappes worth the noting, in such a wonderfull chaunce as happened? But *Strabo* the Philosopher writeth, that diuers men were seene going vp and downe in fire: and furthermore, that there was a slaue of the souldiers, that did cast a maruelous burning flame out of his hande, insomuch as they that saw it, thought he had bene burnt, but when the fire was out, it was found he had no hurt. *Caesar* himselfe also doing sacrifice vnto the goddes, found that one of the beastes which was sacrificed had no hart: and that was a strange thing in nature, how a beast could liue without a hart.

Plutarch proceeds to describe the warning of the Soothsayer, and Calpurnia's dreams of Caesar being slain, and the falling of the pinnacle on his house. At the end of the Life of Caesar, Plutarch mentions other portents:

> Againe, of signes in the element, the great comet which seuen nightes together was seene very bright after *Caesars* death, the eighth night after was neuer seene more. Also the brightnes of the sunne was darkened, the which all that yeare through rose very pale, and shined not out, whereby it gaue but small heate: therefore the ayer being very clowdy and darke, by the weaknes of the heate could not come foorth, did cause the earth to bring foorth but raw and vnrype fruits, which rotted before it could rype.

Of the portents used by Shakespeare, Plutarch mentions only nine and he does not state that the bird in the Capitol was an owl. Shakespeare omits some of Plutarch's portents; but for his remaining ones he had recourse to other sources. In the last book of Ovid's *Metamorphoses* (xv) there is a long account of the portents, thus translated by Golding:

> For battels fighting in the clouds with crashing armour flew,
> And dreadfull trumpets sounded in the aire, and hornes eeke blew,
> As warning men before hand of the mischiefe that did brew.
> And *Phoebus* also looking dim did cast a drowzie light
> Vpon the earth, which seem'd likewise to be in sorie plight:
> From vnderneath amid the starres brands oft seem'd burning bright.
> If often rained drops of blood. The morning starre lookt blew,
> And was besotted heere and there with speckes of rustie hew.
> The Moone had also spots of blood. The screechowle sent from hell
> Did with hir tune vnfortunate in euerie corner yel.
> Salt teares from iuorie images in sundrie places fell,
> And in the chappels of the gods was singing heard, and words
> Of threatning. Not a sacrifice one signe of good affoords,
> But great turmoile to be at hand hir hartstrings doo declare,
> And when the beast is ripped vp, the inwards headlesse are.
> About the Court, and euerie house, and churches in the nights
> The dogs did howle, and euerie where appeered ghastlie sprights,
> And with an earthquake shaken was the towne.   (879–96)

Ovid, in addition to mentioning several of the portents in Plutarch's list, mentions several of the other Shakespearian portents – the war in heaven causing dews of blood, the earthquake, and the owl. The spots of blood on the moon may have suggested Shakespeare's lunar eclipse, although Lucan, as we shall see, has a description of such an eclipse.

In another well-known passage about Caesar's murder, Virgil in *Georgics* I lists a number of portents:[22]

> Quum caput obscura nitidum ferrugine texit
> Impiaque æternam timuerunt sæcula noctem . . .
> Armorum sonitum toto Germania cælo
> Audiit; insolitis tremuerunt motibus Alpes.
> Vox quoque per lucos vulgo exaudita silentes
> Ingens; et simulacra modis pallentia miris
> Visa sub obscurum noctis; pecudesque locutæ;
> Infandum! sistunt amnes, terraeque dehiscunt,
> Et maestum illacrimat templis ebur, æraque sudant . . .
> Per noctem resonare lupis ululantibus urbes,
> Non alias cælo ceciderunt plura sereno
> Fulgura; nec diri toties arsere cometæ.

Here we have an eclipse of the sun, earthquake, ghosts, wolves howling in towns, thunder and lightning, and comets. Shakespeare's thunder and lightning may have been suggested by this passage; and his lion may have derived partly from Virgil's wolves and partly from Lucan's wild beasts in the streets of Rome. For Shakespeare seems also to have been acquainted with Lucan's description of the portents connected with Caesar's crossing of the Rubicon, possibly in Marlowe's translation, although this was not yet published when *Julius Caesar* was first performed:[23]

> Strange sights appear'd, the angry threatning gods
> Fill'd both the earth and seas with prodegies;
> Great store of strange and vnknown stars were seene
> Wandering about the North, and rings of fire
> Flie in the ayre, and dreadfull bearded stars,
> And Commets that presage the fal of kingdoms.
> The flattering skie gliter'd in often flames,
> And sundry fiery meteors blaz'd in heauen:
> Now spearlike, long; now like a spreading torch:
> Lightning in silence, stole forth without clouds,
> And from the northren climat snatching fier
> Blasted the Capitoll: The lesser stars
> Which wont to run their course through empty night
> At noone day mustered; *Phoebe* hauing fild
> Her meeting hornes to match her brothers light,

Strooke with th'earths suddaine shadow waxed pale,
Titan himselfe throand in the midst of heauen,
His burning chariot plung'd in sable cloudes,
And whelm'd the world in darknesse, making men
Dispaire of day . . .
Crownes fell from holy statues, ominous birds
Defil'd the day, and wilde beastes were seene,
Leauing the woods, lodge in the streetes of Rome . . .
Soules quiet and appeas'd sigh'd from their graues,
Clashing of armes was heard, in vntrod woods,
Shrill voices schright, and ghoasts incounter men.

Lucan describes other portents, including prodigious births and a sacrificial beast with strange entrails. It will be observed, in the lines quoted, that he has a striking eclipse of the moon, and a parallel to 'stars with trains of fire'. He provides what is perhaps the nearest parallel to the lion in the Capitol; but it should be mentioned that Plutarch describes how Cassius' lions were let loose at the siege of Megara.

Some portents, too, are mentioned by Appian, including Calphurnia's dream in which she saw Caesar 'all to be goared with bloude', 'manye fearefull tokens' in the sacrifices, and 'there was no harte, or as some say, no heade of the entrailes'. Caesar then asks the diviner to sacrifice again, but with no better result.[24] Some of these portents appear also in *Caesar's Revenge*. Other possible sources for the portents have been suggested. Those preceding the fall of Jerusalem in Nashe's *Christ's Tears*[25] and others described by Dekker in *Canaan's Calamitie*[26] are not connected with Caesar, and they are less close to Shakespeare's than the ones discussed above.[27]

21

AS YOU LIKE IT

THOMAS LODGE'S *Rosalynde*, published in 1590, is his masterpiece, and one of the most attractive tales of the period. Sir Walter Greg was probably right in thinking that if it had not provided Shakespeare with a plot there would have been more chance of its receiving a genuinely critical appreciation. It is not, of course, great literature, 'but in its own particular style and within the limits of its kind the romance of Arden falls not far short of complete success'.[1]

Lodge's own source was presumably *The Tale of Gamelyn* in which he would have found the story of Sir John of Bordeaux and his three sons, the wrestling match, and the hero's flight to join a band of outlaws; but the events in the forest and even Rosalynde herself were Lodge's own additions. To his source he added the 'basic ingredients of Elizabethan romance'; and Dr J. D. Hurrell is right in thinking that there is no need to suppose that Lodge was drawing on an Italian novel.[2] He adhered to the ordinary conventions of the genre, and the merits of *Rosalynde* are due to his skill in the manipulation of conventional material, to the charming pastoral atmosphere, and to the quality of some of the interspersed poems. The prose, though it sometimes reminds us that the sub-title of the book is 'Euphues' Golden Legacie', is less mannered and artificial than Lyly's.

The story begins with Sir John's legacy to his three sons, the largest share going to the youngest, Rosader. The eldest, Saladyne, ill-treats Rosader, making him his foot-boy for two or three years, and then bribes a Norman wrestler to put him permanently out of action in a tournament held at Torismond's court. Rosader, however, defeats the champion in a match watched by Alinda, Torismond's daughter, and Rosalynde, daughter of the banished Gerismond, the rightful king. Rosader and Rosalynde fall in love. Rosader quarrels with Saladyne and soon afterwards is chained up as a madman; but he escapes by the help of Adam Spencer. After nearly dying of starvation they join Gerismond's band of outlaws in the forest of Arden. Meanwhile Rosalynde is banished and Alinda, who speaks in her defence, is banished too. They make their way to the forest, Rosalynde taking the name of Ganymede and posing as Aliena's (Alinda's) page. They find poems carved on the barks of trees written by Montanus to Phoebe; they overhear an eclogue between Montanus and Coridon, and they buy Coridon's farm from his landlord. Torismond, coveting Saladyne's estates, has him thrown into prison. There he repents of his misdeeds and, on being released and banished, he sets out in quest of his brother. Meanwhile Rosader meets Ganymede and Aliena, and Rosader plays at wooing Ganymede. Saladyne arrives in the forest and falls asleep, watched by a lion who waits to attack him. Rosader kills the lion but is not recognized by his brother. Saladyne reveals his change of heart and Rosader makes himself known. A few days later Rosader and Saladyne save the girls from a gang of ruffians, and Aliena and Saladyne fall in love. When Rosalynde tries to assist Montanus with his suit, Phoebe falls in love with her and gets Montanus to deliver a letter to her; but Rosalynde visits her in her sickness and makes her promise to marry Montanus when her passion for Ganymede has been quenched by reason. At the marriage of Saladyne and Aliena, Rosalynde reveals her identity to her father; she marries Rosader, and Phoebe marries Montanus. Then Fernadine, Sir John's second son, arrives on the scene to announce that the twelve peers of France are up in arms in support of Gerismond, and that Torismond has arrived at the edge of the forest, ready to give battle. The three brothers distinguish themselves in the battle; Torismond is slain; Gerismond is restored to the throne; Saladyne recovers his father's lands; Rosader is made heir-apparent; Montanus is made lord of the forest of Arden; Adam Spencer is made captain of the King's guard; and Coridon is made master of Alinda's flocks.

It will be seen that Shakespeare retained the main outlines of the story, but he made a number of significant changes. Some are of no importance. He altered many of the names. The three brothers become Oliver, Jaques, and Orlando; Alinda becomes Celia, a name less likely to be confused with Aliena; King Torismond becomes Duke Frederick; Montanus becomes Silvius, and Coridon, Corin. More significant are the additional characters – Le Beau, who adds a nice satirical touch to the usurper's court; Touchstone,[3] who provides a companion to the ladies on their arduous journey and a satirical commentator on the other characters; Amiens and Jaques (unfortunately given the same name as the second son of Sir Rowland de Boys), who lend variety to the outlaws; Audrey and William, whose function is discussed below; and Sir Martin Martext. Another change is of considerable importance: Shakespeare makes the usurper brother to the rightful Duke, so that Rosalind and Celia are cousins. This provides a parallelism in the two plots, since Orlando, too, is cheated of his rights by a villainous brother. Both villains repent in Shakespeare's play: in *Rosalynde* only one.

Shakespeare constructed his play with practised skill. In a crowded first act he introduces us to all the main characters, except the outlaws; and before the end of the act he has shown us the wrestling match, the mutual attraction of Rosalind and Orlando, and the decision of Rosalind and Celia to seek the outlaws. But, as many critics have complained, the exposition is outrageously clumsy, for at the beginning of the play Orlando tells Adam a number of facts with which he must be perfectly acquainted. Perhaps Shakespeare regarded this speech as a kind of prologue in which he was solely concerned, in a non-naturalistic way, with acquainting the audience with the situation; but it seems much more likely that he was laughing at the theatrical conventions he was using, and alerting the audience to the numerous improbabilities they would be asked to swallow.

Rosader is persuaded by his brother to challenge the wrestler: Oliver in the play has heard that Orlando is intending to challenge him. Shakespeare adds a conversation between Rosalind and Celia, which exhibits their mutual affection and Rosalind's grief for her father. Then Touchstone and Le Beau are introduced in turn. The killing of the Franklin's three sons by the wrestler is distanced in a way proper for comedy by having it described by Le Beau; and the reactions of Rosalind and Celia to the 'good sport' show them to be humane and sensitive. Shakespeare then inserts the incident where the ladies, at the Duke's suggestion, try to dissuade Orlando from the match. The Norman is slain by Rosader; Charles is merely put out of action by Orlando. When Lodge's monarch hears of Rosader's parentage, he embraces him; when Frederick hears of Orlando's, he is displeased. This reminds us that Frederick is a usurper and that the rightful Duke is an outlaw; it prepares the way for Orlando's decision to go to the forest of Arden; and it provides Rosalind and Celia with an excuse for speaking kindly to Orlando. Rosalynde takes a jewel from her neck and sends it to Rosader by a page; Shakespeare's Rosalind takes a chain from her neck and gives it directly to Orlando. Rosader sends Rosalynde a 'sonnet'; Orlando is allowed a single exclamation at the end of the scene, 'But heavenly Rosalind!' The direct expression of love is severely curtailed; but Shakespeare is able to convince us that, if his lovers talk less about their passion, they feel more.

Shakespeare omits Lodge's account of Rosader's return with his friends to his brother's house, only to find the door barred against him, of his breaking into the house to give a party, and of Adam Spencer's temporary reconciliation of the two brothers. Oliver makes no pretence of reconciliation.

Lodge gives a long soliloquy to Rosalynde on the banishment of her father and on her love for Rosader; she sings 'Love in my bosom like a bee', the best of Lodge's lyrics; Torismond enters and banishes her; Alinda makes a euphuistic oration in defence of her friend, and she too is banished; Alinda comforts Rosalynde and they decide to disguise themselves and seek out the banished King. Shakespeare condenses all this material into the third scene of the play. In place of Rosalynde's soliloquy and song, there is a short dialogue with Celia; in place of Alinda's oration, Celia is given a speech of only eight lines; and as the Duke does not banish her, her decision to accompany Rosalind appears as a positive act of affection.

For Act II Shakespeare rearranges his source-material. Lodge, after describing the arrival of Ganymede and Aliena in the forest and their discovery of Montanus' verses on the bark of a pine-tree, gives us the Montanus–Coridon eclogue, and goes on to describe the purchase of the farm. This, much condensed, is the substance of Shakespeare's fourth scene in which, however, Rosalind and Celia actually overhear Silvius complaining to Corin of Phebe's cruelty. Lodge then describes how Rosader is chained as a madman, his escape with Adam's assistance, his killing of some of his brother's guests, and his departure with Adam. For this Shakespeare substitutes the simpler version of his third scene. Lodge continues with the collapse of Adam – there is a long moralizing speech on fortune, which may have suggested Touchstone's remarks in II. vii – and Rosader's succour by the outlaws. The banished King asks for tidings of Rosalynde. This material, except for the last item, Shakespeare utilized in the last two scenes of the act, in which, too, Jaques discourses on the world as a stage, and Amiens sings his two songs. The first scene of this act introduces us to the outlaws; and in the second scene the usurper hears of his daughter's flight and is told of the rumour that she and Rosalind have gone off in Orlando's company. This provides a link with Frederick's wrath with Oliver in the next act. In Lodge's story there is no connection between Rosader's flight and Torismond's seizure of Saladyne's estates; in the play the Duke seizes Oliver's property in revenge for Orlando's disappearance. In the source Saladyne is banished ostensibly for the wrongs he has done his brother: Shakespeare makes use of this motive, incidentally but delightfully, when Frederick replies to Oliver's declaration that he had never loved his brother, 'More villain thou!'

In the novel Orlando carves his poems on the barks of trees; in the play, for obvious reasons, he hangs his poems on the trees. Aliena and Ganymede see Rosader at the same time; in the play the two girls discover two of Orlando's poems, and Celia reveals that she has seen him in the forest. Orlando enters with Jaques, and after the latter's departure, Rosalind addresses Orlando as 'forester'. (In the novel

Rosader has been appointed as forester by Gerismond.) Before the end of the scene, 'Ganymede' offers to play the part of Rosalind, ostensibly to cure Orlando of his love, though she hopes not to succeed. In the novel the eclogue between Rosalynde and Rosader takes place at their second meeting, and there is no suggestion that it will cure him of his love. The love-making is carried on in a pastoral vein, so that there is no contrast between the Montanus–Phoebe scenes and the Rosader–Rosalynde ones; but both Rosalind and Orlando retain their wit and humour – though they are fathoms deep in love they are able to joke about it. Rosalind not merely satirizes the behaviour of her own sex, but she is also witty at Orlando's expense.

The third scene of Act III is devoted to Touchstone's wooing of Audrey, not in the source. In the fourth scene Rosalind mentions a meeting with her father, in which he had failed to recognize her; and in the fifth she intervenes on Silvius' behalf, and Phebe falls in love with her. This complication occurs much later in the novel: Shakespeare wished to have the maximum complication by the end of his third act – Silvius loving Phebe, who loves Ganymede, who loves Orlando, who loves Rosalind. (In *Twelfth Night* the complications come even earlier in the play: Cesario loving Orsino, who loves Olivia, who loves Cesario.)

In IV. i we have the mock wooing and the mock marriage, suggested by Rosalind and not, as in Lodge's tale, by Aliena. After the second scene, which is an excuse for another song, Silvius delivers Phebe's poem to Rosalind, whose pretence that the latter is full of chiding is a Shakespearian addition. Oliver enters to recount his rescue by Orlando from a snake, impishly added by Shakespeare, and a lioness. Orlando's hesitation before saving his brother is mercifully condensed from a tedious soliloquy in the novel. Shakespeare omits Saladyne's failure to recognize his brother, which has little point, and his long confession. In the novel Rosader takes his brother to Gerismond; in the play, more dramatically, Oliver is sent with the bloody napkin to excuse his broken promise to Ganymede. The scene ends with Rosalind nearly betraying herself by her swoon.

Shakespeare omits the attack by ruffians on Ganymede and Aliena and makes Celia fall in love with Oliver without such an occasion for gratitude. He omits, too, the tedious love-making of Saladyne and Aliena, Phoebe's sickness, and Ganymede's visit to her. He complicates Touchstone's wooing by the introduction of his easily intimidated rival, William. He adds the quartet of lovers – Silvius, Phebe, Orlando, and Rosalind – and has Rosalind boast that she is a magician, not that she has a friend who is one. He inserts another scene for the sake of 'It was a lover and his lass'. In place of the wedding in Church, he has the masque of Hymen; and the play concludes with the arrival of Jaques de Boys to announce the conversion and abdication of Duke Frederick. There is no mention of the twelve peers of France and no battle.

The name of Orlando Shakespeare probably took from Ariosto's poem, though Rosalind's lover is never exactly *furioso*. Coridon was possibly changed to Corin under the influence of *Syr Clyomon and Clamydes* in which a princess in man's dress takes service with a shepherd of that name.[4] Although there was a forest of Arden near Stratford, which some think Shakespeare conflated with the Ardennes, the pastoral world of the play owes more to literary tradition than it does to the Warwickshire countryside. In a sense the play can be regarded as a critique on pastoralism and, as the pastoral was, amongst other things, a mode of love-poetry, a critique on love. There are, as critics have noted,[5] several levels of conventionality. There is, first, the noble outlaw convention, satirizing both Court life and the exiles who profess to disdain it. Then there is the pastoral convention, going back to Theocritus, and, as Bullough remarks,[6] 'stereotyped in the Renaissance'. The love-sick swain enamoured of the hard-hearted shepherdess is satirized by Rosalind when she attacks Phebe. Thirdly we have Rosalind and Celia, great ladies rôle-playing as shepherd and shepherdess, a convention which found its culmination in the Trianon. Fourthly we have country bumpkins such as Audrey and William as imagined by the town; and these are taken off by Touchstone. Lastly we have a portrait of a shepherd seen without prejudice, Corin being untouched by Touchstone's gibes. There is, in fact, an extraordinary complexity of cross-satire in the play. Jaques satirizes the Duke, Orlando, and Touchstone; Touchstone, as his name indicates, satirizes everyone; Rosalind satirizes not merely Jaques and Phebe, but also the whole convention of romantic love and the waywardness of her own sex. It need hardly be said that, to mock the illusions and conventions of love, as Shakespeare does in nearly all his comedies, to believe that most loving is mere folly, is not a denial of love. Shakespeare is rescuing the reality of love from the fashionable counterfeits and distortions of his age. 'True love', it has been said, 'undergoes the refining process of satire, and survives in a less questionable and ambiguous form'.

✤

✤ 22 ✤

TWELFTH NIGHT

TWELFTH NIGHT, it has been said, is a masterpiece of recapitulation.[1]
Shakespeare had already used the device of the mistaken identity of
twins in *The Comedy of Errors*; in *Twelfth Night*, as in many Italian
plays, the twins are of different sexes. In *The Two Gentlemen of Verona* a
girl, disguised as a page, had acted as emissary from the man she loves
to the woman he loves. In *Love's Labour's Lost* we hear the story of a
woman who died of unrequited love (v. ii. 13–15) and her fate may
have suggested the 'Patience on a monument' speech. In *The Merchant
of Venice* we have Antonio's love for Bassanio, which is paralleled by
the love of the later Antonio for Sebastian. In *As You Like It* we have a
Fool and a singer; in *Twelfth Night* we have a singing Fool. In *Much
Ado About Nothing* Beatrice and Benedick are tricked into loving each
other, or into admitting their love; Malvolio is tricked into believing
that Olivia is in love with him. Sir Toby is a reduced version of
Falstaff, though without his wit or cowardice; and Sir Andrew was
perhaps developed from Slender.

There were, of course, sources apart from Shakespeare's previous
plays. John Manningham in his diary[2] mentions that he saw a performance of the play at the Middle Temple and says that it was 'much
like the *Comedy of Errores*, or *Menechmi* in Plautus, but most like and
neere to that in Italian called *Inganni*'. There are three plays of that
title, one of them later than *Twelfth Night*. *Gl'Inganni* of Curzio
Gonzaga (1592) has some links with Shakespeare's play. The disguised
woman takes the name of Cesare and the author's name reminds us of
'The Murder of Gonzago', the play 'written in very choice Italian'
performed before Claudius. Secchi's play[3] (published 1562) has a
woman, Ginevra, disguised as a man, Ruberto, in love with Gostanzo.
To cure him of his infatuation with a courtezan, Ruberto tells him
that a woman is in love with him:[4]

> *Gost.* Where is she?
> *Rub.* Near you. . .
> *Gost.* How do you know that she loves me?

Rub. Because she often discusses her love with me.
Gost. Do I know her?
Rub. As well as you know me.
Gost. Is she young?
Rub. Of my age.   (I. 9)

In a later scene, as Helen A. Kaufman points out,[5] Gostanzo asks Ruberto why he is so upset by the girl's suffering, and she replies that she loves the girl as much as she does herself. Given the situation of a girl disguised as a man in love with her master, repeated in other plays and stories, the resemblance in actual dialogue is not particularly striking.

Another of Secchi's plays, *L'Interesse*, also has some resemblances to *Twelfth Night*, although the plot is totally different. Years before the opening of the play, Pandolfo wagered that his pregnant wife would bear a son. When the baby is born, although a girl, he brings her up as a boy and calls her Lelio. Lelio in due course falls in love with one of her sister's suitors, named Fabio; disguises herself as her sister and becomes pregnant by Fabio. As Miss Kaufman shows,[6] we have here the central situation of *Twelfth Night* where a girl, disguised as a man, is in love with one who loves another woman. Fabio is told that Lelio is challenging him to a duel. Secchi may therefore have suggested to Shakespeare the comic possibilities of involving Cesario in a duel. A scrap of dialogue, in which Fabio asks Lelio about her love, is close to the one quoted from Secchi's other play, and also to the Cesario–Orsino exchange:

Fabio. Is she young?
Lelio. About your age.
Fabio. Is she beautiful?
Lelio. A sweet face, and comely as yours.

There is also in the same scene an account by Lelio of a girl who is pining away from unrequited love.

Another play, the anonymous *Gl'Ingannati* (1538), resembles *Twelfth Night* so closely that it is likely that Manningham was really referring to this when he spoke of *Inganni*. The comedy is in prose. Lelia, the heroine, with the help of the nuns of the convent where she has been living, disguises herself as a man and takes the name of Fabio; she does this for love of Flaminio, whose mistress she had been, and in whose household she takes service as a page. Flaminio sends her on love-embassies to Isabella, who forthwith falls in love with her. Lelia, less scrupulous than Viola, kisses Isabella and allows her to hope. Then Fabrizio, Lelia's lost brother, comes to Modena with his tutor, who shows him the chief sights of the town.[7] Lelia's father learns of her disguise and he and Isabella's father meet Fabrizio and take him for Lelia. Thinking him mad, they lock him up in Isabella's room, where he becomes her lover. The play ends with the marriages of Fabrizio to Isabella and of Flaminio to Lelia. There is no shipwreck in the play, Fabrizio having been separated from his family at the sack of Rome. Some have thought[8] that the farcical element in the play had some influence on *Twelfth Night*: but I see no resemblance between Stragualcia's dealings with Piero and those of Sir Toby with Malvolio, or between the tricking of Giglio by Pasquelia and the gulling of Malvolio by Maria; nor is it easy to see Malvolio as a combination of Gherardo, Giglio, and Piero.[9] On the other hand, a phrase in the prologue, 'La notte di Beffana [Epiphany]', presumably gave Shakespeare his title, even if (as is often assumed) the play was first performed on Twelfth Night.

The same story of Lelia was told by Bandello[10] and in the translation by Belleforest: Shakespeare doubtless knew one of these. The closest parallel is with Orsino's confession that men's fancies are more giddy and unfirm than women's, and Viola's confession that she knows

> Too well what love women to men may owe.
>
> (II. iv. 104)

So Nicuola speaks to Lattanzio of the girl he once loved, that is herself. The following is Belleforest's version:[11]

> Et que scavez vous si ceste fille languist encor pour l'amour de vous, et vist en destresse? Car i'ay ouy dire que les filles en leurs premieres apprehensions aiment d'vne vehemence tout autre, et plus grande qui ne font les hommes, et que malaisement on estaint ceste flamme ainsi viuement esprise, ayant trouue suiet non occupe en autre chose.

Bandello's phrase, 'l'amoroso verme voracemente con grandissimo cordoglio le rodeva il cuore', may have suggested Viola's lines:

> She never told her love
> But let concealment, like a worm i'th'bud,
> Feed on her damask cheek.   (II. iv. 109)

The story of Lelia is to be found also in Cinthio's *Hecatommithi* (v. 8), the source of *Othello* and a possible source of *Measure for Measure*. This version contains a shipwreck; but there is a shipwreck too in the version of the story given in *Riche his Farewell to Militaire Profession* (1581) which is properly regarded as the main source of Shakespeare's play. It may be mentioned that Riche, in other parts of the book, uses three words not previously used by Shakespeare, and three not used by him after *Twelfth Night*. In Riche's fifth story a man tries to reform his shrewish wife by treating her as a lunatic:

> he tied her in a darke house that was on his backside, and then callyng his neibours about her, he would seeme with greate sorrowe to lament his wiues distresse, telling them that she was sodainly become Lunatique.

This incident bears some slight resemblance to the treatment of Malvolio; but Shakespeare seems also to have remembered John Darrell's exorcisms of Nicholas Starkey's children, as described in his *True Narration* (1600):

> Theis .4. especially .3. of them vsed much light behauiour and vayn gestures, sundry also filthy scurrilous speaches, but whispering them for the most part among themselues, so as they were no let to that holy exercise we then had in hand. Sometimes also they spake blasphemy calling the word preached, *bible bable, he will neuer haue done prating, prittle prattle.*   (p. 10)

Feste, as Sir Topas, urges Malvolio to leave his vain bibble-babble. Samuel Harsnett, whose later pamphlet directed against the catholic exorcists Shakespeare perused, exposed the puritan exorcisms in his *Discouery of the Fraudulent Practises of John Darrel* (1599). It may be worth noting that Shakespeare borrows the words of the alleged demoniacs for his bogus priest.

Riche in his epistle dedicatory to gentlewomen confesses that he is not a good dancer:

> As firste for Dauncyng, although I like the Measures verie well, yet I could neuer treade them a right, nor to vse measure in any thyng that I went aboute, although I desired to performe all thynges by line and by leauell, what so euer I tooke in hande.
>
> Our Galliardes are so curious, that thei are not for my daunsyng, for thei are so full of trickes and tournes, that he whiche hath no more but the plaine Sinquepace, is no better accoumpted of then a verie bongler, and for my part, thei might assone teache me to

make a Capricornus, as a Capre in the right kinde that it should bee.

For a Ieigge my heeles are too heauie: And these braules are so busie, that I loue not to beate my braines about them.

A Rounde is too giddie a daunce for my diet, for let the dauncers runne about with as muche speede as thei maie: yet are thei neuer a whit the nier to the ende of their course, vnlesse with often tourning thei hap to catch a fall. And so thei ende the daunce with shame, that was begonne but in sporte.

This passage seems to have contributed to the picture we get of Sir Andrew in I. iii. Sir Andrew has 'the back-trick simply as strong as any man in Illyria', he can cut a caper, and Sir Toby asks him:

Why dost thou not go to church in a galliard, and come home in a coranto? My very walk should be a jig; I would not so much as make water but in a sink-a-pace.

His later question, 'Were we not born under Taurus?' may likewise have been suggested by Riche's reference to Capricorn.

The following is a summary of Riche's tale of Apolonius and Silla: Silla, the daughter of Duke Pontus, the governor of Cyprus, falls in love with Duke Apolonius while he is her father's guest. Apolonius, ignorant of her feelings, sails for Constantinople. Silla persuades her servant Pedro to accompany her to Constantinople, and she travels as his sister. On the voyage Silla is saved from rape at the hands of the lascivious captain by a shipwreck in which both he and Pedro are drowned. Silla gets ashore, clinging to the Captain's sea-chest, which contains money and apparel. She dresses as a man and calls herself by the name of her twin brother, Silvio. On arriving at Constantinople she takes service with Apolonius, who employs her on a love-embassy to a wealthy widow, Julina; Julina falls in love with Silla and enjoins her not to say anything more on behalf of Apolonius: 'from hence-forthe either speake for your self, or saie nothyng at all'. Meanwhile Silvio, returning from the wars, hears of his sister's flight and goes in search of her. Arriving at Constantinople and 'walkyng in an euenyng for his own recreation, on a pleasaunte greene yarde, without the walles of the Citie', he encounters Julina who invites him to supper. Surprised at being addressed by his own name by a complete stranger, he nevertheless consents; and after supper Julina invites him to stay the night. She comes to share his bed and in the morning, 'for feare of further euiles', Silvio goes off to seek for his sister 'in the partes of

Grecia'. When Apolonius demands an answer to his suit, Julina says she is pledged to another. Hearing from his servants that his page is his successful rival, Apolonius casts Silla into a dungeon. Julina, finding herself with child, hastens to the Duke's palace and confesses her love. Apolonius reproaches Silla for her breach of trust; but she urges Julina to confess that she had been faithful to her trust. Julina urges her to acknowledge the truth.

> Now is the tyme to manifest the same vnto the worlde, whiche hath been done before God, and betwene ourselues.

Hearing that Julina is pregnant, Apolonius threatens to kill Silla if she does not marry her. Silla explains to Julina that she is a woman; Apolonius forthwith agrees to marry Silla; and Silvio, hearing of the marriage, and ashamed of his desertion of Julina, agrees to marry her.

The only close echo of Riche's tale is to be found in Olivia's words to Cesario:

> I have said too much unto a heart of stone,
> And laid mine honour too unchary out.
>
> (III. iv. 191–2)

This resembles Julina's reproach, just before Silla reveals her sex:

> Ah vnhappie and aboue all other most vnhappie, that haue so charely preserued myne honour, and now am made a praie to satisfie a yong mans lust.　　　　(Bullough, II, 360)

Yet it cannot be doubted that Shakespeare had read Riche's story. The shipwreck, Silvio's acceptance of Julina's invitation, Julina's revelation of her betrothal, her criticism of Silvio's fearful refusal to acknowledge it, and the Duke's anger are sufficiently close to the corresponding incidents in *Twelfth Night* to make it apparent that this was the main source.

Manningham refers to Olivia as a widow. It is possible that the play originally followed Riche in this respect; but it is more likely that Manningham remembered her mourning while forgetting the cause. In any case the advantages of having Olivia young and inexperienced are obvious: it would not have suited the atmosphere of the play to have had Olivia and Sebastian sharing a bed without benefit of clergy,[12] nor is Olivia deserted as Julina is. Shakespeare's sea-captain, moreover, is anything but lustful.

Riche's story has no underplot, nor have the Bandello and Belle-forest versions. In complicating his play by the introduction of Sir Andrew's wooing of Olivia, his reluctant challenge to Cesario, and the gulling of Malvolio, Shakespeare may have taken a very slight hint from the two absurd suitors in *Gl' Ingannati*; but the Malvolio plot is more likely to have been suggested by the topical story of the Comp-troller of the Household, Sir William Knollys, who demonstrated against a noisy party in the small hours of the morning by walking amongst the revellers, clad only in his shirt, with a copy of Aretine in his hand.[13] Like Malvolio, he complained of bear-baiting; he was connected with Banbury, a place noted for its cakes and ale, as well as for its puritans; his father is known to have defended the puritans; and Malvolio speaks of his 'austere regard of control'. Malvolio's name was probably suggested by the phrase 'male voglia' which recurs frequently in Bandello's version of the story.[14]

In Emmanuel Forde's *Parismus* (1598) there is a Violetta who is ship-wrecked while following her lover in disguise; and there is also an Olivia; but the viola was the flower symbolizing faithfulness and the *viola de braccia* was Apollo's instrument and the symbol of passion and chastity.[15] Fitzroy Pyle and others have suggested[16] that Shake-speare drew on Sidney's *Arcadia* for certain details; but women dis-guised as men and men who are tricked by forged letters are not uncommon. Nor, I think, is there much evidence that Shakespeare was influenced either by *Syr Clyomon and Clamydes* or by *Common Conditions*.

Such were the materials on which Shakespeare set to work. It is difficult to accept Hotson's theory[17] that the play was written, rehearsed, and acted within a fortnight, though it would have been possible for the poet to have adapted a play already written to suit the topical occasion of Virginio Orsino's visit. Shakespeare was not as prolific as the Spanish dramatists with whom Hotson compares him. If he could have written a masterpiece in ten days his company would have expected more than two plays a year from him. In any case it seems unlikely that Orsino, Elizabeth's guest, would have felt flattered by the portrait of his namesake. Whether *Twelfth Night* was first per-formed on this occasion remains doubtful and perhaps the following year, after Orsino's visit, is more likely. At least we can be sure that it was performed on 6 January: there are various references to the Epiphany in the course of the play.[18]

Shakespeare adopts a new setting for his play, abandoning Modena (the scene of *Gl'Ingannati*) and Constantinople (Riche's choice), and choosing Illyria, a geographical compromise, and a conveniently obscure location. The social *milieu* of his characters is closest to that of Riche's novel, although Olivia's household is essentially Elizabethan. From Riche, too, Shakespeare borrowed the shipwreck as a convenient way of separating the twins and starting Viola on her career. She is not, like Silla, pursuing the man she loves at the time of the shipwreck, nor has she been jilted as Lelia had been. Indeed, Shakespeare makes her decide to take service with Orsino only when she has no chance of serving Olivia. Viola dresses as her brother, and this makes it more plausible that each should be mistaken for the other. It is dramatically important that Sebastian should think that Viola is drowned, as he would otherwise jump to the conclusion that he had been mistaken for her. Silvio, although he is searching for a sister he believes is alive, never puts two and two together.

Shakespeare wisely dispenses with the parents of both Lelia and Isabella whose father Gherado is Lelia's unwelcome suitor. Sebastian and Viola are orphans and Olivia is alone in the world. The courage and self-reliance of Viola are thus increased; and the isolation of Olivia allows both Sir Andrew and Malvolio to aspire to her hand.

In the first act of *Gl'Ingannati* we have the situation presented to us of Isabella falling in love with Lelia, who is in love with Flaminio, who loves Isabella; and Gherado wants to marry Lelia. By cutting out Gherado, Shakespeare is able, by the end of his first act, to reach the same point in his plot, with Olivia in love with Viola, Viola in love with Orsino, and Orsino in love with Olivia – 'too hard a knot' for Viola to untie. But in Act I we have also been introduced to the characters of the underplot; Sir Andrew's pretensions to Olivia's hand prepare the way for his duel with Cesario and Malvolio's scorn for Feste makes him determine on revenge.

Lelia's brother does not appear until the third act of *Gl'Ingannati*; Shakespeare introduces Sebastian much earlier, at the beginning of Act II; and, in the same act, we have the interruption of the revellers, the hatching of the plot against Malvolio, and a scene in which Viola is able indirectly to express her love for Orsino. In the second act of *Gl'Ingannati* Flaminio hears of the favours granted to his page, and wishes to kill both Isabella and Lelia; in Riche's version Apolonius does not become jealous until after Silvio has been seduced by Julina: Shakespeare does not let Orsino be aware of Olivia's love for Cesario until the last scene of the play and he then proposes to sacrifice the lamb he loves to spite Olivia. It is obvious that unconsciously he loves Cesario more than he has ever loved Olivia; and this, together with Cesario's theatrical willingness to die for love, prepares the way for the sudden transfer of Orsino's affections. To make possible the postponement of Orsino's knowledge of Olivia's love, it was necessary to postpone her declaration of love until the third act, and Sebastian's meeting with her until the fourth. The intervening scenes are full of matter for a May morning – Malvolio's appearance in yellow stockings and his treatment as a madman, Sir Andrew's challenge, the intervention and arrest of Antonio, and Viola's realization that her brother is alive. In the second half of the play Shakespeare owes nothing to the complicated intrigue of *Gl'Ingannati*, which, indeed, more resembles the farce of *The Comedy of Errors*; but by having Sir Toby, Sir Andrew, and the Fool, as well as Olivia, all mistake Sebastian for Cesario, he makes a similar use of mistaken identity. In *Gl'Ingannati* Lelia and Fabrizio are never on the stage together and they could be played by a single actor or actress. In 'Apolonius and Silla' Silvio does not discover his lost sister until after her marriage. Shakespeare has the more exciting and moving confrontation of brother and sister and the revelation of Cesario's sex in the last act of the play.

T. W. Baldwin has shown with what skill *Twelfth Night* is constructed 'on the *Andria* variety of the Terentian formula';[19] and he pointed out that the interest of *Gl'Ingannati* falls off after the second act when we reach the epitasis of the more interesting story and have to wait for the catastrophe for more than two acts. Shakespeare, on the other hand, delays the epitasis both of the Viola–Olivia situation, and of Malvolio's hope of marrying Olivia until Act III. But although we may well admire the art with which Shakespeare has constructed his play, its superiority to all its sources is displayed more obviously in the subtler characterization, in the humour of the prose scenes, and above all in the poetic texture of the play as a whole. *Gl'Ingannati* is not merely written in prose: it is, comparatively, prosaic.[20]

✳ 23 ✳

TROILUS AND CRESSIDA

THE MAIN SOURCE of Troilus and Cressida, as we might expect, was Chaucer's great poem, *Troilus and Criseyde*.[1] But, like all Elizabethans, Shakespeare was also acquainted with Henryson's bitter sequel, *The Testament of Cresseid*, in which the heroine suffers as a leper for her unfaithfulness. For the other incidents of the play, those relating to the siege of Troy, Shakespeare consulted the first instalment of Chapman's translation of the *Iliad*, published in 1598, and he may have looked at Hall's translation as well. He also knew part, at least, of Virgil's *Aeneid*. He had read Caxton's *Recuyell of the Historyes of Troye*, translated from the French, and Lydgate's *Troy Book*. Golding's translation of Ovid's *Metamorphoses*, moreover, deals with some incidents of the Tale of Troy.

The main outlines of the love-plot are to be found in Chaucer's poem. In Book I, Troilus falls in love with Criseyde and enlists Pandarus' help to woo her; in Book II Pandarus carries out this plan; in Act I of the play, Troilus is already in love with Cressida, and Pandarus is already engaged in furthering his suit. In Book III the lovers meet at the house of Deiphebus and their love is consummated in Pandarus' house; in Act III the lovers are united at the house of Pandarus. In Book IV of the poem the Trojans agree to exchange Criseyde for Antenor, Pandarus contrives another meeting, and the lovers part; in Act IV of the play news is brought that Cressida is to be exchanged, and on the morning after the lovers have been united, Diomed arrives to conduct Cressida to the Greek camp. In Book V Criseyde is wooed by Diomed and eventually she yields, she writes to Troilus, and he seeks to drown his grief in fighting and revenge on Diomed; In the last act of the play, Troilus is a witness of Cressida's unfaithfulness, Cressida writes to him, and he fights desperately, seeking to avenge himself on Diomed, and also to avenge the murder of Hector by Achilles.

The action of the poem, as becomes a narrative, is leisurely. Shakespeare makes it more dramatic by beginning his play just before Cressida yields to Troilus. He ends it only three days later after

Cressida has yielded to Diomed. This telescoping has the effect of intensifying Cressida's unfaithfulness. Chaucer treats his heroine with gentleness and sympathy; she is a young widow, charming, pliable, and timid. Chaucer evades any direct explanation of her unfaithfulness and excuses her as much as he can. We are led to understand that she turns to Diomed, not out of sexual desire, but because she is lonely and isolated in the Greek camp and because she is always tempted to take the line of least resistance. Shakespeare's Cressida has not been married and she is a coquette by temperament, sharpening the appetite of both men by her tactics. Chaucer's poem is written in the tradition of courtly love which laid down an elaborate code of behaviour for the lover, especially secrecy and fidelity. The code had nothing to do with the love of husband and wife, and the aim of the man was not marriage but faithful service and, if the lady consented, a love-affair which was frowned upon only if it became public. The basis of courtly love was adultery, because marriages were all of convenience; and there was often a complete separation of love and marital duties.[2] Shakespeare wrote his play more than two centuries later, by which time the code of society had changed radically. The Elizabethan writer, whether aristocratic or bourgeois, usually assumed that the proper end of love was marriage. Astrophel felt guilty about his pursuit of Stella and Donne's persona's adulteries were meant to shock. The dramatists all frowned on adultery, except occasionally in farcical comedy. Shakespeare was placed in something of a difficulty in dramatizing the story of Troilus and Cressida. On the one hand, Troilus was the pattern of a faithful lover; on the other hand, he did not in any of the sources marry Cressida. Shakespeare clearly retains the secrecy demanded by the code of courtly love, and he never raises the question of marriage at all. One critic has argued that the meeting of the lovers before a witness constituted a common-law marriage, but this appears to contradict the impression one gets not only from this scene but from the whole play. An honest and devoted lover, as Troilus undoubtedly is – he is not the Italianate roué described by Oscar Campbell – one who gives and demands eternal faithfulness, might be expected to marry the object of his love. Shakespeare made the affair clandestine, but nowhere suggests that a prince would be forbidden to marry the daughter of a traitor. He is deliberately vague about Trojan marriage customs: they are different from those implied by Chaucer, but they also differ from the customs current in Elizabethan drama.

Editions of Chaucer in the sixteenth century included Henryson's sequel, in which Cresseide, after she has been abandoned by Diomed and become the mistress of a succession of Greek warriors, is smitten with leprosy and reduced to beggary. Under the influence of this poem, 'Cressid' had become a synonym not merely for an unfaithful woman, but for a harlot. Pistol, with his usual flamboyance, calls Doll Tearsheet 'the lazar kite of Cressid's kind' and Feste mentions that Cressida was a beggar.[3] There is one slight indication that Shakespeare had read Henryson's poem. There Cynthia speaks of Cresseide's 'voice sa cleir'; and Cresseide herself speaks of her 'cleir voice'.[4] So in Shakespeare's play, when Cressida is told that she must go to the Greek camp, she says:

> I'll go in and weep . . .
> Tear my bright hair, and scratch my praised cheeks,
> Crack my clear voice with sobs.   (IV. ii. 104 ff.)

The character of Troilus in Chaucer's poem is very similar to that of Shakespeare's hero. His prowess as a warrior, second only to Hector's, is mentioned by both poets, and so too are his faithfulness in love, and his attempt to forget his love in battle. Both hope to be killed. Chaucer's Troilus cries:

> Myn owen deth in armes wol I seche,
> I recche nat how soone be the day! (v. 1718–19)

Shakespeare echoes these words in the line:

> I reck not though I end my life today. (v. vi. 26)

Chaucer's Pandarus is younger and pleasanter than Shakespeare's. He is the chief vehicle for Chaucer's irony and humour, and he brings the lovers together because he is fond of them and wants them to be happy. Shakespeare's Pandarus also acts without hope of reward, but he gets a vicarious pleasure from the affair, he is sentimental and silly, and he indulges continually in leers and innuendoes. He serves as a bawdy chorus to the love-scenes of the play, and his earthy conception of sex is contrasted with the idealism of the hero. The coarsening of Pandarus was necessary to Shakespeare's purpose. He is depicted in such a way as to fit the word derived from his name, and also with the less sympathetic portrayal of Cressida. In the scene where Pandarus brings the lovers together, the three characters are presented for a moment as types of faithful lover, wanton, and pander. The primitive morality technique is used by Shakespeare with extreme sophistication to exhibit, as it were, the birth of a legend.[5] It should, perhaps, be mentioned that the syphilitic Pandarus of the epilogue is also outside the framework of the play, even though he casts a retrospective light on the character we have seen inside the framework.

Shakespeare's Diomed is also a coarsened version of Chaucer's. Whereas in Chaucer's poem he is a noble warrior who wins Criseyde by his long and eloquent wooing, in Shakespeare's play he hardly bothers to woo Cressida. He never pretends to love her and obviously despises her. This degrading of Diomed's character is a corollary to the alteration in Cressida's. She has to fall to the first man who bothers to seduce her – and the cruder his advances the more violent the contrast between her vows and her actions. One can understand why the New Shakespeare Society was shocked when Bernard Shaw declared that she was Shakespeare's first real woman.

The general outline of the love-plot is therefore to be found in Chaucer's poem, but of the four main characters only Troilus is left more or less unchanged, and the atmosphere of the play, as everyone recognizes, is totally different from that of the poem. This is partly due to the accretions of legend, partly to the change of customs and idea in the intervening centuries, partly perhaps to the Inns of Court audience for which the play was probably written, partly to the tone of the plays being written by Jonson and Marston about the same time, and partly, perhaps, to the influence of the War of the Theatres.

For his other plot Shakespeare used at least three sources – Lydgate's *Troy Book*, Caxton's *Recuyell*, and Chapman's translation of some books of the *Iliad*. Lydgate's poem is very long and somewhat tedious; but Shakespeare would have found in it character-sketches of all his chief personages. Hector, for example, was not merely an outstanding warrior, but also wise and temperate –

> Sadde and discret and prudent neuer-the-les.
>
> (II. 4804)

He was magnanimous in battle and wise in counsel:

> For he was aye so iuste and so prudent,
> So wel avysed and so pacyent,
> And so demened in his gouernaunce,
> That hym was lothe for to do vengeaunce,
> Where as he myght in easy wyse treate,
> For to reforme thynges smale and greate;

> For lothe he was, this noble worthy knyght,
> For any haste to execute ryght,
> Or causeles by rygour to condempne.   (II. 1129–37)

Shakespeare mentions that Hector spares his fallen enemies; he refers to his patience 'as a virtue, fix'd', and in the council-scene he makes him advise the surrender of Helen because the Trojan case was morally bad. Caxton does not mention these characteristics, though he states that 'ther yssued neuer oute of his mouthe a vyllaynous worde' and that 'ther was neuer knyght better belouyd of his peple than he was'. He also mentions that Hector lisped – a peculiarity Shakespeare had used in his portrayal of Hector.

Caxton says that Helenus was 'a man of grete scyence [252^v] and knewe all the Artes lyberall'. Lydgate adds that he 'in clergie and science' was expert, and

> toke but litel hede
> Of alle the werre, knyghthod, nor manhede.
> > (II. 4859–60)

Shakespeare also mentions that Helenus is a priest with a dislike of war.
Lydgate and Caxton both refer to Troilus as a second Hector:

> And called was Hector the secounde. . .
> Excepte Ector, ther was nat swiche another. . .   (II. 288, 4895)
> In force and gladnesse hee resamblid much to Hector, And was
> the second after hym in prowesse.

Lydgate also emphasizes that Troilus

> was alwey feithful, iust, and stable,
> Perseueraunt, and of wil immutable. . . .
> In his dedis he was so hool and pleyn;   (II. 4879 ff.)

and that in battle –

> He was so fers thei myght him nat withstonde
> Whan that he hilde his bloody swerde on hond.
> > [*bloodly* 1513]

So Ulysses, in his portrait of Troilus, mentions that he was 'firm of word' and more dangerous than Hector in battle; and Troilus himself remonstrates with his brother for his 'vice of mercy', urging his fellow Trojans to 'leave the hermit Pity with our mother' (V. iii. 37, 45).

Both Lydgate and Caxton mention two characters of the name of Ajax. Ajax Telamonius has no resemblance to Shakespeare's character, though in the *Iliad* he is compared to a mill-ass.[6] Lydgate's Oileus Ajax is large in size,

> And of his speche rude and rekkeles:
> Ful many worde in ydel hym asterte,
> And but a cowarde was he of his herte.
>
> (II. 4578–80)

Shakespeare's Ajax is not cowardly, but he is described as a brainless, blockish, scurvy-valiant ass, sodden-witted, and slow as the elephant. Lydgate and Caxton both refer to Ulysses' cunning and eloquence, and Lydgate also mentions his discretion and prudence; but his subtlety and wisdom were proverbial. Both Lydgate and Caxton, unlike Chaucer, speak of Diomed's lecherous disposition,

> lecherous of complexioun,
> And had in loue ofte sythes his part,
> Brennynge at hert with Cupides darte. . .
>
> (II. 4618–20)

There are a number of similarities[7] between the incidents in Shakespeare's play and those in the *Troy Book*. Lydgate mentions an encounter between Hector and Ajax which Hector breaks off when he discovers that he is fighting his cousin, and in the play Hector has only one bout with Ajax for the same reason. Caxton has the same incident (Bullough, VI. 198), and like Shakespeare uses the term 'cousin-german'. Both Lydgate and Caxton mention Andromache's dream in which she has a premonition of Hector's death, and the fruitless attempt of Priam, Cassandra, Hecuba, and Helen to dissuade him from the battle. Both Lydgate and Caxton describe the incidents leading up to Hector's death – the fight between Hector and Achilles, in which Achilles is worsted, the fight between Hector and the Greek in sumptuous armour – in Lydgate Hector kills him, in Caxton he takes him prisoner – and the killing of Hector, while he is unprepared, by Achilles. Lydgate inserts some moralizing on the sin of covetousness which led to Hector's death. Shakespeare increases Achilles' guilt and the horror of Hector's murder by having Hector disarm Achilles at the first encounter, and by making Achilles and his myrmidons murder Hector, an incident borrowed from the death of Troilus as described by Lydgate and Caxton:[8]

And afore that Achilles entryd in to the bataylle he assemblid his
myrondones And prayd hem that they wolde entende to none other
thynge but to enclose troyllus and to holde hym wyth oute fleynge
tyll he cam And that he wolde not be fer fro hem. And they pro-
mysid hym that they so do wolde. And he smote in to the bataylle. . . .
Than the myrondones . . . threstid in amonge the troians and
recouerid the felde . . . and sought no man but troyllus, they fonde
hym that he foughte strongly and was enclosid on all parties, but he
slewe and wounded many. And as he was all allone amonge hem
and had no man to socoure hym they slewe his horse And hurte
hym in many places And araced of his heed his helme And his
coyffe of yron And he deffended hym the beste wyse he cowde.
Than cam on Achilles when he sawe troyllus alle naked And ran
upon hym in a rage and smote of his heed And caste hit vnder the
feet of the horse And toke the body and bonde hit to the taylle of
his horse And so drewe hit after hym thurgh oute the ooste.

Lydgate and Caxton both describe Hector's visit to the Greek camp,
and 'Achilles behelde him gladly, forasmuch as hee had neuer seen him
vnarmed'. So in the play Achilles wishes 'to see the great Hector
unarmed'. Lydgate mentions the wounding of Paris by Menelaus,
and in the play the incident is referred to by Aeneas. Caxton describes
how Diomed fought with Troilus and took his horse, and sent it as a
present to Cressida. This incident also appears in the play. Caxton,
but not Lydgate, mentions that Achilles had refused to go to battle
one day because he was in love with Polyxena and he had promised
Priam and Hecuba 'that he sholde helpe no more the Grekes'. Achilles,
in the play, mentions his love of Polyxena and his vow, but it is
apparently not his main motive for keeping to his tent.

The debate in Troy about the restoration of Helen is to be found in
Caxton, and the arguments used by Hector, Paris, Helenus, and Troilus
correspond to those used in the play. But in Caxton the debate takes
place before the outbreak of the war. Its position in the play is determined by the position of a similar debate in Book VII of the *Iliad*.[9]

E. M. W. Tillyard added a few more parallels with Caxton and
Lydgate.[10] He suggested that the speech on time seems to be based on
Ulysses' appeal to Achilles in Lydgate's poem:

> By youre manhod, that is spoke of so ferre
> That your renoun to the worldis ende
> Reported be, wher-so that men wende,

> Perpetuelly, by freshnes of hewe
> That the triumphe of this highe victorie
> Be put in story and eke in memorie,
> And so enprented that foryetilnes
> No power haue by malis to oppresse
> Youre fame in knyghthod, dirken or difface,
> That shyneth yit so clere in many place
> With-oute eclipsynge, sothly, this no les;
> Which to conserve ye be now rekeles
> Of wilfulnes to cloude so the lyght
> Of youre renoun that whilom shon so bright
>
> (IV. 1770–83)

Tillyard likewise pointed out that Lydgate condemns the Trojan war because of its trivial cause:

> We trewly may aduerten in oure thought
> That for the valu of a thing of nought
> Mortal causes and werris first by-gonne;
> Strif and debate, here vnder the sonne,
> Wer meved first of smal occasioun,
> That caused after gret confusioun,
> That no man can the harmys half endite. (II. 123–9)

Caxton blames Hector for yielding to a request to call off the day's battle when victory was in his power:

> There is no mercy in battaill. A man ought not to take misericorde,
> But take the victorye who may gete hit.

So Troilus in the play blames his brother for his mistaken chivalry.

These parallels are sufficient proof that Shakespeare made use both of Lydgate and of Caxton. But for many of the incidents and characters Shakespeare must have gone to Chapman's translation of Homer. Thersites is to be found in Homer, but not in Chaucer, Lydgate, or Caxton. He is thus described in the 1598 edition – there are considerable differences in later editions:

> A man of tongue, whose rauenlike voice, a tuneles iarring kept,
> Who in his ranke minde coppy had of vnregarded wordes,
> That rashly and beyond al rule, vsde to oppugne the Lords,
> But what soeuer came from him, was laught at mightilie:
> The filthiest Greeke that came to *Troy*: he had a goggle eye;

Starcke-lame he was of eyther foote: his shoulders were contract
Into his brest and crookt withall: his head was sharpe compact,
And here and there it had a hayre.   (II. 206–13)

He is not only a filthy deformed railer, but also a coward who weeps
when he is chid by Ulysses. Shakespeare keeps these characteristics and
even uses the same epithet 'rank'. Later Thersites says he will croak
like a raven, suggested by the opening lines of the above quotation.

The account of the dissension in the Greek army is based on the
Homeric account. Shakespeare follows Homer in making Achilles
withdraw from the battle through excessive pride, though he omits
the reason for his resentment of Agamemnon, and adds the motive of
love of Patroclus (derived partially from Homer) and love of Polyxena
(derived from Caxton). Shakespeare can be vague about the cause of
the quarrel since, as he declares in the prologue, he begins in the middle
of the story. But in the first act he shows us the results of the feud, and
then passes on to the matter of Book VII, the challenge of Hector to
Ajax and the debate in Troy about the restoration of Helen. In Book VII
Shakespeare would have found the device of the lottery, though this is
Nestor's suggestion. Shakespeare invents the idea of the manipulation
of the lottery by Ulysses and his use of the challenge to arouse Achilles.
In all the sources the embassy to Achilles is merely a suit: in the play
it is part of Ulysses' plot, and it is linked with Hector's challenge.
Shakespeare treated the combat between Hector and Ajax differently
from any of his predecessors, though the incident itself is a combination
of elements derived from his sources. In Book XI Ulysses and Phoenix
give advice to Achilles; Shakespeare again strengthens the importance
of Ulysses' part by omitting Phoenix. The death of Patroclus was
derived from *Achilles Shield* (*Iliad*, XVIII): in Caxton the killing of
Patroclus by Hector takes place much earlier and is not related to the
slaying of Hector by Achilles in revenge for the death of his friend.
Here Shakespeare is indebted to Homer alone.

In depicting Nestor Shakespeare relied on Chapman rather than on
Caxton. In his portrait of Menelaus Shakespeare follows Homer's
conception. In his complete translation (though not in 1598) Chapman
describes Menelaus as 'short-spoken after his countrie the Laconicall
manner, yet speaking thicke and fast' (Bk II, Commentarius). Shakespeare's Menelaus is also laconical. He utters only two words on his
first appearance and six on his second.

Certain Homeric details Shakespeare took from parts of the *Iliad* not yet translated. He might have read the poem in a French or Latin translation, but the treatment of Hector's dead body by Achilles he could have found in the *Aeneid* or in a classical dictionary. Achilles surveys Hector in order to find the best place to kill him, very much as Achilles chooses the death stroke in the *Iliad* (Bk XXII).

Hector's visit to the Greek camp is derived from Caxton, but it seems to have been amplified from Greene's collection of stories and debates entitled *Euphues his Censure to Philautus* (1587).[11] In a description of a similar visit to the Greek camp during a truce Greene mentions that Hector walked with Achilles and Troilus with Ulysses, as in the play. The same book contains a discussion on which qualities are most necessary for a soldier – wisdom, fortitude, or liberality. Helenus, in arguing for the necessity of wisdom in a soldier, uses language similar to Ulysses', when he speaks of the way the Greeks scorn the work of the staff officer:

> For suppose the captaine hath courage enough to braue the enemy in the face, yet if hee knew not by a wise and deepe insight into his enemies thoughts, how with aduantage to preuent such ambushes as may be layed to preiudice his army, had hee as great courage as the stowtest champion in the worlde, yet might the defect of wisedome in the preuention of such perills, ruinate both him selfe, his honour, and his Souldiers.

There is another discussion on the question of whether Helen should be restored, in the course of which she is referred to as a gem, a pearl, and as a piece. In Shakespeare's play Troilus speaks of her as a pearl, and Diomed speaks of her as a piece. Hector's argument that 'Nature ... hath taught vs ... to mayntayne my Brothers deede with the Swoorde, not to allow such a fact honorable, but as holding it princely, with death to requite an iniury' is not unlike Hector's attitude in the play. He condemns the rape of Helen, but agrees to continuing the war because it 'hath no mean dependence upon [their] joint and several dignities'.

Greene mentions Hecuba's dream that she has given birth to a fire-brand; one of his characters criticizes the Trojans for being ignorant of moral philosophy; as Hector accuses his brothers of being unfit to hear it; he mentions the definition of virtue as a mean between two extremes (which is usually thought to be the point of the line 'Between whose endless jar justice recides' (I. iii. 119)); he refers to the palace of Ilium (though this is also in Caxton); and he makes Ulysses critical of

women: 'An ounce of giue in a Ladies ballaunce, weygheth downe a
pound of loue mee'. Finally it may be mentioned that one character
speaks of beauty as metaphysical, much as Troilus claimed that beauty
was an absolute value; Cressida is described as 'tickled a little with a
selfe conceipt of hir owne wit'; and a lustful woman in one of the
illustrative tales mislikes 'hir olde choyce, through the tickling desire of a
new chaunge'. Ulysses, speaking of Cressida, uses the epithet 'tickling'[12]
or 'ticklish'. It may be argued that Shakespeare took a good deal of
atmospheric detail from Greene's book.

In Ulysses' famous speech on degree Shakespeare appears to have
combined[13] a number of different sources. From Homer he took the
general idea of the speech:

> wretch keepe thy place and heare
> Others besides thy Generall that place aboue thee beare:
> Thou art vnfit to rule and base without a name in war
> Or state of counsaile: nor must Greekes be so irregular
> To liue as euery man may take the scepter from the king:
> The rule of many is absurd, one Lord must leade the ring.
>
> (II. 193–8)

Agamemnon says that the Greeks would have conquered Troy if they
had not quarrelled amongst themselves, and Homer also uses the
image of bees. The Greeks hastening to the council are compared to
tribes of thronging bees.[14] So Ulysses in the play asks

> When that the general is not like the hive,
> To whom the foragers shall all repair,
> What honey is expected?   (I. iii. 81–3)

Virgil[15] also uses the image of the bees repairing to their hive, and
Shakespeare had used it before in *Henry V*. He was also acquainted
with Elyot's *The Governour* in which the bee image is explicitly related
to the question of order[16] and to Ulysses' speech on the need for order:

A publike weale is a body lyuyng, compacte or made of sondry
astates and degrees of men, whiche is disposed by the ordre of equite
and gouerned by the rule and moderation of reason. . . . For as
moche as *Plebs* in latin, and comminers in englisshe, be wordes only
made for the discrepance of degrees, wherof procedeth ordre:
whiche in thinges as wel naturall as supernaturall hath euer had
such a preeminence, that therby the incomprehensible maiestie of

god, as it were by a bright leme of a torche or candel, is declared
to the blynde inhabitantes of this worlde. More ouer take away
ordre from all thynges what shulde then remayne? Certes nothynge
finally, except some man wolde imagine eftsones *Chaos*: whiche of
some is expounde a confuse mixture. Also where there is any lacke of
ordre nedes must be perpetuall conflicte: and in thynges subiecte to
Nature nothynge of hym selfe onely may be norisshed; but whan
he hath distroyed that where with he dothe participate by the ordre
of his creation, he hym selfe of necessitie muste than perisshe, wherof
ensuethe uniuersall dissolution. But nowe to proue, by example of
those thynges that be within the compasse of mannes knowledge, of
what estimation ordre is, nat onely amonge men but also with god,
all be it his wisedome, bounte, and magnificence can be with no
tonge or penne sufficiently expressed. Hath nat he set degrees and
astates in all his glorious warkes? . . .

Beholde also the ordre that god hath put generally in al his
creatures, begynnyng at the most inferiour or base, and assendynge
upwarde: he made not only herbes to garnisshe the erthe, but also
trees of a more eminent stature than herbes, and yet in the one and
the other be degrees of qualitees; some pleasant to beholde, some
delicate or good in taste, other holsome and medicinable, some
commodious and necessary. . . So that in euery thyng is ordre, and
without ordre may be nothing stable or permanent; and it may nat
be called ordre, excepte it do contayne in it degrees, high and base,
accordynge to the merits or estimation of the thyng that is ordred.
Nowe to retourne to the astate of man kynde. . . . It is therfore
congruent, and accordynge that as one excelleth an other in that
influence, as therby beinge next to the similitude of his maker, so
shulde the astate of his persone be aduanced in degree or place
where understandynge may profite: which is also distributed in to
sondry uses, faculties, and offices, necessary for the lying and
gouernance of mankynde. . . .

The populare astate, if it any thing do varie from equalitie of
substance or estimation, or that the multitude of people haue ouer
moche liberte, of necessite one of these inconueniences muste happen:
either tiranny, where he that is to moche in fauour wolde be eleuate
and suffre none equalite, orels in to the rage of a communaltie,
whiche of all rules is moste to be feared. For lyke as the communes,
if they fele some seueritie, they do humbly serue and obaye, so
where they imbracinge a licence refuse to be brydled, they flynge

and plunge: and if they ones throwe downe theyr gouernour, they ordre euery thynge without iustice, only with vengeance and crueltie: and with incomparable difficultie and unneth by any wysedome be pacified and brought agayne in to ordre. Wherfore undoubtedly the best and most sure gouernaunce is by one kynge or prince. . . For who can denie but that all thynge in heuen and erthe is gouerned by one god, by one perpetuall ordre, by one prouidence? One Sonne ruleth ouer the day, and one Moone ouer the nyghte; and to descende downe to the erthe, in a litell beest, whiche of all other is moste to be maruayled at, I meane the Bee, is lefte to man by nature, as it seemeth, a perpetuall figure of a iuste gouernaunce or rule: who hath amonge them one principall Bee for theyr gouernour, who excelleth all other in greatnes, yet hath he no pricke or stinge, but in hym is more knowledge than in the residue. . . The capitayne hym selfe laboureth nat for his sustinance, but all the other for hym; he onely seeth that if any drane or other unprofitable bee entreth in to the hyue, and consume the the hony, gathered by other, that he be immediately expelled from that company. . .

The Grekes, which were assembled to reuenge the reproche of Menelaus . . . dyd nat they by one assent electe Agamemnon to be their emperour or capitain: obeinge him as theyr soueraine durying the siege of Troy? . . . They rather were contented to be under one mannes obedience, than seuerally to use theyr authorities or to ioyne in one power and dignite; wherby at the last shulde haue sourded discention amonge the people, they beinge seperately enclined towarde theyr naturall souerayne lorde, as it appered in the particuler contention that was betwene Achilles and Agamemnon for theyr concubines, where Achilles, renouncynge the obedience that he with all other princes had before promised, at the bataile fyrst enterprised agaynst the Troians. For at that tyme no litell murmur and sedition was meued in the hoste of the grekes, whiche nat withstandyng was wonderfully pacified, and the armie unscatered by the maiestie of Agamemnon, ioynynge to hym counsailours Nestor and the witty Ulisses.

The importance of order is stressed by many authors Shakespeare is known to have read. In *Troilus and Criseyde*, for example, Chaucer celebrates the power of Love to hold all things together, even to restrain the greedy sea from overflowing – [17]

To drenchen erthe and al for evere-mo.

In the Homily on obedience, Shakespeare would have heard order in the state connected with order in the universe, and the dangers resulting from the destruction of order are similar to those stressed in Ulysses' speech:[18]

Almighty God hath created and appointed all thinges in heauen, earth and waters, in a most excellent and perfect order. In heauen, hee hath apponted distinct and seuerall orders and states of Arch-aungels and Aungels. In earth hee hath assigned and appointed Kinges, Princes, with other gouernoures vnder them, in all good and necessary order. The water aboue is kept, and rayneth downe in due time and season, The Sunne, Moone, Starres, Rainebow, Thunder, Lightning, Cloudes, and all Birdes of the aire, doe keepe their order. The Earth, Trees, seeds, plants, herbs, corne, grasse, and all manner of beasts, keep themselues in order, al the partes of the whole yeare, as Winter, Summer, Monethes, nights and dayes, continue in their order: all kindes of Fishes in the Sea, Riuers, and Waters, with all Fountaines, Springes, yea, the Seas themselues keep their comely course and order: and man himselfe also hath all his parts both within and without, as soule, heart, minde, memory, vnderstanding, reason, speech, with all singular corperall members of his bodye, in a profitable, necessary, and pleasaunt order: euery degree of people in their vocation, calling and office, hath appointed to them their duety and order: some are in high degree, some in low, some Kings and Princes, some inferiors and subiects, Priests, and lay-men, Maisters and Seruauntes, Fathers and Children, Husbandes and Wiues, riche and poore, and everyone haue neede of other, so that in all things is to be lauded and praised the goodly order of God, without the which, no house, no Citye, no common-wealth can continue and endure or last. For where there is no right order, there raigneth all abuse, carnal libertie, enormitie, sin, and Babilonicall confusion. Take away Kings, Princes, Rulers, Magis-trats, iudges, and such estates of Gods order, no man shall ride or goe by the high way vnrobbed, no man shal sleep in his own house or bed vnkilled, no man shal keep his wife, children, and possessions in quietnes, all things shall be common, and there must needs follow all mischiefe, and vtter distruction both of soules, bodies, goods, commonweales.

Shakespeare had also read Hooker's treatise *Of the Lawes of Ecclesiasticall Politie* (1593), for in the first book, in a context which uses the image of the untuned string and the phrase 'degrees in schools' (both used by Shakespeare), Hooker has a famous and eloquent passage on the necessity of Order:

> His [God's] commanding those things to be which are, and to be in such sort as they are, to keepe that tenure and course which they doe, importeth the establishment of Natures Law. . . And as it commeth to passe in a kingdome rightly ordered, that after a Law is once published, it presently takes effect far and wide, all States framing themselues thereunto; euen so let vs thinke it fareth in the naturall course of the World: since the time that God did first proclaime the Edicts of his Law vpon it, Heauen and earth haue harkned vnto his voyce, and their labour hath bin to do his will: *He made a Law for the Raine*, He gaue *his Decree vnto the Sea, that the Waters should not passe his commandment*. Now, if nature should intermit her course, and leaue altogether, though it were but for a while, the obseruation of her own Lawes; if those principall and Mother Elements of the World wherof al things in this lower World are made, should lose the qualities which now they haue; if the frame of that Heauenly Arch erected ouer our heads should loosen and dissolue it selfe; if Celestiall Spheres should forget their wonted Motions and by irregular volubilitie turne themselues any way as it might happen; if the Prince of the Lights of Heauen, which now as a Gyant doth run his vnwearied course, should as it were through a languishing faintnesse begin to stand and to rest himselfe; if the Moone should wander from her beaten way, the times and seasons of the yeere blend themselues by disordered and confused mixture, the Winds breathe out their last gaspe, the Clouds yeeld no Raine, the Earth be defeated of Heauenly Influence, the Fruits of the Earth pine away as Children at the withered brests of their Mother, no longer able to yeeld them reliefe; what would become of Man himselfe, whom these things now doe all serue? See wee not plainly that obedience of Creatures vnto the Law of Nature is the stay of the whole World?   (I. 3)

Many other sources have been suggested for Ulysses' speech, naturally enough since the ideas expressed in it were widely diffused. Florio, in his translation of Montaigne, uses the word 'imbecility'[19] (as Shakespeare does) and refers to cannibalism in a passage about the necessity of obedience; but it is by no means certain that Florio's translation was published before the first performance of *Troilus and Cressida*. One critic suggested that Shakespeare may have remembered the introductory stanzas to Book v of *The Faerie Queene* on the subject of justice;[20] but there is only one, not very striking, verbal parallel. Hanford argued[21] that Shakespeare was influenced, directly or indirectly by Plato's analysis of the evils of democracy in the eighth book of *The Republic*. T. W. Baldwin claimed[22] that Shakespeare was influenced by Cicero's *Tusculans* which discusses the origin and foundation of society and uses the analogy of the planets. Shakespeare may have read it in the original since he uses here, and only here, the word 'insisture', apparently derived from a note on 'institiones', 'cum insistere videntur'. 'Course', the next word in the line, translates 'cursus', but neither word is used in Dolman's translation. Green thought that Shakespeare remembered one of Whitney's *Emblems*,[23] representing Chaos, with the winds, waters, and stars mingling in confusion. Henderson[24] pointed out that Lydgate uses the word 'degree' three or four times, and that his Agamemnon delivers a long speech against the indiscipline of the Greek army. Lydgate comments on the mischief of

> varyaunce
> Among lordes, whan thei nat accorde. . .
> Envie is cause of suche dyvysyoun,
> And covetyse of domynacyon . . .
> That everyche wolde surmounte his felawe.
>
> (III. 2342 ff.)

So Shakespeare speaks of the envious fever of Emulation.

It is not necessary to believe that Shakespeare deliberately, or even unconsciously, combined material from all the books I have mentioned. He was writing within a tradition, and the speech was a collection of common-places. Elsewhere he follows Chaucer in claiming that it is love that prevents chaos. But the nature of the situation in *Troilus and Cressida*, as well as the example of Lydgate and Elyot, would make him stress degree as a concomitant of order. Few would accept Baldwin's curious arguments that the speech is un-Shakespearian. The conclusion of it, with disorder leading to cannibalism, can be paralleled in *Coriolanus*, *King Lear*, and the scenes in *Sir Thomas More* generally accepted as Shakespeare's.

Our examination of the sources, not only of this speech but of the play as a whole, suggests that Shakespeare followed his usual custom in reading all the accessible material on his theme and using one book to amplify another. Chaucer, Henryson, Homer, Lydgate, and Caxton all contributed to themes and incidents in the play; and one critic, Miss Theleman,[25] even argues that Shakespeare must have consulted De la Lande's translation of Dictys, since his play has certain similarities of treatment with this work which are not to be found in Lydgate or Caxton.

It should be added, however, that there was at least one play on the same theme before Shakespeare's, and some of the apparent similarities with De la Lande may have been derived from this play. But Shakespeare, as a general rule, took more pains than his contemporaries in the collection of source-material, and he is more likely than Chettle and Dekker to have gone to Caxton's source.

Shakespeare organized his material in the form of a tragical satire, at the time when Jonson and Marston were writing comical satires.[26] The play is complete in itself and there is no evidence to support the view that the poet intended it as the first part of a trilogy, the second part dealing with the death of Troilus, and the third with the fall of Troy.[27] Both the Greeks and Trojans are depicted less heroically than they are by Caxton and Homer, but, as befits a play with a Trojan hero, his countrymen are presented more sympathetically. This was in accordance with the medieval tradition, stemming ultimately from Virgil, and with the legend that survivors from the siege of Troy landed in Britain.[28]

IV
TRAGIC PERIOD

24

HAMLET

SHAKESPEARE'S *Hamlet* was based on a lost play of the same title, perhaps by Shakespeare himself, perhaps by an unknown dramatist, but since *The Spanish Tragedy*, one of the most popular plays of the age, which kept its place on the stage in spite of ridicule and parody, resembles *Hamlet* closely, it would appear that the source-play – the *Ur-Hamlet* as it has been called – was written by Kyd, or by a close imitator of his.[1] Both plays begin with a ghost demanding vengeance; both are concerned with the madness, real or assumed, of the avenger; both contain the death of an innocent woman; both heroes blame themselves for their procrastination; both contain a play within the play.[2] We know very little about the *Ur-Hamlet*: the Ghost is said to have cried like an oyster-wife, 'Hamlet, revenge!' and Hamlet is alleged to have said, 'There are things called whips in store'. This, however, looks suspiciously like a misquotation of a passage from one of the late additions to *The Spanish Tragedy*:

> And there is *Nemesis* and Furies,
> And things called whippes,
> And they sometimes do meete with murderers.

Perhaps, Armin, who quotes the phrase, may have confused the two plays.[3]

Although, therefore, we have no certain knowledge of the *Ur-Hamlet*, we can deduce a good deal about its contents from a study of other versions of the Hamlet story. Its author was doubtless attracted to the plot because it enabled him to use some of the popular ingredients of *The Spanish Tragedy*. Instead of a father seeking to avenge his murdered son, he was provided with a son seeking to avenge his murdered father. The story as given by Saxo Grammaticus and in Belleforest's *Histoires Tragiques* is substantially the same. In the former the father of Amleth, a governor of Jutland, had married Gerutha, the daughter of the King of Denmark, and had won fame by slaying the King of Norway in single combat. His brother, Feng, murders him, seizes his office, and marries his widow, thus 'adding incest to unnatural murder'. Young Amleth determines to avenge his father, but to allay his uncle's suspicions he puts on an antic disposition, so that he seems completely lethargic. In his feigned madness he 'mingled craft and candour in such a way that, though his words did not lack truth', there was nothing to reveal 'how far his keenness went'. Two attempts are made to pierce his disguise. A beautiful woman, a childhood friend of his, is instructed to seduce him; but he is warned of the plot both by his foster-brother and by the woman herself. Then one of Feng's friends undertakes to spy on him, while he is talking with his mother in her chamber. From this trap Amleth is saved by pretending to be a cock, crowing and flapping his arms, till he finds the spy hidden under the straw mattress. He pierces him with his sword, cuts up the body into little pieces, cooks them, and flings them to the pigs. He upbraids his mother for her lascivious conduct, urging her to lament her own guilt rather than his madness. The mother repents and is won over to Amleth's side. Feng next despatches Amleth to Britain with two retainers, bearing a letter with a demand that the King should put Amleth to death. While the retainers are asleep, Amleth searches their belongings, finds the letters, and substitutes fresh instructions, as in Shakespeare's play. Amleth's companions are duly hanged and he marries the British princess. A year later he returns to Jutland and, having made Feng and his followers drunk, he sets fire to the palace. He changes swords with Feng, his own having been tampered with, and slays him. Feng's followers are burnt alive. The version of the story given by Belleforest is much the same, except that Gertrude and Feng had committed adultery before the murder of her husband and that Amleth's excessive melancholy is mentioned.

Whichever source the author of the *Ur-Hamlet* used, he would have found the germ of all the main characters, except Laertes – Claudius, Gertrude, Polonius, Ophelia, Horatio, Rosencrantz, and Guildenstern – as well as the basis for the feigned madness, the interview with Ophelia, the closet-scene, the voyage to England, and the changing of weapons in the final duel. If he used Belleforest, he would have found too Amleth's melancholy and Gertrude's adultery. But in neither of these sources was there a ghost, a *Mousetrap*, a Laertes, or a Fortinbras; there were no drowning of Ophelia, no pirates, no grave-digger scene, and no Osric. We may be reasonably sure that the author of the *Ur-Hamlet*, imitating *The Spanish Tragedy*, invented the *Mousetrap*, the Ghost, and the madness and death of Ophelia. The introduction of Fortinbras, Laertes, and Pyrrhus provided Shakespeare with a trio of avengers of fathers to contrast with his hero.

Some other characteristics of the source-play may be deduced from a study of the piratical First Quarto of Shakespeare's play, which is apparently contaminated by memories of an earlier version. It is also probable that *Der Bestrafte Brudermord*, performed in Germany, was derived confusedly from the pre-Shakespearian play.

From the bad quarto, it would seem that the character of the Queen was modified by Shakespeare. After the death of Corambis (i.e. Polonius) she blames herself for Hamlet's madness and believes either that she is thereby punished for her incestuous remarriage, or else that her marriage, by depriving Hamlet of the crown, has driven him mad from thwarted ambition. Hamlet urges her to assist him in his revenge, in order to purge her soul of guilt. She replies:

> *Hamlet*, I vow by that maiesty
> That knowes our thoughts, and lookes into our hearts,
> I will conceale, consent, and doe my best,
> What stratagem soe're thou shalt deuise.
>
> (III. iv) (Sh. Q. Facsimiles scene-division)

Later on, when Hamlet returns from England, she sends him a warning message by Horatio:

> Bid him a while
> Be wary of his presence, lest that he
> Faile in that he goes about.   (IV. vi)

Thus in the *Ur-Hamlet* the Queen apparently took positive steps to aid the Prince in his revenge, whereas in Shakespeare's play she conceals her son's secret and probably keeps herself from her husband's bed, without doing anything more positive to assist her son.

The version of the voyage to England given in *Fratricide Punished* (as the German play is usually called) differs from Belleforest's and also from Shakespeare's. Hamlet embarks for England with his escort and they are forced by contrary winds to anchor by an island, not far from Dover. They land to take air and exercise and the two ruffians inform Hamlet that they have orders to kill him. He pleads with them in vain; he attempts, without success, to seize a sword; and he finally escapes by a trick. The men plan to shoot him, one from each side; Hamlet obtains permission to say a last prayer and proposes to raise his hands when he is ready to die; but, on raising his hands, he throws himself forward so that his executioners shoot each other. Hamlet finishes them off with their own swords. He then searches them and finds a letter from the King, commanding that, should the first attempt on his life miscarry, he should be put to death by the King of England. There is nothing about the forged commission, and nothing about the pirates. Hamlet makes his own way back to Denmark. It has been argued[4] that some such scene must have been in the *Ur-Hamlet* because of the lines in the bad quarto:

> Being crossed by the contention of the windes,
> He found the Packet sent to the king of *England*. . .
> He being set ashore, they [the others] went for *England*,
> And in the Packet there writ down that doome
> To be perform'd on them poynted for him. (IV. vi)

There is nothing here to suggest the shooting of Rosencrantz and Guildenstern on the island; but, on the other hand, Hamlet being set ashore conflicts with the account of the voyage given by Shakespeare. If there were, indeed, a scene on the island in the *Ur-Hamlet*, such as in *Fratricide Punished*, Shakespeare must have realized its absurdity and he may have been worried by the fact that the play was already too long. Here, then, he may have gone to Belleforest for the business of the forged commission and the deaths of Rosencrantz and Guildenstern, the encounter with the pirate ship being his own invention, though possibly suggested by an incident in *Arcadia*.[5]

The *Ur-Hamlet*, then, so far as it can be reconstructed, seems to have been fairly close to Shakespeare's play in its main outlines. The revelation of the Ghost, the feigned madness, the play-scene, the closet-scene, the killing of Polonius, the voyage to England, the madness and suicide of Ophelia,[6] and the duel with Laertes were probably all to be found in the old play, and Shakespeare's additions (the pirates, Fortinbras, and the gravediggers), important as they are, are less significant than his intensification and subtilization of themes and motives present in his source – the effect of a mother's guilt on a son, the malcontent's satire under the guise of madness, the self-laceration caused by enforced delay, the contrast between the avengers, and the friendship between Hamlet and Horatio.

It used to be thought that the real problem of *Hamlet* is not due to the complex character of the hero, but to the confusions caused by Shakespeare's inability to transform the intractable material of the old play, so that we have motives and incidents from the *Ur-Hamlet* (such as the murder of Rosencrantz and Guildenstern, and Hamlet's callous attitude to it) side by side with the feelings and experience of the civilized poet. There are, too, certain discrepancies, such as Hamlet's age – eighteen or thirty – and the varying knowledge displayed by Horatio, which have been thought to indicate revision. It has been argued that in an earlier version of the play 'To be or not to be' belonged to Act I (before Hamlet's meeting with the Ghost) and that the graveyard-scene was an afterthought.[7] Santayana, for example, declared[8] that 'some of Hamlet's actions and speeches' are apparently survivals from the original play and that these 'give a touch of positive incoherence to Hamlet's character'. The view that Shakespeare was hampered by his source-play was expressed in its bluntest form by J. C. Squire, who complained[9] that *Hamlet* was 'crowded with faults. There are scenes which lead nowhere and the main theme is very confusingly handled'. He went on to suggest that once the Ghost was invented – though it was probably in the *Ur-Hamlet* – the feigned madness was unnecessary. Shakespeare, Squire declared, was too lazy, or thought he was too busy, to undertake the necessary revision, so that we have 'new wine in an old bottle'. A. J. A. Waldock likewise believed[10] that

> an old plot is wrenched to new significances, significances, in places, that to the end it refuses to take. It was, perhaps, inevitable that the play should show signs, in fissures and strain, of all this forceful bending.

T. S. Eliot, to take a last example, under the baleful influence of J. M. Robertson, the disintegrator, believed at one time that the play was 'certainly an artistic failure'.[11] But, whatever the defects of the play, we ought not to ascribe them to the intractability of the source-material. This material, complex but not intractable, had outstanding advantages, so obvious that one hesitates to enumerate them. It was familiar, popular, and thrilling, and required less adaptation than the sources of *Othello* or *King Lear*. Although some characteristics of the play may be survivals from the *Ur-Hamlet*, there is no reason to believe that Shakespeare retained them casually and carelessly, or merely to please the groundlings. It seems likely that he wrote some passages so that he could fully express his conception of the play, even though he knew that his work would be mangled by cuts in the theatre. Such a concern with his art could hardly have existed side by side with the slapdash methods critics have imputed to him. We cannot properly explain the coarseness of Hamlet's words to Ophelia, both in the nunnery-scene and in the play-scene, by the fact that her prototype was a lady of easy virtue. If, as is probable, Ophelia went mad in the *Ur-Hamlet*, she is unlikely to have been looser in her morals than Shakespeare's character; and, even if she were, we can no more explain the coarseness of the words used by Shakespeare's Hamlet by this fact, than we can Othello's brutality by the character of the Moor in Cinthio's tale. Nor can we explain the callousness of Hamlet's epitaph on Polonius by recalling that Amleth fed his dismembered body to the swine. The simple answer to these critics who say that Shakespeare's Hamlet could never have said such things, or done such things as murder his schoolfellows, is that Shakespeare's Hamlet did, and that we ought to try and explain these things in terms of the existing play. Shakespeare made himself responsible for any incidents or character-istics that he retained from the source-play.

It is obvious that Shakespeare realized the dramatic advantages of contrasting the 'barbaric nature of his material' with 'the modern refinement and sophistication of his hero'.[12] Nor was Shakespeare alone in this. By 1602, the revenge play had become a more complex and sophisticated genre than it had been fifteen years earlier; and in the revenge plays of Marston, written about the same time as *Hamlet*, and in those of Webster, Tourneur, and Chapman, written soon afterwards, we can see something of the same complexity in the characters of the avengers. Whether *Antonio's Revenge* was a debased version of Shakespeare's *Hamlet*, or *Hamlet* a refined version of Marston's play is immaterial to our present purpose, since both were ultimately derived from *The Spanish Tragedy* and the *Ur-Hamlet*. The greater nobility and, indeed, humanity of Shakespeare's hero are due largely to his doubts. Antonio pursues his revenge without misgiving and complacently pronounces after its achievement that

> Sons that reuenge their fathers blood, are blest.   (v. v)

But in *The Malcontent*, acted by Shakespeare's company, and published in the same year as the Second Quarto of *Hamlet*, the hero is a melancholy malcontent who is too proud in the end to take his revenge:

> Slaue, take thy life.
> Wert thou defenced through blood and woundes,
> The sternest horror of a ciuell fight,
> Would I atcheeue thee: but prostrate at my feete
> *I scorne to hurt thee: tis the heart of slaues*
> *That daines to triumph ouer peasants graues.*
>
> (ed. H. H. Wood, 1. 214)

In *The Pilgrim*, by Beaumont and Fletcher, a man is spared by his enemy for the same reason as Claudius is spared by Hamlet; in *The Maid's Tragedy*, Amintor is deterred from revenge by his superstitious belief in the divine right of kings; in *The Revenger's Tragedy*, Vindice is presented as morbid and unbalanced; and in *The Atheist's Tragedy*, the Ghost urges his son to 'leaue reuenge vnto the King of Kinges': God intervenes at the end, so that when the villain lifts an axe to execute the hero he providentially strikes out his own brains. In *The Revenge of Bussy D'Ambois* we have another variation on the revenge formula: Chapman's hero, Clermont, accepting the duty of avenging his brother's death, sends Montsurry a challenge, which is refused; he doubts whether a private man should take the law into his own hands; and in the end he slays his enemy in fair fight and bids both him and his brother to rest in peace. These different treatments of the revenge formula show that Shakespeare was not circumscribed by the expectations of his audience. The villain could be forgiven, as *Measure for Measure* and *The Malcontent* prove; revenge could be treated as a duty, or as a sin; and the avenger could refrain from vengeance out of Senecan pride, or as a Christian duty. The fascination of the revenge theme to the Elizabethans and to the dramatists was the manifest conflict between the revenge code and the teaching of classical moralists and Christian preachers.[13] Private vengeance was forbidden by Church and State, and their prohibition was reinforced by classical writers. Seneca, for example, in his essay on Anger,[14] declared that the offender should be corrected 'by admonition, forcible reprehensions, friendly but effectuall speech'. We ought to forgive; personal revenge is always wrong; and we ought to be too proud to stoop to it.

> It is the part of a great mind to despise iniuries: it is a contumelious kinde of reuenge, that he thought him vnworthy to reuenge himself on. . . That man is great and noble, that after the manner of a

mightie wilde beast, listneth securely the barking of lesser Dogges. . .
So then we ought to auoid wrath whether it bee with our equall,
with our superiours, or inferiours. To striue against our equals is a
matter doubtful, against our superiours is furie, against our inferiours
is basenes. Anger . . . is the canker of humane nature. . . A man that is
truely valiant, and that knoweth his owne worth, reuengeth not an
iniurie, because he feeleth it not. . . How farre more worthy a
thing is it to dispise all iniuries and contumelies, as if the minde were
impregnable. Reuenge is a confession of paine. The minde is not
great which is animated by iniurie.

Of course the view of preachers and moralists on the subject of revenge
was not necessarily identical with that of an audience. It has even been
suggested that the popularity of the revenge play is a sign of the
survival of more primitive modes of thought; and the prevalence of
duelling, particularly after the accession of James I, both on and off the
stage, is a sign that popular feelings about vengeance differed from the
more official views. Many dramatists seem to have assumed that
revenge was a kind of wild justice; and, though the avenger usually
has to expiate his deeds, especially if they have resulted in the death of
innocent people, the dramatist seldom flatly condemns revenge.[15]

Shakespeare was fully conscious of the difference between religious
and popular views on revenge; but the revenge play had become so
varied that we could not, even if Shakespeare were not unique, predict
the precise way in which he would treat the Hamlet story. We do not
know the attitude of the author of the Ur-Hamlet; we do not know
what playgoers who had seen it would expect of Shakespeare's version;
and we do not know the extent to which he fulfilled or cheated their
expectations. Just as Athenian audiences would be interested in the
varying treatments of the Orestes story by Aeschylus, Sophocles, and
Euripides, and just as the better-educated members of Racine's audiences would be intrigued by his variations on a theme of Euripides, so
Shakespeare's audiences must have expected him to present variations
on the themes of Leir or Amleth. They would not mind alterations if
they justified themselves by their effectiveness. The extent to which
Hamlet's madness was real or assumed, the extent of the Queen's
complicity in the murder of his father, the nature of Hamlet's love for
Ophelia, and many other details could be settled in accordance with
Shakespeare's dramatic design. The character of his hero could vary
from that of a primitive avenger who unquestioningly carried out his

father's commands to that of a Stoic or a Christian who disapproved of revenge. There is nothing improbable in John Lawlor's argument[16] that an Elizabethan audience would suppose that Hamlet's failure to act was due to a scruple about the morality of revenge. The wonder is not that Shakespeare retained so little of the spirit of the earlier play, but that he was able to make use of so many of its episodes. The primitive materials formed a strange basis for such a sophisticated play; and nothing better illustrates Shakespeare's genius than the way he made use of primitive episodes for his own purposes. In the *Ur-Hamlet*, for example, the hero spared the King at his prayers to avoid sending him straight to heaven: Shakespeare's hero offers precisely the same avowed reason – but hardly any critic believes him.

The main outlines of his plot being settled by the source-play, Shakespeare concerned himself with the re-creation of his characters. As part of this process he turned to Timothy Bright's *Treatise of Melancholie*. Shakespeare could, of course, have picked up his information about melancholia from a variety of books, but the evidence that he had read Bright is quite substantial.[17] Bright tells us, for example, that

> the ayre meet for melancholicke folke, ought to be thinne, pure and subtile, open, and patent to all winds: in respect of their temper, especially to the South, and Southeast.   (p. 257)

This lends point to Hamlet's remark:

> I am but mad north-north-west; when the wind is southerly I know a hawk from a handsaw.   (II. ii. 374–5)

More significant is the echo of Bright's phrase, 'the braine as tender as a posset curd' (p. 13) in the Ghost's account of the operation of poison on his body:

> And with a sudden vigour it doth posset
> And curd, like eager droppings into milk.
>   (I. v. 68–9)

Bright uses Hamlet's phrase 'custom of exercise'. He shows how the melancholy man ponders and debates long, but when he does act, he acts vigorously (p. 13). Unnatural melancholy, Bright tells us, destroys 'disposition of action'. Melancholy men sometimes suffer from a combination of desperate fury and fear:

Which so terrifieth, that to auoid the terrour, they attempt sometimes to depriue them selues of life: so irksome it is vnto them
through these tragicall conceits, although waighing and considering
death by it self without comparison, and force of the passion, none
more feare of it then they.   (p. 111)

This 'sharpe kind of melancholie' makes 'rage, reuenge, and fury' to
possess both heart and head, and the whole body is 'carried with that
storme, contrarie to persuasion of reason' (pp. 111–12). The melancholy
man is dull of deed, with a reasonably good memory (p. 124),

firme in opinion, and hardly remoued wher it is resolued: doubtfull
before, and long in deliberation . . . giuen to fearefull and terrible
dreames: in affection sad, and full of feare.   (p. 124)

Yet he is sometimes apparently merry 'through a kinde of Sardonian,
and false laughter' (p. 102). He is apt to see 'phantasticall apparitions'
(p. 103) and he is apt to be

doubtfull, suspitious, and thereby long in deliberation, because
those domesticall feares, or that internall obscuritie, causeth an
opinion of daunger in outwarde affaires, where there is no cause of
doubt.   (p. 131)

Finally, 'the whole force of the spirite' being 'closed vp in the dungion
of melancholy darkenes, imagineth all darke, blacke and full of feare'.
One is reminded of numerous passages in the play – of Hamlet's fear
that the devil is making use of his melancholy to abuse him with a
'phantasticall apparition'; of his bad dreams and suicidal thoughts; of
his belief that the world is nothing but a foul and pestilent congregation
of vapours; of his wit and sardonic humour.[18] Shakespeare seems to
have used many of the traits of Bright's case-histories.

For his treatment of the supernatural Shakespeare relied partly on
Reginald Scot and partly on Lavater's *Of Ghosts and Sprites*. In his
account of the drinking habits of the Danes he seems to have been
echoing Nashe's *Pierce Penilesse*. Indeed, as Arnold Davenport pointed
out,[19] that pamphlet left its mark on several scenes of the play. Nashe
compares a foppish Dane to a swarm of butterflies (ed. McKerrow, I.
172), as Hamlet calls Osric a water-fly. He refers to the Danes as sots,
as 'this surley, swinish Generation' (I. 180), and as 'foule drunken
swine' (I. 205). So Hamlet confessed:

They clepe us drunkards, and with swinish phrase
Soil our addition.   (I. iv. 19–20)

He points out that this particular vice detracts from their virtues:

> A mightie deformer of mens manners and features, is this vnnecessary
> vice of all other. Let him bee indued with neuer so many vertues,
> and haue as much goodly proportion and fauor as nature can
> bestow vppon a man: yet if hee be thirstie after his owne destruction,
> and hath no ioy nor comfort, but when he is drowning his soule in a
> gallon pot, that one beastly imperfection will vtterlie obscure all
> that is commendable in him; and all his good qualities sinke like
> lead down to the bottome of his carrowsing cups, where they will
> lie like lees and dregges, dead and vnregarded of any man.
>
>   (I. 205)

So Hamlet, after describing how the King 'takes his rouse', goes on to
show how the 'dram of eale' corrupts all the noble substance. Nashe
refers (I. 208) to Rhenish wine and uses the epithet 'heauie-headed'
(I. 210), both used by Hamlet in the same context. Then Nashe has a
long passage attacking the use of cosmetics, by which women 'will
haue their deformities newe plaistred ouer' (I. 181), as Claudius speaks
of the 'harlot's cheek, beautied with plast'ring art' and as Hamlet in
two scenes inveighs against cosmetics. Nashe declares that Sloth brings
'Nobilitie, Courtiers, Schollars' (I. 210) into contempt, but that
emulation of 'the onely myrrour of our Age' (I. 211) overcomes sloth.
So Ophelia speaks of Hamlet as courtier, soldier, scholar, and the glass
of fashion. In the same context Nashe speaks of those who will not be
awakened by any indignities, 'but suffer euery vpstart groome to
defie him, set him at naught, and shake him by the beard vnreuengde'
(I. 210–11). Nashe adds 'he shall be suspected of cowardise' (I. 211). So
at the end of Act II, Hamlet asks 'Am I a coward?/Who . . ./Plucks off
my beard, and blows it in my face?' (ii. 565–7).

For Shakespeare's account of the portents – in *Julius Caesar* as well
as in *Hamlet* – he combined hints, as we have seen, from Plutarch,
Virgil, Ovid, and Lucan. Polonius' advice to Laertes is a tissue of
commonplaces – parallels have been found, for example, in Lyly's
Euphues and Greene's *Gwydonius* – but it seems likely that both the
name and character of that prating councillor was suggested by
Grimaldus Goslicius, the Polish statesman, whose dreary book, *The
Counsellor*, had been published in an English translation in 1598.[20] For
Aeneas's tale to Dido, Shakespeare used Marlowe's play, probably
Virgil as well, and possibly Seneca's *Agamemnon* and *Troas* in the trans-
lations of Studley and Jasper Heywood.[21] For Hamlet's soliloquy in

Act III Scene i, he may have made use of Thomas Bedingfield's version of *Cardanus Comforte*,[22] though he hardly needed a source for such ideas as that death is a sleep, and that sleep is sometimes disturbed by dreams. More plausibly, it has recently been argued that the tone of the play was considerably influenced by Erasmus' *Praise of Folly*.[23] The attack on cosmetics in the nunnery-scene is similar to a passage in Pettie's translation of Guazzo's *Civill Conversation*:[24]

> And hereto that bewty breedeth temptation, temptation dishonour: for it is a matter almost impossible, and sieldome seene, that those two great enimies, bewty and honesty agree togither. . . And though it fall out often that bewty and honesty are joyned togither, yet is falleth out sieldome, but that exquisite bewty is had in suspition.

Guazzo goes on to say that 'Those which vse artificial means, displease God much', and that a woman who paints is behaving like a harlot. Hamlet implies the same thing; and he tells Ophelia that 'the power of beauty will sooner transform honesty from what it is to a bawd than the force of honesty can translate beauty into his likeness' (III. i. 111–13). The scene with Osric may be based, as Malone suggested, on Florio's *Second Frutes* (1591):

> G.   Why do you stand barehedded? You do your self wrong.
> E.   Pardon me good sir, I doe it for my ease.
> G.   I pray you be couered, you are too ceremonious.
> E.   I am so well, that me thinks I am in heauen.
> G.   If you loue me, put on your hat.
> E.   I will doe it to obay you, not for any pleasure that I take
>
> in it.
>
> (p. 111)

These examples out of many will be enough to suggest the range of reading which contributes to the richness of the play. In some cases Shakespeare must have been unconscious that he was echoing something he had read. When, for example, Laertes cautions his sister against the Prince, it is unlikely that Shakespeare was deliberately echoing Henry Swinburne's *Briefe Treatise of Testaments and Last Willes* (1590)[25]. Swinburne had pointed out several times that even when a man swears never to revoke his last will and testament, he can nevertheless do so. There is 'no *cautele* vnder heauen, whereby the libertie of making or reuoking his testament can be vtterly taken away' (p. 61), 'nether is there any cautele vnder the sunne to preuent this libertie' (p. 263), 'neither is there any cautele vnder heauen' (p. 265ᵛ). Before and after these passages Swinburne points out that 'it is not lawfull for legataries to carue for themselues' (pp. 50, 288). So Laertes tells Ophelia:

> Perhaps he loves you now,
> And now no soil nor cautel doth besmirch
> The virtue of his will; but you must fear,
> His greatness weigh'd, his will is not his own. . .
> He may not, as unvalued persons do,
> Carve for himself.   (I. iii. 14 ff.)

We have, of course, to remember that the main source of *Hamlet* was the lost play, and that echoes of books published before 1589 may have been present before Shakespeare took a hand.[26]

ALL'S WELL THAT ENDS WELL

THE SOURCE of *All's Well that Ends Well* was either Boccaccio's tale in the *Decameron* (III. 9) or William Painter's version of the same tale in *The Palace of Pleasure* (1566) (I. 38). The two versions differ very little. Painter tells how the Count of Rossiglione, being an invalid, keeps a personal physician in his house, named Gerardo of Narbona. Beltramo, the Count's son, is brought up with Gerardo's daughter, Giletta. She falls in love with the boy, 'more than was meet for a maiden of her age'. When the Count dies, Beltramo, 'left under the royal custody of the King', is sent to Paris. Gerardo dies shortly afterwards, and Giletta is prevented by her kinsfolk from following Beltramo to Paris. She is rich, but she refuses many suitors. When she hears that the King suffers from a fistula, she journeys to Paris with one of her father's remedies. After seeing Beltramo, she tells the King she can cure him within eight days 'by the aide and helpe of God'. At first the King refuses to be her patient and she suggests that if she fails to cure him she should be burnt at the stake, the King for his part promising to find her a husband. She stipulates that the husband shall be one of her choosing, 'without presumption of any of your children or other of your bloud'. The cure is successful. Beltramo at first refuses to marry Giletta, but he finally accepts her, under protest. He gets permission to return home to consummate the marriage, but goes instead to take service with the Florentines, then at war with the Siennese. Giletta goes to Rossiglione, where she wins the affection of her subjects by her wise rule. She sends word to Beltramo that if he has abandoned his country because of her, she will depart. He replies that he will not return till she has the ring from his finger and a son in her arms begotten by him. Giletta thereupon assembles the noblest and chiefest of her country and tells them that, to enable Beltramo to return home, she is going to spend the rest of her life in pilgrimages and devotion. She goes to Florence, where she hears that Beltramo is in love with a poor girl. She tells the girl's mother that she will provide a dowry for her daughter if she will demand Beltramo's ring, make an assignation with him, and allow Giletta to take her place in bed. The mother consents and Giletta by this means is able to consummate her marriage. Painter adds that she slept with him many more times: Boccaccio mentions only one occasion. When Giletta knows she is pregnant, she gives the girl money and jewels, and in due course gives birth to twin sons. Meanwhile Beltramo has returned home and when he is about to hold a feast Giletta arrives with her babies. She falls at his feet, explaining how she fulfilled his hard conditions. Beltramo, urged by his friends, acknowledges Giletta as his wife and they live happily ever after.

Helena, unlike Giletta, is poor and Shakespeare makes no mention of her having suitors. She does not see Bertram before her interview with the King. After the cure, the King lines up three or four lords for Helena to choose from, and Bertram had expressed a wish to go to the wars before he is trapped into marriage. Helena receives his harsh letter as soon as she arrives at Rousillon, and not in answer to a letter of hers; and she decides at once to leave for Florence, not after ruling for several months. Shakespeare, however, does not mention, as Painter does, that she hopes to fulfil the two conditions, as this might reduce the sympathy of the audience. She meets Diana and her mother as soon as she arrives in Florence, Shakespeare fusing Helena's hostess and the mother. He complicates the business of the rings by having Diana give Bertram the ring Helena had received from the King. Bertram returns home because of the false news of his wife's death; Helena returns with

Diana and her mother before the birth of her child; and Shakespeare has the King visiting Rousillon at the time. Bertram is about to be married to Lafeu's daughter, to whom he gives Helena's ring. This is recognized by Lafeu and the King, Bertram is arrested on suspicion of murdering Helena; Diana enters and claims his hand, and when he repudiates her as a harlot, she demands her ring. Finally Helena enters and all is explained. These complications in the last act, and Bertram's ordeal, are stage-managed by Helena.

Shakespeare creates several important characters. Bertram's mother, the poet's most sympathetic portrait of an old lady, and Lafeu are two of them; and both express a warm admiration for Helena, feeling that she is really too good for Bertram. The rather gloomy Clown is introduced partly to sing a song about Helen of Troy, implying a contrast between her destructiveness and Helena's healing powers, as revealed in her cure of the King and in her redemption of Bertram. Finally, and most significantly, Shakespeare adds the character of Parolles, the man of words, the *miles gloriosus*, whose exposure is the first shock administered to Bertram's self-conceit and false values. He is shown to be as incapable of choosing a friend as he is of appreciating the woman he has been driven to marry. His false values are still further revealed in his willingness to promise marriage as a means of seduction – unlike Beltramo in this – and his moral bankruptcy is displayed in the last scene when he slanders Diana.

The King's attitude, too, differs from that of his prototype. In the source, the King is reluctant for Giletta to choose Beltramo; but in the play the King has an eloquent speech on the theme that 'virtue is the true nobility'. It may be mentioned that Giovanni Battista Nenna's treatise on nobility, translated by William Jones and published in 1595 under the title *Nennio*, is a debate on the subject of whether true nobility is founded on birth or virtue. The conclusion is that 'true and perfect nobilitie, doth consist in the vertues of the minde'. The supporter of this view points out that 'the body is lesse noble than the minde. Of which two partes nature hath framed man, the one being subiect to corruption, the other eternallie dureable'.[1] Since we are all descended from Adam, nobility does not depend on birth, for 'if Adam was noble, why then we are all noble . . . but if hee were ignoble, and base, we are so likewise'. It follows that 'true and perfit Nobilitie, is deriued from no other fountaine, then the vertues of the minde, and not from the worthinesse of bloud'. A king can ennoble any man he pleases; it follows that the 'dignity of a doctor is equall vnto the degree of a knight which hee obtaineth as a reward of his vertues'. We are reminded of Helena and her father. Indeed, Nenna points out that women too are noble by reason of their virtue:

> a Lady not borne of any noble bloud, but beautified with good conditions, ought farre to be preferred before her, whose birth is noble, and renowmed, and by her vnordinate behauior becommeth base, and infamous.

The King in *All's Well*, who points out that Helena is noble because she is virtuous, and that he can himself give her the rank she lacks, agrees with Nenna and other writers on the subject 'that the nobilitie of the minde, is farre more true, and farre more perfect, then the nobility of blood conioyned with riches'.

Most critics feel dissatisfied with the play, as they are not with the source.[2] Our sympathies are divided between Beltramo and Giletta, and when she succeeds in an apparently impossible task we feel she deserves the hand of the hero. Whether he deserves her is not a question to be raised. Shakespeare transformed the conventional material of the story and, in so doing, gave himself nearly insoluble problems. W. W. Lawrence, indeed, pointed out[3] the folk-tale elements surviving in the play and he argued that the Elizabethans would have applauded Helena's cleverness. The trouble is, as Middleton Murry declared,[4] that Helena is by no means a medieval type, but created with 'delicate hesitation' as well as business-like resolution. Bertram, moreover, unlike Beltramo, is 'a cad, morbidly conscious of his birth, blind in his judgement of others, vicious in his morals, and, when cornered, a cowardly liar' – not, one would think, much of a prize. But Harold S. Wilson was right, I believe, in his interpretation of the play.[5] Shakespeare realized that Helena's actions in the second half of the play were liable to rob her of our sympathy. He arouses our admiration for her in the first acts, both by her own actions and by the comments of others, and in the second half of the play he removes her from the centre of the stage. Bertram's siege of Diana's chastity, the unmasking of Parolles, and the accusation of Bertram in the final scene 'successively provide the focus of interest while Helena works out her designs unobtrusively in the background'. If the title of the play is to be justified, Bertram must be converted, not just trapped; and the function of the Parolles scenes – once the most popular part of the play – and of Bertram's final ordeal, in which he is exposed for what he shamefully is, is to bring him to a self-recognition, and so make him less unworthy of his wife, whom Shaw admired as a forerunner of Ibsen's heroines.[6]

Helena never loses our sympathy, especially when the play is performed. The way she releases the King from his promise, her quiet submissiveness when Bertram repudiates her, and her wish to save him from the dangers of war all prevent us from feeling that she is like Ann Whitfield, hunting down her prey. In the scenes in which Bertram is tricked, the emphasis is mainly on Helena's pathos, and Diana is never merely a puppet. As Wilson said,

> the controlling idea of the play that emerges is the conception of Helena's love as far stronger than Bertram's arrogance, a love which works unobtrusively and with humility toward an end that heaven favors. (p. 239)

We may feel in reading the play that Shakespeare did not quite succeed in humanizing his source-material. Some of the trouble may be due to imperfect revision and a poor text – Violante, for example, is given no words to say, and Bertram's final capitulation is given in an absurd couplet. But it is a play which acts much better than it reads, and the undertones (e.g. the feeling that, apart from Helena, the younger generation are inferior to their elders) and ambiguities, especially in the character of the heroine, may not be evidences of failure on the part of the dramatist but of a deliberate deepening of his theme. If the Clown were given better jokes and Bertram a better speech at the end, the play would leave us with feelings of greater satisfaction.

✳ 26 ✳

MEASURE FOR MEASURE

THE FIRST literary treatment of the plot of *Measure for Measure* was, as far as is known, Claude Rouillet's *Philanira* (1556), a Latin play which was translated into French seven years later.[1] This was followed in 1565 by the version given in Cinthio's *Hecatommithi*, a collection of tales in which Shakespeare found the plot of *Othello*. There was a French translation by Gabriel Chappuys in 1584. Cinthio also dramatized the story under the title *Epitia*: this was never acted, but published post-humously in 1583. Meanwhile George Whetstone's play on the same theme, *Promos and Cassandra*, had been published in 1578, and this was Shakespeare's principal source. Three years later Thomas Lupton retold the story in the second part of *Siuqila*; and in 1582 Whetstone rehandled it in one of the tales in his *Heptameron of Ciuill Discourses*. Other versions of the story need not be listed as they appear to have had no influence, direct or indirect, on Shakespeare's play.

Othello was written just before, or just after, *Measure for Measure*, and Shakespeare may well have read several or many of Cinthio's stories at this time. From them, as Mary Lascelles suggests,[2] he could have derived the idea of giving the story a happy ending, 'of the inclination to pardon which is to be looked for in the man of highest authority', and of the capacity of the victim of intolerable wrong to forgive the villain when he is at her mercy. It was, perhaps, hardly necessary for Shakespeare to go to Cinthio to learn this.

In Cinthio's tale the Emperor leaves Juriste as his deputy to govern Innsbruck. Vico is condemned to death for rape and his sister, Epitia, pleads with Juriste to pardon him. When she returns to hear his decision he offers to spare Vico if she will yield to him, hinting that he may afterwards marry her. On Vico's entreaty, Epitia consents to Juriste's proposal; but on the following morning Vico is executed and the body is sent to his sister. Epitia sets out to appeal to the Emperor; Juriste is brought to confess and he is made to marry Epitia. Epitia then begs for his life and she and Juriste live happily ever after. Here Shakespeare would have found the main outlines of his plot despite obvious differences: Isabella only pretends to assent to Angelo's proposal; Claudio's offence is not rape, but fornication; his life is saved despite Angelo's command; and, although Isabella is brought to plead for Angelo, she does not marry him.

There is some evidence that Shakespeare had read also Cinthio's dramatic version. Professor Madeleine Doran has a convenient list of points in which *Measure for Measure* agrees with *Epitia* while diverging from the other sources.[3] If from these one subtracts two which *Epitia* shares with the narrative version, there remain the following: the name of Juriste's sister, Angela; the fact that the Secretary protests to the Podesta about the harshness of the law and the severity of its prose-cution, and that he soliloquizes on the harshness of those in power; there is discussion in both plays of justice and mercy, power and authority; an evil criminal is substituted for Vico; Angela pleads with

Epitia for Juriste's life, as Mariana does with Isabella, and Epitia distinguishes between the act and the intention; the Captain of the prison announces that Vico has not been killed, as the Provost does in *Measure for Measure*; and Epitia tells the Emperor, as Isabella tells the Duke, that the sentence on her brother was just.

The closest verbal parallels are the following:

> O, I will to him, and pluck out his eyes! . . .
> Unhappy Claudio! wretched Isabel!
> Injurious world! most damned Angelo!
> (IV. iii. 118 ff.)

> Male ne hò detto à Iuriste, e poco meno
> Che non gli habbia cacciati ambiduo gli occhi,
> Accesa da giusta ira, e da vergogna.   (III. ii)

> O sclerato, o traditore Iuriste,
> O dolorosa Epitia, o miserella.   (III. i.)

Whatsoever you may hear to the contrary, let Claudio be executed by four of the clock.   (IV. ii. 114–15)

> Andai al Podestà ratto, ei mostromme
> Lettra di man d'Iuriste, & del sigillo
> Di lui segnata, che gli commetteva,
> Che, senza udir cosa, che fusse detta,
> Levar gli fesse il capo.

There is another reference in the same scene to the hand and seal:

> Lettra, segnata del maggior Sigillo.

Vincentio, in a different context, shows the Provost the hand and seal of the Duke. As Mr Ball says:[4]

The hand and seal, the letter with its order to disregard all other advice, the messenger who is pictured arriving at the prison and bearing death when pardon is expected, are common only to *Epitia* and *Measure for Measure* and are not found in other sources.

The Emperor, on hearing Epitia's story, asks, 'E questo è vero?' and she replies 'Più ver, che il vero'. In the same way Vincentio tells Isabella 'Nay, it is ten times strange' and she replies:

> It is not truer he is Angelo
> Than this is all as true as it is strange;
> Nay, it is ten times true.   (V. i. 43–5)

Later on Vincentio exclaims: 'This is most likely!' and Isabella again replies:

> O that it were as like as it is true!   (v. i. 104)

Professor Schanzer points out[5] that Angela's maid soliloquizes on the power of a beautiful young woman to obtain her petitions, and even take Jove's thunderbolt from his hands:

> che potrà levare
> I fulmini di mano al sommo Giove
> Quando più fier, che mai fulmina, & tuona.

This may have suggested both Lucio's speech on the power of maidens (I. iv. 80 ff.) and Isabella's speech on 'Man, proud man' (II. ii. 106 ff.).

In addition to some points already mentioned, F. E. Budd argues that Epitia's conduct may have suggested Vincentio's justification for the bed-trick (that Angelo and Mariana were betrothed), and that his speaking on the adverse side at the opening of Angelo's trial finds a counterpart only in *Epitia*. Some of these points are somewhat dubious, but there would appear to be enough valid parallels to make it very likely that Shakespeare had read this play.

From Cinthio's story or play, we may suppose, Shakespeare turned to a source nearer home, Whetstone's long and rambling two-part doggerel tragi-comedy, in which Cassandra, a young and virtuous maiden, goes to Promos to solicit for her brother Andrugio's life. He has been condemned theoretically for rape, although his offence was, like Claudio's, mutually committed. Promos agrees to pardon Andrugio and to marry Cassandra, on condition that she sleeps with him first. Andrugio pleads, Cassandra consents, but after she has performed her part of the bargain,

> *Promos*, as feareles in promisse, as carelesse in performance, with sollemne vowe, sygned her conditions: but worse than any Infydel, his will satisfyed, he performed neither the one nor the other: for to keepe his aucthoritye vnspotted with fauour, and to preuent *Cassandraes* clamors, he commaunded the Gayler secretly, to present *Cassandra* with her brothers head. The Gayler, with the outcryes of *Andrugio*, abhorryng *Promos* lewdenes, by the prouidence of God, prouided thus for his safety. He presented *Cassandra* with a Felons head newlie executed, who . . . was so agreeued at this trecherye, that at the pointe to kyl her selfe, she spared that stroke, to be auenged of *Promos*.   (from 'The Argument of the whole Historie')

The argument goes on to describe how Cassandra told the King her story and he ordered that Promos should marry her forthwith and afterwards be executed. But as soon as the marriage was solemnized, Cassandra, 'tyed in the greatest bonds of affection to her husband, became an earnest suter for his life'. The King refuses to grant her suit until the disguised Andrugio discloses his identity.

Shakespeare also read the version of the story in Whetstone's *Heptameron*, in which the tale is recounted by Isabella. Dr Lascelles believes that Shakespeare may also have come across Lupton's version,[6] in which there is a disguised prince, a common enough theme in all literatures, and most recently dramatized in Middleton's *Phoenix*, in which the hero acquaints himself with the crimes and vices of society before throwing off his disguise. Lupton, however, in his odious Utopia, *Siuqila*, hoped to improve people's morals by stern laws and by the encouragement of informers. If Shakespeare read this work, he would have, one supposes, been horrified; and this may have influenced his description of Angelo's rule.

The central situation in *Measure for Measure* has three analogues in one of the sources of *The Merchant of Venice*, Silvayn's *The Orator* (1596). One (no. 54) is about a man who persuaded his sister to cause her ravisher to die; another (no. 61) is concerned with two ravished maidens, one of whom wishes to marry the man responsible; and the third (no. 68) is about a ravished maiden who 'did first require her ravisher for her husband'.[7]

Reading Cinthio's tale or play, or Whetstone's two versions, or all four, Shakespeare would have been struck by the dramatic possibilities of the theme, but he must have realized too that the psychology of the heroine was theatrical and false. It is not easy to accept the spectacle of a virtuous maiden forgiving a man who is both her seducer, a blackmailer, and the supposed murderer of her brother. Such a character could be interpreted only in terms of psychopathology. The marriage at the end of the play could be justifiable only if the character of Promos were whitewashed. Shakespeare was faced, therefore, with two alternatives: he could make a revenge tragedy, ending with the killing of the corrupt deputy; or he could by various means mitigate the guilt of Promos and so be able to end the play with his marriage. But both these solutions would have been comparatively feeble. Shakespeare had already in *Titus Andronicus* written a play in which the innocent heroine is raped, and the result is not properly tragic. In *Lucrece* the raped heroine commits suicide, a tolerable end to a narrative poem, but not, as the failures of Heywood and Obey showed, satisfactory for a play. On the other hand, however much the guilt of Promos were minimized, his marriage with his victim would lay her open to the suspicion that she did not dislike his proposal as much as she pretended. To remove this suspicion altogether, Shakespeare made Isabella a novice with a passionate hatred of sexual vice. He decided to write a play on the subject of forgiveness – not the forgiveness prompted by sexual passion (as in Whetstone), nor even the magnanimity displayed in some of Cinthio's tales, but Christian forgiveness – that is, the forgiveness of enemies.[8]

By making his heroine a novice, Shakespeare ensured that the conflict in her mind should be as violent as possible, thus adding to the dramatic intensity of the plot. On the other hand, it meant that Isabella, whatever the conflict between her rôles as Sister and sister, could not possibly consent to Angelo's proposal. She ought not, even to save a brother's life, commit one of the seven deadly sins; for if he demanded, or even accepted, the sacrifice, she would believe him to be damned. She might, of course, have done it without telling him, like the heroine of Clemence Dane's *The Way Things Happen*; but in that play the man who is saved from prison is humiliated, and furious with the woman who has bought his freedom. Yet Claudio's life had to be saved, so a substitute for Isabella had to be found. Already in the source a substitute on the block is found for the condemned brother; Shakespeare finds a substitute, Ragozine, for this substitute, Barnardine, and a substitute for Isabella in the shape of Mariana.[9] The device was doubtless suggested by the plot of *All's Well that Ends Well*, in which Helena tricks Bertram in the same way, from which the name of Mariana is taken, and in which the bed-trick is an integral part of the story. Shakespeare in both cases uses the situation to exhibit the blindness of sexual passion. Bertram imagined that it would be distasteful to have sexual intercourse with his wife and bliss to sleep with Diana; yet, as Helena comments,

> O strange men!
> That can such sweet use make of what they hate,
> When saucy trusting of the cozen'd thoughts
> Defiles the pitchy night. So lust doth play
> With what it loathes, for that which is away.
>
> (IV. iv. 21–5)

Similarly, Angelo imperils his immortal soul by offering to spare

Claudio's life in exchange for a single night with a woman who loathes him, and yet in the dark is unable to tell the difference between Isabella and Mariana. Absurd from the point of view of naturalism, the bed-trick is symbolically satisfying.

Shakespeare, then, had to find an apt substitute for Isabella. It had to be someone who loved Angelo and had some right to his bed. What better choice than someone to whom Angelo had been betrothed, and whom he had rejected for some reason appropriate to his character and to the theme of the play? The reason was not far to seek. Claudio, contracted to Juliet, had postponed the marriage ceremony for the sake of the dowry. Angelo, with far less excuse, had repudiated Mariana because her dowry had miscarried. Claudio's fornication, for which he is condemned to death, is shown to be much less sinful than the mercenary behaviour of Angelo, though the latter earns a reputation for uprightness and self-control. It is necessary to the scheme of the play that Angelo should commit the very sin for which he had con-demned another to death. The fact that Isabella is a novice would suggest Angelo's character. He, like Isabella, is something of a puritan. He is a man of severe morals, sincerely respected both by the Duke and by Escalus. He believes himself to be impervious to sexual temp-tations. He is regarded as one

> whose blood
> Is very snow-broth, one who never feels
> The wanton stings and motions of the sense,
> But doth rebate and blunt his natural edge
> With profits of the mind, study and fast.
>
> (I. iv. 57–61)

They say this Angelo was not made by man and woman, after this downright way of creation. . . Some report, a sea-maid spawn'd him; some, that he was begot between two stockfishes.

(III. ii. 97 ff.)

Chastity may proceed from meanness or cowardice: but it would be wrong to regard Angelo as a villain. 'He is betrayed by the subtler temptation that would mean nothing to a grosser man. He is moved by the sight of the beauty of a distressed woman's mind'.[10] Once he falls into temptation, he is betrayed by the sexual instinct he had despised. As Cadoux puts it,[11]

His scheme of life had no decent place for sex, and therefore no foothold from which to fight its indecencies.

It is possible that the puritanical streak in his character was prompted by the self-righteous and frightening rigidity displayed in Lupton's perverted Utopia.

Until recently most critics have objected to Isabella's forgiveness of Angelo. Johnson and Coleridge for once were in agreement; and Bridges thought the ending showed a lack of artistic conscience.[12] W. W. Lawrence excused Shakespeare by saying that in the drama of the period it was customary for the repentant villain to be married to the heroine. If this were all, there would be a good deal to be said for the accusation by Bridges. But Angelo, though morally guilty of lust and murder, and actually guilty of meanness, blackmail, and treachery, is not really a villain; he is a 'sincere self-deceiver'[13] and he repents. Nor is he the central character of the play; and those critics who have sought to justify the ending of the play have done so by showing that Isabella, who had pleaded for mercy for her brother, is put in the position where the test of the sincerity of her religion is whether she can bring herself to forgive the man who has wronged her.

Shakespeare, by making his heroine a novice, involves Claudio also in a searching ordeal, under which he fails; but by having Vincentio returning in disguise to manipulate the action, he ensures that the characters shall be tempted without ultimately tragic results. Even Barnardine is spared; and Lucio alone, who despite his wit and corrupt charm is a cold-hearted lecher, informer, and slanderer, is treated with some severity – he is made to marry the mother of his child. It is difficult to agree with Una Ellis-Fermor[14] that the lowest depths of Jacobean cynicism are touched in this play. It has often been observed that many of the minor characters are depicted sympathetically – the warm-hearted Mariana (who inspired Tennyson), the humane Provost, the saintly Juliet. Shakespeare, indeed, was not without sympathy for Pompey the pimp, for Barnardine the drunken murderer, and for Mistress Overdone who looks after Lucio's bastard.

Tillyard complained,[15] with greater justice, that the play falls into two disparate halves. After the scene between Claudio and Isabella, most of the rest of the play is in prose, and what verse there is, is greatly inferior to that of the first two acts. Theatrical intrigue takes the place of psychological profundity and great poetry. Tillyard was right to point out the change in the second half of the play, but, apart from the fact that the last two acts are highly successful in the theatre, at least in recent years, they can be defended on other grounds. It is, perhaps, the intervention of the divine in human affairs, symbolized by the activities of the Duke, which transforms the style of the second half of the play. The characters become puppets, 'taking part in no common action' (to use Eliot's phrase), and manipulated so that they all find either judgement or salvation. In the first part of the play, it may be said, the characters blunder along in their human way, until they can be saved by Providence Divine. Thereafter they are whirled about so swiftly that they do not have leisure, even for poetry. The poetry is in the action.

However this may be, one cannot deny that there are ironies and ambiguities in the play. Audiences quite naturally laugh at the Duke, and sympathize with Lucio and Barnardine; and although they may be brought to approve of Isabella's refusal to sacrifice her chastity, they may well be taken aback by the savagery of her onslaught on Claudio. Yet to transform the Duke into Lucio's satirical portrait of him, and to depict Isabella as neurotic, as some recent directors have done, hardly does justice to the play's depth and humanity. Shakespeare himself smiles at his play's dramaturgic extravagance, as when he makes the Duke exclaim, 'O, 'tis an accident that heaven provides' (IV. iii. 73), when it is the dramatist, rather than heaven, who has provided the convenient corpse of Ragozine.[16]

27

OTHELLO

THE SOURCE of *Othello* is Giraldi Cinthio's *Hecatommithi* (III. 7). As the same collection contains a version of the story which provided the plot of *Measure for Measure*, and as that play was written about the same time as *Othello*, Shakespeare was presumably scanning Cinthio's book in his search for plots in the early years of the seventeenth century. It is possible that there was an Italian dramatic version of the story[1] but in the absence of evidence for this it is safe to assume that Cinthio's tale was the immediate source of *Othello*. There was, indeed, a French translation by Gabriel Chappuys, but from one passage in the

play, which is marginally closer to the Italian than it is to the French, it
seems likely that Shakespeare read the original.[2] Othello's words –

> Villain, be sure thou prove my love a whore –
> Be sure of it; give me the ocular proof;
> Or, by the worth of man's eternal soul,
> Thou hadst been better have been born a dog
> Than answer my wak'd wrath. . . .
> Make me to see't –   (III. iii. 363–8)

are based on the words Cinthio gives to the Moor:

> Se non mi fai, disse, uedere co gli occhi quello, che detto mi hai,
> viviti sicuro, che ti farò conoscere, che meglio per te sarebbe, che tu
> fossi nato mutulo.

Chappuys's version is simply:

> Si tu ne me fais voir ce que tu m'as dit, assure-toi que je te ferai
> connoistre, que mieux t'eût valu être né muet.

The probability that Shakespeare read the Italian text is reinforced by
his use of the word 'acerbe' (I. iii. 345) – which the Folio changed to
'bitter' – for Cinthio tells how the love of his villain for Disdemona
'turned to the bitterest hatred' – 'in acerbissimo odio'. It has been
argued, too,[3] that Shakespeare derived a phrase in his account of the
handkerchief from Ariosto's description of Cassandra in the last canto
of *Orlando Furioso*:

> Una donzella della terra d'Ilia,
> Ch'avea il furor profetico congiunto,
> Con studio di gran tempo, e con vigilia
> Lo fece di sua man di tutto punto.   (XLVI. 80)

Here again Harington's version does not translate 'il furor profetico'.[4]

In Cinthio's tale Othello is called the Moor, Iago the Ensign, and
Cassio the Captain: only Disdemona is given a name. To avoid confusion between the military terms, it will be convenient in the following
account to give Cinthio's characters their Shakespearian names.

Disdemona is a beautiful and virtuous lady who falls in love with the
Moor, not out of lust but because of his virtues. Her relations try to
persuade her to take another husband, but she marries the Moor and
they live in Venice 'in such harmony and peace . . . that no word ever
passed between them that was not affectionate and kind' (Variorum,

p. 377). The Moor is appointed to the command of the Cyprus garrison and Disdemona insists on accompanying him. The Moor embraces her, exclaiming: 'God keep you long in such love, dear wife!' (Var., p. 378).[5] Iago and his wife and Cassio accompany the Moor and Disdemona to Cyprus, sailing in the same ship. The Moor loves both Iago and Cassio and Disdemona loves the young and beautiful Emilia. Iago is handsome, but depraved:

> Despite the malice lurking in his heart, he cloaked with proud and valorous speech and with a specious presence the villainy of his soul with such art that he was to all outward show another Hector or Achilles.   (Var., p. 378)

Cassio dines often at the house of the Moor, who approves of his wife's friendship with him. Meanwhile Iago falls in love with Disdemona and, meeting with no response, he imagines that she must be in love with Cassio. His love turned to hatred, he determines to destroy Cassio and to prevent the Moor from enjoying Disdemona, since he himself cannot. He therefore plans to accuse Cassio and Disdemona of adultery; but before he has the chance of doing so, Othello deprives Cassio of his rank for wounding another soldier while on duty. Disdemona appeals many times on behalf of Cassio and when Othello tells Iago that he will ultimately consent, Iago begins to hint that Cassio and Disdemona are lovers. As a result, when Disdemona next speaks to Othello on Cassio's behalf, he determines to be avenged. He demands that Iago shall speak openly; and he replies that Disdemona now finds the Moor's colour repugnant and that when Cassio boasted of his conquest he refrained from killing him only because he feared the Moor's anger. Othello demands ocular proof and Iago promises to try to provide it. One day when Disdemona is visiting Emilia and fondling her infant daughter, Iago steals an embroidered handkerchief from her girdle and hides it in Cassio's house. Finding it, and knowing whose it is, Cassio goes to return it; but, hearing Othello's voice, he hurriedly departs without seeing Disdemona, though the Moor thinks he recognizes Cassio.[6] Othello asks Iago to sound Cassio; and one day when the Moor is watching, Iago jests with Cassio and afterwards declares that he was boasting of his conquest,[7] claiming that she had given him the handkerchief on the last occasion when they had slept together. Othello asks his wife for the handkerchief and she searches for it in vain. Commenting on Othello's strange behaviour, Disdemona tells Emilia that she is afraid she may become a warning to others not to marry against the advice of their relations, and not to wed a man 'whom nature, heaven and mode of life estrange from us' (Var., p. 384). Emilia, who knows of Iago's plot, is afraid to disclose it to Disdemona; but she warns her to avoid giving any occasion of suspicion to the Moor.

There is a woman in Cassio's house who is an expert needlewoman and, knowing that the handkerchief is Disdemona's, she decides to copy the embroidery before returning it. Iago takes Othello past her window while she is engaged in this task. Othello then bribes Iago to kill Cassio; and one night when Cassio is coming from a harlot's house Iago wounds him in the leg. Cassio calls for help; Iago flees and mingles with the crowd, to sympathize with the wounded man. Incensed with Disdemona because she grieves for Cassio, Othello plans with Iago to murder her. One night, while he is in bed with her, he tells her to investigate a noise in the adjoining room, where Iago batters her to death with a stocking filled with sand. The two men conceal the crime by making part of the ceiling fall. Othello, however, is stricken with remorse and begins to hate Iago who therefore goes to Cassio to tell him that it was the Moor who wounded him and murdered Disdemona. Cassio accuses Othello before the signiory; the Moor is brought to Venice and tortured, but he denies everything. He is banished for life but is eventually killed by Disdemona's kinsmen. Sometime afterwards Iago is involved in another crime: he dies wretchedly after being tortured. 'Thus did Heaven avenge the innocence of Disdemona', concluded Cinthio, adding that 'all these events were narrated by the Ensign's wife, who was privy to the whole' (Var., p. 389).

At first sight, perhaps, the story seems an unpromising basis for a tragedy: the colourless heroine, the melodramatic villain, the sordid murder, the clumsy nemesis, and the leisurely tempo of the story are all serious obstacles. Above all, the Moor himself lacks most of the dimensions of a tragic hero. But it has often been observed that Shakespeare was stimulated to his greatest efforts by the sheer difficulties confronting him. When the difficulties were not in the source (as in *Macbeth*) he imported them from outside. The problem he set himself in that play was to reveal how a noble character came to commit a murder. The loftier the character and the more atrocious the crime, the more stimulating was the problem to his imagination. So, in reading Cinthio's tale, he would have felt challenged by the magnitude of the difficulties involved in making a tragedy from it, but he would nevertheless have found several hints in the tale itself how the subject might be treated – the suggestion that Disdemona had fallen in love with the Moor's virtues and not from lust, her decision to brave the dangers of the sea, her later remark about mixed marriages, and the statement after the murder that the Moor loved her more than life.

Shakespeare stressed the apparent unnaturalness of the marriage, so unnatural that Brabantio can accuse Othello of having used drugs or witchcraft, and Iago can pretend that Desdemona is a supersubtle Venetian who seeks a new thrill by eloping with a coloured man, and who would inevitably realize the error of her choice when she was sated with his body. Shakespeare blackens the marriage before the audience has actually seen Othello and Desdemona and then cleanses it by Othello's account of his wooing, by his disclaiming that he wishes to take Desdemona to Cyprus to please the palate of his appetite, and by Desdemona's declaration that she 'saw Othello's image in his mind'. Yet the very fact that the marriage has been smeared prepares the way for the operation of Iago's poison. The very feeling of difference, which can be a recurrent miracle in marriage, can also be the seed of distrust. In a marriage of mixed races such a difference can be distorted and warped into alienation; the act of faith and commitment can be interpreted as a perversion; the strangeness can appear as a mask hiding the real self. This was the psychological basis of Iago's plot.[8]

Shakespeare would have seen other opportunities in Cinthio's tale. The contrast between the apparent honesty and the actual villainy of the Ensign provided an opportunity of exploring once again the nature of 'seeming', fresh as the poet was from Hamlet's discovery that one may smile and be a villain, and just before he created the non-villainous seemer, Angelo. Above all he must have been struck by the dramatic possibilities of making a noble hero kill the woman he loved.

Several of Shakespeare's alterations were designed to raise the stature of the hero. He is introduced on the night of his elopement, sought by Brabantio's men, and quelling a brawl with eleven words, and sought at the same time by the Duke's messengers, because of his value to the state. The Turkish danger – invented by Shakespeare – would be associated in the mind of the poet and of his audience with the battle of Lepanto and with James I's poem on the subject.[9] Othello's nobility is manifested by his defence against the charge of witchcraft. For this Shakespeare went to Philemon Holland's translation of Pliny's *Natural History*[10] in which he found the story of C. Furius Cresinus, a former bond-slave, who was accused of acquiring great possessions by 'indirect means, as if he had vsed sorcerie,[11] and by charmes and witch-craft drawne into his owne ground that encrease of fruits'. Cresinus' defence begins with the words 'My Maisters', as Othello's does; and pointing to his plough and other implements, he says:

> Behold, these are the sorceries, charmes and all the inchauntments that I vse. . . . I might besides alledge mine owne trauell and toile that I take, the earely rising and late sitting vp so ordinarie with mee, the carefull watching that I vsually abide, and the painefull sweats which I daily endure.[12]   (Bk 18, Chap. 6)

Other details of Othello's defence – the traveller's tales – may also be derived from another section of Holland's translation.[13] But there is another source of Othello's apologia – Sir Lewes Lewkenor's translation of Cardinal Contareno's *The Commonwealth and Government of Venice* (1599).[14] In his address to the reader, Lewkenor speaks of his pleasure in conversing with travellers:

> Of which sorte it hath been my happinesse to be beholding to many of sundry nations for their friendly conuersation, who neuer were so willing at any time to speake, as I euer was ready to receiue their discourses with an attentiue eare.

Lewkenor also contrasts the 'soft beds' of those who stay at home with the hardships of travellers, the 'many carefull thoughtes, industrious penuries and painefull inconueniences'. He refers to his pleasure in listening to the description of foreign countries, 'especially if they come from the mouth of a wise and well speaking traueller, to whose tongue I should willingly endure to haue mine eares enclined', he confesses that his education has been in the wars; he apologizes in the Epistle Dedicatory for 'the vntuned harshnesse of my disioynted stile', and he speaks of 'the violence of my own fortune'. So Othello apolo-gizes for his rude speech and excuses it by his education in the wars. He speaks of his hardships and contrasts the 'flinty and steel couch of war' with the 'thrice-driven bed of down' enjoyed by civilians. Desdemona would 'seriously incline' to hear his tales and devoured up his discourse with 'a greedy ear'. In the same scene she refers to her 'downright violence and storm of fortunes'. Presumably Shakespeare consulted the book for background information about Venice. He took from it his knowledge of 'officers of the night' (I. i. 183)[15] and possibly borrowed the words 'weaponed' (v. ii. 269)[16] and 'intentiuely'

(I. iii. 155). He may also have made use of Kiffen's dedicatory sonnet for part of Iago's motivation. Venice is praised as a city

> Where all corrupt means to aspire are curbd,
> And Officers for vertues worth elected.
> The contrarie wherof hath much disturbd
> All states, where the like cause is vnrespected.

Iago's complaint that he has been passed over in favour of Cassio is a motive absent in Cinthio's tale, and it is noteworthy that he contrasts the good old days, when promotion was by merit, with the degenerate times in which he lives.

Shakespeare used Holland's Pliny for many details, besides the ones already mentioned, to suggest Othello's alien and exotic experience. Pliny mentions[17] the medicinal gum of the Arabian trees, mines of sulphur, a statue made of chrysolite, mandragora, and coloquintida. It has been argued,[18] however, that Shakespeare read Pliny in Latin, that he did not use Holland's translation, that the Arabian trees come from Ovid (*Metamorphoses*, x. 499–502), that the 'antres vast' come from the *Aeneid* (III. 617), that the actual word 'antres' may come from an unidentified version of Pliny, and that 'deserts idle' comes from the Latin. Despite these arguments, it is surely significant that these echoes appear soon after the publication of Holland's translation. T. W. Baldwin must have revised his opinion if he had read Meyerstein's article, or indeed, mine.[19] In any case, there is no doubt that the simile of the Pontic Sea is based directly on Holland's translation, and is indeed a fusion of several different passages.

There are three references to the Pontic Sea in Pliny. One is quoted by the Cambridge editors:

> Out of Pontus the sea alwaies floweth, and never ebbeth againe.
>
> (IV. 13)

It is, however, notable that in the context of this sentence we read how the Danube 'with a mightie encrease of waters . . . rolleth into Pontus', of the 'vast and wide Ocean lying before Asia, and driven out from Europe', of the 'streights they call *Hellespontus*', from which place 'the Sea groweth wide and broad', of a firth 'frozen and all an yce', of a 'continuall fall of snow', and of 'the workes of frozen cold, and the ycie harboure of the chilling Northerne wind' (IV. 12). This context would thus have provided Shakespeare with two of his epithets, 'icy' and 'wide', and perhaps a hint for 'compulsive course'.

The second passage is the following:

On the banke of Betis there is a towne, the wells whereof as the tyde
floweth, doe ebbe; and as it ebbeth, doe flow: in the mid times
betweene, they stirre not. . . And the sea *Pontus* evermore floweth
and runneth out into *Propontis*, but the sea never retireth backe
againe within *Pontus*.   (II. 97)

Here Shakespeare picked up 'never retireth' and joined it with 'never
ebbeth again' from the first passage. Once again the context is revealing:

Moreover, all tides in the maine Ocean, overspread, couer and
overflow much more within the land, than in other seas besides:
either because the whole and vniversall element is more courageous
than in a part: or for that the open greatnesse and largenesse thereof,
feeleth more effectually the power of the planet, working forcibly
as it doth farre and neere at libertie, than when the same is pent and
restrained within those streights. Which is the cause that neither
lakes nor little riuers ebbe and flow in like manner. . . But these
tides and quick motions of the sea, are found to be about the shores,
more than in the deepe maine sea. For even so in our bodies the
extream and vtmost parts have a greater feeling of the beating of
arteries . . . the Firth Taurominitanum, which ebbeth and floweth
oftener than twice. . . In the same place there is another spring that
keepeth order and time with the motions of the Ocean.

(II. 97)

Pliny's information about the water, 'pent and restrained' within the
straits, his use of the word 'forcibly', and the various words indicating
currents combined to suggest 'current and compulsive course' and
'violent pace'. The words 'feeleth' and 'feeling' support the reading of
the Second Quarto, 'feels'; 'keepeth order' links up with 'keeps due
on'; and 'arteries' links up with Othello's bloody thoughts.

Pliny again returns to the subject of the Pontic Sea at the beginning of
Book VI, where it would catch the eye of anyone idly turning the pages
of Holland's translation. Pliny suggests that Nature has

a wilfull desire to maintaine still the Sea in his greatnesse, and to
fulfill his greedy and endles appetite . . . with exceeding rage overflowing the same . . . it sufficed not, I say, to haue broken through
the mountaines, and so to rush in . . . to haue swallowed up much
more by farre than is left behind to be seene; no nor to haue let

Propontis gush through *Hellespont*, and so to encroach again upon the earth, and gaine more ground: vnless from the streights of Bosphorus also he enlarge himselfe into another huge and vast sea, and yet is neuer content, untill the lake Mœotis also with his streight, meet with him as he thus spreadeth abroad and floweth at libertie.

Here we have 'swallowed up' to suggest 'swallow them up'; several words to suggest 'compulsive course' and 'violent pace'; 'never content untill' to suggest 'ne'er ebb . . . till'; and 'exceeding rage' to link up with 'bloody thoughts' (Iago has just urged Othello to be content). The three passages coalesced in Shakespeare's mind to provide the substance and many of the words of Othello's simile:

> Like to the Pontic sea,
> Whose icy current and compulsive course
> Ne'er feels retiring ebb, but keeps due on
> To the Propontic and the Hellespont;
> Even so my bloody thoughts, with violent pace,
> Shall ne'er look back, ne'er ebb to humble love,
> Till that a capable and wide revenge
> Swallow them up.   (III. iii. 457–64)

Shakespeare continues to emphasize Othello's nobility and importance to the state throughout the play. The discussion of his appointment by the garrison at Cyprus and their enthusiastic welcome show that Iago's views are not shared by other soldiers, and Othello's intervention in the brawl exhibits his calm authority. The worst blot in the character of Cinthio's Moor is eliminated by Shakespeare's treatment of Desdemona's murder: the 'sacrificial' killing is carried out by Othello himself and he makes no attempt to escape responsibility for his deed. Whereas Cinthio's Moor remains ignorant of Disdemona's innocence, and never confesses to the murder, Othello hears the truth about the handkerchief from Emilia – who thus risks her life – tries to kill his betrayer, and commits suicide, believing himself to be damned.

Shakespeare makes fewer changes in the character of his heroine, but these too are significant. She is a motherless girl; she elopes, knowing that Brabantio would not give his consent; and this deception of her father, which breaks his heart, shows her bravery and independence, provides the occasion for Othello's defence against the charge of witchcraft, enables Desdemona to defend the purity of her love, and provides Iago with some plausible evidence that she is a deceiver. Her

arrival at Cyprus, her anxiety for Othello's safety, their reunion, her
solicitude for his headache in the scene where she drops her precious
handkerchief, her warm advocacy of Cassio's reinstatement – which
could be interpreted as interference in military affairs – her lack of
resentment at Othello's brutal behaviour, her refusal to wish that she
had never married him, a wish that is transferred by Shakespeare from
Disdemona to Emilia, and her Christian forgiveness of her murderer
revealed by her final denial of his guilt – all these things display the
depth and purity of her love and her genuine goodness to which even
Iago testifies. Her conversations with Emilia after the brothel-scene and
as she prepares for bed and Cassio's marked distaste for Iago's leering
remarks about her sexuality underline her essential innocence.

The third main character also undergoes significant alterations. The
Ensign's sole motive, as we have seen, was his thwarted lust for Disdemona. Shakespeare retains a trace of this motive, but he adds several
others: his envy at Cassio's promotion, his suspicion that both Othello
and Cassio have seduced his wife, his wish to infect Othello with the
jealousy he has himself experienced, his hatred of goodness. 'Ultimately', says Dame Helen Gardner, 'whatever its proximate motives,
malice is motiveless'.[20] He is introduced at the beginning of the play
in the company of Roderigo, a character doubtless suggested by the
necessity of providing a plausible cause of the brawl in Act II. The
situation is borrowed from *Twelfth Night*, where Sir Toby Belch takes
money from Sir Andrew by holding out hopes of Olivia's hand.
Desdemona's marriage changes the situation and Roderigo now hopes
for adultery rather than marriage; and this provides Iago with an
additional motive for destroying Desdemona, when he is threatened
with exposure. The creation of Roderigo has another effect: the brawl,
instead of being an accident becomes part of Iago's grand design.
Although Iago is an opportunist, who is continually improvising, he
controls events more completely than the villain of the source. It is
he who suggests to Cassio that he should ask Desdemona to plead for
him, and he uses Cassio's visit as the jumping-off place for his temptation
of the Moor. In the novel the Ensign steals the handkerchief because
the jealous Moor has been clamouring for proof. Shakespeare alters
the order of events. Iago asks Emilia to filch the handkerchief and
actually has it in his possession before Othello demands proof; he tells
the story of Cassio's dream, which is not in the source, before mentioning the handkerchief, and hides it in Cassio's lodging afterwards.
Cassio asks Bianca to copy the embroidery – in the novel it is the

woman's own idea – and Bianca brings the handkerchief back to him during the conversation between him and Iago. Shakespeare fuses the characters of the respectable woman in Cassio's house and his whore. The dramatic advantages of these changes are obvious. The events are more closely linked together. Iago's plot becomes at once more plausible and more ingenious, in spite of the obvious element of luck; an unnecessary character is eliminated; the harlot is given a significant rôle, and her jealousy contrasts with that of Othello, Iago, and Roderigo and the production of the handkerchief by Bianca is infinitely more dramatic than a glimpse of it through a window. That Cassio has apparently given the treasured love-token to his whore adds a final touch to Othello's hatred and disgust. In the novel the villain works only on the Moor: in the play he also deceives and manipulates Roderigo, Cassio, and Emilia.

In one respect, however, the Ensign appears to rely less on accident than Iago does. He steals the handkerchief while Disdemona is fondling his child, while Emilia steals the handkerchief only when Desdemona has dropped it. Swinburne thought that Cinthio's account was 'terribly beautiful'[21] and he concluded that Shakespeare discarded it because he could not imagine Iago fathering a child:

> In Shakespeare's world as in nature's it is impossible that monsters should propagate: that Iago should beget, or that Goneril or Regan should bring forth.

However this may be – and Goneril is surely pregnant when her father curses her – a good case can be made out for the superiority of Shakespeare's version of the loss of the handkerchief. There is, first, a purely theatrical reason. Shakespeare's stage-children are never as young as this one would need to be. Moreover, to make Desdemona visit Emilia's house would have altered the relationship between the two women, and it may be said that our opinion of Desdemona would suffer if we thought of her as an intimate friend of the worldly Emilia. Shakespeare allows Desdemona to forget the handkerchief in the only circumstances where her neglect of the love-token is an additional proof of her love. Her attention is concentrated on Othello's supposed headache which the handkerchief fails to alleviate. 'By that one change', declared Middleton Murry,[22] 'it is the perfection of Desdemona's love for Othello that destroys her'. The handkerchief is, of course, a symbol of love; and the magic in the web of it, in which Othello, and possibly Desdemona, believe, symbolizes the fate that brings them together and later destroys them. Because of what he believes, or partly believes, about the handkerchief, Othello accepts fatalistically, when Desdemona loses it, that his marriage is destroyed; and Desdemona's half-belief in the magic accounts for her foolish lie which Othello naturally takes as a further proof of her guilt.

There are some modifications in the character of the villain's wife. Emilia, unlike her prototype, is ignorant of Iago's real character, and as soon as she realizes the truth she sacrifices her life for love of her mistress. Yet she is cynical and coarse-grained; she purloins the handkerchief to please her 'wayward husband', as she thinks him; and she does not confess to finding the handkerchief, in spite of Desdemona's distress and Othello's rage.

Cassio's inability to hold his liquor was Shakespeare's invention; it is used to explain his misconduct without too much alienation of our sympathies. The main lines of his character were determined by his innocent admiration of Desdemona, by his appointment as Othello's lieutenant, and by the fact that he is wounded in returning from a harlot's house. Shakespeare adds his love for Othello and his assistance to him in his wooing; he adds also his appointment to succeed Othello, when the emergency is over, thus confirming that Iago's resentment was unjustified. The invention of Roderigo enables Iago to incite him to remove Cassio; but Roderigo bungles the job, and Iago kills him, wounds Cassio from behind, and accuses Bianca of being an accomplice.

The manner of Desdemona's murder, as we have seen, was Shakespeare's invention. The ending of the story is transformed by a number of alterations: by the insertion of the willow-song scene, by Othello's opening speech in the final scene, by Desdemona's forgiveness, by the immediate discovery of the murder, by Emilia's exposure of Iago, by Othello's remorse, and by Iago's punishment for his crimes – not, as in the source, for another crime altogether.

It has often been observed that Shakespeare was compelled to speed up the plot because once Othello were to confront Desdemona with his suspicions, Iago's lies would be exposed. He does not accuse her directly until the brothel-scene, and even then does not mention the name of her supposed lover. If Othello had confronted her earlier in the play, we should have wondered why Desdemona did not make the enquiries which would have exposed Iago. In reading the play we are struck by the improbability of Iago's luck – the luck of the devil; but in seeing the play we are impressed rather by the diabolical ingenuity of his scheming.

Shakespeare speeds up the action for other reasons. By making the elopement take place on the same night as Othello's appointment to the command in Cyprus, he not merely economizes in time – a single meeting of the Senate dealing with Brabantio's accusation and the Turkish threat – but also he increases the dramatic tension by having a succession of night-scenes. But the greatest dramatic advantage afforded by the change is that it eliminates the period of happy married life in Venice: by not allowing Othello to obtain this day-to-day knowledge of his wife, he provides the only possible basis for Iago's plot. Othello is despatched to Cyprus on the day of his elopement and before the consummation of his marriage. Whereas Cinthio allows time in Cyprus for Iago to fall in and out of love with Disdemona, and for her to get into the habit of visiting his wife, more time before Disdemona notices the loss of the handkerchief, more time before the Moor asks to see it, more again before he sees the woman copying the embroidery, more before the attack on Cassio, and more before the murder of Disdemona, Shakespeare astonishingly condenses the Cyprus scenes into a couple of days. Iago's temptation begins a few hours after Cassio's dismissal, the handkerchief is seen in Bianca's hands a few hours after that, and the final tragedy comes before nightfall. The sheer technical mastery displayed throughout the play is admitted by all critics, even by those, such as Bridges and Stoll, who resent the way that Shakespeare hypnotizes us into believing impossibilities. The poet, indeed, laid up trouble for himself by his determination to achieve speed at all costs, and presumably he felt that, apart from the desirable intensity so achieved, it was necessary to leave no time for Othello, or the audience, to ask inconvenient questions.

As many critics have observed, there was no occasion when Cassio and Desdemona could have committed adultery: they travel to Cyprus on different ships and Iago begins his accusations on the morning after Othello's marriage has been consummated. How are we to answer this point? Are we to assume that Shakespeare made an absurd blunder, and that he ought to have made Cassio and Desdemona travel on the same ship? Or, as Bridges suggested, that Othello's ship should have been delayed for a week by the storm? Or that we are meant to think that Othello was dreadfully stupid? Or should we accept the theory of double-time, that Shakespeare was using two clocks so as to increase the apparent speed of the action, and that he relied on getting away with this trick in the theatre?

There is certainly a deliberate confusion of the time-scheme. Shake-

speare has on the one hand to suggest extreme rapidity of action, since
the success of Iago's plot depends on it; on the other hand, he has to
allow for news to reach Venice of the dispersion of the Turkish fleet
and for Lodovico thereafter to travel from Venice to Cyprus. By one
clock Bianca can complain that Cassio has absented himself for a week;
by the other clock Cassio has arrived on the island less than two days
previously. As Peter Alexander wisely said:[23]

> Shakespeare had set before himself a much more 'philosophical' end
> than the realization of historical probability. He has to reveal the
> heart of a human situation, a situation in which, he makes clear to us,
> the seeds of suspicion and jealousy might easily take root. To create
> an elaborate replica in material terms to satisfy the intelligence,
> when the imagination can gather all it needs of the situation from
> what Shakespeare can spare for mere exposition, would be a breach
> of artistic economy, and would distract attention from the inner
> train of events.

Alexander goes on to suggest that not only do the liberties Shakespeare
takes with time pass unnoticed during a performance, but also that
they are the means he employs, as legitimate as perspective, to con-
centrate on the essentials of his story.

This is not, perhaps, the whole truth about double-time. Othello
accuses Desdemona of committing 'the act of shame' with Cassio a
thousand times, which implies a long-standing liaison; but other
passages, such as Iago's account of Cassio's dream, imply that the
alleged intrigue dates from after Desdemona's marriage. The fact is
that Shakespeare deliberately deprives Othello of the slightest rational
ground for jealousy and Iago makes no attempt to provide even the
flimsiest of evidence until Othello is no longer able to think rationally.
In the early part of the temptation scene Iago seems to imply that
Cassio and Desdemona were too friendly during Othello's wooing.
When Iago returns, he finds that Othello has gone much further in his
imagination than he had gone in his accusations. He then gives the
fabricated account of Cassio's dream, and from Othello's reactions to it
he knows that he can now safely mention the handkerchief. By this
time, and until he has murdered his wife, Othello is so blinded by
passion that he can believe impossibilities.

No one in the theatre notices the existence of Shakespeare's two
clocks. It is true, nevertheless, that *Othello* is 'a tragedy built upon a
comic structure', as one recent critic has argued.[24] It was Rymer's

sense of this that made him call the play 'a bloody farce'. Most of the difficulties we have been discussing could be explained, but not explained away, by Ned B. Allen's ingenious theory[25] that Shakespeare wrote the last three acts first, keeping close to Cinthio's tale, and that, at some later date, he added the first two acts, without realizing the discrepancies between the two halves of the play – e.g. in Act I Cassio is apparently ignorant of Othello's marriage; in Act III, Othello says 'he went between us very oft'.

The general effect of Shakespeare's alterations is more important than the various things we have discussed – the speeding up of the action, the tightening of the plot, the alteration of the characters, and the increasing of the dramatic tension. Cinthio, except for one remark, is without the dramatic irony which is so pervasive in the play – the entrusting of Desdemona to Iago, the iteration of the word 'honest' throughout the play, and such famous strokes as 'If it were now to die, 'Twere now to be most happy'. Cinthio is also without the complex patterns of imagery so well analysed by Spurgeon, Clemen, Bethell, and Heilman. It is ultimately by means of the poetry that Shakespeare completely transforms the sordid story with a commonplace moral into a universal tragedy of love.

KING LEAR

WE DO NOT KNOW what first gave Shakespeare the idea of writing a play about King Lear. It is possible that the original inspiration came not from the Lear story at all but from Sidney's story of the Paphlagonian King and his two sons in *Arcadia*.[1] He may even have been prompted by the topical story of Brian Annesley who in October 1603, about a year before Shakespeare began his play, was reported to be unfit to govern himself or his estate. Two of his daughters tried to get him certified as insane, so that they could get hold of his estate; but the youngest daughter, Cordell, appealed to Cecil, and when Annesley died the Court of Chancery upheld his will. Although Cordell after-

wards married Sir William Harvey, the step-father of the Earl of
Southampton and, in the opinion of some, Mr W.H., the 'only
begetter' of Shakespeare's sonnets, and although it has been suggested[2]
that the Fool's remark, 'Winter's not gone yet if the wild geese fly that
way' is an allusion to Cordell's unkind sister, Lady Wildgoose, the
resemblances to the Lear story may not have been the reason why
Shakespeare decided to dramatize it.[3]

Years before, when he was writing the Histories, Shakespeare would
have come across the Lear story both in Holinshed's *Chronicles* and in
A Mirror for Magistrates. In 1590 he would have read Spenser's brief
account in *The Faerie Queene*. He may have known the version in
Gerard Legh's *Accedens of Armory* (1562); and, about the time he was
writing the play, Camden was retelling the story in his *Remaines*.
There was, finally, the old play of *King Leir*, with which the poet was
certainly familiar. As this appears to have been published only because
of the success of Shakespeare's play, he must have seen it in manuscript
or on the stage. Too little is known about Shakespeare's early career
for us to be certain that he never belonged to the company which
owned the old play.

I have examined elsewhere[4] the evidence that Shakespeare was
acquainted with all these sources, but it will be necessary to summarize
it here. Camden's *Remaines* (1605) was probably published too late to
influence the play. The evidence that Shakespeare knew Legh's book is
inconclusive. It is quite possible that he knew Geoffrey of Monmouth's
account; for France's confession, 'My love should kindle to inflam'd
respect' (I. i. 255), seems to echo 'Amore virginis inflammatus'; and
there are other similarities.[5] With the other sources we are on more
certain ground. Sir Walter Greg detailed[6] some forty parallels between
King Lear and the old chronicle play, and few of these are at all doubtful.
One example will be sufficient to show how well Shakespeare knew the
old play. Perillus (Kent) upbraids Gonorill with the words:

> Nay, peace thou monster, shame vnto thy sexe:
> Thou fiend in likenesse of a humane creature.
>   (Bullough, VII. 400, 2581–2)

Shortly afterwards Leir asks Ragan, 'Knowest thou these letters?' She
snatches them and tears them up. In one scene of *King Lear* Albany
urges his wife in similar terms:

> See thyself, devil!
> Proper deformity shows not in the fiend

> So horrid as in woman. . .
> Thou changed and self-cover'd thing, for shame!
> Be-monster not thy feature . . .
>   howe'er thou art a fiend,
> A woman's shape doth shield thee.   (IV. ii. 59 ff.)

In the last scene of the play he says to her:

> Shut your mouth, dame,
> Or with this paper shall I stopple it. . . .
> Thou worse than any name, read thine own evil.
> No tearing, lady; I perceive you know it. . .
>   Most monstrous! O!
> Know'st thou this paper?   (V. iii. 154 ff.)

In both plays we have 'shame' and 'fiend'; 'monster' is echoed in 'be-monster' and 'monstrous'; 'sex' in 'woman'; and 'Knowest thou these letters?' in 'Know'st thou this paper?' The action of tearing is echoed in Albany's 'No tearing'.

From Holinshed's *Chronicles* Shakespeare took the titles of Cornwall and Albany (Albania) and perhaps a hint for Goneril's first speech: 'She loued him more than toong could expresse'. From *The Faerie Queene* Shakespeare derived the form of Cordelia's name, and the manner of her death, by hanging: in Holinshed, she stabs herself. From *A Mirror for Magistrates* Shakespeare took some ten minor details, including the title 'King of France', and there is one interesting parallel. The lines describing Cordila's life in prison –

> From sight of princely wights, to place where theues do dwel:
> From deinty beddes of downe, to be of strawe ful fayne –
>   (Bullough, VII. 330)

may be compared with Cordelia's lines (IV. vii):

> And wast thou fain, poor father,
> To hovel thee with swine and rogues forlorn
> In short and musty straw?   (IV. vii. 38–40)

Oddly enough, there is some evidence[7] that Shakespeare had perused both the 1574 and 1587 editions of *A Mirror for Magistrates*, since some of the echoes are from one edition, and some from the other.

It has been argued[8] that the play may have been influenced by *Gorboduc*, a play which is likewise concerned with the division of the kingdom in a legendary period of British history. It was written to advocate Queen Elizabeth's marriage; and *King Lear* was written at the time when James was advocating the union of England and Scotland:

> In both plays there is an old king who wants to rest and thinks it is time for his children to bear the burden of responsibility. . . . In both, the division of the kingdom has already been planned when the plays open and, before the court scenes, it is discussed, in *Gorboduc* by Videna and Ferrex, in *King Lear* by Kent and Gloucester. In both plays, too . . . the two kings act against the ponderous advice from wise counsellors.

On the whole it seems likely that the idea of redramatizing the Lear story came from Shakespeare's acquaintance with the old chronicle play, though he must have recognized from the first that the plot needed considerable modification. The author of *King Leir* had dramatized only part of the story, ending the play with the restoration of Leir to the throne, and omitting the tragic sequel in which Cordelia, deposed by her nephews, commits suicide in prison. Here Shakespeare was faced with a real difficulty. Cordelia's death takes place so long after the main events of the story that the dramatist would have had to introduce new characters – Cordelia's nephews – and sacrifice dramatic unity, apart from the fact that the suicide of the virtuous heroine would outrage our feelings. On the other hand, to end the play with the restoration of Lear would seem, to those who knew the sequel, only an interim conclusion. The problem confronting the poet was clear: he had to avoid the gap between the restoration of Lear and the death of Cordelia, he had to make her death connected causally with Lear's initial error, he had to make Lear fully aware of the ultimate results of this error, and since the suicide of Cordelia would be intolerable, she would have to be murdered.

Shakespeare solved the problem by bringing forward the death of Cordelia, so that she dies before her father; and the man who orders her murder does so because he hopes for the throne. This situation can arise only if Cordelia's army is defeated, not by her nephews, but by the armies of Goneril and Regan. If Lear and Cordelia are to die, the wicked sisters must die too; and since they win the battle they must be destroyed by the working out of their own evil passions. Shakespeare makes them quarrel not merely about their shares of the kingdom, but also about Edmund; so he makes one sister poison the other and kill herself – as the Cordelia of the *Chronicles* had done. So Shakespeare makes Goneril's husband a man of integrity and already one can see the character of Albany emerging, and one can also see the need for an attractive upstart by whom both sisters will be sexually attracted. Shakespeare even makes use of the version of Cordelia's death given by his sources by making it the 'official' story, spread by Edmund as a cover to the murder.

For the scene of the division of the kingdom Shakespeare relied mainly on the old play,[9] but he condensed no less than eight scenes into the second part of his own first scene. Leir plans a sudden stratagem to trick Cordella into marriage; the plot is betrayed to Gonorill and Ragan, who promise to marry anyone their father chooses; Leir divides the kingdom between the wicked daughters though he does not banish Cordella; the Gallian King visits Brittayne in disguise and woos Cordella. In the meanwhile Perillus makes an unsuccessful attempt to prevent Cordella from losing her share of the kingdom. Unlike Kent, Perillus is not banished. Shakespeare, by his ruthless telescoping, leaves Lear's motives in some obscurity and does not imply that Goneril and Regan knew beforehand of the love-test. The test is, in fact, an afterthought, not a device to persuade Cordelia to marry. He may well have felt that on the stage Lear's irrationality would be more credible than Leir's stupid cunning; and as he was adding a complex underplot, and continuing the main plot to the death of Cordelia, he could not afford more time for exposition. Kent's banishment and subsequent return to serve Lear are more dramatic than Perillus's continuation in Leir's service.

Shakespeare borrowed comparatively little from the remainder of *King Leir*. He omits the episode in which a murderer, hired by Ragan, is stricken with remorse. He omits the meeting of Leir and Perillus, faint with hunger, with the Gallian King and Cordella; but he remembered the scene of reconciliation between Cordella and her father. The older dramatist had been somewhat hampered by the presence of the Gallian King, like Cordella disguised; and he was hampered still more by the presence of the comic Mumford who kneels in parody of the other characters. The four of them kneel and rise in a ludicrous way in the space of fifty lines. But the scene was not without pathos, and Shakespeare retained its most memorable feature, where Lear and Cordelia kneel to each other (IV. vii). As Granville-Barker said,[10] it is 'a daring and unmatchable picture, for it is upon the extreme edge of beauty; one touch further and it might topple over into the absurd', as of course it does in *King Leir*. After the scene the Gallian King invades Britain, defeats the armies of Cornwall and Cambria, and reinstates Leir. There are no underplot, no storm, no Fool, no madness, and no deaths.

Shakespeare's play opens with the introduction of Edmund to Kent. For the story of Gloucester and his sons, Shakespeare borrowed an episode from Sidney's *Arcadia*, which provided a neat parallel to the Lear story. He helped the audience to accept retrospectively Lear's foolish conduct in the first scene by duplicating it in the subsequent conduct of Gloucester in the second scene. The two plots are closely linked throughout the play. Plexirtus, rechristened Edmund, provided Shakespeare with a lover of the two evil sisters and a murderer of the good one. His brother, Edgar, becomes the immediate cause of Lear's insanity, the man who exposes Goneril to Albany, and a commentator on the action. Gloucester's fortunes are linked with those of the King, and he is blinded when he takes Lear's side. In both plots we have a credulous father – Geoffrey's 'credulus . . . pater' – who believes the evil child and disinherits the good; in both plots the father receives ill from the favoured, and good from the disinherited, child. Lear's madness is suitably balanced with Gloucester's blindness; for Lear acquires wisdom when he is apparently mad and Gloucester sees clearly only when he has been blinded. In a sense, then, the scene which has been regarded as dramatically unnecessary – the meeting of the blind Gloucester with the mad Lear – is the symbolic climax of the play.

Shakespeare picked out from his sources the most suitable incidents, inventing them when no suitable ones were to hand. To make Edmund boast of his bastardy, for example, and to let him overhear Gloucester's lighthearted comments on his mother, prevents him from being a mere stage-villain. Unlike Plexirtus, he finally repents; and Shakespeare had the tact not to make him assist at the blinding of his father. Not only did Shakespeare take the outlines of his underplot from the story of the Paphlagonian King, but he also took some hints from it for the main plot. The death of Lear, for example, owes something to Sidney's account of the death of the Paphlagonian King, 'his hart broken with vnkindnes and affliction, stretched so farre beyond his limits with this excesse of comfort' (Bullough, VII. 407). So Gloucester dies after his reconciliation with Edgar, and Lear in the delusion that Cordelia is alive. It has been argued, moreover, that the duel between Edgar and Edmund may have been suggested by other episodes in *Arcadia*, and that the stratagem by which Edmund deludes his father may be derived

from the story of Plangus.[11] Between this story and that of the Paphlagonian King there is a dialogue in verse between Plangus and Basilius
on suicide, on the justice of the gods, and on the slaughter of the
innocent, which is reflected in Gloucester's attempted suicide and in the
treatment of the death of Cordelia. For Gloucester's attempted suicide
Shakespeare may also have remembered the opening scene of Seneca's
Thebais in which Oedipus asks Antigone to let him fall over a preci-
pice,[12] and a scene in Marston's *The Malcontent* in which Pietro, in
disguise, describes his own feigned suicide by leaping from a cliff into
the sea (IV. iii). But the leap from Dover cliff certainly owes something
to a passage in Holinshed's *Chronicles*, a few pages before the Leir
story, in which there is an account of how Corineus wrestled with
Gogmagog. He

> did so double his force that he got the vpper hand of the giant, and
> cast him downe headlong from one of the rocks there, not farre
> from Douer, and so dispatched him: by reason whereof the place
> was named long after, *the fall or leape of Gogmagog*, but afterward it
> was called *The fall of Douer*.

It is possible, too, that Edgar's description of the imaginary fiend with
eyes like two full moons was influenced by Holinshed's account of the
giant.[13]

The storm, for which there is in the source-play only a rudimentary
thunder-clap which deters Ragan's emissary from the murder of Leir,
may have been suggested by the 'extreame and foule storm' and the
'fury of the tempest' in the *Arcadia* episode; but the storm-scenes owe
most to Harsnett's *Declaration of Egregious Popishe Impostures*. Samuel
Harsnett, Chaplain to the Bishop of London, had already exposed
John Darrell, a puritan exorcist, when in 1603 he turned to attack the
Jesuit exorcists. As Theobald pointed out,

> The greatest part of Edgar's dissembled lunacy, the names of his
> devils, and the descriptive circumstances he alludes to in his own
> case, are all drawn from this pamphlet, and the confessions of the
> poor deluded wretches.

Later editors have pointed out that Shakespeare's indebtedness was
even more extensive than Theobald realized.

One of the first things that is likely to strike a reader of Harsnett's
Declaration is his detailed knowledge of the theatre, not merely of
Plautus and Seneca, but also of miracle plays and of various stage

technicalities. His description of the Vice is one of the most vivid we
have. He continually compares the tricks of the exorcists to a stage
performance and there are as many as 230 theatrical terms in the first
170 pages of his book. Whether he was a playgoer or not, he had to
read plays as part of his job of licensing books for the press.

The events described in Harsnett's *Declaration* had taken place seven-
teen years previously, but the examination by the Ecclesiastical Com-
missioners had been delayed until 1598 and 1602. As I have listed the
parallels with Harsnett in my edition of the play, there is no need for me
to give more than a brief selection here.

Marwood, one of the alleged demoniacs, is described as 'pinched
with penurie, & hunger' (p. 24). Harsnett speaks of the victims as
'poore seely creatures' (p. 41); he mentions 'what wind or weather so
euer' (p. 52), thunder, lightning, and hail (p. 136); he describes the
roaring of the devils possessing the demoniacs (p. 38); he tells how two
needles were thrust into one girl's leg, and a pin into another girl's
shoulder (p. 214); he tells of a demoniac who imagined he was 'rent
with a thousand nayles' (p. 73) and of another who thought he had
'many fiery needles in his skin at once' (p. 93); and he uses the phrase
'mortified patience' (p. 41). So Edgar decides to disguise himself as

> the basest and most poorest shape
> That ever penury in contempt of man
> Brought near to beast.   (II. iii. 7–9)

He speaks of

> The winds and persecutions of the sky . . .
> – Bedlam beggars, who, with roaring voices,
> Strike in their numb'd and mortified bare arms
> Pins, wooden pricks, nails.   (II. iii. 12 ff.)

Harsnett, like Lear, speaks of 'Hysterica passio' and uses a number of
words Shakespeare uses for the first time in this play: 'meiny', 'pro-
pinquity', 'auricular', 'carp', 'gaster', 'benediction', 'yoke-fellow',
'vaunt-courier', and 'asquint'.

When we turn to the storm-scenes Shakespeare's indebtedness to
Harsnett is much more obvious. It may even be suggested that the
storm itself may owe something to his tract. As we have seen there is
one clap of thunder in *King Lear* and a storm in *Arcadia*; but Harsnett
mentions 'a shelter against what wind or weather so euer' (like the
hovel in *King Lear*), 'lightning from heauen', 'thunder, and lightning

to bring *Iupiter* vpon the stage', 'the huge thunder cracke of adiuration' (p. 108). He mentions a violent devil that 'will ruffle, rage, and hurle in the ayre . . . and blow downe steeples, trees, may-poles' (p. 18). Shakespeare twice uses the word 'ruffle'. Harsnett's words 'all these sensible accidents should be made pendulous in the ayre' led to Shakespeare's sole use of the word 'pendulous':

> Now all the plagues that in the pendulous air
> Hang fated o'er men's faults.   (III. iv. 66–7)

Marwood, not unlike Poor Tom,

> did lie but a night, or two, abroad in the fieldes, and beeing a melancholicke person, was scared with lightning, and thunder, that happened in the night.   (p. 24)

Edgar's speech (III. iv. 50 ff.) –

> Whom the foul fiend hath led through fire and through flame, through ford and whirlpool, o'er bog and quagmire; that hath laid knives under his pillow and halters in his pew. . . Bless thee from whirlwinds, star-blasting, and taking! Do poor Tom some charity, whom the foul field vexes –

is a combination of several passages in Harsnett's book. Sara Williams waded 'through a brooke, halfe a yard deepe' (p. 43); Friswood Williams mentioned an apothecary who brought from London 'a new halter, and two blades of kniues' and 'did leaue the same vpon the gallerie floare in her Maisters house' (p. 219). Mainy thought the devil was tempting the demoniacs to commit suicide. One of them cried out 'How doost thou vexe, how doost thou wring me?' (p. 73). Harsnett does not use the word 'star-blasting', but he has 'devil-blasting', 'sprite-blasting', and 'owle-blasted', and he refers to whirlwinds several times.

Harsnett tells us that the devils

> went out in the forme of those creatures, that haue neerest resemblance vnto those sinnes: as for example; the spirit of *Pride* went out in the forme of a *Peacocke* (forsooth): the spirit of *Sloth* in the likenesse of an *Asse*: the spirit of *Enuy* in the similitude of a *Dog*: the spirit of *Gluttony* in the forme of a *Woolfe*.   (p. 141)

Although only the wolf represents the same sin in Harsnett and Shakespeare, Edgar's description of himself as 'hog in sloth, fox in stealth, wolf in greediness, dog in madness, lion in prey' is similar in style; and he confessed that he curled his hair, as Mainy did, and was accused of being Pride. Fliberdigibbet is mentioned several times by Harsnett; Smulkin appears as Smolkin, who appeared in the form of a mouse; Modo and Mahu are derived from Harsnett's Modu and Maho, the devils of Maynie and Sara Williams. Edmund Blunden showed[14] that Modo recalled to Shakespeare lines from one of Horace's *Epistles*:

> Ille per extentum funem mihi posse videtur
> Ire poeta, meum qui pectus inaniter agit.
> Irritat, mulcet, falsis terroribus implet,
> Ut magus, et modo me Thebis, modo ponit Athenis.
>
> (II. I. 210–13)

These lines apparently led to the later mention of 'learned Theban' and 'good Athenian' and to the allusion to 'Persicos odi, puer, apparatus'. T. W. Baldwin pointed out[15] that *magus* in Cooper's *Thesaurus* is described as 'a great learned philsoopher' in Persia; and Harsnett quotes from Horace's next epistle:

> Somnia, terrores magicos, miracula, sagas,
> Nocturnos lemures portentaque Thessala rides –
>
> (II. ii. 208–9)

a passage he versifies in the lines:

> Dreames and Magicall affrights,
> Wonders, Witches, walking sprights,
> What Thessalian Hags can doe,
> All this seems a iest to you.   (p. 137)

It would seem that Harsnett's Modo, one of Horace's odes and passages from two of his epistles, one quoted by Harsnett, lie behind Shakespeare's words.

In the next storm-scene, Edgar declares that 'Frateretto calls me, and tells me Nero is an angler in the lake of darkness'. Nero as an angler comes from 'The Monk's Tale' of Chaucer;[16] but Harsnett, before mentioning Frateretto, Fliberdigibbet and Hoberdidance, speaks of the 'Stygian lake', and soon afterwards mentions a fiddler who comes in to provide music in hell. Nero, of course, was famed as a fiddler and he was accused of matricide as Edgar was accused of attempted parricide.

Edgar's fears that his tears will mar his counterfeiting may echo Harsnett's mention of spectators who are 'brought into such commiseration and compassion, as they shal all weepe, crie and exclaime' and his use of such phrases as 'marred the play' and 'the play be marred'. Finally, the five fiends mentioned by Edgar in IV. i are all to be found in Harsnett's book, Obidicut being a corruption of Hoberdicut. The phrase 'mopping and mowing' in the same speech echoes one or more of the following passages:

> to mop, now, iest, raile, raue, roare . . . make anticke faces, girne, mow, and mop like an Ape, tumble like a Hedgehogge . . . A Sisternity of mimpes, mops, and idle holy women . . . the mowing of an apish wench.   (pp. 38, 136, 166)

The Harsnett influence lasted right down to the end of Shakespeare's career and left traces on *Pericles* and *The Tempest*.[17]

Lear's madness, as we have seen, may have been suggested by the Annesley story, but Shakespeare took some details from his own earliest tragedy, *Titus Andronicus* – the gilded fly, the archery, the imaginary petition, and the words 'I am not mad; I know thee well enough'.

From the fact that Shakespeare uses for the first time more than a hundred words to be found in Florio's translation of Montaigne,[18] it seems probable that he had been reading it not long before he wrote *King Lear* and several critics have argued that certain ideas in the play were derived from Montaigne, or at least that Shakespeare had discovered a kindred spirit.[19] He exposes the weakness of unaccommodated man, he considers the influence of the stars on human destiny, he discusses the effect of dizzy heights, and he may have provided some of the material for the clothing imagery pervasive in the play, for the consideration of Nature, and for Lear's attacks on authority and on the moral imperfections of society.

Shakespeare, then, created *King Lear* from the most heterogeneous materials. As was his custom, he amplified and complicated his original fable by using incidents, ideas, phrases, and even words from a variety of books. He found material for his purposes in the most unlikely places. Some critics, indeed, have complained that the play suffers from structural weakness, Bradley comparing it in this respect with *Timon of Athens*; others have said that Shakespeare was content to use the loose episodic structure of the chronicle play. Nothing could be further from the truth. There is no more impressive example of Shakespeare's skill as a dramatic craftsman. The way in which he combined a chronicle play, one or more prose chronicles, two poems, and a pastoral romance without any sense of incongruity is masterly, and the resulting tragedy is deeply interfused with ideas and phrases from his own early work, from Montaigne, and from Harsnett. Although the setting is prehistoric, the play deals continually with topical ideas – the dangers of a disunited kingdom, exorcism, the plight of the beggar, the conflict between two theories of nature, and what has been called the crisis of the aristocracy.[20] The invention of the storm, Edgar's disguise as Poor Tom, and the creation of a part for Robert Armin, the subtle Fool, enabled Shakespeare to present the madness of the elements as a projection of King, Fool, and feigned demoniac. The two plots are ingeniously linked together. In the third act, for example, the blinding of Gloucester is a punishment for his helping the King, and the death of Cornwall disposes of one of the villains and thus intensifies the jealousy of Regan and Goneril. Edmund forthwith intrigues to gain absolute power. The death of Cornwall, moreover, puts the command of the British forces into the hands of Albany, while the news of the blinding of Gloucester fills him with revulsion for his evil associates. Cornwall is killed by a servant, who is driven to rebel by his master's cruelty, so that the working out of the plot depends on the extent of the servant's acquiescence in evil.[21]

There is one simple test to apply to the structure of a play. If in producing this play you begin cutting scenes and speeches, you are soon brought to realize how impossible it is to find a superfluous line. Shakespeare's fellows – one hopes after his retirement – made a number of cuts and each one is disastrous. They cut, for example, the mock trial of Goneril and Regan, a scene which is as necessary for our understanding of Lear's development as it is essential for the symbolic pattern of the play. Then they cut – as Peter Brook was later to do – the dialogue between the servants at the end of the blinding-scene. How much the scene loses by the omission of this choric comment by ordinary humanity on the savage cruelty of Regan and Cornwall, how necessary it is to end the scene quietly, and how essential it is to prepare the way for Poor Tom's meeting with Gloucester! Then the actors omitted the whole of IV. iii, a scene in which a gentleman describes to Kent the grief of Cordelia when she hears how her father has been treated. Cordelia's part is so tiny, and her absence from the stage has been so long, that her next brief appearance requires careful preparation. The ineffectiveness of some recent Cordelias has been partly due to the omission of this preparatory scene. Apart from this, the audience needs to be informed of the reason why Lear refuses to see Cordelia; and Kent's comment on the influence of the stars, although it is not the whole truth, is necessary to the atmosphere of the play:

It is the stars,
The stars above us, govern our conditions;
Else one self mate and make could not beget
Such different issues.   (IV. iii. 32–5)

It is therefore absurd to suppose that the structure of the play is loose
and episodic. The main plot and the sub-plot are not merely parallel:
they are closely linked. In the first act Lear is deceived by Goneril and
Regan into disinheriting Cordelia and banishing Kent, and Gloucester
is deceived by Edmund into disinheriting Edgar. Edgar, like Kent,
returns in disguise to succour the man who has wronged him. In the
third act the outcasts of the main plot encounter the outcast of the
sub-plot; Lear goes mad and Gloucester, for helping him, is blinded.
In the fourth act the mad Lear encounters the blind Gloucester; the
fathers are succoured by the wronged children; and the evil daughters
quarrel over the evil son. In the last act both fathers die after being
reconciled to the children they have wronged; and Edgar brings about
the destruction of the three evil children. The only real accident in the
play – the only event which does not spring from man's greed, lust,
pride, or love – is the encounter between Edgar and Oswald, which
brings to light the plot to murder Albany; and even this accident
parallels the encounter between Kent and Oswald and is used by
Shakespeare to throw light on Oswald's character.[22]

29

MACBETH

IT IS REASONABLE to assume that Shakespeare chose the subject of
Macbeth because James I was reputed to be descended from Banquo.
On 27 August 1605 the King witnessed at Oxford Matthew Gwinn's
playlet in which three sibyls prophesied to Banquo's descendants
'imperium sine fine'.[1] Three days later, the Queen – but not James –
saw a performance at Christ Church of Samuel Daniel's *Arcadia
Reformed* – published in 1606 as *The Queenes Arcadia* – which is appar-

ently echoed in Macbeth's conversation with the Doctor.[2] Daphne
consults a quack, but afterwards decides that physic can do nothing

> to cure that hideous wound
> My lusts haue giuen my Conscience.

This, she declares,

> keeps me waking, that is, it presents,
> Those ougly formes of terror that affright
> My broken sleepes, that layes vpon my heart
> This heauy loade that weighes it downe with griefe.
>   (f. 2^v)

So Macbeth, before ordering that physic should be thrown to the
dogs, asks the doctor if he cannot

> minister to a mind diseas'd,
> Pluck from the memory a rooted sorrow,
> Raze out the written troubles of the brain,
> And with some sweet oblivious antidote
> Cleanse the stuff'd bosom of that perilous stuff
> Which weighs upon the heart.   (v. iii. 40–5)

Another slight indication that Shakespeare knew something about the
royal visit to Oxford is that among the subjects suggested for debate
before James were whether babies were influenced in their characters
by their nurses' milk, and whether tobacco had medicinal uses, two
subjects on which the King had strong views.[3] Shakespeare seems to
have echoed James's pamphlet against tobacco and the play contains
many references to breast-feeding.

Between August 1605 and August 1606, when *Macbeth* was performed before James I and King Christian of Denmark, perhaps in a
shortened form, Shakespeare had familiarized himself with James's
Daemonologie and some of his other works, and he had read the account
of Macbeth's career in Holinshed's *Chronicles*. It must have been
immediately obvious to him that he would have to depart from the
historical facts: he could not have James's ancestor conspiring with
Macbeth to assassinate Duncan. He hit on the brilliant idea of fusing
the account of the murder of Duncan, by Macbeth, Banquo, and
others, with the account of Donwald's murder of King Duff. The
fusion was made easier by the fact that both Donwald and Macbeth had
ambitious wives, and that witchcraft was an element in both stories.

The murder of a king while he was a guest of the murderers was a more promising dramatic subject than the assassination of Duncan. Between the story of Donwald (pp. 149 ff.) and the story of Macbeth (pp. 168 ff.), Holinshed tells of a supernatural voice heard by King Kenneth after he has slain his nephew (p. 158) and this may have suggested the voice Macbeth thought he had heard after the murder of Duncan.

There are some indications that Shakespeare consulted two other accounts of Macbeth's reign,[4] by George Buchanan and John Leslie. In Buchanan's *Rerum Scoticarum Historia* the description of the voice heard by Kenneth – 'whether in truth an audible voice from heaven addressed him, as is reported, or whether it were the suggestion of his own guilty mind, as often happens to the wicked' (VI. 309–10) – is slightly closer than Holinshed to the passage in the play. Buchanan's summary of Macbeth's character resembles Shakespeare's portrait, though a poet, in creating a tragic hero, would naturally make him as noble as possible, so as to obtain the maximum dramatic contrast between the man and his deeds. Buchanan tells us that Macbeth's mind 'was daily excited by the importunities of his wife', an idea which could readily have occurred to Shakespeare once he had decided to fuse the Donwald and Macbeth stories. Buchanan explains the degeneration of Macbeth's reign into a tyranny by his feelings of guilt, but here Holinshed seems to be closer to Shakespeare:

> For the pricke of conscience (as it chanceth euer in tyrants, and such as atteine to anie estate by vnrighteous means) caused him euer to feare, least he should be serued of the same cup, as he had ministred to his predecessor.

Many editors have compared Macbeth's lines before the murder:

> This even-handed justice
> Commends th'ingredience of our poison'd chalice
> To our own lips.   (I. vii. 10–12)

Holinshed mentions in the margin of his comment that Macbeth's cruelty was caused by fear. Perhaps the closest parallel between Buchanan's and Shakespeare's words is in the passage describing the elevation of Malcolm to Prince of Cumberland:

> The Prince of Cumberland! that is a step,
> On which I must fall down, or else o'erleap,
> For in my way it lies.   (I. iv. 48–50)

Buchanan remarks:

> This appointment highly incensed Macbeth, who thought it an
> obstacle thrown in the way of his ambition, which – now that he had
> obtained the two first dignities promised by his nocturnal visitors –
> might retard, if not altogether prevent, his arriving at the third, as
> the command of Cumberland was always considered the next step
> to the crown.   (VII. 331)

Buchanan mentions that Macbeth invited Banquo and Fleance to
supper, in a friendly manner ('familiariter'), and this may have suggested Shakespeare's treatment of the invitation.[5]

The other account is by Bishop John Leslie, whose *De Origine,
Moribus, et Rebus Gestis Scotorum* (1578) Shakespeare probably read.[6]
Leslie says that it was devils disguised as women ('seu potius Dae-
monorum qui mulierum personas ementiti') who told Macbeth that
Banquo's descendants would be kings.

Leslie makes no mention of Macbeth's having accomplices in the
murder of Duncan – presumably because he, like Shakespeare, wished
to hush up Banquo's part in it – but he stresses Lady Macbeth's influence
and how she overcomes her husband's fears by producing a practical
plan. He refers to Duncan as 'most holy' and gives a vivid account of
Macbeth's reign of terror, after he had begun by 'indulging the common
people with beneficial laws';

> In the end, however, the conscience of his hideous deeds so worked
> upon him and caused him such fear for his life from those about him,
> that his mildness changed to ruthlessness. He began either openly to
> execute his nobles or to induce them by his cunning to intrigue one
> another's deaths. . . In short, like any tyrant, he went in fear of all
> men, and all men of him.   (tr. Collard, NA, p. 189)

The last sentence is a variation on a famous line of Seneca's.

The strongest reason, however, for believing that Shakespeare had
read Leslie's book is the genealogical tree of Banquo's descendants,
with roots, leaves, and fruit, which appears to have left its mark on the
imagery of Acts III and IV.[7]

There is a good deal of evidence that Shakespeare had been rereading
some of Seneca's plays. There are a number of echoes from *Hercules
Furens*[8] – 'three pairs of neighbouring passages paralleling three pairs
of neighbouring passages' in Seneca's play. One of the echoes, indeed,
is closer to the original than to Jasper Heywood's translation, and it is

fused with an echo from *Hippolytus* in which Tanais is mentioned too.

It has been suggested that the contents of the witches' cauldron were derived from classical sources – Lucan, Ovid's *Metamorphoses* (VII. 262 ff.) or Studley's version of *Medea*. Here there is a herb 'snepped of in depe of sylent nyght', 'the squesed clottered blood/Of serpentes', filthy birds, and the 'durtye stynkyng guttes' of a screech-owl, and Medea invokes Hecate. Professor Inga-Stina Ewbank has persuasively argued[9] that Lady Macbeth's invocation of evil spirits, her desire to be unsexed, and her attempt to stiffen her husband's resolution by declaring that she would have dashed out the brains of her babe, were influenced by Medea's invocation of Hecate, her actual murder of her children, and her desire before the murder to be unsexed.

> If ought of auncient corage still doe dwell within my brest,
> Exile all foolysh Female feare, and pity from thy mynde. . . .
> What euer hurly burly wrought doth *Phasis* vnderstand,
> What mighty monstrous bloudy feate I wrought by Sea or Land:
> The like in *Corynth* shalbe seene in most outragious guise,
> Most hyddious, hatefull, horrible, to heare, or see wyth eyes,
> Most diuelish, desperate, dreadfull deede, yet neuer knowne
>   before,
> Whose rage shall force heauen, earth, and hell to quake and
>   tremble sore . . .
>   sith my wombe hath yeelded fruict, it doth me well behoue,
> The strength and parlous puissaunce of weightier illes to proue. . . .
> How wilt thou from thy spouse depart? as him thou followed hast
> In bloud to bath thy bloudy handes.
>   (*Tenne Tragedies* (1927), II. 57)

As Professor Ewbank says:[10]

> Medea's thoughts move from witchcraft, to royal murder, and to the slaying of her own children, with the courage and cruelty which this requires. The key-line comes in her desire to lose her woman's nature – stressing the 'feare, and pity' which we know are thematic words in *Macbeth* – and a little later this recurs in the cruel paradox that the very fact of her having been the source of life . . . is being turned into a further reason to kill. But before then we have heard how, unsexed and tigerish, she will do bloody deeds, too terrible (as is the case with both Macbeth and Lady Macbeth) to 'see wyth eyes', and how these deeds 'shall force heaven, earth, and hell to

quake and tremble sore', in the kind of universal confusion which Macbeth envisages in the witch-scene (IV. i. 50 ff.). The Medea passage leads up to the central *Macbeth* image of hands bathed in blood.

In Act IV, as Professor Ewbank points out, there is a scene 'in which a mother's breast is linked with the massacre of her own tender children'. Medea 'sheds her own blood as a sacrifice to Hecate, so that she may harden herself to that massacre':

> With naked breast and dugges layde out Ile pricke with sacred
> blade
> Myne arme, that for the bubling bloude an issue may bee made,
> With trilling streames my purple bloude let drop on Th'aulter
> stones
> My tender Childrens crusshed fleshe, and broken broosed bones
> Lerne how to brooke with hardned heart.
> (*Tenne Tragedies* (1927), II. 90)

Another of Seneca's plays, *Agamemnon*, gave Shakespeare another model for Lady Macbeth in the shape of Clytemnestra. Her adage –

> The safest path to mischiefe is by mischiefe open still –

is echoed by Macbeth:[11]

> Things bad begun make strong themselves by ill.
> (III. ii. 55)

The Nurse's adage –

> The thing he feares he doth augment who heapeth syn to syn –
> (*Tenne Tragedies*, II. 108)

might almost be taken as an epigraph for *Macbeth*. Cassandra's fore-seeing of the future in Act V has affinities with two memorable passages in *Macbeth*: the aside in which he describes the onset of temptation and the soliloquy about the imaginary dagger:

> my prophesying spright
> Did neuer yet disclose to mee so notable a sight:
> I see the same. . .
> No vision fond fantasticall my senses doth beguile . . .
> shiuering heere I stande.
> O shall a King be murthered. . . ?

> The gubs of bloude downe dropping on the wynde shall powred
> bee.
>
> (*Tenne Tragedies*, II. 133)

So Macbeth conceives the murder of Duncan:

> My thought, whose murder yet is but fantastical,
> Shakes so my single state of man . . .   (I. iii. 138–9)

and in the later soliloquy he addresses the dagger:

> Art thou not, fatal vision, sensible
> To feeling as to sight? or art thou but
> A dagger of the mind. . . ?
> I see thee yet. . .
> Mine eyes are made the fools o'th'other senses,
> Or else worth all the rest. I see thee still;
> And on thy blade and dudgeon gouts of blood.
>
> (II. i. 36 ff.)

in between these passages Macbeth surmises that Pity

> Shall blow the horrid deed in every eye,
> That tears shall drown the wind.   (I. vii. 24–5)

Cassandra, who sees gouts of blood 'dropping on the wynde', speaks of the murder of Agamemnon as a 'detestable deed'. Apart from these passages, Shakespeare seems to have been influenced by the first chorus of the play, which contains possible germs of 'Tomorrow and tomorrow and tomorrow' ('To morrow . . . One clod of croked care another bryngeth in'); of 'When the hurly-burly's done' ('One hurly burly done'); of 'the way to dusty death' ('downe in dust to lye'), and of several other phrases. It is possible that Shakespeare reread Seneca's plays with the intention of writing a more classical play than his previous tragedies had been and (in Sidney's phrase) to write a play which would make kings fear to be tyrants.[12]

There are some resemblances between *Arden of Feversham* and *Macbeth*.[13] The conscience-stricken soliloquies of Michael before the murder of Arden, Mosbie's soliloquy before the murder (III. v), and the knocking (v. i) were doubtless known to Shakespeare and may have influenced his treatment of Duncan's murder. It has often been pointed out that there are echoes of earlier works of Shakespeare himself in *Macbeth*: parallels have been noted between the stanzas describing Tarquin's rape of Lucrece and Macbeth's murder of Duncan – Macbeth himself makes the comparison;[14] between *2 Henry VI* and several passages in *Macbeth* – here the link was the theme of witchcraft;[15] and between Richard III and Macbeth, both of whom wade through slaughter to a throne, and both of whom are overthrown by the forces of liberation.[16]

But, when all is said, Shakespeare's main source was Holinshed. The major alterations he made are easily explicable on dramatic grounds. Once he had decided to graft on the story of Donwald, he would make Duncan more virtuous and deprive Macbeth of a legitimate grievance. Banquo's innocence was determined by both poetic and politic necessity. Several changes can be explained by reasons of dramatic economy: the battles at the beginning and end of the play are condensed, though it is possible that the confusion in the second scene is due to abbreviation. The ten years of good rule by Macbeth, which earned the praise of the judicious Hooker, are omitted; Macduff offends Macbeth by not attending the coronation and by refusing to come to Court, not as in Holinshed by his refusal to assist in the building of Dunsinane Castle; and the prophecies in Act IV are economically ascribed to the weird sisters, not to 'a certeine witch, whom hee had in great trust' nor to 'certeine wizzards, in whose words he put great confidence'.

Law lists[17] thirty-five incidents not to be found in Holinshed, but most of these resulted inevitably from a dramatization of the story – the initial appearance of the weird sisters, Macbeth's letter, Lady Macbeth's welcome to Duncan, and Banquo's suspicion that Macbeth had murdered Duncan. Others are more significant. According to Holinshed, Macduff comes to England, knowing that his family have been murdered. By making Ross bring the news after the testing of Macduff by Malcolm, Shakespeare makes the scene more plausible, since Malcolm could hardly suspect Macduff of being a spy if he knew that Macbeth had murdered his wife and family.

There is nothing in Holinshed to suggest Lady Macbeth's invocation of the murdering ministers, her sleep-walking, or her death; but, as we have seen, the first of these was probably suggested by Seneca's *Medea*, interfused with ideas of demonology suggested by James I's book and Holinshed's account of the weird sisters. Holinshed has nothing about the knocking on the gate or about the Porter, who doubtless originated in the Porter of Hell Gate,[18] while his references to the trial of Father Garnet and to the practice of equivocation were topical at the time Shakespeare was writing.[19]

Holinshed does not mention the appearance of Banquo's ghost and this may have been suggested by Le Loier's *Treatise of Specters*, the English translation of which was published in 1605.[20] He tells us that after tyrants have put to death 'men of noted vertue and honestie' they are 'perplexed and terrified with a million of feares' (p. 112). Such murderers

> haue bin troubled and tormented with most horrible phantosmes and imaginations, which do com into their heads both sleeping and waking... How often haue they supposed and imagined, that they haue seene sundry visions and apparitions of those whom they haue murthered, or of some others whom they haue feared? (p. 112)

Le Loier gives as an example how King Thierry, having slain Simmachus, saw

> on an euening as hee sate at supper . . . the face of Simmachus in a most horrible shape and fashion, with mustachoes, knitting his browes, frowning with his eyes, biting his lippes for very anger, and looking awry vpon him. (p. 112^v)

From this anecdote and from the invitation of Banquo to the solemn supper, mentioned by Holinshed and Buchanan, Shakespeare created the banquet-scene, but adding the arrival of the murderer, the pledging of the absent guest, the double appearance of the ghost, Lady Macbeth's attempt to control the situation, and the exhaustion of the guilty pair after the departure of the guests.

The testing of Macduff by Malcolm is given in full by Holinshed, following Boece, Bellenden, and Stewart; but Shakespeare omits the fable of the Fox and the Flies and adds other vices to Malcolm's self-accusation, so as to provide contrasting pictures of the good and bad ruler.[21] The passage about Edward the Confessor's touching for the King's Evil comes from the English section of the *Chronicles* and this provided Shakespeare with a good supernatural to contrast with the evil of the weird sisters, as well as a holy king to contrast with the ruler of Scotland. As James I was beginning reluctantly to 'touch'[22] the episode had a topical interest; and dramatically it was a useful bridge between the distrust of Malcolm and Macduff, and the news of the killing of Macduff's family which converts him into an avenger.

James I's *Daemonologie* has clearly left its mark on all those scenes in which the Weird Sisters appear, although Shakespeare probably derived some of his information from Reginald Scot's *Discovery of*

Witchcraft (1584). He would naturally have paid particular attention to his royal patron's views.[23] He would have read that 'as to the diuells foretelling of things to come, it is true that he knows not all things future, but yet that he knowes parte' (Bk I, Cap. 1); that witches might 'foretell what commonweales shall florish or decay; what persons shall be fortunate or vnfortunate, what side shall winne in anie battell' (Bk I, Cap. 4); that the Devil makes himself 'so to be trusted in these little thinges, that he may haue the better commoditie thereafter to deceiue them in the end with a tricke once for all; I meane the euerlasting perdition of their soul and body' (Bk I, Cap. 5); that 'he will make his schollers to creepe in credite with Princes, by foretelling great thinges; parte true, parte false. For if all were false he would tyne credite at all handes; but alwaies doubtsome, as his Oracles were' (Bk I, Cap. 6); that 'at their thirde meeting, he makes a shew to be carefull to performe his promises' (Bk II, Cap. 2); and that he is able to 'decaue vs to our wracke' (Bk I, Cap. 2). So Banquo explains that

> oftentimes, to win us to our harm,
> The instruments of darkness tell us truths,
> Win us with honest trifles, to betray's
> In deepest consequence.   (I. iii. 123–6)

The richness of Macbeth depends partly on the fact that Shakespeare was making use of deeply rooted ideas and images – recalling his earliest experiments as a poet and dramatist, his school reading, and his long familiarity with the Bible. All these things combined with the programme of reading he carried out for the specific purpose of writing the play. He may have read several of James I's works,[24] but his instinct led him to borrow only what he needed for his play. Not the least remarkable thing about Shakespeare's method is that one can always find a good dramatic reason for the inclusion of material that critics have ascribed to the demands of patronage.

✤

✤ 30 ✤

TIMON OF ATHENS

THERE ARE still a large number of unsolved problems with regard to
Timon of Athens – its text, its date, its relationship to the anonymous
Timon, the contrast between the best scenes and the worst, and various
loose ends. This account of the sources of the play must therefore be
very tentative.

Berowne in *Love's Labour's Lost* refers to 'critic Timon'.[1] When
Shakespeare was writing *Julius Caesar*, if not before, he would have
read the account of Timon in Plutarch's Life of Antonius. At some time
he had read Painter's account which mentions Timon's wish to be
buried on the shore 'that the waues and surges mighte beate and vexe
his dead carcas'.[2] These words are echoed by Shakespeare. Plutarch's
Life of Alcibiades is paired with that of Coriolanus, and Shakespeare
used it somewhat perfunctorily for the scenes in which Alcibiades
appears. From the Life of Antonius he took some details of prodigality
and generosity, transferring the incidents to Timon.[3]

The relationship of the anonymous *Timon* to Shakespeare's play is
uncertain. Some think there was a common source; others suppose
that the anonymous writer imitated Shakespeare's play. It was generally
argued that Shakespeare was unlikely to have known a play which was
clearly not the work of a professional. The most probable explanation,
however, is that the play was performed at one of the Inns of Court,
and that Shakespeare had seen it. James C. Bulman has recently argued[4]
that

> the two plays have a number of similarities which cannot be
> accounted for by their sharing of a source – neither Lucian, nor
> Plutarch, nor any Renaissance treatment of the Timon legend.
> Among these similarities are a strong emphasis on Timon in pros-
> perity (three acts in each play); scenes in which his parasitic friends
> refuse to reciprocate his generosity; a mock-banquet at which Timon,
> destitute, rails at them (he pelts them with stones . . .); and the
> presence of a faithful steward who remonstrates against his extra-
> vagance, follows him into exile, and helps him to drive off the
> parasites.

Bulman goes on to suggest that Shakespeare derived 'most, if not all, of his Lucian source material through' the anonymous play. There are, however, a number of points[5] in which Shakespeare appears to be imitating Lucian, whose dialogue was available in Latin (translated by Erasmus), French, and Italian. Honigmann thinks that Shakespeare read it in French or Italian, since *Richesse* and *Richezza* are feminine and Plutus is masculine. But since Plutus meets his dupes dressed in embroideries, wearing a lovely mask, so that they fall in love with his beauty, there is the same suggestion of prostitution in all three versions.[6] Lucian compares the right use of wealth to marriage and prodigality to prostitution. All the women in Shakespeare's play are prostitutes or masquers, since in Athenian society love like everything else is a mere commodity. Even the amiable Timandra, the concubine who buried Alcibiades out of affection for him, becomes a diseased whore. Plutarch tells how[7]

> Timandra went and tooke his bodie which she wrapped vp in the best linnen she had, and buried him as honorably as she could possible, with suche things as she had, and could get together.

Shakespeare doubtless read Montaigne's essay 'Of Democritus and Heraclitus' in which the cynicism of Diogenes is preferred to Timon's misanthropy.[8] He would know, too, the portrait of Diogenes in Lyly's *Campaspe*; but it would appear that Shakespeare introduced Apemantus as a foil to the nobler disillusionment of Timon.

The iterative image, linking flatterers, dogs, and sweets,[9] may serve to indicate that Shakespeare's theme, at least in part, was how to tell a flatterer from a friend, on which Plutarch had a memorable essay;[10] and the gold symbolism, stressed by Wilson Knight,[11] is a means of showing the corruption of society in which the cash-nexus is predominant.[12]

It seems impossible that the play was ever performed in the text which has come down to us. There are bad joins, unexplained incidents, long gaps between announced and actual entrances, and whole scenes which read more like first drafts than memorial reconstructions. Under the circumstances a study of Shakespeare's use of sources is not particularly revealing.

* 31 *

ANTONY AND CLEOPATRA

THE MAIN SOURCE of *Antony and Cleopatra* was, of course, Plutarch's
Life of Antonius. Shakespeare's portrait of his hero is very close to
Plutarch's, much closer, indeed, than the Antony portrayed in *Julius
Caesar*. He made use of almost every incident in the later years of
Antony's life, except the long, absorbing, but irrelevant, account of
the Parthian campaign. One passage, contrasting Antony's present
luxuriousness with his former powers of endurance, is taken from
Plutarch's account of an earlier campaign. Another passage used by
Shakespeare, describing the first meeting of the two lovers, refers to
events before the opening of the play. Both these flashbacks are
exceptionally full of verbal reminiscences, as a comparison will show:[1]

> . . . and moreouer sent *Hircius* and *Pansa*, then Consuls, to driue
> *Antonius* out of Italy. These two Consuls together with *Caesar*, who
> also had an armye, went against *Antonius* that beseeged the citie of
> *Modena*, and there ouerthrew him in battell: but both the Consuls
> were slaine there. *Antonius* flying vpon this ouerthrowe, fell into
> great miserie all at once: but the chiefest want of all other, and that
> pinched him most, was famine. Howbeit he was of such a strong
> nature, that by pacience he would ouercome any aduersitie, and the
> heauier fortune lay vpon him, the more constant shewed he him
> selfe. . . . It was a wonderfull example to the souldiers, to see *Antonius*
> that was brought vp in all finenes and superfluitie, so easily to drinke
> puddle water, and to eate wild frutes and rootes: and moreouer it is
> reported, that euen as they passed the Alpes, they did eate the barcks
> of trees, and such beasts, as neuer man tasted of their flesh before.

> Antony,
> Leave thy lascivious wassails. When thou once
> Was beaten from Modena, where thou slew'st
> Hirtius and Pansa, consuls, at thy heel
> Did famine follow; whom thou fought'st against,
> Though daintily brought up, with patience more
> Than savages could suffer. Thou didst drink

The stale of horses and the gilded puddle
Which beasts could cough at. Thy palate then did deign
The roughest berry on the rudest hedge;
Yea, like the stag when snow the pasture sheets,
The barks of trees thou brows'd. On the Alps,
It is reported thou didst eat strange flesh,
Which some did die to look on. And all this –
It wounds thine honour that I speak it now –
Was borne so like a soldier that thy cheek
So much as lank'd not.   (I. iv. 55–71)

Although Shakespeare follows North's translation very closely, his additions make all the difference: the lines about the 'stale of horses and the gilded puddle', the line about the stag, and the final phrase of the passage.

The Cydnus passage is put into the mouth of Enorbarbus at the moment in the play when Antony is to marry Octavia and desert Cleopatra. The tribute of the cynical soldier to the Queen's enchantment, driving him to conceits which are not in the source, is a masterly dramatic stroke.[2]

Therefore when she was sent vnto by diuers letters, both from *Antonius* him selfe, and also from his frendes, she made so light of it, and mocked *Antonius* so much, that she disdained to set forward otherwise, but to take her barge in the riuer of *Cydnus*, the poope whereof was of gold, the sailes of purple, and the owers of siluer, which kept stroke in rowing after the sounde of the musicke of flutes, howboyes, citherns, violls, and such other instruments as they played vpon in the barge. And now for the person of her selfe: she was layed vnder a pauillion of cloth of gold of tissue, apparelled and attired like the goddesse *Venus*, commonly drawen in picture: and hard by her, on either hand of her, pretie faire boyes apparelled as painters doe set forth god *Cupide*, with little fannes in their hands, with the which they fanned wind vpon her. Her Ladies and gentlewomen also, the fairest of them were apparelled like the nymphes *Nereides* (which are the mermaides of the waters) and like the *Graces*, some stearing the helme, others tending the tackle and ropes of the barge, out of the which there came a wonderfull passing sweete sauor of perfumes, that perfumed the wharfes side, pestered with innumerable multitudes of people. Some of them followed the barge all alongest the riuers side: others also ranne out of the citie to see her comming in. So that in thend, there ranne such multitudes of people one after an other to see her, that *Antonius* was left post alone in the market place, in his Imperiall seate to geue audience: and there went a rumor in the peoples mouthes, that the goddesse *Venus* was come to play with the god *Bacchus*, for the generall good of all *Asia*.

> The barge she sat in, like a burnish'd throne,
> Burn'd on the water. The poop was beaten gold;
> Purple the sails, and so perfumed that
> The winds were love-sick with them; the oars were silver,
> Which to the tune of flutes kept stroke, and made
> The water which they beat to follow faster,
> As amorous of their strokes. For her own person,
> It beggar'd all description. She did lie
> In her pavillion, cloth-of-gold, of tissue,
> O'erpicturing that Venus where we see
> The fancy out-work nature. On each side her
> Stood pretty dimpled boys, like smiling Cupids,
> With divers-colour'd fans, whose wind did seem
> To glow the delicate cheeks which they did cool,
> And what they undid did.
> *Agr.*   O, rare for Antony!
> *Eno.* Her gentlewomen, like the Nereides,
> So many mermaids, tended her i'th'eyes,
> And made their bends adornings. At the helm
> A seeming mermaid steers. The silken tackle
> Swell with the touches of those flower-soft hands
> That yarely frame the office. From the barge
> A strange invisible perfume hits the sense
> Of the adjacent wharfs. The city cast
> Her people out upon her; and Antony,
> Enthron'd i'th'market-place, did sit alone,
> Whistling to th'air; which, but for vacancy,
> Had gone to gaze on Cleopatra too,
> And made a gap in nature.   (II. ii. 195–222)

The vivid opening lines are an addition of the poet. He also adds the description of the sails and the oars, 'metaphysical' hyperboles which 'diffuse a tone of luxury and sensuousness throughout the passage';[3] and in these additions and in the last three lines of the passage[4]

the successive elements – the winds, the water, the air – are represented all as succumbing to the enchantment of love which breathes
from the great Queen and her burning barge; and by this varied
return on a single motive North's inconsequential panorama is
given an organic unity.

Most striking of all, perhaps, is the suggestion that Cleopatra was more
beautiful than Venus herself. Plutarch mentions that Antonius was
reputed to be descended from Hercules, that Cleopatra dressed as the
goddess Isis, and that there was a rumour after the first meeting of the
lovers that Venus was come to play with Bacchus 'for the general
good of all Asia'. Shakespeare makes use of all these suggestions of
divinity, but mainly indirectly. Antony refers to the death of Hercules
when he is himself meditating suicide; the mysterious music under the
earth is said to signify the departure of Hercules from Antony; and
Cleopatra is termed 'our terrene moon'.

The character of Enobarbus is virtually Shakespeare's creation.
Plutarch tells us little about him except that

> he being sicke of an agewe when he went and tooke a little boate to
> goe to *Caesars* campe, *Antonius* was very sory for it, but yet he sent
> after him all his caryage, trayne, and men: and the same *Domitius*,
> as though he gaue him to vnderstand that he repented his open
> treason, he died immediately after.

This was before the battle of Actium. In the play Enobarbus refuses to
desert even after this battle. It is not until the end of Act III that he
decides to leave his master. He is still present when Antony says farewell
to his servants (IV. ii), and Antony's commendation of their loyalty
has therefore a note of unconscious irony. Shakespeare makes Enobarbus die, not of an ague, but of a broken heart.

A number of other works have been suggested as subsidiary sources
of the play. It has been argued,[5] for example, that in his treatment of
Cleopatra's death Shakespeare was influenced by Chaucer's treatment
of her as one of love's martyrs, and also by the ode of Horace celebrating
the battle of Actium (I. 37).[6] There Cleopatra's courage and nobility
are portrayed by an admiring enemy, and Horace shows her determination to avoid being exhibited in a Roman triumph:

> Quae generosius
> perire quaerens nec muliebriter
> expavit ensem nec latentis

classe cita reparavit oras;
ausa et iacentem visere regiam
voltu sereno, fortis et asperas
tractare serpentes, ut atrum
corpore combiberet venenum,
deliberata morte ferocior;
saevis Liburnis scilicet invidens
privata deduci superbo
non humilis mulier triumpho.

But although Shakespeare was doubtless acquainted with this poem, and certainly acquainted with Chaucer's, he could have developed independently from Plutarch's account his presentation of Cleopatra's suicide.

Professor Ernest Schanzer in *Shakespeare's Appian* (1956) and again in *The Problem Plays of Shakespeare* (1963) has convincingly argued that Appian was another source. The fifth book of Appian's history deals with events up to the death of Sextus Pompeius. The passages relating to Lucius, Antony's brother, in the play can hardly be based on Plutarch alone, for he does not make clear, as Shakespeare and Appian both do, that Lucius had republican sympathies. Antony asks Octavius:

> Did he not rather
> Discredit my authority with yours,
> And make the wars alike against my stomach,
> Having alike your cause?   (II. ii. 52–5)

Appian, but neither Goulard nor Plutarch, shows that Lucius was fighting against the triumvirate for the restoration of the republic: he never claimed to be fighting in Antony's name, and Antony is justified in claiming that he had the same cause as that of Octavius. But Fulvia, on the other hand, as Appian makes clear, used Antony's grievances as her justification for her wars, although her real motive was the desire to get him to return to Italy, so as to detach him from Cleopatra. The different war-aims of Lucius and Fulvia are thus reflected in the play. As Antony states, 'my brother never/Did urge me in his act' (II. ii. 49–50); and Fulvia 'To have me out of Egypt made wars here' (II. ii. 99). The last point, however, is made by Goulard in his life of Octavius, as well as by Appian.

The borrowings from Appian, relating to Sextus Pompeius, are equally significant, and they are fully discussed by MacCallum.[7]

Plutarch mentions very briefly Sextus Pompeius' inroads on Italy.
Appian gives this account of his followers:

> Out of *Italy* all things were not quiet, for *Pompey*, by resorte of
> condemned Citizens, and auntient possessioners, was greatly
> increased, both in mighte, and estimation: for they that feared their
> life, or were spoyled of their goodes, or lyked not the present state,
> fledde all to hym . . . beside a repayre of yong men, desirous of
> gayne and seruice, not caring vnder whome they went, bycause
> they were all *Romanes*, sought vnto him.
>
> (Schanzer, *Shakespeare's Appian*, Bk v, 76–7)

This appears to be the source of two passages in the play:[8]

> The condemn'd Pompey,
> Rich in his father's honour, creeps apace
> Into the hearts of such as have not thriv'd
> Upon the present state, whose numbers threaten;
> And quietness, grown sick of rest, would purge
> By any desperate change . . .   (I. iii. 49–54)

and 'flush youth revolt' (I. iv. 52). The verbal parallel ('present state')
and the absence of any such account in Plutarch are fairly conclusive.

Antony expresses indignation at Pompey's murder (III. v. 18–19).
Plutarch does not mention the murder; Goulard states that it was
carried out by Antony's commandment; Appian, however, tells us:

> There bee that saye, that *Plancus* and not *Antony*, did commaunde
> hym to dye, whyche beeyng president of *Syria*, had *Antonyes* signet,
> and in great causes wrote letters in hys name. Some thynke it was
> done with *Antonyes* knowledge, he fearyng the name of *Pompey*, or
> for *Cleopatra*, who fauoured *Pompey* the great.

Appian at least allows the possibility of Antony's innocence.

There is some evidence that Shakespeare had read *Antonie*, the
Countess of Pembroke's translation of Garnier's *Marc Antoine*.[9] The
clearest parallel was pointed out by John Dover Wilson.[10] In the
Argument, it is said that Antony 'for knitting a straiter bond of amitie
betweene' him and Octavius 'had taken to wife *Octavia*'. Agrippa in
Shakespeare's play in proposing the marriage uses a similar phrsae:

> To hold you in perpetual amity,
> To make you brothers, and to knit your hearts

> With an unslipping knot, take Antony
> Octavia to his wife.   (II. ii. 129–32)

In a later scene Enobarbus prophesies that

> You shall find the band that seems to tie their friendship together
> will be the very strangler of their amity.   (II. vi. 116–18)

The verbal links are substantial: 'knitting'/'knit'; 'bond'/'band';
'amity'; 'take to wife'.

In the first scene of *Antonie* the hero speaks of breaking from
Cleopatra:

> Thou breakest at length from thence, as one encharm'd
> Breakes from th'enchaunter –   (79–80)

lines which, as Professor Schanzer has shown,[11] may well have suggested the line:

> I must from this enchanting Queen break off.
>   (I. ii. 125)

One chorus in *Antonie* describes the operations of the Nile, mentioning
'*Nilus*' mire', the 'fatt slime' left behind, and the resulting rich harvest:

> making therby greatest growe
> busie reapers ioyfull paine,
> when his flouds do highest flow.

Shakespeare likewise speaks of 'Nilus' slime' and 'Nilus' mud', and
mentions also that the greater the flood the greater is the harvest:

> The higher Nilus swells
> The more it promises; as it ebbs, the seedsman
> Upon the slime and ooze scatters his grain,
> And shortly comes to harvest.   (II. vii. 20–3)

Cleopatra's lines –

> Thy eies, two Sunnes, the lodging place of loue,
> Which yet for tents to warlike *Mars* did serue –
>   (1941–2)

and the line describing Cleopatra –

> Her beamy eies, two Sunnes of this our world – (715)

may have suggested the opening speech in Shakespeare's play:[12]

> Those his goodly eyes,
> That o'er the files and musters of the war
> Have glow'd like plated Mars, now bend, now turn
> The office and devotion of their view
> Upon a tawny front . . .   (I. i. 2–6)

and also the description of Antony in the last scene:

> His face was as the heav'ns, and therein stuck
> A sun and moon . . .
>   his rear'd arm
> Crested the world.   (V. ii. 79 ff.)

Finally, as MacCullum noted,[13] the lines at the very end of *Antonie* –

> A thousand kisses, thousand thousand more
> Let you my mouth for honors farewell giue –
>   (1997–8)

spoken by Cleopatra about the dead Antonius, resemble words spoken by the dying Antony in Shakespeare's play:

>   until
> Of many thousand kisses the poor last
> I lay upon thy lips.   (IV. xv. 19–21)

There is stronger evidence that Shakespeare made use of Daniel's *Cleopatra* and his *Letter from Octavia*. The latter poem, which first appeared in 1599, has an Argument containing an account of Antony's marriage to Octavia:[14]

> For *Antonie* hauing yet vpon him the fetters of *Ægypt*, layd on by the power of a more incomparable beauty, could admit no new Lawes into the state of his affection, or dispose of himselfe, being not himselfe, but as hauing his heart turned Eastward, whither the poynt of his desires were directed, toucht with the strongest allurements that ambition, and a licentious soueraignty could draw a man vnto: could not truly descend to the priuate loue of a ciuill nurtred Matron, whose entertainment bounded with modesty, and the nature of her education, knew not to clothe her affections in any other colours, then the plaine habit of truth.

So, in the play, Antony exclaims:

> These strong Egyptian fetters I must break,
> Or lose myself in dotage.   (I. ii. 113–14)

Later on, when the marriage with Octavia has been arranged, Antony says:

> though I make this marriage for my peace,
> I'th'East my pleasure lies   (II. iii. 40–1)

Maecenas refers to Octavia's modesty (II. ii. 245) and Enobarbus points out that since she 'is of a holy, cold, and still conversation' (II. vi. 119), Antony 'will to his Egyptian dish again'.

Octavia in Daniel's poem (st. 2) imagines how her letter will reach Antony:

> Although perhaps, these my complaints may come
> Whilst thou in th'armes of that incestuous Queene,
> The staine of Ægypt, and the shame of Rome
> Shalt dallying sit, and blush to haue them seene:
> Whilst proud disdainfull she, gessing from whome
> The message came, and what the cause hath beene,
>   Will scorning say, Faith this comes from your Deere,
>   Now Sir you must be shent for staying heere.

This may have given a hint for Cleopatra's words about the messengers from Rome in the first scene of the play:

> Nay, hear them, Antony.
> Fulvia perchance is angry. . . .
> Call in the messengers. As I am Egypt's Queen,
> Thou blushest, Antony, and that blood of thine
> Is Caesar's homager. Else so thy cheek pays shame
> When shrill-tongu'd Fulvia scolds.   (I. i. 19–20, 29–32)

In a later stanza (36) Octavia imagines Cleopatra's wiles:

> She armes her teares, the ingins of deceit
> And all her batterie, to oppose my loue,
> And bring thy comming grace to a retreit,
> The power of all her subtilty to proue:
> Now pale and faint she languishes, and strait
> Seemes in a sound, vnable more to moue:
>   Whilst her instructed fellowes ply thine eares
>   With forged passions, mixed with fained teares.

This is a good description of the Cleopatra presented in I. iii, II. v, and in Act IV, and although Plutarch gives a similar account, Daniel's is closer to Shakespeare's.

It is probable that Shakespeare had read the earlier version of *Cleopatra*.[15] There are a number of details common to both plays, which are not to be found in Plutarch. Daniel in his first act stresses Cleopatra's determination to hoodwink Caesar by committing suicide. She is particularly concerned at the thought of Octavia watching her disgrace:

> I that liu'd and raign'd a Queene,
> Do scorne to buy my life at such a rate,
> That I should vnderneath my selfe be seene,
> Basely induring to suruiue my state:
> That Rome should see my scepter-bearing hands
> Behind me bound, and glory in my teares;
> That I should passe whereas *Octauia* stands,
> To view my misery, that purchas'd hers.   (63–70)

So in Shakespeare's play Cleopatra tells Antony:

> Your wife Octavia, with her modest eyes
> And still conclusion, shall acquire no honour
> Demuring upon me.   (IV. xv. 27–9)

Later on, she tells Proculeius:

> Know sir, that I
> Will not wait pinion'd at your master's court,
> Nor once be chastis'd with the sober eye
> Of dull Octavia.   (V. ii. 52–5)

Daniel makes Cleopatra say (50–4) that Caesar:

> seekes to entertaine my life with wiles.
> But *Caesar*, it is more then thou canst do,
> Promise, flatter, threaten extreamity,
> Imploy thy wits and all thy force thereto,
> I have both hands, and will, and I can die.

The last line combined with several references to resolution – 'For who can stay a minde resolu'd to die' (1183); 'For what I will I am resolu'd' (1449–1450); 'her resolution' (1592) – to make Shakespeare's line (IV. xv. 49):

> My resolution and my hands I'll trust . . .

and the last lines of Act IV:

> we have no friend
> But resolution, and the briefest end.

As Professor Farnham points out,[16] Shakespeare follows Daniel in making Proculeius advise Cleopatra to sue for Caesar's grace, in making her refer to the violation of her privilege of dying, and in having her send a message to Caesar, declaring that she wishes to die.

Cleopatra temporizes with Caesar and soothes his pleasure (89) for the sake of her children. Shakespeare makes Caesar threaten to kill her children if she commits suicide (v. ii. 130–1).

One scene in the play, where Seleucus accuses Cleopatra of lying about the amount of her treasure is sometimes misinterpreted by commentators. Plutarch makes it perfectly clear – and this was certainly Shakespeare's intention also – that Cleopatra is acting a part:

> Then she sodainly altered her speache, and prayed him to pardon her, as though she were affrayed to dye, and desirous to liue . . . and so he tooke his leaue of her, supposing he had deceiued her, but in deede he was deceiued him selfe.

This is reinforced by the marginal gloss: 'Cleopatra finely deceiueth Octauius Caesar, as though she desired to liue'. In other words Cleopatra had fully determined on suicide: she pretended about the treasure to make Caesar believe she wished to live. The versions given by Daniel, by Jodelle in *Cleopatre captive*, and by Shakespeare are closely based on Plutarch's account. Daniel is the only one of the four writers who does not suggest that Cleopatra was tricking Caesar:[17]

> Alas, said she, O *Caesar*: is not this a great shame and reproche, that thou hauing vouchsaued to take the peines to come vnto me, and hast done me this honor, poore wretche, and caitife creature, brought into this pitiefull and miserable estate: and that mine owne seruants should come now to accuse me, though it may be I have reserued some iuells and trifles meete for women, but not for me (poore soule) to set out my selfe withall, but meaning to giue some pretie presents and gifts vnto *Octauia* and *Liuia*, that they making meanes and intercession for me to thee, thou mightest yet extend thy fauor and mercie vpon me?

Daniel has the following version of the speech (684–94):

> Ah *Caesar*, what a great indignity
> Is this, that here my vassall subiect stands

T'accuse me to my Lord of trechery?
If I reseru'd some certaine womens toyes,
Alas it was not for my self (God knowes),
Poore miserable soule, that little ioyes
In trifling ornaments, in outward showes.
But what I kept, I kept to make my way
Vnto thy *Liuia* and *Octauias* grace,
That thereby in compassion moouèd, they
Might mediate thy fauour in my case.

The corresponding passage in Jodelle's play is as follows:[18]

CLE. A! faux meurdrier! a! faux traistre! arraché
Sera le poil de ta teste cruelle.
Que pleust aux Dieux que ce fust ta cervelle!
Tien, traistre, tien.

SEL.   O Dieux!

CLE.   O chose detestable!
Un serf, un serf!

OCT.   Mais chose émerveillable
D'un coeur terrible!

CLE.   Et quoy, m'accuses tu?
Me pensois tu veufve de ma vertu
Comme d'Antoine? a a! traistre.

SEL.   Retiens la,
Puissant Cesar, retiens la doncq.

CLE.   Voila
Tous mes biensfaits. Hou! le dueil qui m'efforce
Donne a mon coeur langoureux telle force,
Que je pourrois, ce me semble, froisser
Du poing tes os, et tes flancs crevasser
A coups de pied.

OCT.   O quel grinsant courage!
Mais rien n'est plus furieux que la rage
D'un coeur de femme. Et bien, quoy, Cleopatre?
Estes vous point ja saoule de le battre!
Fuy t'en, ami, fuy t'en.

CLE.   Mais quoy, mais quoy?
Mon Empereur, est-il un tel esmoy
Au monde encor que ce paillard me donne?
Sa lacheté ton esprit mesme estonne,

Comme je croy, quand moy, Roine d'ici,
De mon vassal suis accusee ainsi,
Que toy, Cesar, as daigné visiter,
Et par ta voix à repos inciter,
He! si j'avois retenu des joyaux,
Et quelque part de mes habits royaux,
L'aurois-je fait pour moy, las, malheureuse!
Moy, qui de moy ne suis plus curieuse?
Mais telle estoit ceste esperance mienne
Qu'à ta Livie et ton Octavienne
Des ces joyaux le present je feroy,
Et leurs pitiez ainsi pourchasseroy
Pour (n'estant point de mes presens ingrates)
Envers Cesar estre mes advocates.   (III. 244–78)

Shakespeare's lines are as follows:

O Caesar, what a wounding shame is this,
That thou vouchsafing here to visit me,
Doing the honour of thy lordliness
To one so meek, that mine own servant should
Parcel the sum of my disgraces by
Addition of his envy! Say, good Caesar,
That I some lady trifles have reserv'd,
Immoment toys, things of such dignity
As we greet modern friends withal; and say
Some nobler token I have kept apart
For Livia and Octavia, to induce
Their mediation, must I be unfolded
With one that I have bred?   (v. ii. 158–70)

Daniel reduces the violence of Cleopatra's attack on her treasurer, and disposes of it in three lines; the epithet 'ungrateful', though a natural addition to Plutarch's words, could have been suggested by 'Voila/Tous mes biensfaits'; he uses Jodelle's word, 'vassal'; and he follows him in inverting Plutarch's 'unto Octavia and Livia' and in using the pronoun 'thy':

à ta Livie et ton Octavienne . . .
Unto thy *Livia* and *Octavias* grace.

Shakespeare, in the corresponding scene, follows North's translation closely. He transfers Cleopatra's physical violence to another scene

(II. v) where she maltreats the messenger from Rome. But the verbal parallels with North are sufficiently obvious: 'shame' (158); 'vouche-saved'/'vouchsaving' (159); 'mine own servant' (161); 'trifles' (164). Shakespeare also echoes two of Daniel's words – 'toys' (165), 'mediate'/'mediation' (169) – and he, like Daniel and Jodelle, stresses the ingratitude of Seleucus.

In one respect Shakespeare is closer to Jodelle than he is to North or Daniel. North does not put any abusive language into Cleopatra's mouth; Daniel's Cleopatra calls Seleucus a 'vile, ungrateful wretch', a 'vassal', and a 'caitife' – the last is transferred from Cleopatra's words about herself. But Jodelle's heroine calls Seleuque a variety of names – 'faux meurdrier . . . faux traistre . . . un serf . . . ce paillard' – and she refers to his 'lacheté'. So Shakespeare's Cleopatra says:

> O slave, of no more trust
> Than love that's hir'd! . . .
> Slave, soulless villain, dog!
> O rarely base!   (v. ii. 153–4, 156–7)

Plutarch makes a good deal of the fact that Dolabella 'did beare no euil will vnto Cleopatra' and of his warning that she was to be sent to Rome within three days. Daniel's Dolabella expresses his admiration of Cleopatra to Octavius and sends her a love-letter with the information she wants. Shakespeare, more dramatically, makes Dolabella inform Cleopatra by word of mouth, but his love is not directly expressed. Daniel's treatment, however, left one impression on Shakespeare. Cleopatra says (1094–6):

> I thanke the man, both for his loue and letter;
> The one comes fit to warne me thus before,
> But for th'other, I must die his debter.

So Shakespeare's Cleopatra tells Dolabella:

> I shall remain your debtor.   (v. ii. 204)

Daniel's Cleopatra complains of the difficulty of suicide (1174–83):

> But what haue I saue these bare hands to do it?
> And these weake fingers are not yron-poynted:
> They cannot pierce the flesh being put vnto it,
> And I of all meanes else am disappointed.
> But yet I must a way and meanes seeke, how
> To come vnto thee, whatsoere I do,

O Death, art thou so hard to come by now,
That we must pray, intreate, and seeke thee too?
But I will finde thee wheresoere thou lie,
For who can stay a minde resolu'd to die?

There are similar passages in Shakespeare:

My resolution and my hands I'll trust (IV. xv. 49)

Quick, quick, good hands!   (V. ii. 39)

Where art thou, Death?
Come hither, come!   (V. ii. 46–7)

mine nails
Are stronger than mine eyes   (V. ii. 222–3)

The Messenger describes how Cleopatra decks herself for death:

Euen as she was when on thy cristall streames,
Cleare *Cydnos*, she did shew what earth could shew; . . .
Even as she went at first to meete her loue.
So goes she now at last againe to finde him.
But that first, did her greatnes onely proue,
This last her loue, that could not liue behind him. (1447 ff.)

So Shakespeare's Cleopatra declares:

I am again for Cydnus
To meet Mark Antony.   (V. ii. 227–8)

Daniel's Cleopatra speaks several times of the easy death afforded by the asps –

That with one gentle touch canst free our breath
(1518)

thou best freest vs from our liues worst terror,
In sweetly bringing soules to quiet rest.   (1523–4)

That open canst with such an easie key
The doore of life; come gentle cunning thiefe. . .
(1534–5)

But still in one same sweet vnaltered cheare. . .
(1617)

Shakespeare's Cleopatra describes her death

As sweet as balm, as soft as air, as gentle. . .

(v. ii. 309)

Daniel describes how Honour leads forth (1579–81)

> Bright Immortalitie in shining armour:
> Thorow the rayes of whose cleare glory, she
> Might see lifes basenesse. . .

and Cleopatra speaks of 'That enemy, base Life' (1600). Shakespeare's Cleopatra likewise contrasts her 'immortal longings' (v. ii. 280) with her baseness in dying after Iras (v. ii. 299).

The touch of the asp proves that the gold of Cleopatra's love is pure (1612) as the death of Shakespeare's Cleopatra makes her Antony's wife. As Daniel's Cleopatra dies (1651–4) –

> in her sinking downe she wries
> The Diademe which on her head she wore:
> Which *Charmion* . . . espies,
> And hastes to right it as it was before.

Charmian in the corresponding scene in Shakespeare's play says:

> Your crown's awry;
> I'll mend it and then play.   (v. ii. 316–17)

The evidence that Daniel revised his play after seeing a performance of Shakespeare's is much less conclusive. The date of the latter is not known, and it may have been written after the 1607 edition of Daniel's play. Daniel in this revision presents the death of Cleopatra on the stage instead of describing it by messenger and he introduces Dircetus (as Garnier had done) to relate the death of Antony to Octavius. The account of the hoisting of his body into the monument may owe something to a stage performance:[19]

> Shee drawes him vp in rowles of taffaty
> T'a window at the top, which did allow
> A little light vnto her monument.
> There *Charmion*, and poore *Eras*, two weake maids
> Foretir'd with watching, and their mistresse care,
> Tug'd at the pulley, hauing n'other aydes,
> And vp they hoise the swounding body there
> Of pale *Antonius* showring out his blood
> On th'vnder-lookers, which there gazing stood.

(244–52)

There are two fairly close parallels. Cleopatra, tugging on the pulley, is said to be heavier by her grief:

> when shee a fresh renewes
> Her hold, and with reinforced power doth straine,
> And all the weight of her weake bodie laies,
> Whose surcharg'd heart more then her body wayes.

In the same circumstances, Shakespeare's Cleopatra cries:

> How heavy weighs my lord!
> Our strength is all gone into heaviness;
> That makes the weight.   (IV. xv. 32–4)

Later in the same scene Dircetus quotes Antony's warning:

> And none about Octauius trust, said hee,
> But *Proculeius*: he's an honest man.   (280–1)

Shakespeare's Antony likewise says:

> None about Caesar trust but Proculeius.
>
> (IV. xv. 48)

North's version is not so close: 'that chiefly she should trust *Proculeius* aboue any man else about *Caesar*'. There would seem to be no way of proving which poet was indebted to the other; but it is possible that Shakespeare imitated Daniel's first version of *Cleopatra* and that Daniel then returned the compliment.

We are assured that the portrait of Cleopatra owes 'more to a study of prostitutes than to a knowledge of how even the worst queens behave'. One of the scenes which occasioned this verdict is the one where Cleopatra questions the Messenger about Octavia, asking him the colour of her hair, her height, her voice, her gait, her age, and her face. It so happens that when Mary, Queen of Scots, sent James Melville to the English Court, Elizabeth asked a whole series of questions about her rival:[20]

> Who, she asked, was the fairer, Mary or she? a question Melville tried to dodge by declaring that she was the fairest Queen in England and theirs the fairest Queen in Scotland. As Elizabeth was not to be put off, he replied that they were both the fairest ladies of their courts, but the Queen of England was whiter. . . . Next she wanted to know who was the higher. Mary was, answered Melville. Then is

she over high, retorted Elizabeth; she herself being neither over high nor over low.

Questions followed about Mary's skill in playing and dancing, and Elizabeth later demonstrated her own skill in both respects. When one considers, too, Elizabeth's occasional acts of violence, one is bound to wonder whether Shakespeare was so ignorant of how queens, good or bad, behave.

Another critic, Daniel Stempel, thinks that 'lass unparalleled' is a sign that Cleopatra cannot rise above the vices of her sex; and, in commenting on her self-description, –

> a woman, and commanded
> By such poor passion as the maid that milks
> And does the meanest chares –   (IV. xv. 73–5)

declares that the lines mean that she is 'governed by no specifically noble passion'.[21] Once again Elizabeth's own words show that Shakespeare knew better than his critic. In a speech to Parliament in 1576, Elizabeth replied to a petition that she should take a husband:

> If I were a milk-maid, with a pail on my arm, whereby my private person might be little set by, I would not forsake that poor and single state to match with the greatest monarch.

It is not, of course, claimed that Shakespeare had heard of Elizabeth's enquiries about her rival, or even that he was echoing her speech to Parliament. It is merely suggested that in two scenes where Cleopatra's conduct has been stigmatized as unregal, Shakespeare came uncannily close to contemporary examples of queenly behaviour – closer, indeed, than Samuel Daniel did in his statuesque portrait.

Michael Lloyd has shown[22] that Shakespeare consulted Plutarch's essay in his *Moralia* on Isis and Osiris and that he refreshed his memory of *The Golden Asse* with its account of the worship of Isis.

Finally, it may be mentioned that Dr Ethel Seaton pointed out some curious echoes of the book of Revelation.[23] It is possible that the apocalyptic imagery was designed to raise the stature of the protagonists, but the echoes are more likely to have been unconscious.

32
CORIOLANUS

SHAKESPEARE's knowledge of the Coriolanus story probably dated from his schooldays. The story is told by Livy (Bk 2) and Shakespeare could have refreshed his memory of it when Philemon Holland's translation of it was published in 1601. But the fable of the Belly and the Body's Members is to be found not only in Livy, but also in Erasmus' *Copia*, in Aesop's *Fables*, and in a collection by Caxton, as well as in Plutarch's *Lives*. In later years Shakespeare came to know the versions given by Sidney in his *Defence of Poesy* and by Camden in his *Remaines*, as we can tell from verbal echoes of both;[1] and, of course, he read the whole of the Coriolanus story as given by Livy and Plutarch. At some time between 1588 and 1608, he had come across William Averell's *Meruailous Combat of Contrarieties* in which the fable was used as a warning against sedition at the time of the Spanish Armada.[2] The actual vocabulary of Menenius' fable owes more to Averell's version than to any other. Averell's Tongue, for example, asks:

> Will you see the patterne of a gluttonous Pantrey, then looke vpon the Bellie, for he is a smoking kitchin of variable viands . . . the breathing Lunges, like blowing bellowes, lie by the Liuer as by a Forge . . . and the entrayles like a sinck conuay the filth downe the Fundament. . . . Wherefore Bretheren, and fellow members, let vs not be subiect to two such Cormorants, which regarde not our benefit, but theyr owne profit. (f. A3^{v})

Apart from the identical words – 'viands', 'lungs', 'sink', and 'cormorant' are all used in Shakespeare's retelling of the fable (I. i. 94–152) – 'Pantrey' may have suggested 'cupboarding' and 'storehouse'. On other pages of Averell's pamphlet all the significant words used by Menenius appear, except 'smile' (105) and 'gulf' (96).

The story of Coriolanus was frequently used in the years immediately before Shakespeare wrote his play by writers on political theory. Some account of these will give an idea of the climate of opinion to which the play was a deliberate contribution.

In 1604 a volume was published entitled *Foure Paradoxes, or Politique Discourses*, containing two essays by Thomas Digges, and two by Dudley Digges, his son, and the stepson of Shakespeare's testamentary overseer.[3] One of Dudley's essays is in praise of the soldier's profession. In the other he argues 'That warre sometimes' is 'lesse hurtfull, and more to be wisht in a well gouernd State than peace'. War, he declares, is better than 'luxurious idleness' and peace is apt to lead to

> dissention, when idlenesse ministers each actiue humour fit occasion of working, to the indangering of diseased, to the distempering of most healthfull bodies, when quiet security giues busie heads leasure to deuide the common-wealth into contentious factions.
>
> (p. 102)

With this may be compared the dialogue on the advantages of war in *Coriolanus*, IV. v. Digges proceeds to discuss the use of war as a means of curing internal dissensions, his main example being the story of Coriolanus, taken directly from North's Plutarch, though with the insertion of one phrase from Livy:[4]

> These enmities haue been instruments in most Countries ouer-throwes, they ouertake vs in our securitie like secret fiers in the night, and are therefore more to be feared, they steale on vs by degrees hidden in the deepnesse of our rest, like the consumption in a body vnpurged, vnexercised, that is indeed lesse painefull yet proues more mortall than most diseases . . . a perfect remedie to dissipate the other, if wee bee not to our selues defectiue; to wit, forreine warre, a souereigne medicine for domesticall inconueniences. . . The generall daunger will soone withdraw mens mindes from intestine garboiles to resist the generall mischief, both which appeared in that wise proceeding of the *Senate* of *Rome* in *Coriolanus* time that by this means appeased all diuisions, euen then when as *Liuie* obserues heat of contention betwixt the people and nobilitie had made, *Ex vna ciuitate duas*. . . . For the populousnesse of that Citie, by reason of their peace occasioning a dearth and famine, and their idlenesse stirring vp lewd felowes to exasperate the desperate need and enuious malice of the meaner sort, against the nobility, whose pride and luxurie grown through sloth intolerable, caused them to contemne and iniure the poorer people, in the end the fire brake forth hard to be quenched, and then the *Senate* hauing as I may say bought wit by this deare experience, were at length

enforced to flie to this medicine, which wisely applied before, had well preuented all those causes, and their vnhappie effectes. Then they resolued on a warre with the *Volsces* to ease their City of that dearth, by diminishing their number, and appease those tumultuous broyles, by drawing poore with rich, and the meane sort with the Nobilitie, into one campe, one seruice, and one selfesame daunger: sure means to procure sure loue and quietnesse in a contentious Commonwealth, as that of *Rome* was at that time.

Yet euen then there wanted not home tarrying hous-doues, two peace-bred tribunes *Sicimus* [*sic*] and *Brutus*, hindred that resolution calling it crueltie, and it may be some now will condemne this course, as changing for the worse: some that wil much mislike a body breaking-out should take receipts of quick-siluer or mercurie, that may endanger life: yet they cannot but knowe euen those poysons outwardly applied are souereigne medicines to purge and clense, and therefore hauing a good Physition, I must professe, I thinke it much better to take yeerely Physicke.   (pp. 103–5)

We cannot be sure that Shakespeare had read *Foure Paradoxes*, though he might have done so out of neighbourly interest. In *Coriolanus* he uses the metaphor of 'breaking out' in three places, though his use of it is not confined to this play:

> Proceed by process,
> Lest parties – as he is belov'd – break out,
> And sack great Rome with Romans. (III. i. 314–16)

> On a dissension of a doit, break out
> To bitterest enmity.   (IV. iv. 17–18)

This lies glowing, I can tell you, and is almost mature for the violent breaking out.   (IV. iii. 22–3)

The image in the third passage is taken from a fire, in the first and second from either fire or disease. Digges uses the phrase in both senses, as indeed Shakespeare had done in earlier plays; but before 1604 and as late as *The Two Noble Kinsmen*, Shakespeare thought of war in the same medical terms as Dudley Digges – an idea made easy to his contemporaries by the theory of correspondences between the body politic and the microcosm,[5] as well as by the fact that physicians had frequent recourse to bleeding. As many critics have observed, there is a great deal of disease imagery in *Coriolanus*. More significant is the stress laid by Shakespeare in this play and in *Antony and Cleopatra* on the glory of the 'royal occupation' of soldiering. Plutarch, it is true, tells us that 'in those dayes valliantnes was honoured in Rome aboue all other vertues' (p. 238); but Dudley Digges devotes a whole essay to this theme. Plutarch, again, mentions that the Consuls hoped 'by the meanes of forreine warre, to pacifie their sedition at home' (p. 243); but Digges uses this as one of his main arguments in favour of war, and it is his sole reason for retelling the Coriolanus story. Shakespeare, of course, was familiar with the idea: Henry IV, it will be recalled, advises Hal to 'busy giddy minds with foreign quarrels'. Coriolanus rejoices in the war because it will enable Rome to vent her 'musty superfluity', an argument mentioned by Digges, but only indirectly by Plutarch.

Digges, who does not refer to Volumnia, adopts an attitude not unlike hers – exemplified in her remarks on her son's wounds (I. iii. 29–42) – as in a passage in the third essay, in which he prophesies that in the future the country will

> motherlike respect those sonnes that are hir Champions, and seeke
> to perchase her ease with painefull industrie, her honor with effusion
> of their bloude, her safety with losse of life.   (p. 95)

Although, therefore, Shakespeare could have developed his conception of the play from Plutarch's *Lives*, Digges may well have contributed to the atmosphere of the play with his praise of the military hero, his claim that 'the discommoditie of our long peace opprest by luxurie' is 'worse farre than warre', and his retelling of the Coriolanus story as an example of the way foreign wars can be used to cure sedition.[6]

Another book, published two years later, contains a significant reference to Coriolanus. This is Richard Knolles's translation of Bodin's *Six Bookes of a Commonweale*.[7] Bodin, after describing 'how dangerous a matter it is in euerie commonweale to banish a great man', goes on to mention Coriolanus who 'cast into exile, brought the Romans to such extremitie, as that had he not suffered himselfe to haue beene ouercome with the prayers and teares of his mother, and the other women whom the Romans had sent vnto him, the Roman State had there taken end'. Bodin has a long analysis of the disadvantages of democracy, including the fickleness and ingratitude of the people. This context illustrates the main significance the Coriolanus story would have for most of Shakespeare's original audience.

A third book, also published in 1606, has some links with *Coriolanus*.

This was entitled *A Comparative Discourse of the Bodies Natural and Politique. Wherein out of the principles of Nature, is set forth the true forme of a Commonweale, with the dutie of Subiects, and the right of the Soueraigne.*[8] As its title implies, this book by Edward Forset is an elaborate comparison between the human body and the body politic, its starting point being Menenius' fable:

> This similitude was both fitly and fortunatly enforced by *Menenius Agrippa*, who being imployed in the appeasing and persuading of the seditious reuolting commons of Rome, did by a very tale of this proportionable respectiuenes of the parts in mans body, and the mutualitie of kindnes and ayd afforded from each to other, so sensibly shew them their errour, that surseasing their malignant enuy wherewith they were inraged against their rulers (whom they accounted as the idle belly that swallowed the labors of their hands) they discerned at the last that their repining against, and their pining of that belly, whence was distributed vnto them their bloud and nourishment, necessarily tended to their owne destruction; and were thereuppon forthwith reclaymed into their bounds of obedience.[9]   (To the Reader)

Forset compares the king both to the head and the heart; and just as Averell wrote to advocate patriotic unity at the time of the Armada, so Forset attacks the gunpowder conspirators (pp. 51–2). In the last section of the book there is a discussion of the diseases of the commonwealth, magistrates being compared to physicians and surgeons; and in view of the numerous disease images in *Coriolanus* it is interesting to observe Forset's extended comparison between the diseases of the body and those of the commonwealth:

> Diseases arise as in the body naturall by distemper of humours; so in the politicall, by disorder of manners: and as in the bodie naturall they doe hinder, peruert, and corrupt the orderly actions of nature; so in the politicall they do impeach, infringe, and resist the proceedings and regiment of a iust gouernance.   (p. 72)

Forset proceeds to discuss the remedies in both cases:

> As against all diseases of the naturall bodie the skill and application of Phisicke is ordained; so against the corruption of manners in the politicall bodie, wholesome lawes be prouided: whereof where the more bee made, the more it argueth the sinfullnesse of that people,

as the vse of much phisicke argueth much distemper. . . So the
lawes and prouisions against offences in the State (like to a well
directed Phisicke) are to range vnder the regiment of the Soueraigne
with a seruiceable subalternation, recognizing him as the principall
Phisicion for the redressing or remedying the maladies of the bodie
politique.   (p. 73)

Constables, bailiffs, jurors, 'and such like' act as physicians to the civil
body; and just as the incompetence of some doctors makes people
regard their 'professions and practise, as vnnecessarie', so there are
many

> that taking offence at the vnsufficiencie or corruptions of some magis-
> trats and officers of iustice, either vtterly denie the lawfulnesse of
> their calling, or at the least spurne and repine at their administration.
>   (pp. 74–5)

Just as the physician should endeavour to keep people healthy, and
cure them when they fall ill, so the function of a magistrate 'is either to
hold all vpright when the state is in a good case, or to recouer and
recure that which shall become vnsound' (p. 75). Like the physician,
the magistrate has different remedies according to the nature of the
trouble – 'drying consumers, to waste away the superfluous confluence
of any annoying matter', 'attractiue openers, to loose and draw forth
any inwardly infixed festerings', 'dispersers and dissoluers of any
gathered together or swelling putrifactions', 'repercussiues, to suppresse
and repell all beginning outrages', and 'expellers of all that is hurtfull
and burdenous, cleansing the verie fountaynes of euill' (p. 76). Forset
argues that the faults of great men are most dangerous, as disease in an
important part of the body causes the whole body to be

> vexed with giddinesse and tumults: So when great men of a better
> condition, and higher degree, shall grow humerous, opinionate,
> and factious . . . they doe not only seduce the vnskilfull and vnruly
> Commons, but also traine on with their suggestion of colourable
> causes, some officers of publique trust . . . to adhere vnto them in
> their misconceiuing aduentures, till all be endangered by such
> mutinous confusion. . . The forenoted diseases setled in the nobler
> parts, are the more principally to be prouided for, and it is ordinarie
> to withdraw the anguish thereof, to some of the lesse principall, yea
> though it should be with torments of incision, burning or ligature.
>   (pp. 80–1)

Just as the patient has to be prevented from eating hurtful food, so 'traiterous complotters and the vngouerned' have to be restrained from 'riches and honor' – a mild punishment of traitors! But where a disease is 'particular only to one part', amputation is necessary:

> the part wherunto such paine sticketh & is so affixed, as that it cannot be remoued or remedied, were better to be pulled out, cut of, & disseuered from the bodie: howbeit much extremitie is to be abidden, and many waies for healing are to be tried befor it com to so hard a passe, as to harden the heart to endure such violence.

> (p. 84)

So when Sicinius says that Coriolanus is a 'disease that must be cut away', Menenius pleads:

> O, he's a limb, that has but a disease –
> Mortal, to cut it off: to cure it, easy.

> (III. i. 296–7)

A few lines later Sicinius repeats the idea of amputation:

> The service of the foot,
> Being once gangren'd, is not then respected
> For what before it was.

There is a good deal of disease imagery in the early acts of the play, but the significant images from the present standpoint, those relating to the sickness of the commonweal, are concentrated into the first scene of the third act. Coriolanus speaks of the contagion of democracy:

> those measles
> Which we disdain should tetter us, yet sought
> The very way to catch them.   (III. i. 78–80)

He speaks of those that prefer

> A noble life before a long, and wish
> To jump a body with a dangerous physic
> That's sure of death without it.   (III. i. 153–5)

Brutus, like Forset, realizes that desperate diseases of the state require desperate remedies:

> Sir, these cold ways,
> That seem like prudent helps, are very poisonous
> Where the disease is violent.   (III. i. 220–2)

A senator urges Coriolanus to leave the patricians 'to cure this cause', and Menenius adds:

> For 'tis a sore upon us
> You cannot tent yourself.   (III. i. 235–6)

Brutus speaks of Coriolanus' treason as an infection (III. i. 310). Shakespeare had previously referred to the sickness of the state (e.g. in *2 Henry IV, Hamlet*, and *Macbeth*) but Forset's book may have retriggered this imagery. At least we may suppose that some of Shakespeare's audience would have known about 'diseases setled in the nobler parts' and perhaps have been more critical of Coriolanus' conduct than some Shakespearian commentators have been.[10] On the other hand they would have had little sympathy with democratic ideas. Machiavelli alone seems to have condemned Coriolanus, without attempting to mitigate his guilt.[11]

Two more books may be mentioned briefly. Laurentius Grimaldus Goslicius, in his *Commonwealth of Good Counsaile*, as the 1607 translation was called, discussing natural patriotism, mentions that 'euen the wicked and most vnnatural subiects, attempting the subuertion of their country' have 'stayed their handes from performing so wicked an enterprise' as soon as they see their native soil. He illustrates the point by showing how easily Veturia (i.e. Shakespeare's Volumnia) dissuaded her son from destroying Rome; but, with the ambivalence of most writers on Coriolanus, he commends his piety in pardoning his country 'which through the crueltie of the *Tribunes*, at that time persecuting the Nobilitie, had beene to him vnthankefull'. Goslicius declares that it is dangerous for magistrates to 'be chosen by the multitude' and deplores the creation of the office of tribune:

> In *Rome* likewise the multitude not induring the dignitie of the Senate ... in the ende created *Tribunes*, by whose furie and insolency, the authoritie of the Senate was diminished, and by sedition and troubles brought the state to vtter destruction.
>
> (pp. 32, 67, 80–1)

Finally, William Fulbecke in *The Pandeçtes of the Law of Nations* (1602) alludes to the banishment of Coriolanus in his chapter on the evils of democracy:

> It is against the nature of the people to beare rule: for they are as vnfitte for regiment, as a mad man to giue counsaile. . . This beast of many heades hath a threeforked tongue: with the one part it

tickleth the eares of them whom they flatter: with the other it licketh their woundes: with the last, and sharpest it pricketh their hearts. . . The wayward people may be iustly compared to a bundell of thornes, which will beare vp a great man, but will pricke him if he leane or lie vpon it.   (ff. 29, 30ᵛ, 31)

Attempts have been made to link the writing of *Coriolanus* with the Midlands insurrection of 1607, and certainly the increased emphasis given to the shortage of corn suggests that this had a topical significance to Shakespeare's original audience. It is clear from the books that we have been considering that the poet was writing within a tradition, that he was less one-sided than most writers on the subject, and that the play exhibits, as Coleridge pointed out, the wonderful impartiality of Shakespeare's politics. Nevertheless, I believe that Andrew Gurr has shown that by the alterations made by Shakespeare in the Menenius fable, and his elimination of the riots about usury, he 'tightened up the parallel with the Midlands food riots and gave the belly metaphor a more precise relevance'. He refers to Zeeveld's comparison of the defenders of common rights in the House of Commons with the Tribunes in the play and he concludes that

> What Shakespeare seems to have done is to take two quite separate events and link them through the body-politic concept so that they independently confirm the fallaciousness of the organic analogy.

Perhaps Shakespeare was reacting against the extravagancies of Edward Forset.[12]

In any case Shakespeare takes the main incidents of his play from Plutarch's Life, though he selects and rearranges them. He omits, for example, the departure of the common people from Rome, which Plutarch gives as the occasion for Menenius Agrippa's fable. The people agree to return to Rome on condition that they are allowed to elect Tribunes to safeguard their interests; but in the play Brutus and Sicinius are already established in their offices. Shakespeare likewise omitted the plan to colonize Velites with the surplus Roman population – a more humane method than using them as cannon-fodder. In some ways, perhaps, Shakespeare tends to minimize the genuine grievances of the citizens, so as to arouse sympathy for his hero. He enlarges considerably on the cowardice of the common soldiers. On the other hand, the spokesman for the citizens in the first scene is no Jack Cade: he is given an eloquent and educated speech about their plight, resembling, it is said, the complaints of the Warwickshire peasants. There is nothing in Plutarch to suggest the intolerable behaviour of Coriolanus during his candidature, and his banishment occurs, not immediately after the revocation of his election, but after some later corn riots.

Shakespeare invents the episode of the boy Marcius chasing the butterfly, so as to throw an oblique light on the immaturity of the hero. He omits two acts of trickery by the Tribunes, though in other ways he blackens their characters. He makes Coriolanus go into exile alone – 'like a lonely dragon '– not with three or four of his friends. Plutarch introduces Aufidius only at this point in the story: Shakespeare introduces him earlier as a rival, following the suggestion of North's words:

> bicause that many times in battells where they met, they were euer at the encounter one against another, like lustie coragious youthes, striuing in all emulation of honour. (p. 219)

This chivalric touch, Murry argued,[13] led Shakespeare to depict the meeting of the exiled Coriolanus with Aufidius in such a way that the nobility of the Volscian is inconsistent with his previous character and with the envious plotter required for the last scene of the play. Plutarch's Aufidius is not present when Coriolanus agrees to spare Rome: by introducing him in this scene Shakespeare prepares the way for the assassination. Plutarch describes three successive embassies to Coriolanus before that of the women. The first consisted of his 'familiar friends' who are presented with hard conditions of peace and are told to give an answer within thirty days. At the end of that time a second embassy refuses the terms and is given three days to reconsider them. A third embassy consists of priests and soothsayers. The women's embassy is suggested by Valeria, a point Shakespeare does not use. Shakespeare condenses the first three embassies into single appeals by Cominius and Menenius. Shakespeare does not specify the terms of peace, but refers to them merely as

> The first conditions, which they did refuse
> And cannot now accept. (v. iii. 14–15)

Instead he concentrates on Coriolanus' obsessive desire to burn Rome.

Of great significance, however, is the development of the characters of Menenius and Volumnia. Menenius Agrippa's sole function in Plutarch is to tell the 'pretty tale' of the belly and the body's members. In the play his plebeian origins are not mentioned: he acts as the hero's

friend and adviser, appearing in thirteen scenes, and he is in some sense
the *raisonneur* of the piece. Volumnia is hardly mentioned by Plutarch –
except that she brought up Caius Martius – until she goes to plead with
him. There is nothing in Plutarch to suggest the fatal relationship
between mother and son, on which Shakespeare based his play.

Three brief examples, all mentioned by George Wyndham,[14] will
serve to illustrate the closeness with which Shakespeare follows North's
translation. In II. iii the First Folio prints the meaningless lines:

> And Nobly nam'd, so twice being Censor,
> Was his great Ancestor.

North supplies the missing words:

> *And Censorinus that was so surnam'd*
> And nobly nam'd so, twice being Censor.

The second example shows how Shakespeare was led into anachronism
by his misunderstanding of North, who says that Coriolanus

> was euen such another, as *Cato* would haue a souldier and a captaine
> to be: not only terrible, and fierce to laye about him, but to make the
> enemie afeard with the sound of his voyce, and grimness of his
> countenaunce.   (p. 240)

The corresponding passage in the Folio reads (with an obvious misprint):

> Thou wast a Souldier
> Euen to *Calues* wish, not fierce and terrible
> Onely in strokes, but with thy grim lookes, and
> The Thunder-like percussion of thy sounds
> Thou mad'st thine enemies shake.   (I. iv)

The third example is even more curious. North mentions that 'a
goodly horse with a capparison' (p. 242) is offered to Coriolanus. In the
play, Lartius hails Coriolanus with the words:

> Oh Generall:
> Here is the Steed, wee the Caparison.   (I. ix)

Several of the longer speeches in the play are based directly on Plutarch
– Coriolanus' attack on the distribution of free corn, and on the
Tribunes (III. i), his speech to Aufidius at Antium (IV. v), and Volumnia's
appeal to him to spare Rome are notable examples. An examination of
the last of these will exhibit how Shakespeare transformed great prose
into greater verse.[15]

If we helde our peace (my sonne) and determined not to speake, the
state of our poore bodies, and present sight of our rayment, would
easely bewray to thee what life we haue led at home, since thy exile
and abode abroad. But thinke now with thy selfe, howe much more
vnfortunatly, then all the women liuinge we are come hether,
considering that the sight which should be most pleasaunt to all
other to beholde, spitefull fortune hath made most fearefull to vs;
making my selfe to see my sonne, and my daughter here, her
husband, besieging the walles of his natiue countrie. So as that which
is thonly comforte to all other in their aduersitie and miserie, to
pray vnto the goddes, and to call to them for aide: is the onely thinge
which plongeth vs into most deepe perplexitie. For we can not (alas)
together pray, both for victorie, for our countrie, and for safety of
thy life also: but a worlde of grieuous curses, yea more then any
mortall enemie can heape vppon vs, are forcibly wrapt vp in our
prayers. For the bitter soppe of most harde choyce is offered thy
wife and children, to forgoe the one of the two: either to lose the
persone of thy selfe, or the nurse of their natiue contrie. For my selfe
(my sonne) I am determined not to tarie, till fortune in my life time
doe make an ende of this warre. For if I cannot persuade thee, rather
to doe good vnto both parties, then to ouerthrowe and destroye the
one, preferring loue and nature, before the malice and calamitie of
warres: thou shalt see, my sonne, and trust vnto it, thou shalt no
soner marche forward to assault thy countrie, but thy foote shall
treade vpon thy mothers wombe, that brought thee first into this
world.   (ed. 1895, pp. 256–7)

This is Shakespeare's version:

> Should we be silent and not speak, our raiment
> And state of bodies would bewray what life
> We have led since thy exile. Think with thyself
> How more unfortunate than all living women
> Are we come hither; since that thy sight, which should
> Make our eyes flow with joy, hearts dance with comforts
> Constrains them weep, and shake with fear and sorrow
> Making the mother, wife, and child to see
> The son, the husband, and the father, tearing
> His country's bowels out. And to poor we
> Thine enmity's most capital: thou bar'st us
> Our prayers to the gods, which is a comfort

That all but we enjoy. For how can we,
Alas, how can we for our country pray,
Whereto we are bound, together with thy victory,
Whereto we are bound? Alack, or we must lose
The country, our dear nurse, or else thy person,
Our comfort in the country. We must find
An evident calamity, though we had
Our wish, which side should win; for either thou
Must as a foreign recreant be led
With manacles through our streets, or else
Triumphantly tread on thy country's ruin,
And bear the palm for having bravely shed
Thy wife and children's blood. For myself, son,
I purpose not to wait on fortune till
These wars determine; if I can not persuade thee
Rather to show a noble grace to both parts
Than seek the end of one, thou shalt no sooner
March to assault thy country than to tread –
Trust to't, thou shalt not – on thy mother's womb,
That brought thee to this world.   (v. iii. 94–125)

The argument in both speeches is identical and the ideas follow one
another in the same order. Shakespeare often makes use of North's
phraseology. There are three chief differences: Shakespeare condenses
the sentences describing the difficulty of prayer; he tightens up the
structure by rhetorical devices; and he inserts some metaphorical
phrases in place of North's more prosaic ones. As examples of rhetorical
ordering of the argument, we may instance the lines –

> Making the mother, wife, and child, to see
> The son, the husband, and the father –

or the repetition in the lines –

> Whereto we are bound, together with thy victory,
> Whereto we are bound –

or the equally effective repetition:

> The country, our dear nurse, or else thy person,
> Our comfort in the country.

The metaphorical additions go a long way towards increasing the
vividness and dramatic effectiveness of the speech. Instead of 'besieging

the walls of his native country', Shakespeare uses the violent image, 'tearing/His country's bowels out'. Then he presents the effects of victory and defeat more concretely than Plutarch had done:

> for either thou
> Must as a foreign recreant be led
> With manacles through our streets, or else
> Triumphantly tread on thy country's ruin,
> And bear the palm for having bravely shed
> Thy wife and children's blood.

Another example from the same scene will illustrate the way Shakespeare transformed what he borrowed. After Coriolanus' surrender, he cried out in North's version:

> Oh mother, what haue you done to me? And holding her hard by the right hande, oh mother, sayed he, you haue wonne a happy victorie for your countrie, but mortall and vnhappy for your sonne: for I see my self vanquished by you alone.   (p. 257)

Shakespeare seized on the significant points in this passage, as we can see by the original stage direction *Holds her by the hand silent*, by the repetition of the words 'O mother', and by the lines:

> You have won a happy victory to Rome;
> But for your son – believe it, O, believe it! –
> Most dangerously you have with him prevail'd,
> If not most mortal to him.   (v. iii. 186–9)

But whereas Plutarch's Coriolanus is thinking only of the shame of surrendering to his mother, Shakespeare's hero knows that the surrender will lead to his own death. Equally significant is the insertion of the lines – the last of a series of images drawn from acting –

> Behold, the heavens do ope,
> The gods look down, and this unnatural scene
> They laugh at.   (v. iii. 183–5)

Coriolanus, with all his faults, is portrayed more sympathetically by Shakespeare than by Plutarch. Plutarch records that his host in Corioli, for whom he intervenes, was an 'honest wealthie man': Shakespeare makes him a poor man.[16] More significantly, Plutarch actually condemns him for giving in to his mother, while Shakespeare tacitly approves.

V
LAST PLAYS

✱
✱ 33 ✱
PERICLES

THERE ARE still many unsolved problems in connection with *Pericles* but there is now fairly general agreement that the text of the 1609 quarto, bad as it manifestly is, was based on an earlier play and that Wilkins's novel – *The Painfull Adventures of Pericles* – was based on the same play, rather than on Shakespeare's rewriting of it.[1] It would also seem, from the difference of style between the first two acts and the last three, and from the novel's divergencies from the later acts, that Shakespeare made few changes in the early acts, but that he rewrote the remainder of the play, from the birth of Marina to the end.[2] The authorship of the source-play is still a matter for debate, Heywood and Day being the present favourites; but Dryden's statement[3] that

> *Shakespear's* own Muse her *Pericles* first bore;
> The Prince of *Tyre* was elder than the *Moore*

has been used to support the view that the *Ur-Pericles*, as it has been called, was written by Shakespeare himself. Dryden, however, wrote these lines some sixty years after the play was performed and he may have assumed it was an early work merely because of its episodic structure, or even because Jonson described it as 'a mouldy tale'. It is true that *Pericles* has something in common with *The Comedy of Errors*. Ægeon is separated from his wife during a sea-voyage; Æmelia takes refuge in a nunnery; and Thaisa becomes a priestess in the temple of Diana, both at Ephesus. Presumably Shakespeare had read the story of Apollonius of Tyre, the ultimate source of *Pericles*, before he wrote

The Comedy of Errors. As we have seen, that is the only one of Shakespeare's plays which is based on a Latin comedy; but it has been pointed out[4] that Palaestra, the heroine of the *Rudens* of Plautus, is, like Marina, stolen by pirates and sold by them to a pimp. The play also contains a shipwreck and the marriage of the heroine to a young man who had originally intended to buy her as his mistress.[5]

There are three reasons for rejecting the theory that *Pericles* was written at the beginning of Shakespeare's career. The verse of the first two acts, though unlike that of Shakespeare's maturity, has little resemblance to that of *The Comedy of Errors*;[6] the *Rudens*, although we need not doubt that Shakespeare read it, is an analogue rather than a source since the kidnapping by pirates and the sale of the heroine to a brothel are features of the Apollonius story; and there is no real evidence of a play on the subject as early as 1590.

The story itself was indeed a mouldy tale existing in many versions from the ninth century onwards. The only versions which the author of *Pericles* must have read are those given by Gower in *Confessio Amantis* and by Lawrence Twine's *Pattern of Painful Adventures*.[7] The play owes most to Gower, as the choice of that poet as presenter makes clear. The naming of characters – Helicanus, Dionyza, and Lychorida – follows Gower rather than Twine; Leonine is master of the brothel in Gower's poem, though Shakespeare uses the name for a different character; Philoten is mentioned by Gower, but not by Twine; and Gower's Thaise, Appolinus' daughter, becomes the name of Pericles' wife. The archaic style of the choruses is an imitation of Gower's; and there are two striking verbal echoes. When Appolinus' wife is resuscitated, she asks:[8]

> Wher am I?
> Where is my lorde, what worlde is this?

Thaisa in the play uses the same words:

> O dear Diana,
> Where am I? Where's my lord? What world is this?

There is nothing to correspond to this in Twine's novel. In the reunion-scene, Thaise says to Appolinus:

> My lorde, I am a mayde,
> And if ye wyst, what I am,
> And out of what linage I cam,
> Ye wolde not be so salvage.

So Marina tells Pericles:

> I am a maid,
> My lord . . .
> I said, my lord, if you did know my parentage
> You would not do me violence.

It has been suggested[9] that the name of the hero was derived from Pericles of Athens, who was noted for his patience. Whether Shakespeare's hero should be credited with this virtue is a moot point: his despair on the report of Marina's death tells against it. It is surely more likely that the name was derived from Sidney's Pyrocles, who is ship-wrecked like Pericles, and who nearly strikes the unrecognized Philoclea who rebukes him for his excessive grief at her supposed death, as Pericles strikes Marina.[10]

Shakespeare had certainly read *The Orator* of Alexander Silvayn; and Professor Bullough quotes[11] Declamation 53 about a nun who preserves her chastity in a brothel; but Twine provides a much closer parallel to the brothel-scenes of the play.

It is possible, as I have suggested elsewhere,[12] that Shakespeare took the name of Marina from the account of a Mexican girl who was baptised under that name. She had been sold by her own mother to some Indians and she afterwards became an interpreter to Cortez and forgave her cruel mother in a way which would have appealed to Shakespeare during his final period.

As we do not know the exact nature of the original *Pericles*, we cannot know precisely how much Shakespeare took from it, and how much from Gower and Twine; but if Wilkins's novel was based on the old play – and not, as some believe, on Shakespeare's revision of it – we can estimate the kind of changes he made. The bad text of the play, however, makes this a hazardous task. It may be suggested, for example, that some of Shakespeare's intentions have been blurred by omissions. In Act II Scene v Simonides informs Thaisa's suitors that she will not marry for at least a year:

> One twelve moons more she'll wear Diana's livery.
> This by the eye of Cynthia hath she vow'd,
> And on her virgin honour will not break it.

Presumably Simonides invented the vow to rid himself of the suitors, so as to leave the field free for the favoured Pericles. It is worth noting that Diana is mentioned several times in the Shakespearian parts of the

play and once, as Lucina, in the first scene for which he was probably
not responsible. Pericles prays to Lucina during his wife's labour –

> Divinest patroness, and midwife gentle
> To those that cry by night –

and his prayer is unavailing. When Thaisa is restored to life, her first
words are addressed to the same goddess – 'O dear Diana!' – and,
assuming irrationally that she will never see Pericles again, she decides
to put on a vestal livery, in accordance with her alleged pre-marital
vow, and serve as priestess in the temple of Diana. Pericles vows,
again by Diana, not to cut his hair. Marina prays to Diana to protect
her chastity in the brothel. The goddess appears to Pericles in a vision,
telling him to visit her temple, and there he is reunited to Thaisa. He
promises to 'offer night-oblations' to the goddess. He might well cry,
in scriptural phrase, 'Great is Diana of the Ephesians!' I suggested[13]
some years ago that it looks as though Thaisa's time in the temple was
intended to be a means of expiating the sin of taking in vain the name
of Diana. Professor Hoeniger has rightly pointed out that 'such an
interpretation is irreconcilable with any known form of the story'.[14]
To which we may reply that sources are not a branch of predestination
and that the continual references to Diana, added by Shakespeare,
presumably had some thematic function. We may well agree that
Pericles is more like Job than Leontes; that his trials, and those of his
wife and daughter, are 'a means of testing them'; and their final reunion
is in accordance with Jupiter's pronouncement in *Cymbeline*:[15]

> Whom best I love I cross; to make my gift,
> The more delay'd, delighted.

Shakespeare was trying, it not altogether successfully, to convert the
wheel of fortune into the wheel of providence.

If has often been pointed out that in the brothel-scene Wilkins gives
more eloquent speeches to Marina than she is allowed in the play:[16]

If as you say (my Lorde) you are the Gouernour, let not your
authoritie, which should teach you to rule others, be the meanes to
make you misgouerne your selfe: If the eminence of your place
came vnto you by discent, and the royalty of your blood, let not
your life prooue your birth a bastard: If it were throwne vpon you
by opinion, make good, that opinion was the cause to make you
great. What reason is there in your Iustice, who hath power ouer all,

to vndoe any? If you take from mee mine honour, you are like him, that makes a gappe into forbidden ground, after whome too many enter, and you are guiltie of all their euilles: my life is yet vnspotted, my chastitie vnstained in thought. Then if your violence deface this building, the workemanship of heauen, made up for good, and not to be the exercise of sinnes intemperaunce, you do kill your owne honour, abuse your owne iustice, and impouerish me.

After a short speech by Lysimachus, Marina continues:

It is not good . . . when you that are the Gouernour, who should liue well, the better to be bolde to punish euill, doe knowe that there is such a roofe, and yet come vnder it. Is there a necessitie (my yet good Lord) if there be fire before me, that I must strait then thither flie and burne my selfe? Or if suppose this house (which too too many feele such houses are) should be the Doctors patrimony, and Surgeons feeding; folowes it therefore, that I must needs infect my self to giue them maintenance?

This extract is sufficient for the purpose of comparison with the corresponding scene in Shakespeare's play. Professor Philip Edwards rightly calls attention to the brevity of Marina's two crucial speeches and shows how absurd it is for Lysimachus to praise her wisdom and eloquence on the strength of what she is given to say.[17]

Several explanations have been offered.

(1) Marina's speeches as given by Wilkins drop into blank verse only occasionally and accidentally. They do not closely reproduce what was heard on the stage before or after Shakespeare's revision but rather represent Wilkins's variations on what he heard. This I find incredible. As several critics have noted,[18] Wilkins's speeches are thinly concealed blank verse, revealed in such tell-tale repetitions as

which too too many feele such houses are.

(2) Wilkins reproduces a more accurate version of the scene than the corrupt quarto[19] and therefore his version should be printed in a modern text of the play. This I believe to be impossible, because the verse preserved by Wilkins is quite unlike the kind written by Shakespeare in the seventeenth century.

(3) Wilkins reproduces substantially the scene as performed before its revision by Shakespeare, whereas the quarto reproduces the scene after revision. G. A. Barker, whose view this is,[20] thinks that Shakespeare,

unlike the earlier dramatist, was not concerned with the qualities of a good ruler and is

> intent on making Lysimachus into a more desirable suitor for Marina by removing as much of the blemish from him as possible without doing violence to the plot of the old play. We have, therefore, the rather improbable situation of Lysimachus's denying that he came to the brothel with any ill intentions. Consequently, Shakespeare has to strike out most of Marina's argument, since Lysimachus does not need conversion. Yet he can still show his admiration for Marina's speech in words that clearly show Shakespeare's revision:

> > Had I brought hither a corrupted mind,
> > Thy speech had altered it.

We may agree that Shakespeare wished to provide Marina with a more satisfactory husband than he is in the source-play; but Professor Edwards's objection still stands,[21] that Marina does not earn the right to be complimented on her eloquence. Nor can it be maintained that Lysimachus does not need conversion. It is obvious from the way he is greeted by the Bawd and Boult that he is an old customer; there is nothing in his early exchanges with Marina to suggest that he is, like Gladstone, attempting to rescue fallen women; and the words quoted by Barker read like a shame-faced excuse. In other words Lysimachus did need to be converted, and he was converted.

(4) This leaves the most probable explanation; that whatever changes were made by Shakespeare in the scene it is very unlikely that the quarto gives a faithful reproduction of it. We may suppose that Marina was given more eloquent speeches, if not so extended as the ones provided by Wilkins. It seems likely that Shakespeare made the brothel-scenes more sordid and realistic than they had been in his source.

One other alteration may be mentioned. In the recognition-scene, Appolinus smites his daughter (according to Gower); and, according to Twine, he 'stroke the maiden on the face with his foote, so that shee fell to the ground, and the bloud gushed plentifully'; and, in Wilkins, who probably reflects the source-play, he struck her on the face so that she swooned. In Shakespeare's gentler version Pericles pushes Marina roughly back.

As we cannot be certain how much Shakespeare derived from the source-play, there seems to be little point in discussing the numerous minor sources which have been listed by Professor Hoeniger[22] and others; but it is fairly certain that the author of II. i, whether John Day or another, was echoing Day's *Law Tricks*.[23]

34

CYMBELINE

SAMUEL JOHNSON dismissed *Cymbeline* in a sentence:[1]

> To remark the folly of the fiction, the absurdity of the conduct, the confusion of the names and manners of different times, and the impossibility of the events in any system of life, were to waste criticism upon unresisting imbecillity, upon faults too evident for detection, and too gross for aggravation.

Harley Granville-Barker did not go as far as Johnson in his condemnation, yet even he spoke of Shakespeare as a wearied artist.[2] A study of the poet's manipulation of his sources shows, however, that he was not too wearied to take considerable pains. He was looking, we may suppose, for a plot through which he could express the theme of forgiveness and reconciliation. Realizing the weakness of *Pericles*, in which the hero and his family suffer undeserved trials at the hands of fortune, he wanted a story in which the disasters were caused more directly by human agency. Perhaps the popularity of *Mucedorus*, a feeble old play revived in 1607, led Shakespeare, or his company, to search for similar old romantic plays worth revival or adaptation, or for similar 'mouldy' plots which could be dramatized. Shakespeare had been reading Plutarch's *Lives* while he was writing the Graeco-Roman plays, and in the last of these, *Timon of Athens*, the hero, after his self-imposed banishment, lives in a cave. A cave also figures in *The Rare Triumphs of Love and Fortune*, then nearly thirty years old, written and published while the poet was still at school.[3] In this play, which opens with a debate between Jupiter and the other gods and goddesses, the Princess Fidelia is in love with Hermione, a supposed orphan who had been brought up at court by his father, King Phizantius. Fidelia's boorish brother, Armenio, discovering their love, fights a duel with Hermione, which is interrupted by the King. Hermione is banished. The name of the princess was adapted by Shakespeare for that assumed by Imogen (Fidele); Hermione, which Shakespeare well knew was properly a woman's name, served as the heroine of his next play; the position of Posthumus Leonatus is not unlike that of Hermione in the old play; and Cloten's pursuit of Imogen may be roughly compared with Armenio's pursuit of Fidelia. In Act III we meet Hermione's father, the exiled Bomelio, who resembles Belarius in some ways and, since he practises magic, Prospero in others. At the end of the play, by the intervention of Jupiter, the lovers are reunited and the King is reconciled with Bomelio. One may compare the vision of Jupiter in *Cymbeline* and the reconciliation of the King with Belarius. Of course, as J. M. Nosworthy says,[4]

> It would be unwise to attach too much weight to such parallel features as a banished lover, a banished duke, a cave, and a sleeping potion, for these are part of the stock-in-trade of every writer of romance.

What is more significant is that both plays

> present the banished lover as a pauper brought up at Court, both include a boorish brother, and both introduce Jupiter and use him, flagrantly as a *deus ex machina*. Just as Belarius recognizes Cloten though he has not seen him for many years, so Bomelio recognizes Armenio, and just as Imogen offers her breast for the mortal stroke, so does Fidelia.

The old play, therefore, provided Shakespeare with hints for his initial situation, for his pastoral scenes, and for his last act. But clearly it would not do as it stood. The plot was inorganic and arbitrary, with too little complication and not enough dramatic tension. It lacked also solidity of background. This Shakespeare provided by setting his scene in the early legendary period of British history, known to Elizabethans from Holinshed's *Chronicles*, *The Faerie Queene*, *Albion's England*, *The Mirror for Magistrates*, and from numerous plays from *Gorboduc* to *King Leir*, including the popular *Locrine* and *Mucedorus*. Shakespeare, as we have seen, had consulted some of these works a few years before, while he was writing *King Lear*.

There were considerable differences between the various accounts of

Cymbeline. In *The Mirror for Magistrates* there is a fanciful tale of how Guiderius defeated a Roman army, thirty thousand strong, and of his challenge to meet Claudius in single combat. Holinshed tells how Cymbeline became king in 33 B.C. and that he reigned for thirty-five years; and that Christ was born during his reign is the only fact recorded by Spenser. As Cymbeline had been brought up in Rome, he was excused by Augustus from paying tribute. At some later date the tribute was again demanded and refused; but Holinshed, after some hesitation, ascribes this refusal to Guiderius. Holinshed mentions that British chroniclers claimed that the Romans were twice defeated, but that Latin historians claimed that the Romans were ultimately victorious. Spenser makes Arviragus the brother of Cymbeline. Shakespeare follows Holinshed in making Cymbeline the father of both Guiderius and Arviragus, though he makes him, and not Guiderius, refuse to pay the tribute.

Cymbeline's reign coincided with the peace of Augustus; and it has been argued[5] that the peace with which the play ends, and Cymbeline's decision, despite the British victory, to pay the neglected tribute, may reflect James I's rôle as peace-maker. Indeed, the play contains a number of references to more recent events. The significance of Milford Haven, not mentioned in the play's sources, is that it was the place where Henry Tudor had landed to defeat Richard III and so found the Tudor dynasty. Daniel and Drayton, among others, referred to Milford in contexts which show that their readers, and Shakespeare's original audience, would appreciate the significance. It has been suggested,[6] moreover, that

> With Imogen and the two boys out of Wales, audiences are expected to associate the Princess Elizabeth, Prince Henry and Prince Charles: Shakespeare signposts this message clearly in his repeated references to Milford Haven.

The legendary history of Brute, the son (or grandson) of Aeneas, described by the chroniclers, and touched on by poets and preachers, was linked in people's minds with 'the apocalyptic destiny of Britain' and the aims of James I's foreign policy.[7]

Professor Harold F. Brooks has shown[8] conclusively that Shakespeare made extensive use of *The Mirror for Magistrates* in his dramatization of the refusal to pay tribute – not merely of Blenerhasset's 'Guidericus', but also of four tragedies by Higgins in the 1587 edition. The lines (III. i. 46–7) –

> Till the injurious Romans did extort
> This tribute from us, we were free –

echo Higgins's lines:

> I sayd I would not pay them tribute, I,
> They did extort the same by force, perdy . . .
> Hee should not beare our freedom so away.

Earlier in the same scene the Queen speaks of Britain, fenced

> With sands that will not bear your enemies' boats
> . . . A kind of conquest
> Caesar made here; but made not here his brag
> Of 'came, and saw, and overcame'. With shame –
> The first that ever touch'd him – he was carried
> From off our coast, twice beaten; and his shipping –
> Poor ignorant baubles! – on our terrible seas,
> Like egg-shells mov'd upon their surges, crack'd
> As easily 'gainst our rocks.   (21–9)

Higgins's Caesar speaks of 'our shatter'd ships . . . that else had bulg'd themselues in sand'; and he admits:

> I haue no cause of *Britayne* conquest for to boast
> Of all the Regions first and last with whome I werd.

Nennius speaks of how Caesar

>   for all his bragges and boste:
> Flew backe to shippes . . .
> The *Monarche Caesar* might haue bene ashamde
> From such an Islande with his shippes recoyle.

Irenglas makes the same point in similar wards:[9]

> When *Caesar* so, with shamefull flight recoylde,
> And left our *Britayne* land vnconquerde first.

The killing of Cloten and Posthumus' fighting in disguise may both have been suggested by Higgins's story of Hamo, a Roman who puts on British garments so as to have the opportunity of killing Guiderius. He is afterwards slain and

> hewde in pieces small:
> Which downe the cleeues they did into the waters cast.

Holinshed mentions that Arviragus slew Hamo near a haven (and that Southampton was named after him) but he omits the hewing in pieces. Cloten's head is thrown into 'the creek behind our rock', but his headless body has to be preserved so as to delude Imogen.

For the battle Shakespeare went to the Scottish section of Holinshed's *Chronicles*, to the story of how a peasant named Hay with his two sons helped to defeat the Danes at the battle of Luncarty in A.D. 976. This story Shakespeare would have read at the time he was collecting materials for *Macbeth*, as it is sandwiched between the accounts of Donwald and Duncan. Perhaps the episode was intended as a tribute to Sir James Hay who 'became Knight of the Bath on 4 June 1610, at the installation of the Prince of Wales'.[10]

Shakespeare still needed a plot to combine with those he had already, one which would dramatically postpone the reunion of the lovers and make it a reconciliation as well as a reunion. The obvious resource was a story of jealousy, and he looked for one like *Othello* or *Much Ado about Nothing* in which a husband is made to believe that his wife has been unfaithful by the slander of an Italianate villain. Boccaccio's *Decameron* was available to Shakespeare in a French translation, though he could as easily have read the original. Here, in the ninth tale of the second day, Shakespeare found the popular tale of a wager on a wife's chastity. Some Italian merchants at an inn in Paris deride the idea of a female chastity and Bernabo of Genoa is provoked by Ambrogiuolo to bet on the chastity of his wife, Ginevra. On going to Genoa, Ambrogiuolo realizes that he cannot seduce Ginevra. Concealed in a chest, he is able to observe the pictures of her bedroom, to steal a ring and other belongings, and to observe a mole on the lady's breast. Bernabo is convinced that he has lost the wager and he orders his servant to murder Ginevra. The servant, convinced of her innocence, spares her. She dresses in his clothes and takes service with the Soldan. One day she sees her purse and girdle in a stall in the market-place. When the truth comes to light, Ginevra reveals herself to her husband and forgives him. The villain is tortured to death:[11]

> the verie same day that hee was impaled on the stake, annointed with honey, and fixed in the place appointed, to his no meane torment: he not onely died, but likewise was deuoured to the bare

bones, by Flies, Waspes, and Hornets, whereof the Countrey notoriously aboundeth.

As Iachimo is forgiven, this torture is not used in *Cymbeline*; but in *The Winter's Tale* Autolycus tells the Clown:

He has a son – who shall be flay'd alive; then 'nointed over with honey, set on the head of a wasp's nest; then stand till he be three quarters and a dram dead; then recover'd again with aquavitae or some other hot infusion; then, raw as he is, and in the hottest day prognostication proclaims, shall he be set against a brick wall, the sun looking with a southward eye upon him, where he is to behold him with flies blown to death. (IV. iv. 772 ff.)

There is no doubt, from this single parallel, that Shakespeare had read the Boccaccio tale; and there are, in fact, many resemblances between the wager plot in *Cymbeline* and the story of Ginevra – the circumstances of the wager, the realization by the seducer that he cannot win it, the concealment in a chest, the description of the pictures and furniture, the mole on Ginevra's left breast, the stealing of a jewel, the plot to kill the heroine, the relenting of the servant, the disguise of Ginevra as a man, and the final exposure of the slanderer are to be found in Shakespeare as in Boccaccio. But just as the poet went to Blenerhasset and Higgins as well as to Spenser and Holinshed for the historical material in *Cymbeline*, so it is now established that he went to an English version of the wager story. This was entitled *Frederyke of Jennen*, published originally in 1518, but reprinted in 1560. The story in its essentials is the same as Boccaccio's, but it differs in a number of details. In the *Decameron* all the merchants present at the wager are Italian: in *Frederyke of Jennen* there are four merchants from different countries – Spain, France, and Italy. This may explain why in the corresponding scene in *Cymbeline* there are a Frenchman, an Italian, a Dutchman, and a Spaniard, the last two without speaking parts. In *Frederyke of Jennen*, as in *Cymbeline*, the wager is first suggested by the villain, and the odds are even, not five to one as in Boccaccio. The villain declares that he has lost the wager as soon as he sees the heroine; she is told that the chest contains jewels and plate, and agrees to keep it in her own chamber; the villain, on seeing the mark on her body, realizes that this 'privy token' will be convincing evidence; on his return he claims to have won his wager in the presence only of the holder of the stakes; the servant sends a bloody cloth soaked in the blood of a lamb as a proof of his murder of Ambrose's wife; and Ambrose repents before he knows of her innocence. In all these details Shakespeare follows the English tale instead of the *Decameron*. There is no doubt that Shakespeare used both versions.

The joining of the wager story with *The Rare Triumphs of Love and Fortune*, in which the heroine is a princess, and the linking of both with the historical material from various sources, meant that the atmosphere of the wager story was completely changed; but it has been argued[12] that the bourgeois setting of the wager story led to the iterative imagery of the play – buying selling, jewels etc. If so, it is clear that Shakespeare uses the imagery for the purpose of defining spiritual and moral, as well as material, values.

In Shakespeare's manipulation of these heterogeneous materials there is no sign of the wearied artist of Granville-Barker's imagination. One might, indeed, complain of the dramatist's sheer virtuosity as being too clever to be good. He displays extraordinary ingenuity throughout the play, as for example in the way in which Imogen is made to awaken beside the body of a headless corpse dressed in her husband's garments. We are asked to accept the drug, like Juliet's, which counterfeits death, Cloten's desire to rape Imogen in her husband's clothes, the curious funeral customs prevailing in the Welsh mountains, the juxtaposition of the loved and hated bodies, and Imogen's delusion about the identity of the corpse. It is a measure of Shakespeare's skill that we do accept these improbabilities, at least when Peggy Ashcroft or Vanessa Redgrave is playing Imogen. The acceptance is made easier by Imogen's insult to Cloten in the phrase which rankles so deeply – 'his meanest garment'. Equally cunning is the wager-scene, so written that a refusal by Posthumus to bet on Imogen would seem to be a lack of faith in her. A third example is the extraordinary final scene in which more than a score of knots are unravelled. Bernard Shaw complained that the surprises surprise nobody; but, of course, they are not meant to surprise the audience. The gradual unravelling is the performance of a ritual of reconciliation and forgiveness.

The theatrical virtuosity has been ascribed to 'coterie dramaturgy' with its deliberate self-consciousness,[13] and in particular to the influence of Beaumont and Fletcher's work. Certainly, as Thorndike pointed out long ago,[14] there are many resemblances between *Philaster* and *Cymbeline*. In both plays there is a princess who is destined by her father to marry a boor, and there is the same contrast between Posthumus and

Cloten as there is between Philaster and Pharamond. Both heroes are driven from Court and both denounce the female sex. Imogen is lost in the wilds like Arethusa, and dresses as a boy like Bellario, a name similar to Shakespeare's Belarius, and to Bellaria, the heroine of Greene's *Pandosto* who was rechristened by Shakespeare as Hermione. Both plays contain pastoral scenes and both were performed by Shakespeare's company. The resemblance between the two plays extends to individual speeches, although it is not so great as some critics have pretended. The most striking verbal parallel is, in fact, between *Philaster* and *The Winter's Tale*.[15] But it is by no means certain that *Philaster* preceded *Cymbeline*. Shakespeare had already turned his back on tragedy in *Pericles*; and though *Philaster* may have been written as early as 1608, it may have been as late as 1610. As Shakespeare later collaborated with Fletcher in *The Two Noble Kinsmen* and the lost *Cardenio*, it would be unreasonable to deny a reciprocal influence. It is quite possible that they saw each other's work during the process of composition.[16]

It may be said, however, that even if the technique of *Cymbeline* was not greatly influenced by Fletcher, there are signs that Shakespeare was exhausted as a poet. The play is full of echoes of his own earlier work and the style is sometimes strangely contorted. The echoes, however, may be explained as due to the poet's 'desire to gather up the strands of all his work and knit them together in the pattern of his new vision'.[17] There are echoes of *Lucrece*, *As You Like It*, *Troilus and Cressida*, *Othello*, and *Antony and Cleopatra*. Shakespeare was treating afresh several of the themes he had dealt with during his career, and considering them again in the light not merely of his new intuitions, but also of the demands of the genre of tragi-comedy.

Of course the play is an odd mixture. The material taken from British legendary history is vastly different in kind from the *Decameron*; the masque-like vision contrasts violently with the scenes of the Roman invasion; classical Rome is mingled with Renaissance Italy; and there are other extraordinary disparities. The play is, in one sense, a bridge between the English Histories and the Roman plays;[18] in another sense it is a link between pastoral romance and tragedy. Shakespeare's task was rendered easier by the calculated anachronism in Renaissance painting and Elizabethan literature, as well as by a certain historical innocence. But it seems probable that the confusion of genres was designed to assist the creation of an imaginary world in which the poet's new symbolic method could have unrestricted scope. The

interpenetration of opposites gave a moral significance to the romantic
material and set free the poet and his audience from the restrictions of
realism.[19]

❖

❖ 35 ❖

THE WINTER'S TALE

THE SOURCE-MATERIAL of *The Winter's Tale* forms a great contrast
to that of *Cymbeline*. Instead of going to six different works Shakespeare
relied very largely on Greene's romance, *Pandosto*, published in 1588.[1]
   Greene devotes some pages to an explanation of Pandosto's jealousy.
His wife, Bellaria, often went into Egistus' bed-chamber

> to see that nothing should be amis to mislike him. This honest
> familiarity increased dayly more and more betwixt them: for
> *Bellaria*, noting in *Egistus* a princely and bountifull minde, adorned
> with sundrie and excellent qualities, and *Egistus* finding in her a
> vertuous and curteous disposition, there grew such a secret vniting
> of their affections, that the one could not well be without the
> company of the other.

Pandosto, not unnaturally, became jealous. Shakespeare gives Leontes
no such excuse. The scene can be played with Leontes jealous from the
start, or becoming jealous at l. 108 on the words 'Too hot, too hot!'
The latter way, with its sudden destruction of love and friendship, is
the one that Shakespeare probably intended; but we should remember
that Hermione is visibly pregnant, that Polixenes' first line mentions a
nine-month stay in Sicilia, and that at this point the audience 'cannot
fail to wonder whether the man so amicably addressing this expectant
mother may not be the father of her child'.[2] It has been well said that
Leontes is his own Iago[3] and it was this that made Shaw regard the
depiction of jealousy in this play as more realistic than that in *Othello*.[4]
   Shakespeare follows the earlier part of his source fairly closely.
Greene describes how when the guard was sent to arrest Bellaria, 'they
found her playing with her yong sonne'. On this hint Shakespeare
constructed the scene in which Mamillius begins his interrupted tale;

but Leontes himself, not merely the guard, comes in to order Hermione's arrest.

In the novel it is Bellaria who appeals to the oracle; the contents, already known to the reader, are read out at the trial; Pandosto immediately recognizes its truth and forthwith repents; word is brought of the death of his son; and Bellaria is killed by the news. This order of events is quite satisfactory in a prose narrative, but it lacks dramatic tension. Shakespeare must have realized that it would spoil the trial-scene, in which Hermione appeals to the oracle, if she were allowed to make the appeal in a previous scene; so he makes Leontes himself decide to send a deputation to Apollo's temple at Delphos, not to confirm his suspicions, but rather to satisfy other people. The substance of the oracle is not known to anyone, nor revealed to the audience, till it is read out at the trial. The King, instead of accepting it, declares that it is false. News is then brought that Mamillius has died, and we assume, as Leontes himself does, that this is a punishment for his blasphemy against Apollo. Hermione faints, and Paulina brings word that she is dead. Bellaria has indeed died; but Hermione, unknown to Leontes, or to the audience, recovers. This is almost the only occasion when Shakespeare conceals from the audience an essential fact. Paulina swears that Hermione is dead; Leontes says later that he viewed the bodies of wife and son; and Antigonus' dream, in which it appears that the spirit of Hermione chooses a name for her daughter, and prophesies the death of Antigonus, all these things reinforce the conviction that Hermione has died. For the audience to share in Leontes' feelings in the last scene of the play, it was necessary for Shakespeare to indulge in unprecedented obfuscation.

The only substantial borrowing of the actual words of Greene's novel is of Bellaria's speech at her trial:

If the deuine powers be priuy to humane actions (as no doubt they are) I hope my patience shall make fortune blushe, and my vnspotted life shall staine spightfull discredit. For although lying Report hath sought to appeach mine honor, and Suspition hath intended to soyle my credit with infamie: yet where Vertue keepeth the Forte, Report and suspicion may assayle, but neuer sack: how I haue led my life before Egistus comming, I appeale Pandosto to the Gods, and to thy conscience. What haue passed betwixt him and me, the Gods onely know, and I hope will presently reueale: that I loued Egistus I can not denie, that I honored him I shame not to confesse:

to the one I was forced by his vertues: to the other for his dignities. But as touching lasciuious lust, I say Egistus is honest, and hope my selfe to be found without spot: for Franion, I can neither accuse him, nor excuse him: for I was not priuie to his departure, and that this is true which I haue heere rehearsed, I referre my selfe to the deuine Oracle.   (Bullough, VIII. 170–1)

Shakespeare uses nearly all this speech, though he breaks it up with interruptions by Leontes:

>   *Her.* Since what I am to say must be but that
> Which contradicts my accusation, and
> The testimony on my part no other
> But what comes from myself, it shall scarce boot me
> To say 'Not guilty'. Mine integrity
> Being counted falsehood shall, as I express it,
> Be so receiv'd. But thus – if pow'rs divine
> Behold our human actions, as they do,
> I doubt not then but innocence shall make
> False accusation blush, and tyranny
> Tremble at patience. You, my lord, best know –
> Who least will seem to do so – my past life
> Hath been as continent, as chaste, as true,
> As I am now unhappy; which is more
> Than history can pattern, though devis'd
> And play'd to take spectators; for behold me –
> A fellow of the royal bed, which owe
> A moiety of the throne, a great king's daughter,
> The mother to a hopeful prince – here standing
> To prate and talk for life and honour 'fore
> Who please to come and hear. For life, I prize it
> As I weigh grief, which I would spare; for honour,
> 'Tis a derivative from me to mine,
> And only that I stand for. I appeal
> To your own conscience, sir, before Polixenes
> Came to your court, how I was in your grace,
> How merited to be so; since he came,
> With what encounter so uncurrent I
> Have strain'd t'appear thus; if one jot beyond
> The bound of honour, or in act or will
> That way inclining, hard'ned be the hearts

Of all that hear me, and my near'st of kin
Cry fie upon my grave!

 Leon.   I ne'er heard yet
That any of these bolder vices wanted
Less impudence to gainsay what they did
Than to perform it first.

 Her.   That's true enough;
Though 'tis a saying, sir, not due to me.

 Leon. You will not own it.

 Her.   More than mistress of
Which comes to me in name of fault, I must not
At all acknowledge. For Polixenes,
With whom I am accus'd, I do confess
I lov'd him as in honour he requir'd;
With such a kind of love as might become
A lady like me; with a love even such
So and no other, as yourself commanded;
Which not to have done, I think had been in me
Both disobedience and ingratitude
To you and toward your friend; whose love had spoke
Even since it could speak, from an infant, freely,
That it was yours. Now for conspiracy;
I know not how it tastes, though it be dish'd
For me to try how; all I know of it
Is that Camillo was an honest man;
And why he left your court, the gods themselves,
Wotting no more than I, are ignorant.

 Leon. You knew of his departure, as you know
What you have underta'en to do in's absence.

 Her.   Sir,
You speak a language that I understand not.
My life stands in the level of your dreams,
Which I'll lay down.

 Leon.   Your actions are my dreams.
You had a bastard by Polixenes,
And I but dream'd it. As you were past all shame –
Those of your fact are so – so past all truth;
Which to deny concerns more than avails; for as
Thy brat hath been cast out, like to itself,
No father owning it – which is indeed

More criminal in thee than it – so thou
Shalt feel our justice; in whose easiest passage
Look for no less than death.
    Her.   Sir, spare your threats.
The bug which you would fright me with I seek.
To me can life be no commodity.
The crown and comfort of my life, your favour,
I do give lost, for I do feel it gone,
But know not how it went; my second joy
And first fruits of my body, from his presence
I am barr'd, like one infectious; my third comfort,
Starr'd most unluckily, is from my breast –
The innocent milk in it most innocent mouth –
Hal'd out to murder; myself on every post
Proclaim'd a strumpet; with immodest hatred
The child-bed privilege denied, which 'longs
To women of all fashion; lastly, hurried
Here to this place, i'th'open air, before
I have got strength of limit. Now, my liege,
Tell me what blessings I have here alive
That I should fear to die. Therefore proceed.
But yet hear this – mistake me not: no life,
I prize it not a straw, but for mine honour
Which I would free – if I shall be condemn'd
Upon surmises, all proofs sleeping else
But what your jealousies awake, I tell you
'Tis rigour, and not law. Your honours all,
I do refer me to the oracle:
Apollo be my judge!   (III. ii. 20–114)

Into the framework of Bellaria's speech Shakespeare has inserted points from other pages of Greene's novel. Hermione's claim that her past life had been continent, chaste, and true, her statement that to condemn her without proof was rigour and not law, her complaint that she had been proclaimed a strumpet, are all taken from previous pages of *Pandosto*.[5] So, too, is Leontes' statement that those guilty of certain vices have impudence enough to deny them. Hermione's statement that she was the daughter of the Emperor of Russia was suggested by Greene's mention of the fact that Egistus had married the Emperor of Russia's daughter.

In Greene's story the baby, Fawnia, is turned adrift in a boat:

> He caused a little cock-boate to be prouided, wherein he meant to put the babe, and then send it to the mercie of the seas, and the destinies. . . . The gard . . . carried the child to the King, who, quite deuoide of pity, commanded that without delay it should bee put in the boat, hauing neither saile nor rudder to guid it, and so to bee carried into the midst of the sea, and there left to the wind and waue as the destinies please to appoint.   (Bullough, VIII. 166–7)

The baby is carried alone to the coast of Sicily, but Shakespeare, making Leontes King of Sicilia, causes Antigonus to take Perdita to some remote and desert place – in fact, as it turns out, on the coast of Bohemia of which country Polixenes is king. Shakespeare must have felt that it would be hard for an audience to credit that a newly-born infant would survive under such circumstances; but he remembered the passage about the little cock-boat when he described in *The Tempest* the vessel which carried Prospero and his infant daughter to the enchanted island:

> A rotten carcass of a butt, not rigg'd,
> Nor tackle, sail, nor mast.

Not that Shakespeare was unaware of the absurdities of his plot; but he prepared his audience for them by laughing at them himself. The disposal of Antigonus, devoured by a bear, is described in absurd terms by the Clown. As S. L. Bethell pointed out, Shakespeare was deliberately using an antiquated technique.[6] The antiquity of the story is 'pressed home by the employment of out-moded technique'. By the use of exaggerated conventions and by continual reminders that the play is a play – 'like an old tale', as we are told more than once – Shakespeare forbids absorption in the action so that we can 'observe the subtle interplay of a whole world of interrelated ideas'. Bethell also suggested that the antiquated technique is 'not only a means of commanding a special sort of attention, but is also in itself a statement about the nature of reality'. However that may be, we are not meant to be particularly perturbed by the fatal exit of Antigonus. 'Gentlemen usually dine upon animals', Bethell remarked, 'but now the bear will dine upon the gentleman'.[7] The description of the bear's dinner, interspersed with ludicrous references to the shipwreck, marks the point in the play where tragedy is metamorphosed into comedy: it is the hinge dividing the two panels of a diptych.[8]

Bethell also suggested that Shakespeare was fully aware that Bohemia lacked a coastline, for there were contemporary jokes on the subject and at this very time Princess Elizabeth was marrying its ruler. Sterne's famous chapter in *Tristram Shandy* should prevent us from considering the matter too curiously,[9] but it may be worth mentioning that in Emmanuel Forde's *Famous and Pleasant History of Parismus, the valiant and renowned Prince of Bohemia* (1597), the coast of Bohemia is mentioned; and Part 2, entitled *Parismenos* (1599), opens with an attack by a bear on the heroine, Violetta.[10] It has been suggested, too,[11] that Shakespeare may have located the first part of the play in Sicily because Ceres, like Hermione, was queen of that island, and he wished to reinforce the Perdita–Persephone parallel implicit throughout the play.

Greene describes the finding of Fawnia in words closely echoed by Shakespeare:[12]

> It fortuned a poore mercenary Sheepheard . . . missed one of his sheepe, and thinking it had strayed into the couert, that was hard by, sought very diligently to find that which he could not see, fearing either that the Wolues, or Eagles had vndone him . . . wandered downe toward the Sea cliffes, to see if perchaunce the sheepe was browsing on the sea Iuy, whereon they greatly doe feede.
>
> (Bullough, VII. 173)

> They have scared away two of my best sheep, which I fear the wolf will sooner find than the master: if anywhere I have them, 'tis by the sea-side, browsing of ivy.   (III. iii. 66–70)

Greene mentions a proposal to wed Dorastus (Florizel) to the daughter of the King of Denmark.[13] Shakespeare omits this as irrelevant to his purpose. The sheep-shearing feast, of which Fawnia is the mistress, is mentioned in *Pandosto*, but it takes place before her meeting with Dorastus. By presenting the lovers at the feast, by introducing Polixenes and Camillo in disguise, and by confronting Florizel with his father, Shakespeare greatly increases the dramatic effectiveness of the story. Here he may have taken a hint from John Day's *Humour Out of Breath* in which there is a disguised father interrupting the wedding of his sons.[14]

In *Pandosto* the cup-bearer who had helped Egistus to escape has faded from the story, and Dorastus and Fawnia reach Bohemia by another accident. In the play, Camillo's desire to return to his native land provides a plausible motive for his help of the lovers. In *Pandosto* the old shepherd, going to the palace to inform the King of the circumstances of his discovery of Fawnia, is kidnapped and taken to Bohemia with the lovers: in the play, the shepherd and his son are lured to the ship by Autolycus, and Camillo informs the King of the lovers' escape.

In the novel, the fugitives are arrested as spies; and Pandosto, falling in love with his own daughter, promises to free Dorastus if she will yield to him. In the play, on the other hand, Leontes receives the lovers with courtesy and affection and promises to be their advocate with Polixenes. Shakespeare would probably have avoided the incest motive in any case,[15] but nothing could better show his obsession with forgiveness, reconciliation, and restoration than the way in which he transforms the ending of the story. Pandosto commits suicide; Leontes is reunited with Hermione.

It has been suggested that Hermione's resurrection may have been derived at some remove from the story of Alcestis or from that of Pygmalion. Both are given in Pettie's *Palace of Pleasure*; Marston had given a somewhat pornographic version of the Pygmalion story; and it is to be found in the *Metamorphoses*. There are other possibilities. The statue-scene may have been influenced by *Amadis de Gaule* in which there are living statues and characters called Florisel and Perdida;[16] and in *The Tryall of Chevalry* (1605), Ferdinand, supposed dead, poses as his own statue.[17] Possibly the 'resurrection' is a blending of one of these with some variant of the Sleeping Beauty. Professor Glynne Wickham has shown that, as the scene was staged, Hermione would resemble a painted effigy on an Elizabethan tomb.[18]

A number of critics have shown how greatly Shakespeare improved on the loose texture of Greene's novel.[19] By his alterations he was able to bring together all the main characters in the last scene of the play. Polixenes' pursuit of the lovers enables him to be reconciled with Leontes, and Leontes with Hermione, and Perdita to be restored to her parents. In the novel, much more clumsily, after Pandosto's recognition of Fawnia, they all have to embark to pay Egistus a visit. Some critics, indeed, from Johnson onwards, have reproached Shakespeare for not showing on the stage the recognition of Perdita by her father; but Shakespeare, having recently dramatized a similar scene in *Pericles*, decided rightly that our interest ought to be concentrated on the reunion of Hermione and Leontes.[20] Moreover, as Nevill Coghill maintained, the report of the recognition of Perdita is invariably successful in the theatre.[21] Other critics have complained of the theatricality and unreality of the statue-scene; but it has always been successful on the stage, whether played by Mrs Siddons, Helen Faucit, Lillah McCarthy, or Diana Wynyard.[22]

Apart from those passages in the play which could only have been written by Shakespeare with *Pandosto* open on his desk, there are others where he seems to have echoed Greene unconsciously, for the echoes occur in quite different contexts. When, for example, Paulina attacks the courtiers for being yes-men[23] –

> 'Tis such as you,
> That creep like shadows by him, and do sigh
> At each his needless heavings – such as you
> Nourish the cause of his awaking –   (II. iii. 33–6)

Shakespeare borrowed a phrase from a description of the effect of Bellaria's death on the common people: 'They went like shadowes, not men'. And when Leontes decides that it is impossible to keep women chaste –

> Be it concluded,
> No barricado for a belly. Know't,
> It will let in and out the enemy
> With bag and baggage –   (I. ii. 203–6)

he takes a phrase which describes the sudden flight of Egistus:[24]

> For *Egistus* fearing that delay might breede daunger . . . taking bagge and baggage, with the helpe of *Franion*, conueied himself and his men out of a posterne gate of the Citie.

There is one interesting example of a fusion of two sources. Dorastus soliloquizes in *Pandosto*:[25]

> And yet *Dorastus* shame not at thy shepheards weeds: the heauenly Godes haue sometime earthly thoughtes: *Neptune* became a Ram, *Iupiter* a Bul, *Apollo* a shepheard: they Gods, and yet in loue: and thou a man appointed to loue.

The corresponding speech in Francis Sabie's poem, *The Fisshermans Tale* (1595), based on Pandosto, runs as follows:[26]

> Loue conquers all things: it hath conquered
> *Apollo* once, it made him be a swaine.
> Yea mightie *Mars* in armes inuincible,

It forced hath to lay aside his speare,
Loue made the sea-god take a Wesils shape,
Yea mightie *Ioue*, whose rage makes earth to shake,
Loue made to take the snow-white shape of Bull.

The two versions coalesced in Shakespeare's lines:

> The gods themselves,
> Humbling their deities to love, have taken
> The shapes of beasts upon them: Jupiter
> Became a bull, and bellow'd; the green Neptune
> A ram, and bleated; and the fire-rob'd god,
> Golden Apollo, a poor humble swain,
> As I seem now. (IV. iv. 25–31)

The words are spoken not in soliloquy, but to Perdita; and they are made much more vivid than either of the sources by the epithets ('green', 'fire-robed', 'golden') and still more by the realism of the verbs ('bellowed' and 'bleated'). Florizel, unlike Dorastus, is humorous rather than condescending.

The scenes in Bohemia are prevented from being pastorally senti-mental by the invention of Autolycus, 'the snapper up of unconsidered trifles', who might have stepped out of one of the pamphlets of Harman, Greene, or Dekker, exposing the iniquities of the criminal underworld. Several of his tricks do in fact come from Greene's coney-catching pamphlets, written nearly twenty years previously. Greene mentions that the singing of ballads

> is nothing els but a sly fetch to draw many togeather, who listning vnto a harmelesse dittie, after warde walke home to their houses with heauie hearts.

He gives an example of how two rogues[27]

> got vpon a stal singing of balets which belike was some prety toy, for very many gathered about to heare it, and diuers buying, as their affections serued, drew to their purses and paid the singers for them. . . Counterfeit warning was sundrie times giuen by the rogue and his associate, to beware of the cut pursse, and looke to their pursses, which made them often feel where their pursses were, either in sleeue, hose, or at girdle, to know whether they were safe or no. Thus the craftie copesmates were acquainted with what they most desired, and as they were scattered, by shouldring, thrusting,

feigning to let fall something, and other wilie tricks fit for their
purpose: heere one lost his purse, there another had his pocket
pickt. . .

Another of the pamphlets describes two more of Autolycus' tricks – the
stealing of linen[28] and the robbing of the shepherd's son.[29] In this
episode Shakespeare may have remembered the parable of the Good
Samaritan.[30] Greene's account of the qualities necessary for the successful pickpocket seem to be echoed by Shakespeare's rogue.[31] The one
moral Forman extracted from the play was 'Beware of trusting
feined beggars or fawninge fellouss'.

It has been suggested[32] that Autolycus was intended to play some
part in the discovery of Perdita's parentage; but, as the play stands, his
presence in Act v is unnecessary to the plot. Despite Forman's omission
of any mention of the statue-scene, it is fairly certain that this was in
Shakespeare's mind from the start.

The discussion about grafting, which introduces Perdita's catalogue
of flowers, is, as Professor Knight has shown,[33] a microcosm of the
whole play, a discussion on 'great creating Nature'. The cultivated
flowers are contrasted with the natural flowers of the countryside, just
as Perdita's world is contrasted with that of the Court, and just as
Sicilia is contrasted with Bohemia. Polixenes, in arguing the case for
grafting, is unconsciously justifying the marriage of his son to the
supposed country maiden:

> You see, sweet maid, we marry
> A gentle scion to the wildest stock,
> And make conceive a bark of baser kind
> By bud of nobler race. This is an art
> Which does mend nature – change it rather; but
> The art itself is nature.   (IV. iv. 92–7)

The discussion of the relative importance of art and nature is often
found in Elizabethan literature. It has been argued[34] that Shakespeare
had a more profound conception that Bacon. But in any case, as H. S.
Wilson pointed out,[35] the poet seems to be echoing a discussion by
Puttenham in *The Arte of English Poesie* on the relative importance of
nature and art in the composition of poetry. Puttenham argues that in
some cases art is an 'ayde and coadiutor to nature' or 'a meane to
supply her wants, by renforcing the causes wherein shee is impotent
and defectiue'. He goes on to compare the artist or poet with the
gardener:[36]

In another respect arte is not only an aide and coadiutor to nature in all her actions, but an alterer of them, and in some sort a surmounter of her skill, so as by meanes of it her owne effects shall appeare more beautifull or straunge and miraculous, as in both cases before remembred. . . And the Gardiner by his arte will not onely make an herbe, or flowr, or fruite, come forth in his season without impediment, but also will embellish the same in vertue, shape, odour and taste, that nature of her selfe woulde neuer haue done: as to make the single gillifloure, or marigold, or daisie, double: and the white rose, redde, yellow, or carnation; a bitter mellon sweete, a sweete apple, soure; a plumme or cherrie without a stone; a peare without core or kernell, a goord or coucumber like to a horne, or any other figure he will: any of which things nature could not doe without mans help and arte. These actions also are most singular, when they be most artificiall.

Puttenham goes on to justify that which

A Poet makes by arte and precepts rather then by naturall instinct: and that which he doth by long meditation rather then by a suddaine inspiration.

One further borrowing may be mentioned. It is generally accepted that Perdita's speech about flowers was derived from Golding's translation of Ovid:[37]

While in this garden *Proserpine* was taking her pastime,
In gathering eyther violets blew, or lillies white as lime . . .
Dis spide her; lou'd her: caught her vp. . .
The ladie with a wailing voyce afright did often call . . .
And as she from the vpper part her garment would haue rent,
By chance she let hir lap slip downe, and out the flowers went.

Perdita mentions the gathering of violets and lilies and the dropping of the flowers by the frightened girl, but she adds daffodils, primroses, oxlips, and other flowers not mentioned by Ovid:

O Proserpina,
For the flowers now that, frighted, thou let'st fall
From Dis's waggon! – daffodils,
That come before the swallow dares, and take
The winds of March with beauty; violets, dim
But sweeter than the lids of Juno's eyes

> Or Cytherea's breath; pale primroses,
> That die unmarried ere they can behold
> Bright Phoebus in his strength – a malady
> Most incident to maids; bold oxlips, and
> The crown-imperial; lilies of all kinds,
> The flow'r-de-luce being one. O, these I lack
> To make you garlands of, and my sweet friend
> To strew him o'er and o'er!   (IV. iv. 116–29)

The association of Perdita with Proserpine, Flora, and Whitsun Pastorals, and Leontes' greeting to her as 'goddess', 'welcome as is the spring to the earth', have led critics to regard the play as a myth of the seasons. Certainly Shakespeare's neighbour, Leonard Digges, published a few years later a translation of Claudian's *The Rape of Proserpine* (1617) prefixed with an interpretation of the allegory. Shakespeare was doubtless aware of the intermittent allegorical undertones in his play; but it would surely be wrong to interpret the whole play allegorically, or to regard it as a myth of resurrection. Professor Inga-Stina Ewbank has shown how Shakespeare took a hint from the alternative title of *Pandosto* – *The Triumph of Time* – and that by the restoration of Hermione to Leontes,[38]

> time has at last in its triumph brought about its own defeat. This does not efface the human suffering that has gone before, however, and that weighs so heavily on the play right till the very end. Rather than a myth of immortality, then, this play is a probing into the human condition, and – as a whole as well as in details – it looks at what time means and does to man.

❋ 36 ❋

THE TEMPEST

NO SOURCE has been discovered for the main plot of *The Tempest*, though William Collins thought he had found it in a story entitled *Aurelia and Isabella*.[1] It is probable that Shakespeare picked up hints from a number of different places, but the material he was dramatizing was the common stuff of romances. Friar Bacon in Greene's play is one of many magicians who renounce their magic art. Shrimp in *John a Kent and John a Cumber* by Munday has resemblances to both Puck and Ariel: he misleads lovers by playing a tune or speaking in the voice of one of the lovers. In *The Rare Trimphs of Love and Fortune* (already used by Shakespeare in *Cymbeline*), Bomelio's magic books are stolen by his son. There is a Wild Man in *Mucedorus*.[2] Then there are some remarkable resemblances to *The Tempest* in *scenari* of the *commedia dell'arte*.[3] In *Li Tre Satiri* the magician's servants are spirits in the form of wild men; some shipwrecked mariners steal the magician's book and desire the virginal Phillis; and, even more strikingly, Zanni escapes from a rock in which he had been imprisoned by a necromancer for refusing to obey his behests, as Ariel refused to obey Sycorax. In *Il Capriccio* there is an enchanted banquet which is removed by spirits. In *I Forestieri* shipwrecked sailors get drunk; in *Arbore Incantato* the magician has a wild man as a servant; in *Arcadia Incantata* a good magician raises a storm, shipwrecked sailors are tormented by spirits and prevented from eating; and in *Pantaloncino* the magician throws away his wand and book of spells. A German play by Jacob Ayrer, entitled *Die Schöne Sidea* (1618, but written before 1605) contains a dethroned magician, a prince who is made to carry logs, whom Sidea pities and marries, and a spirit-servant. As Ayrer adapted foreign plays this one may be based on one brought to Germany by an English touring company.

Three Spanish books have been suggested as sources.[4] In Antonio de Eslava's *Noches de Invierno* (1609) there is a dethroned magician who leads to his palace – under the sea – the usurper's disinherited son as a bridegroom for his daughter, and a storm raised by magic to destroy the usurper's favoured son now reigning as his successor. In Diego Ortúñez de Calahorra's *Espejo de Principes y Cavalleros*, translated into English as *The Mirror of Knighthood* (1578) there is a princely magician with two children. In Part III (*c.* 1586), the Knight of the Sun lands on an island which had been ruled by a witch, whose son, the present ruler, had been fathered by the devil. Another book is Thomas's *History of Italy* (1549, 1561) in which Shakespeare could have read of Prosper Adorno, Duke of Genoa, who was deposed in 1561, returned in 1577 as deputy for the Duke of Milan, and made friends with Ferdinando, King of Naples, but was again expelled. In the previous century there was an Alfonso, King of Naples, who married the Duke of Milan's daughter, and afterwards abdicated in favour of his son, Ferdinand, to devote himself to 'study, solitariness and religion'. It is probable that Shakespeare had read *The Mirror for Knighthood*, or a work derived from it, and possible that he had dipped into Thomas's *History* (for information about Venice when he was writing his Venetian plays), though the names of Prospero, Alfonso, and Ferdinand he could have obtained elsewhere. He had acted in *Every Man in his Humour* in which there are characters named Prospero and Stephano.

When we turn to travel books we are on much firmer ground. It is fairly certain that Shakespeare found the name of the god Setebos in the account of the devil worshipped by the Patagonians in Richard Eden's *History of the Travayle in the West and East Indies* (1577).[5] There is little doubt that Shakespeare had read three accounts of the Bermudas shipwreck – William Strachey's *True Reportory of the Wracke* (which he must have read in manuscript), Silvester Jourdain's *A Discovery of the Barmudas*, and *A True Declaration of the Estate of the Colonie in Virginia*. The extent of the verbal echoes of these three pamphlets has, I think, been exaggerated. There is hardly a shipwreck in history or fiction which does not mention splitting, in which the ship is not lightened of its cargo, in which the passengers do not give themselves up for lost, in which north winds are not sharp, and in which no one gets to shore by clinging to wreckage. Strachey's account of the ship-wreck is blended with memories of St Paul's – in which too not a hair perished – and with Erasmus' colloquy. Both Strachey and Erasmus mention a ball of fire at the masthead; but as both mention that it used to be called Castor and Pollux, it is likely that Strachey consulted Erasmus to eke out his memories.[6]

The reputation of Bermuda as dangerous and 'given over to Devils and wicked spirits', contrasted with the true facts as detailed in the pamphlets, was echoed by Shakespeare in the contrasting views of the courtiers in II. i. Adrian's words 'uninhabitable and almost inaccessible' conflate Strachey's remark that the island 'had long ere this beene inhabited' but for the difficult entrance, with the words of *A True Declaration* 'a place hardly accessible'. Shakespeare's rejection of Gonzalo's commonwealth may have received some support from the mutiny and laziness described by Strachey, the treason and idleness deplored in *The True Declaration*:[7]

An incredible example of their idlenes . . . *Sir Thomas Gates* . . . hath seen some of them eat their fish raw, rather than they would go a

stones cast to fetch wood and dresse it. . . . God sels vs all things for
our labour, when *Adam* himselfe might not live in paradice without
dressing the garden.

In Gonzalo's commonwealth nature produces food 'without sweat or
endeavour' so that 'all men' are 'idle, all'.

Gonzalo's Utopia is closely based on a famous passage by Montaigne,
one of the few verbal borrowings from Florio's translation which is
generally accepted. There is another, however, discovered by Eleanor
Prosser,[8] who demonstrated that the words in which Prospero re-
nounced his vengeance were based on the opening paragraph of the
essay 'Of Cruelty':

> Methinkes vertue is another manner of thing, and much *more noble*
> than the inclinations vnto Goodnesse, which in vs are engendered.
> Mindes well borne, and directed by themselues, follow one same
> path, and in their actions represent the same visage that the vertuous
> doe. . . He that through a naturall facilitie and genuine mildnesse
> should neglect or contemne injuries receiued, should no doubt
> perform *a rare action* and worthy commendation: but he who being
> *toucht and stung to the quicke* with any wrong or offence receiued,
> should arme himselfe *with reason against this furiously* blind desire of
> reuenge, and in the end after a great conflict yeeld himselfe master
> over-it, should doubtlesse *doe much more*. The first should doe well,
> the other *vertuously*: the one action might be termed goodnesse, the
> other *vertue*. For it seemeth that the very name of Vertue pre-
> supposeth difficultie, and inferreth resistance, and cannot well
> exercise it selfe without an enemie.

So Prospero tells Ariel:

> Though with their high wrongs I am struck to th'quick,
> Yet with my nobler reason 'gainst my fury
> Do I take part; the rarer action is
> In virtue than in vengeance.   (v. i. 25–8)

It is significant that one of the main themes of the play was taken from
one of Montaigne's essays, and the climax from another.

As Professor Kermode has pointed out, 'many elements are mixed
in Ariel, and his strange richness derives from the mixture' – English
folklore, classical mythology, neo-platonism, magical theory, medieval
theology.[9] Kermode dismisses the influence of Isaiah xxix, in which the

name is used; but as Robert Graves and Ann Pasternak Slater have argued, that chapter seems to have coloured several incidents in the play.[10] Equally curious are the echoes from the *Aeneid* – the unexplained references to Dido in II. i, the disguise of Ariel as a harpy in Act III, Ferdinand's first words to Miranda, and Ceres' description of the 'saffron wings' of Iris.[11]

The masque with which Prospero entertains the lovers seems to belong to the general tradition of court masques and one in particular, *Hymenaei*, is thought to have influenced Shakespeare because Jonson refers to the transitory nature of such devices, and because of the cosmic scene and its dissolving. This may have linked up in Shakespeare's mind with the warning by St Peter that 'all these things shall be dissolved'[12] and passages from Alexander's dreary Senecan play, *Darius*:[13]

> Let greatnesse of her glassie scepters vaunt;
> Not sceptours, no, but reedes, soone brus'd, sone broken:
> And let this worldlie pompe our wits enchant.
> All fades, and scarcelie leaues behinde a token.
>
> Those golden Pallaces, those gorgeous halles,
> With fourniture superfluouslie faire:
> Those statelie Courts, those sky-encountring walles
> Euanishe all like vapours in the aire.

These lines are preceded by others in which the glory of Darius' name is said to be

> A meere illusion made to mock the sight,
> Whose best was but the shaddowe of a dreame.

Earlier in the play there is a reference to 'starre-boasting *Babilon*', treasures are described as

> Difficile to obtaine,
> Difficile to retaine,
> A dreame, a breath, a fume . . .

and near the end we are told that the 'pompes and triumphes' of kings are useless:

> Their Arches, Tombes, Piramides hie,
> And Statues are but vanitie.

A last echo, and a more indisputable one, may be mentioned. Immediately after his renunciation of vengeance, Prospero says farewell to his magic art, which he first celebrates in words closely based on Medea's invocation in Ovid's *Metamorphoses* – on the Latin original as well as on the Golding translation.[14] The imitation is so ingeniously done that it is metamorphosed to suit the white magic of Prospero,[15] even if we are surprised to hear that he has raised the dead.

It is, of course, possible that a lost play or an undiscovered tale provided Shakespeare with his plot; but it seems more likely that for once he invented the plot, making use of memories of masques, plays, romances, perhaps examples of the *Commedia*, and books of travel; and that these memories coalesced with others from Virgil and Ovid. In Montaigne and the Bible, as well as from his own previous romances, he would find the principle of the necessity of forgiveness which animates the whole play.

37

HENRY VIII

THERE WERE several earlier plays on the reign of Henry VIII. Shakespeare himself had contributed at least one scene to *Sir Thomas More*. Another play, belonging to Henslowe, was performed in 1598;[1] three years later he commissioned Chettle to write a play about Wolsey: and this was popular enough for him to commission Chettle, along with three other playwrights, to follow it up with a play on the early life of the Cardinal.[2] Finally, in 1604, Samuel Rowley's play, *When You See Me, You Know Me*, was performed at the Fortune Theatre, published in 1605, and reprinted in 1613, the year when Shakespeare's play was first performed. We do not know if *Henry VIII* owed anything to the Henslowe group of plays, for they are lost; but as it was sub-titled 'All is true', and as the prologue deplores the frivolity of some other treatment of the subject, it seems likely that *Henry VIII* was written as a counterblast to Rowley's play which deviates from historical truth more than Shakespeare ever did.

Henry VIII was included as Shakespeare's in the First Folio; but since the middle of the eighteenth century a number of critics have argued that the play was written in collaboration with John Fletcher. It was noticed that the versification of much of the play resembled that of Fletcher's, and that the spelling differences in the alleged shares of the two dramatists cannot be accounted for by the habits of the three compositors who set up the Folio text.³ Some colour was lent to the theory of collaboration by the fact that two plays, excluded from the First Folio – *Cardenio* and *The Two Noble Kinsmen* – were allegedly written by Shakespeare and Fletcher. The alternative theory, that Shakespeare wrote the whole play, but that he had picked up some of Fletcher's mannerisms and rhythms, is attractive to those who hold a high opinion of the play. My own tentative view is that the play is substantially Shakespeare's, but that when the manuscript arrived from Stratford it was handed over to Fletcher, who did a bit of tidying up and added the prologue and epilogue.

It is certain that Shakespeare made use of at least three sources,⁴ namely Holinshed's *Chronicles*, Foxe's *Actes and Monuments* (i.e. the *Book of Martyrs*), and Speed's *History of Great Britaine* (1611). The last of these only provided two images in Wolsey's speeches after his fall – both, incidentally, in passages often ascribed to Fletcher:

> Certaine it is, that Cardinall *Wolsey*, fell likewise in great displeasure of the King, though hee sought to excuse himselfe with want of sufficient authority: but now his Sunne hauing passed the Meridian of his greatnesse, began by degrees againe to decline, till lastly it set vnder the cloud of his fatall eclipse. Formerly wee haue spoken of the rising of this man, who now being swolne so bigge by the blasts of promotion, as the bladder not able to conteine more greatnesse, suddenly burst, and vented foorth the winde of all former fauours. Vaine glorious he was, in state, in diet, and in rich furniture.

Although R. A. Foakes points out⁵ that there is a passage about Wolsey in Holinshed's *Chronicles*, which refers to the 'spirit of swelling ambition, wherwith the rable of popes haue beene bladder like puffed and blowne vp', the juxtaposition of the two images in Speed's *History* makes it certain (as Foakes would agree) that this was the source of the two speeches in the play.

> I have touch'd the highest point of all my greatness,
> And from that full meridian of my glory

I haste now to my setting. I shall fall
Like a bright exhalation in the evening,
And no man see me more.   (III. ii. 223–7)

> I have ventur'd
Like little wanton boys that swim on bladders
This many summers in a sea of glory;
But far beyond my depth: my high-blown pride
At length broke under me, and now has left me,
Weary and old with service, to the mercy
Of a rude stream that must for ever hide me.
Vain pomp and glory of this world, I hate ye.
(III. ii. 358–65)

It will be noticed that the effectiveness of the two echoes is enormously increased by the poet's additions. The 'bright exhalation in the evening' is a splendid reinforcement of the first; and in the second the bursting of the bladder does not merely let out the air of promotion, it is attached to a boy swimming beyond his depth. It may be mentioned, too, that Wolsey in Churchyard's poem in *A Mirror for Magistrates* says that he 'did swim, as dainty as a ducke' and confesses his great pride, 'For which offence, fell *Lucifer* from skyes'. The first line may have been the link between bladders and boys; and the second may have suggested the reference to Lucifer's fall in the second speech.

The influence of Foxe is apparent only in the Cranmer-scenes of Act v. Neither Hall nor Holinshed records the attempt to arrest Cranmer for heresy, his being kept waiting outside the council-chamber, or the King's protection of him. Shakespeare – if it was Shakespeare – appears to have overdone the saintly humility of the Archbishop, which was presumably meant to contrast with the arrogance of Wolsey and the malice of Gardiner, and to prepare the way for his prophetic utterance at the christening of Elizabeth.

The first four acts of the play are based on Holinshed but, as Foakes and Bullough have demonstrated,[6] individual scenes are often indebted to widely separate passages in the *Chronicles*. The first scene incorporates facts from between pages 853 and 872; the second scene from between 852 and 922; Act II scene i from between 850 and 906; and Act III Scene ii from between 796 and 930. As with all the previous Histories, Shakespeare telescoped the facts to obtain a greater unity. The Field of the Cloth of Gold took place in 1520; Buckingham was executed in 1521; the fall of Wolsey took place in 1529; Cranmer became Archbishop of Canterbury in 1532; Henry married Anne in 1533 and Elizabeth was born in the same year; Katherine died in 1536. The actual period covered by the play was therefore sixteen years. Shakespeare takes many liberties. He places Katherine's death, for example, before the birth of Elizabeth. He ascribes to Wolsey a mistake made by the Bishop of Durham who accidentally gave to Wolsey a book treating of his private affairs and of the £100,000 he had managed to acquire by dubious means.

The two scenes in which Shakespeare followed Holinshed most closely – because here the source was more eloquent than usual – were those concerned with Katherine's trial (II. iv) and her interview with the two Cardinals (III. i). How closely can be seen from a comparison of Holinshed's words with the first of these:[7]

And bicause shee could not come to the king directlie, for the distance seuered betweene them, shee went about by the court, and came to the king, kneeling downe at his feet, to whome she said in effect as followeth: Sir (quoth she) I desire you to doo me iustice and right, and take some pitie vpon me, for I am a poore woman, and a stranger, borne out of your dominion, hauing heere no indifferent counsell, & lesse assurance of freendship. Alas sir, what haue I offended you, or what occasion of displeasure haue I shewed you, intending thus to put me from you after this sort? I take God to my iudge, I haue beene to you a true & humble wife, euer conformable to your will and pleasure, that neuer contraried or gainesaid any thing thereof, and being alwaies contented with all things wherein you had any delight, whether little or much, without grudge or displeasure, I loued for your sake all them whome you loued, whether they were my freends or enimies.

I haue been your wife these twentie yeares and more & you haue had by me diuerse children. If there be anie iust cause that you can alleage against me, either of dishonestie, or matter lawfull to put me from you; I am content to depart to my shame and rebuke: and if there be none, then I praie you to let me haue iustice at your hand. The king your father was in his time of excellent wit, and the king of Spaine my father Ferdinando was reckoned one of the wisest princes that reigned in Spaine manie yeares before. It is not to be doubted, but that they had gathered as wise counsellors vnto them of euerie realme, as to their wisedoms they thought meet, who deemed the marriage betweene you and me good and lawfull, &c.

Wherefore, I humblie desire you to spare me, vntill I may know what counsell my freends in Spaine will aduertise me to take, and if you will not, then your pleasure be fulfilled.

Sir, I desire you do me right and justice,
And to bestow your pity on me; for
I am a most poor woman and a stranger,
Born out of your dominions, having here
No judge indifferent, nor no more assurance
Of equal friendship and proceeding. Alas, sir,
In what have I offended you? What cause
Hath my behaviour given to your displeasure
That thus you should proceed to put me off
And take your good grace from me? Heaven witness,
I have been to you a true and humble wife,
At all times to your will conformable,
Ever in fear to kindle your dislike,
Yea, subject to your countenance – glad or sorry
As I saw it inclin'd. When was the hour
I ever contradicted your desire
Or made it not mine too? Or which of your friends
Have I not strove to love, although I knew
He were mine enemy? What friend of mine
That had to him deriv'd your anger did I
Continue in my liking? Nay, gave notice
He was from thence discharg'd? Sir, call to mind
That I have been your wife in this obedience
Upward of twenty years, and have been blest
With many children by you. If, in the course
And process of this time, you can report,
And prove it too against mine honour, aught,
My bond to wedlock or my love and duty
Against your sacred person, in God's name,
Turn me away and let the foul'st contempt
Shut door upon me, and so give me up
To the sharp'st kind of justice. Please you, sir,
The King, your father, was reputed for
A prince most prudent, of an excellent
And unmatch'd wit and judgment; Ferdinand,
My father, King of Spain, was reckon'd one

The wisest prince that there had reign'd by many
A year before. It is not to be question'd
That they had gather'd a wise council to them
Of every realm, that did debate this business,
Who deem'd our marriage lawful. Wherefore I humbly
Beseech you, sir, to spare me till I may
Be of my friends in Spain advis'd, whose counsel
I will implore. If not, i'th'name of God,
Your pleasure be fulfill'd!   (II. iv. 13–57)

Shakespeare used all the ideas, and much of the phrasing of Katherine's speech, as given by Holinshed. He tightens up the syntax and adds one or two points – Katherine's dismissal of her friends if the King did not approve of them, her forceful demand for punishment if she has sinned, and the oath with which she concludes the speech. The superiority of Hermione's defence may partly be due to the superiority of Greene's eloquence to Holinshed's, partly to Shakespeare's wish to arouse sympathy for Katherine without forfeiting our respect for Henry. He lets it be understood that Henry's conscientious scruples about the legality of his marriage were subordinate to his wish to marry Anne, and to Katherine's failure to produce a male heir; but these motives could not be brought into the open.

The play, as several critics have noted,[8] consists of a series of 'falls', like those of *A Mirror for Magistrates* – Buckingham, Wolsey, Katherine. Frank Kermode adds a fourth, that of Cranmer, who is saved by the King's intervention.[9] The falls are loosely related to each other, but the play is nevertheless somewhat episodic. Each of the three who fall acquires a new humility. Many of Shakespeare's audience would know that the sequence of falls continued after the end of the play: Anne, unable to produce a male heir, was executed for alleged adultery, incest, and treason not long afterwards; Cromwell, whom we see rising, was suddenly overthrown and executed; Gardiner was merely imprisoned in the reign of Edward VI; and Cranmer died at the stake in the reign of Katherine's daughter.

NOTES

I Introduction

1 Selma Guttman, *The Foreign Sources of Shakespeare's Works* (1947); Gordon R. Smith, *A Classified Shakespeare Bibliography, 1936–1958* (1963); John W. Velz, *Shakespeare and the Classical Tradition* (1968).

2 *William Shakespeare's Petty School* (1943); *William Shakespeare's Small Latine and Lesse Greeke* (1944); *On the Literary Genetics of Shakespeare's Poems and Sonnets* (1950).

3 J. Dover Wilson, 'Shakespeare's "Small Latin" – How Much?', SS 10 (1957), 12 ff.; F. P. Wilson, 'Shakespeare's Reading', SS 3 (1950), 14 ff.; J. A. K. Thomson, *Shakespeare and the Classics* (1952); G. K. Hunter, Shakespeare's Reading' in *A New Companion to Shakespeare Studies*, ed. K. Muir and S. Schoenbaum (1971), 55 ff.

4 William Beeston, who declared that Shakespeare had been a schoolmaster in the country (E. K. Chambers, *William Shakespeare* (1930), II. 254).

5 J. Dover Wilson, op. cit. But Ezra Pound preferred Golding to Milton.

6 ibid.

7 ibid.

8 *Studies in Elizabethan Drama* (1955), 13 ff.

9 Propertius, II. xii. 1–8.

10 Baldwin, I. 649.

11 J. A. K. Thomson, op. cit., 32–3.

12 *Odes*, III. 7, 29–30.

13 E. I. Fripp, *Shakespeare Man and Artist* (1938), 109–10.

14 Cf. 20, 304 *post*.

15 Cf. 12 *post*.

16 F. McCombie, '*Hamlet* and the "Moriae Encomium"', SS 27 (1974), 59 ff.

17 Rolf Soellner, NQ (1954), 108–9. See also his article, JEGP, LV (1956), 70.

18 Cf. 211 *post*.

19 Cf. I. A. Richards, *Speculative Instruments* (1955), 210.

20 J. Dover Wilson in *Shakespeare's Hand in 'Sir Thomas More'* (1923), 128–9.

21 Shakespeare here misread North's translation.

22 Cf. K. Muir, 'The Dramatic Function of Anachronism', PLPL (1951), 529 ff.

23 S. Schoenbaum, op. cit., 8.

24 Cf. F. Yates, *A Study of Love's Labour's Lost* (1936), 50 ff; J. W. Lever, SS 6, 79 ff.

25 See below, pp. 132, 183.

26 Cf. G. C. Taylor, *Shakespeare's Debt to Montaigne* (1925).

27 Cf. 186 *post*.

28 Cf. 141 *post*.

29 Cf. John E. Hankins, *Shakespeare's Derived Imagery* (1953).

30 Cf. *King Lear*, ed. K. Muir, IV. ii. 49–50n., and F. P. Wilson, n. 3 *ante*.

31 Cf. 169 *post*.

32 Cf. 187 *post*.

33 Cf. 135 *post*.

34 Cf. J. L. Lowes, *The Road to Xanadu* (1927), *passim*.

35 *Shakespeare's Biblical Knowledge* (1935).

36 Thomas Carter, *Shakespeare and Holy Scripture* (1905).

37 *A Specimen of a Commentary*, ed. A. Over and M. Bell (1967), 203–4.

38 A. Hart, *Shakespeare and the Homilies* (1934), 9–77.

39 E. I. Fripp, *Shakespeare Studies* (1930), 98–128.

40 Harold Brooks has provided much information on this subject.

41 Cf. E. Prosser, SSt 1 (1965), 261–4; R. Ellrodt, 'Selfconsciousness in Montaigne and Shakespeare', SS 28 (1975), 37 ff.

42 *Shakespeare and the Arch-Priest Controversy* (1975).

43 J. Isaacs, *Shakespeare's Earliest Years in the Theatre* (1953).

44 Cf. 15, 275 *post*.

45 It has recently been suggested by Warren B. Austin (*A Computer-Aided Technique for Stylistic Discrimination*, 1969) that the pamphlet was written by Chettle.

46 Cf. K. Muir in *Essays on Shakespeare and the Elizabethan Drama*, ed. R. Hosley (1963), 45 ff.

47 K. Muir and S. O'Loughlin, *The Voyage to Illyria* (1937), 49. Perhaps my collaborator was responsible for this passage.

48 Cf. J. C. Maxwell's note in *King Lear*, ed. Muir, II. iv. 119.

49 F. Yates, op. cit., *passim*.

50 Cf. A. Davenport, NQ (1953), 371–4; G. B. Evans, ibid., 377–8.

51 Cf. 'what drugs, what sorceries, what oiles' (Nashe, ed. McKerrow, I. 180) and *Oth.*, I. iii. 90–1. 'Enuie is a Crocodile that weepes when he kils, and fights with none but he feeds on . . . this . . . monster (Nashe, I. 184) and *Oth.*, III. iii. 169–71.

52 *1 Henry IV*, II. iv. 368.

53 Cf. 63 *post*.

54 A. Thaler, *Shakespeare and Sir Philip Sidney* (1947).

55 K. Muir and J. F. Danby, NQ (1950), 49–51; F. Pyle, MLR, XLIII (1948), 449 ff.

56 Cf. 45 *post*.

57 Cf. 227 *post*.

58 Cf. 229 *post*.

59 Cf. 47 ff. *post*.

60 Cf. 208 *post*.

61 But cf. W. B. C. Watkins, *Shakespeare and Spenser* (1950), and Abbie F. Potts, *Shakespeare and 'The Faerie Queene'* (1958).

62 Cf. I. Ribner, NQ (1952), 244–6; J. D. Reeves, ibid., 441–2.

63 Ed. McKerrow, II. 140.

64 E. Holmes, *Aspects of Elizabethan Imagery* (1929), 50.

65 E. A. Fripp, *Shakespeare: Man and Artist* (1938), 86–7.

66 Fripp, op. cit., 87.

67 *Literary Genetics* (1950), 133–5. I have added one detail.

68 Cf. 55 *post*.

69 Cf. J. L. Jackson, SQ, I (1950), 260 ff.

70 But S. M. Pitcher, *The Case for Shakespeare's Authorship* (1961), thinks it was an early play by Shakespeare himself.

II Early Plays

1 THE COMEDY OF ERRORS

1 T. W. Baldwin, *Shakespere's Small Latine* (1944), I. 426.

2 Bullough, I. 4.

3 *Confessio Amantis; The Patterne of Painfull Adventures*.

4 T. W. Baldwin, *Shakespere's Five-Act Structure* (1947), 673–4.

5 Bullough, I. 9.

6 Baldwin, *Five-Act Structure*, 677, 680–1; Bullough, I. 9–10.

7 Bullough, I. 27–8.

8 Q, New Camb. ed. (1922), 77–8, argued that Shakespeare incorporated the work of an earlier dramatist.

9 *Five-Act Structure*, 665–6. See also Leo Salingar's account of Shakespeare's transformation of his sources in *Shakespeare and the Traditions of Comedy* (1974).

10 W. T. Jewkes, *Act-division in Elizabethan and Jacobean Plays 1583–1616* (1958). See also Emrys Jones, *Scenic Form in Shakespeare* (1971), 67; Henry Snuggs, *Shakespeare and Five Acts* (1960); and Mark Rose, *Shakespearean Design* (1972).

11 T. W. Baldwin, *William Shakespeare Adapts a Hanging* (1931).

2 THE TWO GENTLEMEN OF VERONA

1 Bullough, I. 206.

2 E. K. Chambers, *William Shakespeare*, I. 331.

3 René Pruvost, EA (1960), 1–9, discusses the relationship between *T.G.*,
T.N., and *Gl'Ingannati*.

3 THE TAMING OF THE SHREW

1 HLQ, xxvii (1963–4), 289–308. Reprinted in the Signet Shakespeare ed.
The following discussion is greatly indebted to this article.
2 Cf. Bullough, i. 109.
3 Hosley, op. cit., 306.
4 op. cit., 296.
5 ibid., 302.
6 ibid., 303.
7 Hosley, op. cit., 299; R. A. Houk, SAB, xviii (1943), 181–2.
8 J. C. Maxwell (private letter). It comes from *Senatulus*, tr. N. Bailey
(1725), 483.
9 Hosley, op. cit., 302.
10 Cf. Donald A. Stauffer, *Shakespeare's World of Images* (1949), 46; Cecil C.
Seronsy, SQ, xiv (1963), 15–30; Hosley, ed. *T.S.* (Pelican Shakespeare);
Leo Salingar, *Shakespeare and the Traditions of Comedy* (1974).
M. Mincoff, ES, liv (1973), 554 ff., argues forcibly that *T.S.* was written
before *C.E.*

4 TITUS ANDRONICUS

1 'The Authorship of *T.A.*', JEGP, xlii (1943), 55 ff.
2 See New Arden (1961), xxiv–xxvii, and New Cambridge (1948), xxv ff.,
editions.
3 Cf. R. M. Sargent, 'The Source of *T.A.*', SP xlvi (1949), 167 ff., for the
view that the chapbook substantially represents Shakespeare's source.
4 Cf. Bullough, vi. 12.
5 Cf. T. J. B. Spencer, 'Shakespeare and the Elizabethan Romans', SS 10
(1957), 27 ff.
6 Cf. R. A. Law, 'The Roman Background of *T.A.*', SP, xl (1943), 145 ff.
7 ii. i. 135; iv. i. 82–3. Cf. *Hip.*, ll. 1177 and 668.
J. A. K. Thomson, *Shakespeare and the Classics* (1952), 52, points out
that the second of these quotations is modified by an echo from Seneca's
Epistle 107, 'dominator poli' being substituted for 'Magna regnator
deum'.
8 Cf. Bullough, vi. 26.
9 'The Metamorphosis of Violence in *T.A.*', SS 10 (1957), 39 ff.
10 See R. F. Hill, 'The Composition of *T.A.*', SS 10 (1957), 60 ff., for a
sympathetic study of the problems.

5–7 HENRY VI: PARTS 1–3

1 *Shakespeare's Henry VI and Richard III* (1929). Cf. Madeleine Doran,

2 and 3 Henry VI: Their Relation to The Contention and The True Tragedy (1928).

2   e.g. J. P. Brockbank, 'The Frame of Disorder' in *Early Shakespeare*, ed. J. R. Brown and B. Harris (1961), 73 ff.

3   Cf. Chap. I, n. 45.

4   But see J. Dover Wilson, 'Malone and the Upstart Crow', SS 4 (1951), 56 ff.; S. Schoenbaum, *William Shakespeare: A Documentary Life* (1975), 115 ff.

5   J. Dover Wilson, New Camb. ed.; H. C. Hart, Old Arden ed.,; E. K. Chambers, *William Shakespeare* (1930), I. 290–1.

6   L. Abercrombie, *A Plea for the Liberty of Interpreting* (1930).

7   Cf. 167 *post*.

8   *2 Henry VI* (1952), xxvii.

9   Especially if he had acted in any of their plays.

10   Nashe, ed. McKerrow, I. 212.

11   Ed. Part I, ix–xiv.

12   v. v. 103 ff.

13   Even though the fall of France and its causes is the overriding theme.

14   Cf. K. Muir, *Shakespeare the Professional* (1973), 74. The other passage is v. iii 1–4.

15   *Richard II*, v. iii.

16   Bullough, III. 113, 115.

17   Carol Dixon, in a paper read at the International Shakespeare Congress, Washington, 1976, argued that *Henry VI* was influenced by a number of ballads.

8 RICHARD III

1   W. G. Boswell-Stone, *Shakespeare's Holinshed* (1907), 342 ff.; Bullough, III. 249 ff.

2   New Camb. ed. *passim*.

3   Boswell-Stone, 343.

4   ibid., 345.

5   New Camb. ed. (1954), 196.

6   Boswell-Stone, 391.

7   ibid., 417.

8   *Edward V*, f. xxi.

9   Hol. pp. 756–7, Hall, 1550, R3, xxx^v–xxxi.

10   Bullough, III. 310–12.

11   ll. 1873 ff. The speech appears, unlike most of the play, to be reproduced fairly accurately in Q. Shakespeare's debts to the old play were probably more considerable than can be deduced from Q which, we may suppose, was published in order to gain from the popularity of Shakespeare's play.

12   i.e. Ah!

13 J. Dover Wilson, SQ, III (1952), 305.

14 G. B. Churchill, *Richard III up to Shakespeare* (1900), 497 ff.; J. Dover Wilson, op. cit., 299–306; Bullough, III. 237 ff.

15 New Camb. ed., xxv. Shakespeare does not mention that the prophecy comes true, since G could stand for Gloucester. Vaughan, as reported by Hall, *Edward V* (f. xvii), makes this point.

16 In a private letter to me (16 August 1971).

17 III. 313.

18 Cf. K. Muir, *Shakespeare's Tragic Sequence* (1972), 26 ff.
    W. H. Clemen has a detailed commentary on the play in *A Commentary on . . . R. III* (1968).

9 ROMEO AND JULIET

1 See O. H. Moore, *The Legend of R.J.* (1950); R. A. Law, *Texas Studies* (No. 9) (1929), 82–5; Mary M. Mulligan, *The Sources of R.J.* (Unpublished thesis, Liverpool, 1954).

2 J. C. Walker, *Historical Memoir on Italian Tragedy* (1799), 57.

3 ibid., 61.

4 John Masefield, *William Shakespeare* (1927), 70. This was modified in later editions.

5 Peter Alexander, *Shakespeare's Life and Art* (1938), 115.

6 Brooke, op. cit., 254.

7 Law, op. cit.

8 353, 1353, 2710.

9 219, 387.

10 1738–40. T. W. Baldwin, *Shakespeare's Five-Act Structure* (1947), 769, thinks that Marlowe was the debtor.

11 Address to the Reader.

12 Cf. K. Muir, NQ (1956), 241–3, for other sea imagery.

13 *A Specimen of a Commentary*, ed. A. Over and M. Bell (1967), 112, 224.

14 Curiously enough, Q1 of *R.J.* prints 'barge' for 'barke'.

15 Ann Thompson, '*Troilus and Criseyde* and *Romeo and Juliet*', *The Yearbook of English Studies* (1976), 26 ff., has recently shown how much the play owes to Chaucer.

10 RICHARD II

1 Matthew W. Black, ed. *Richard II* (1955), 405 ff.

2 New Camb. ed. (1939), lxxv ff.

3 Peter Ure, NQ (1953), 426–9, and ed. *Richard II* (1961), xxx–li.

4 e.g. Holinshed, 497, 499.

5 e.g. 487–94.

6 See n. 3 *ante*.

7   *Archaeologia* (1824). Text from J. A. Buchon, *Collection des chroniques*, XIV (1826), 336, 341, 371.

8   ibid., 341.

9   ibid., 369.

10 ibid., 372.

11 ibid., 411.

12 ibid., 417.

13 Ed. B. Williams (1846), 49, 52, 56.

14 ibid., 20.

15 ibid., 37, 56–60. Holinshed uses the expression in a different context, 489.

16 L. B. Campbell, *Shakespeare's Histories* (1947), 308 ff., 319 ff. Cf. Bullough, III. 415 ff. Other parallels have been noted by Harold Brooks and Peter Ure.

17 *Shakespeare's History Plays* (1944), 253.

18 'Notes sur les sources . . .', *Revue de l'Enseignement de Languages Vivantes* (1924), 1 ff., 54 ff., 106 ff., 158 ff.

19 ed. cit., liv ff. [Berners' Froissart, ed. W. E. Henley (1903), 336].

20 ibid., lvi [Henley, 311].

21 Ed. *Woodstock* (1946), 50 ff.

22 ed. cit., xxxv, xl.

23 Cf. Black (n. 1 *ante*), Reyher (n. 18), and *The Civile Wars*, ed. L. Michel (1958), 8–21.

24 Michel, 146, gives Daniel's revised text.

25 ed. cit., xlix.

26 Hall (1550), *Henry IV*, f. vi (echoed by Holinshed).

27 ibid., f. xv.

28 Holinshed, 508.

29 Froissart, ed. Henley, 398. Cited by Tillyard, 295.

30 K. Muir, RES, x (1959), 283–9.

31 *Shakespere's Small Latine* (1944), II. 427–8.

32 *Fasti*, I. 493–4.

33 Bullough, I. 323.

34 See 4 *ante*.

35 J. Lyly, *Works*, ed. Bond, I. 313–14, 316. Cited by Ure.

36 v. 97.

37 v. 74. Malone cited a Lyly passage given above.

38 In a private communication.

39 See 51 *ante*.

40 Ed. Rossiter, IV. i. 143 ff.

41 ibid., III. ii. 108–9, v. i. 127–8.

42 SS 6 (1953), 79 ff.

43 NQ (1953), 374 ff.

44 J. Sylvester, III. ii. 2.

45 Unpublished thesis, University of Liverpool (1956), 16–17.
46 Ed. E. Gosse (1883), I, *An Alarum against Usurers*, 86.
47 op. cit., 86, 87, 88, 88, 86, 89, 90.
48 Harold F. Brooks, SQ, XIV (1963), 195–9, argues that among the sources of the political allegory of the garden-scene is Elyot's *Boke of the Gouernour*, I. xxiii. He speaks of 'improfytable weedes' as the gardener proposes to root away the weeds 'which without profit suck/The soil's fertility'. In the same article Brooks suggests that the incident of Richard's horse was derived from Elyot too. See II. xiii.

II A MIDSUMMER-NIGHT'S DREAM

1 *Works*, ed. McKerrow, III. 324.
2 Bullough, I. 388.
3 *Collected Poems*, ed. Muir and Thomson (1969), 73.
4 Bullough, 389.
5 *Sixteen Plays of Shakespeare*, ed. Kittredge (1948), 148.
6 E. Schanzer, UTQ, XXIV (1954–5), 234 ff.
7 E. K. Chambers, *William Shakespeare* (1930), I. 363.
8 E. I. Fripp, *Shakespeare Man and Artist* (1938), 394.
9 *The Petite Pallace*, ed. H. Hartman (1938), 125.
10 IV. 95.
11 III. 1331 ff.
12 3960 ff.
13 Cf. R. B. McKerrow, *The Library* (1924–5), 17–18; McKerrow and Ferguson, *Title Page Borders* (1932), 80.
14 Thomson (see below) calls it a mantle.
15 *A Gorgious Gallery of Gallant Inventions*, ed. H. E. Rollins (1926), 112.
16 T. Mouffett, *Of the Silkewormes and their Flies* (1599), 13.
17 *Thisb* was altered to *Thisbe* in later editions.
18 Golding's 'Tumbe' may have suggested Thisbe's rhyme, 'dumbe'/'tombe'
19 *Mythology and the Renaissance Tradition* (1932), 58.
20 As Bush suggests (59), Shakespeare may also have been influenced by Howell's version of the story of Cephalus and Procris, mentioned by Pyramus and Thisbe, since Sephalus calls on the sisters three when he finds Procris dead:

> He curst the gods that skies possesst,
> The Systers three and all the rest.

21 'Then made he mone'. Cf. v. i. 325.
22 Dunstan Gale's *Pyramus and Thisbe* was not published until after November 1596.
23 *c*. 1545.
24 Cf. 'wicked cruell wall' (*Gorgious Gallery*).
25 Bullough, I. 375, is unconvinced.

26 op. cit., 28.

27 Three passages may have influenced Theseus' first speech in Act v.

28 Many of the parallels with Mouffet's poem were pointed out by M. L.
Farrand (SP, xxvii (1930), 233 ff.) and, more effectively, by A. S. T.
Fisher (NQ (1949), 376 ff.). D. Bush, MLN, xlvi (1931), 144–7, replied
to the first of these.

29 M. C. Bradbrook, *Shakespeare and Elizabethan Poetry* (1951), 98, 256.

30 Cf. Anne Righter, *Shakespeare and the Idea of the Play* (1962), *passim*.

31 In his forthcoming edition of *M.N.D.*, Harold Brooks provides a
remarkably full account of the sources. In addition to those mentioned
above, he lists as probable sources three of Seneca's plays – *Oedipus*,
Medea, and especially *Hippolytus* – and passages from Spenser's *Shep-
heardes Calender*. An article by Leah Scragg on the influence of Lyly's
Gallathea on *M.N.D.* is to appear in SS 30 (1977).

12 LOVE'S LABOUR'S LOST

1 Bullough, I. 425 ff.

2 Cf. M. C. Bradbrook, *The School of Night* (1936), 153 ff.; F. A. Yates,
A Study of 'Love's Labour's Lost' (1936); R. David, ed. *L.L.L.* (1951),
xxxviii ff.; G. Ungerer, *Anglo–Spanish Relations* (1956).

3 *Riverside Shakespeare* (1974), 174.

13 KING JOHN

1 William M. Matchett in the Signet edition supports Honigmann. Dr S.
Carr (Unpublished thesis, Liverpool, 1974) has convincingly argued that
Shakespeare's play was based on *The Troublesome Raigne*. The matter is
discussed by Bullough, iv. 1 ff., and by R. L. Smallwood, Penguin ed.
(1974), 365 ff.

2 Bullough, iv. 22.

3 Edward Rose, 'Shakespeare as an Adapter', *Macmillan's Magazine* (1878).

4 Honigmann ed. (1954), xv–xvi.

5 E. C. Pettet, 'Hot Irons and Fever', EC, iv (1954), 128 ff.

6 'Commodity and Honour in *K.J.*', UTQ, xxix (1959–60), 341 ff. R. L.
Smallwood, ed. *K.J.* (1974), 45–6.

III Comedies and Histories

14 THE MERCHANT OF VENICE

1 E. Honigmann, MLR, xlix (1954), 293 ff.

2 Ed. J. R. Brown (1955), xxx, n.5.

3 Bullough, I. 463.

4 Bullough, I. 482; J. R. Brown, ed. cit., xxxi, 168.

5 Bullough, I. 486. The ballad is printed by J. R. Brown.
6 J. R. Brown, ed. cit., xxxi.
7 Bullough, I. 449.
8 Ed. F. Bowers, II. i. 47–8, 54.
9 J. Dover Wilson, *Shakespeare's Happy Comedies* (1962), 94 ff.
10 Cf. Bullough, I. 456, 497. But it is unlikely that Shakespeare knew this tale.
11 J. R. Brown, ed. cit., xxxii, 173.
12 J. Dover Wilson, op. cit., 114.

15–16 HENRY IV: PARTS 1–2

1 Scenes concerned with rebellions would be cut sooner than those dealing with Hal's exploits.
2 e.g. W. G. Zeeveld's article, ELH, III (1936), 317 ff.
I am indebted to Pauline Dalton's unpublished thesis (Liverpool, 1965).
3 Hall, f. xx.
4 Bullough, IV. 196 ff.
5 Hall, f. xxi.
6 Holinshed, 498/2/3.
7 E. Seaton, K. M. Lea, RES, XXI (1945), 319–22.
8 Ed. L. Michel, 320. Daniel later altered this stanza.
9 Pointed out by Theobald in his edition of Shakespeare (1733).
10 Theobald, cited New Var. (1936), I. i. 70–3n.
11 Dalton, op. cit., 187.
12 J. Dover Wilson in *The Library*, XXVI (1945), 2 ff.
13 J. J. Elson, SP, XXXII (1935), 177 ff.
14 Bullough, IV. 164, seems to suggest that it is Prince John's bravery which is being rewarded.
15 Bullough, IV. 251 ff.
16 E. B. Benjamin, 'Fame, Poetry . . .' SR, VI (1959), 64 ff.
17 NQ (1954), 238 ff.
18 A. E. Morgan, *Some Problems of . . . Henry the Fourth* (1922), 4–5.
19 ibid., 26–43. Cf. W. W. Greg, *Henslowe Papers* (1907), 57–8. Some readings are dubious and the spelling has been modernized.
20 Ed. G. B. Harrison (1922), 54, 74.
21 Cf. C. A. Greer, NQ (1954), 53 ff.

17 THE MERRY WIVES OF WINDSOR

1 See H. J. Oliver's ed. (1971), lv.
2 J. L. Hotson, *Shakespeare Versus Shallow* (1931), 85–7.
3 J. M. Nosworthy, *Shakespeare's Occasional Plays* (1965), 93 ff.
4 F. G. Fleay, followed by New Camb. ed.
5 Dorothy Hart Bruce, SP, XXXIX (1942), 265 ff.

6 Bullough, II. 26.
7 Bullough, II. 6–7.
8 R. S. Forsythe, MP, XVIII (1920), 401 ff. Cf. Oliver, ed. cit., lix ff.
9 IV. iii. 29.
10 Hotson, op. cit., 113 ff.; Oliver, ed. cit., xlvi ff.; Bullough, II. 11 ff.; F. Yates, *The Rosicrucian Enlightenment* (1975), 31–2.
11 J. Crofts, *Shakespeare and the Post-Horses* (1937), *passim*.
12 Hotson, op. cit., *passim*.

18 HENRY V
1 Bullough, IV. 376 ff., gives extracts from all these.
2 Ed. *Henry V* (1954), xxxv.
3 Walter, ed. cit., xxxvi, and note on IV. iii. 16–18.
4 Bullough, 357.
5 Walter, ed. cit., 91.
6 Bullough, IV. 362, 408.
7 TLS (1974), 12 July.
8 J. H. Walter, MLR, XLI (1946), 237 ff.
9 Two recent interpretations may be mentioned: Gordon Ross Smith, 'Shakespeare's *Henry V*: Another Part of the Critical Forest', *Journal of the History of Ideas*, XXXVII (1976), 3 ff.; Andrew Gurr, SS 30 (1977), forthcoming.

19 MUCH ADO ABOUT NOTHING
1 C. T. Prouty, *The Sources of 'M.A.'* (1950).
2 Bullough, II. 134, prints some of *Fedele and Fortunio* as an analogue.
3 D. J. Gordon, SP, XXXIX (1942), 279 ff.
4 op. cit., 71–2.
5 op. cit., 70.
6 Mary A. Scott, PMLA, XVI (1901), 475 ff.
7 Abbie Findlay Potts, SAB, XVII (1942), 103–11, 126 ff.
8 J. Masefield, *Shakespeare* (1911), 134.
9 F. C. Kolbe, *Shakespeare's Way* (1930), 87–9.

20 JULIUS CAESAR
1 Among editors: J. D. Wilson (1949), T. S. Dorsch (1955). Among critics: M. W. MacCallum, *Shakespeare's Roman Plays* (1910); E. Schanzer, *Shakespeare's Problem Plays* (1963).
2 *M.N.D.*, II. i. 77–80.
3 *Henry V*, IV. vii. 25 ff. Caesar and Alexander are parallel lives.
4 One can be fairly sure that Shakespeare had not read Muret's Latin play or that of Jacques Grévin, or even Pescetti's *Il Cesare*, despite one or two interesting parallels (Calpurnia fears, as Brutus hopes, that the

assassination of Caesar will be performed in the theatre; as in Shakespeare's play, it is Cassius who urges that Antony should be killed, and Brutus replies that after the death of Caesar, Antony, a mere limb, would be powerless. Cf. Bullough, v. 32, and his reference to A. Boecker, 30 ff.). The anonymous *Caesar's Revenge*, although not published until 1607, was probably written before Shakespeare's play – it is discussed below. Only the epilogue of *Caesar Interfectus* has survived.

5   K. Muir, *Shakespeare the Professional* (1973), 33.

6   As in *Caesar's Revenge*.

7   Douglas Bush, MLN, II (1937), 407–8. J. C. Maxwell, NQ (1956), 147, showed that in Decius Brutus' flattery of Caesar (II. i. 203–8) he used an illustration from Elyot's *The Governor*.

8   *Shakespeare's Appian* (1956), ed. E. Schanzer, 14.

9   ibid., 15–16.

10   ibid., 19.

11   ibid., xx.

12   ibid., 44.

13   ibid., 45–6.

14   Ed. 1578, Sig. N2^v.

15   Cf. E. Schanzer, op. cit., 18–19. Joan Rees thinks that the inconsistency of Kyd's Caesar, both boastful and heroic, may have stimulated Shakespeare to explore the deeper implications of the character. MLR, L (1955), 135–41.

16   Ed. Boas.

17   Some other parallels are given in *Shakespeare's Sources*, I, 194–5.

18   NQ (1954), 196–7.

19   ibid.

20   A. Bonjour, *The Structure of J.C.* (1958), Chap. I.

21   Cf. *J.C.*, ed. T. S. Dorsch, 58, 62.
     Harold Brooks has supplied me with another echo from the *Mirror* ('Shore's Wife', ed. L. B. Campbell, 378):
     > Duke Haniball in all his conquest greate,
     > Or Ceaser yet, whose triumphes did excede,
     > Of all their spoyles.

     (Cf. *J.C.*, III. viii. 149–51).

22   I. 467 ff.

23   522 ff.

24   Ed. E. Schanzer, 18, 20.

25   J. Dover Wilson, ed. *J.C.* (1949), I. iii. 5–28n.

26   T. S. Dorsch, ed. cit., II. ii. 19–22n. Cf. Dekker, ed. A. Grosart, I. 13 ff.

27   Bullough, v. 141 ff., prints extracts from Sallust, Velleius Paterculus, Tacitus, Suetonius, and Florus. I agree that these are analogues rather than sources.

Sidney Homan's recent article, SSt VIII (1975), 195 ff., has an interesting
discussion of the influence of the parallel lives in Plutarch – Dion,
Alexander, Demetrius – on Shakespeare's portrayal of Brutus, Caesar,
and Antony respectively.

21 AS YOU LIKE IT

1 W. W. Greg, ed. *Rosalynde* (1907), x, xiv.
2 Unpublished thesis, University of Birmingham.
3 Apparently the name he assumes in the forest of Arden.
4 Bullough, II. 155–6, 257.
5 E.g. H. Gardner, 'A.Y.L.I.' in *Shakespeare: The Comedies*, ed. K. Muir
   (1965), 58 ff.; E. C. Pettet, *Shakespeare and the Romance Tradition* (1949),
   128–31.
6 Bullough, II. 155.

22 TWELFTH NIGHT

1 Barrett Wendell, *William Shakespeare* (1894), 209.
2 S. Race, NQ (1954), 380–3, thinks this is a Collier forgery.
3 Bullough, II. 339, prints the argument.
4 ibid., 342.
5 SQ (1954), 271 ff.
6 ibid.
7 *T.N.*, III. iii. 41–2.
8 M. Luce, ed. Riche's *Apolonius and Silla* (1912), 11–12.
9 A Latin version of this play was performed at Queen's College, Cambridge, in 1595 under the title of *Laelia*.
10 *Novelle* (1554), II. 36.
11 *Histoires Tragiques*, IV (1571), 229–30.
12 Still less would Shakespeare have followed *Gl'Ingannati* in having little
   Cittina describe the union of Lelia and Flaminio (v. v) or in having
   Pasquella describe how she and Isabella discover that Fabrizio is a man
   (IV.5): 'e trovai che s'abbraciavano e si baciavano insieme. Io ebbi voglia
   di chiarirmi se era o maschio o femina. Avendolo la padrona disteso in
   sul letto, e chiamandomi ch'io l'aiutasse mentre ch'ella gli teneva le
   mani, egli si lasciava vincere. Lo sciclsi dinanzi: e, a un tratto, mi sentii
   percuotere non so che cosa in su le mani; né cognobbi se gli era un
   pestaglio o una carota o pur quell'altra cosa. Ma, sia quel si vuole, e' non
   è cosa che abbia sentita la grandine. Come io la viddi cosi fatta, fugge,
   sorelle, e serra l'uscio! E so che, per me, non ve tornarei sola; e, se
   qualcuna di voi non mel crede e voglia chiarirsene, io gli prestarò la
   chiave'.
13 E. K. Chambers, *Shakespeare: A Survey* (1925), 178; L. Hotson, *The
   First Night of 'T.N.'* (1954), 98 ff.

14   Probably not from Malevolti of *Il Sacrificio*, performed and published with *Gl'Ingannati*.
15   Hotson, op. cit., 131.
16   MLR (1948), 449 ff.; Var. ed. *T.N.*, 375–6.
17   Hotson, op. cit., *passim*.
18   ibid., 145 ff.
19   T. W. Baldwin, *Shakespere's Five-Act Structure* (1947), 715.
20   Bullough, II. 278.

23 TROILUS AND CRESSIDA

1   The sources of the play are discussed in R. K. Presson's *Shakespeare's T.C. and the Legends of Troy* (1953) and Robert Kimbrough, *Shakespeare's T.C. and its setting* (1964). There are wider surveys in the New Var. ed. (Hillebrand and Baldwin) and in Bullough, VI. I am also indebted to an unpublished Liverpool thesis by Mary F. Bruce (1948).
2   C. S. Lewis's views, as expressed in *The Allegory of Love* (1936), on which this account is based, have since been questioned.
3   *Henry V*, II. i. 74; *T.N.*, III. i. 53. Pistol's phrase was a quotation.
4   338, 435.
5   Cf. L. C. Knights, TLS (1932), 408.
6   XI. 485 ff.
7   All listed by Presson, op. cit.
8   Bullough, VI. 214.
9   Presson, op. cit., 91 ff., and New Var., II. ii. 421n.
10 *Shakespeare's Problem Plays* (1950), 33 ff., 149.
11 Cf. C. H. Herford, *N.S.S. Trans.* (1888), 186, and K. Muir, NQ (1955), 141. For quotations, see Grosart's ed. of Greene, VI, 209, 165, 167, 155, 169, 239, 236, 263, 160, 166, 195.
12 Readings of Q and F.
13 There is a full discussion in the New Var. ed., 389 ff., and a briefer one in Dobrée's, pp.116–17.
14 *Seaven Bookes*, II. 83 ff.
15 *Aen.* I. 430.
16 Chaps. I, II.
17 III. 1744 ff.
18 Cf. A. Hart, *Shakespeare and the Homilies* (1934), 33–4.
19 Temple, ed., II. 275, IV. I.
20 Steevens, ed. (1793).
21 SP, XIII (1916), 100–9. I. A. Richards, *Speculative Instruments* (1955), 198 ff.
22 New Var. ed., 401.
23 H. Green, *Shakespeare and the Emblem Writers* (1870), 448 ff.
24 W. B. D. Henderson, *Parrott Presentation Volume*, ed. H. Craig (1935), 142–4.

25 *Archiv*, CXXXIII (1915), 91–6.
26 Cf. Oscar J. Campbell, *Comicall Satyre and Shakespeare's T.C.* (1938).
27 T. W. Baldwin in New Var. ed., 451–3.
28 The influence of *Lucrece* and the *Sonnets* on the imagery of the play is discussed by K. Muir, SS 8 (1955), 28 ff.

IV Tragic Period

24 HAMLET

1 Nashe's preface of Greene's *Menaphon* is thought by most critics to imply that Kyd was the author of the original *Hamlet*.
2 Bullough, VII. 16–17, lists a number of further resemblances between the two plays.
3 R. Armin, *A Nest of Ninnies* (1608), sig. G3^v.
4 G. I. Duthie, *The 'Bad' Quarto of Hamlet* (1941), 186 ff.
5 Bullough, VII. 48, 188–9.
6 When Shakespeare was fifteen, a Katherine Hamlet was drowned in the Avon at Tiddington, and in July of the same year a William Shakespeare, of Warwick, was drowned in the Avon while bathing.
7 W. J. Lawrence, *Speeding up Shakespeare* (1937), 55 ff. As the soliloquy stands at present, Hamlet refers to the bourne from which no traveller returns, after he has seen the Ghost; but he could be implying that the devil had appeared in his father's shape, or that a ghost is not the same thing as a real return in flesh and blood form.
8 *Life and Letters*, 1 (1928), 18.
9 *Shakespeare as a Dramatist* (1935), 77 ff.
10 *Hamlet: A Study in Critical Method* (1931), 97.
11 *Selected Essays* (1932), 143. Eliot later retracted.
12 E. M. W. Tillyard, *Shakespeare's Problem Plays* (1950), 29.
13 F. Bowers, *Elizabethan Revenge Tragedy* (1940), *passim*.
14 Tr. T. Lodge (1614), 520, 547–8, 556–7.
15 Bowers, op. cit.
16 J. J. Lawlor, RES (1950), 97. Cf. *The Tragic Sense in Shakespeare* (1960), 47 ff.
17 J. Dover Wilson, *What Happens in Hamlet* (1935), 309–20, sets out most of the evidence.
18 T. Bright, op. cit., 257, 13, 130, 111–12, 124, 102–3, 131.
19 A. Davenport, NQ (1953), 371–4, and G. B. Evans, ibid., 377–8.
20 Bullough, VII, 44–5.
21 ibid., VII. 159 ff.
22 H. Craig, HLB (1934), 17 ff.
23 Frank McCombie in SS 27 (1974), 59 ff.

24   Tudor translations ed. ii. 10–13.

25   K. Muir, NQ (1957), 285–6.

26   A. P. Stabler has three useful articles on the remoter sources of *Hamlet*: SP, LXII (1965), 654 ff.; *Research St.*, XXXII (1964), 207; PMLA, LXXXI (1966), 207 ff. See also Bullough, VII. 5 ff.

     W. Montgomerie, *Hibbert Journal*, LIX (1960), 67 ff., suggests the influence of Tacitus' account of the Emperor Claudius.

25 ALL'S WELL THAT ENDS WELL

1   op. cit., 29, 28, 32, 58, 92, 94, 97.

2   The critical history of the play is admirably surveyed in Joseph G. Price's *The Unfortunate Comedy* (1968).

3   *Shakespeare's Problem Comedies* (1931), 51 ff.

4   *Shakespeare* (1936), 302.

5   HLQ, XIII (1949), 217 ff.

6   *Prefaces* (1934), 155.

26 MEASURE FOR MEASURE

1   Mary Lascelles, *Shakespeare's 'Measure for Measure'* (1953), gives the best and fullest treatment of the sources. Bullough, II. 399 ff., adds some points. Three earlier treatments are not altogether superseded: F. E. Budd, *Rev. de Lit. Comp.*, (1931), 711–36; R. H. Ball, *Univ. Colorado St.* (1945), 132–46; L. Albrecht, *Neue Untersuchungen zu Shakespeares Mass für Mass* (1914).

2   op. cit., 35.

3   *Endeavors of Art* (1954), 385–9. Cf. E. Schanzer, *The Problem Plays of Shakespeare* (1963), 86.

4   op. cit.

5   Privately.

6   op. cit., 22 ff., 36 ff. Cf. Bullough, II. 514.

7   Bullough, VI. 371.

8   R. W. Chambers, *Man's Unconquerable Mind* (1939), 301 ff.

9   Isabella refers to another substitution, that of Christ for the sinner. Cf. J. Black's article in SS 26 (1973), 124.

10   John Masefield, *William Shakespeare* (1911), 178.

11   A. T. Cadoux, *Shakespearean Selves* (1938), 81.

12   R. Bridges, *The Influence of the Audience* (1927), 13.

13   J. I. M. Stewart, *Character and Motive in Shakespeare* (1949), 14.

14   *The Jacobean Drama* (1936), 260.

15   *Shakespeare's Problem Plays* (1950), 132.

16   Cf. J. W. Bennett, *Measure for Measure as Royal Entertainment* (1966). I have suggested elsewhere (NQ (1956), 424–5) that Shakespeare consulted Erasmus' *Funus* to obtain background material about friars and

nuns. Erasmus tells us that a dying man's younger son is dedicated to St Francis, his elder daughter to St Clare: *Filius minor dicaretur S. Francisco, filia maior S. Clarae.* This passage may have suggested making Isabella a votaress of St Clare, as Francisco suggested Francisca, Isabella's interlocutor. In the same context Erasmus tells us that the dying man is visited by Bernardine, a Franciscan friar, and Vincentius, a Dominican friar. On the page following the reference to St Clare, Erasmus speaks of *Barnardino [sic] tanundem Vincentio*, which may have given Shakespeare two of his characters' names.

27 OTHELLO

1 Mario Praz, *Machiavelli and the Elizabethans* (1928), (*Proc. Brit. Acad.* 49–97), points out (68) that Cinthio's *Altile* has a villain who ruins Norrino by his treachery, his motive being his thwarted love for Altile.

2 Cf. W. Wokatsch, *Archiv*, CLXII (1932), 118–19.

3 J. S. Smart, *Shakespeare: Truth and Tradition* (1928), 183n.

4 J. Sylvester, however, also uses the phrase 'prophetic fury'. It may be mentioned that the tent, embroidered by Cassandra, described in several stanzas of Ariosto's poem, seems to have suggested the magic in the web of Desdemona's handkerchief.

5 Cf. II. i. 187–92.

6 III. ii. 29–41.

7 III. iii. 243–4, IV. i.

8 K. Muir, Penguin ed. (1968), 33.

9 Cf. Emrys Jones's article, SS 21 (1968), 47–52, and G. R. Hibbard, ibid., 39–46. Shakespeare could have read about the Turkish wars in R. Knolles's *Generall Historie of the Turks* (1603) and in W. Thomas's *Historie of Italie* (1549). Cf. Bullough, VII. 212.

10 Cf. E. H. W. Meyerstein, TLS (1942), 72.

11 I. iii. 111: 'indirect and forced courses'.

12 I. iii. 77, 91–4, 169, 232.

13 V. 2. But see PMLA (1934), 807–9, and PQ (1938), 351 ff.

14 K. Muir, RES (1956), 182.

15 Malone's note.

16 Hart's note, ed. 1903, V. iii. 264.

17 XII. 14, 15, 25, XXXV. 15, XXXVIII. 8, XXV. 13, XIX. 5, XX. 3.

18 T. W. Baldwin, 'Shakespeare's Use of Pliny', *Parrott Presentation Vol.*, ed. H. Craig (1935), 157 ff.

19 K. Muir, MLR, LIV (1959), 224–5; NQ (1953), 513–14.

20 H. Gardner, *The Noble Moor* (*Proc. Brit. Acad.*, 1955, 189–205).

21 A. C. Swinburne, *Three Plays of Shakespeare* (1909), 34.

22 *Shakespeare* (1936), 315–16.

23 *Shakespeare's Life and Art* (1938), 166.

24 Barbara H. de Mendonca, SS 21 (1968), 31–8.

25 SS 21 (1968), 13 ff.

28 KING LEAR

1 Bullough, VII. 402.

2 Ed. K. Muir (1972), II. iv. 45n.

3 Bullough, VII. 270–1, 309–11.

4 Ed. K. Muir, xxiv ff.

5 ibid., xxxii–iii.

6 *The Library*, XX (1939–40), 386–97.

7 Ed. K. Muir, xxxi–xxxii, and n. 6 *ante*.

8 Barbara Heliodora de Mendonça, SS 13 (1960), 41 ff.

9 Bullough, VII. 337.

10 G. B. Harrison and H. Granville-Barker, *A Companion to Shakespeare Studies* (1934), 77.

11 D. M. McKeithan, *Univ. Texas Bull.*, 8 July 1934, 45–9.

12 ll. 114–21.

13 K. Muir ed., xxx–xxxi.

14 'Shakespeare's Significances' in A. Bradby, *Shakespeare Crit. 1919–35*, 331.

15 *Shakespere's Small Latine and Lesse Greeke* (1944), II. 520.

16 F. E. Budd, RES, XI (1935), 421 ff.

17 *Per.*, IV. vi. 118; *Temp.*, II. ii. 5–12.

18 K. Muir, ed. cit., 235; G. C. Taylor, *Shakespeare's Debt to Montaigne* (1925).

19 Cf. R. Ellrodt's article in SS 28 (1975), 37 ff.

20 Rosalie L. Colie, 'Reason and Need' in Colie and Flahiff, *Some Facets of 'King Lear'* (1974), 185 ff. Professor Colie refers to Lawrence Stone's *Crisis of the Aristocracy* (1965). A number of other essays in *Some Facets* by Bridget Gellert Lyons (23 ff.), by F. D. Hoeniger (89 ff.), by Rosalie Colie (117 ff.) and by F. T. Flahiff (221 ff.) are relevant to a study of the sources of the play.

21 A. J. Price, NQ (1952), 313–14.

22 See K. Muir, *Shakespeare's Tragic Sequence* (1972) and my review of S. L. Goldberg's *An Essay of King Lear*, RQ, XXVIII (1975), 284 ff.

29 MACBETH

1 H. N. Paul, *The Royal Play of Macbeth* (1950), 17–22; Bullough, VII. 470–2.

2 K. Muir, *Sources I*, 167n. But see New Arden notes where additional sources are suggested for this speech: Seneca, *Her. Fur.*, 1261–2, 1077–81; Seneca, *Agam.*, Chorus 1; Timothy Bright, *A Treatise of Melancholie*, 189. T. W. Baldwin cites *Ciceronis Sententiae*.

3 Paul, op. cit., 388–90.

4 ibid., 202–9; Bullough, vii. 438–43, 509 ff., 517 ff.; New Arden ed., xxxv.

5 Paul, op. cit., 218–19.

6 ibid., 171–6, 212.

7 ibid., 174.

8 Ed. Grierson and Smith (1914), 105, ed. J. Dover Wilson, xliii.

9 SS 19 (1966), 82 ff.

10 ibid., 85.

11 K. Muir, NQ (1949), 214–16.

12 P. Sidney, *The Defence of Poesie*, E4^v.

13 B. J. Burden, cited New Arden, xxxvi.

14 New Arden, 189.

15 ibid., 190. Based on G. Wilson Knight.

16 ibid., 190.

17 R. A. Law, *Texas St.* (1952), 35–41.

18 Glynne Wickham, 'Hell-Castle and its Door-keeper', SS 19 (1966), 68 ff.

19 Paul, op. cit., 237 ff.; New Arden, xv ff.

20 Paul, op. cit., 56–9.

21 New Arden, liv.

22 Paul, op. cit., 367 ff.

23 Cf. W. M. Merchant, 'His Friend-like Queen', SS 19 (1966), 75 ff.

24 e.g. *Basilikon Doron, The Trew Law of Free Monarchies, Daemonologie*.

30 TIMON OF ATHENS

1 *L.L.L.*, iv. iii. 166.

2 Bullough, vi. 294.

3 E. A. J. Honigmann, 'Timon of Athens', SQ, xii (1961), 3 ff.

4 SS 27 (1974), 111 ff. A second article by Bulman, SS 29 (1976), 103 ff., again argues that the anonymous *Timon* was the main source of Shakespeare's play. Honigmann, op. cit., 12–13, argues that the mock banquet could have been suggested by Lucian, that the throwing of stones derives from his account of the later stoning of the parasites, and that the faithful steward was expanded from Plutarch's Life of Antonius.

5 Cf. Honigmann, op. cit.

6 Bullough, vi. 263 ff., translated from the Italian.

7 *Lives*, ed. G. Wyndham, ii. 143.

8 W. Farnham, *Shakespeare's Tragic Frontier* (1950), 65.

9 C.F.E. Spurgeon, *Shakespeare's Imagery* (1935), 198–9.

10 *Moralia* (tr. Holland, 1603), 83. Cf. P. Ure, *Shakespeare: The Problem Plays* (1961), 47.

11 *The Wheel of Fire* (1930), 208.

12 Cf. K. Muir, 'Timon of Athens and the Cash Nexus' (1947). Reprinted in *The Singularity of Shakespeare* (1977).

31 ANTONY AND CLEOPATRA

1 Bullough, v. 267.
2 ibid., 274.
3 W. A. Edwards, *Plagiarism* (1933), 110.
4 J. Middleton Murry, *Countries of the Mind* (1922), II. 11–12.
5 *The Legend of Good Women.*
6 P. D. Westbrook, PMLA, LXII (1947), 392–8.
7 *Shakespeare's Roman Plays* (1910), 648–52.
8 E. Schanzer, *Shakespeare's Appian*, 76–7.
9 E. Schanzer, NQ (1956), 152–4.
10 Ed. *Antony and Cleopatra* (1950), x, n2.
11 op. cit., 154.
12 E. Schanzer, op. cit., 153; J. Dover Wilson, 236.
13 op. cit., 44, 47, 58.
14 Cf. R. C. Bald, TLS (1924), 776; W. Farnham, *Shakespeare's Tragic Frontier* (1950), 172–3; H. Norgaard, NQ (1955), 56–7.
15 The best account is by Willard Farnham, op. cit., 157 ff. He shows that Daniel's Cleopatra and Shakespeare's have the same mixed motives: to avoid being led in triumph; to safeguard her children; and to be loyal to Antony. Both refer to Antony as Atlas.
16 op. cit., 167.
17 Bullough, v. 314, 424.
18 Ed. F. Gohin (1925), 75–7. Joan Rees, MLR, XLVII (1952), 1–10, discusses Daniel's debt to Jodelle.
19 Cf. Joan Rees, SS 6 (1953), 91 ff.
20 Cf. Helen Morris, 'Queen Elizabeth I "shadowed" in Cleopatra', HLQ (1969), 271–8. K. Muir, 'Elizabeth I, Jodelle and Cleopatra', RD (1969), 197 ff.
21 SQ, VII (1956), 59 ff.
22 SS 12 (1959), 88 ff.
23 RES (1946), 219 ff.

32 CORIOLANUS

1 K. Muir, NQ (1953), 240–2.
2 E. Honigmann called my attention to this book.
3 L. Hotson, *I. William Shakespeare* (1937), *passim.*
4 He uses some of North's phraseology.
5 Cf. Leonard Barkan, *Nature's Work of Art* (1975), *passim.*
6 Cf. G. R. Waggoner, 'An Elizabethan attitude towards peace and war', PQ, XXXIII (1954), 20 ff.

7 J. E. Phillips, Jr, *The State in Shakespeare's Greek and Roman Plays* (1940), has a good summary of Bodin's views.

8 ibid., 69 ff.

9 It may be mentioned that 'persuade', 'accounted', and 'idle' are used in this first scene, and that 'enforced', 'repined', 'surcease', and 'sensibly' occur elsewhere in the play.

10 e.g. F. N. Lees, RES, I (1950), 114 ff.; George Saintsbury, CHEL (1932), v. 198.

11 *Discourses*, ed. B. Crick (1970), 124–5, 183.

12 SS 28 (1975), 63–9; MLR, LVII (1962), 321 ff. Cf. E. C. Pettet, 'Coriolanus and the Midland Insurrection of 1607', SS 3 (1950), 34 ff.

13 J. M. Murry, *Discoveries* (1924), 267–8.

14 *Essays in Romantic Literature* (1919), 220–1.

15 Bullough, v. 539.

16 Cf. H. Heuer, SS 10 (1957), 50 ff.

V Last Plays

33 PERICLES

1 Wilkins, however, referred to the performance by Shakespeare's company and used Shakespeare's names for the characters.

2 Cf. Kenneth Muir, *Shakespeare as Collaborator* (1960), 56 ff.

3 *Poems and Fables*, ed. J. Kinsley (1962), 160.

4 Percy Simpson, *Studies in Elizabethan Drama* (1955), 17–22. First noted by Malone.

5 See discussion of Lysimachus' behaviour, p. 257 *post*.

6 R. W. Pease III, in an unpublished dissertation (University of Texas, 1972), 'The Genesis and Authorship of Pericles', suggests that Shakespeare began a play on the subject early in his career and took it up again after a lapse of nearly twenty years.

7 But it is curious, as F. D. Hoeniger points out (New Arden ed., xviii) that in a French MS Apollonius assumes the name of Perillie, and that in a 14th-century German poem Cerimon's assistant is called Filominus.

8 *Confessio*, VIII. 1214 ff., 1704 ff.; (Bullough, VI. 401, 414).

9 J. M. S. Tompkins, RES, III (1952), 323.

10 III. 23.

11 Bullough, VI. 546.

12 *Shakespeare as Collaborator*, 78–9.

13 ibid., 80.

14 op. cit., lxxxi.

15 *Shakespeare as Collaborator*, 82.

16 Cf. Bullough, VI. 535.

17 SS 5 (1952), 44.
18 K. Muir, op. cit., 65 ff.; Bullough, VI. 549 ff. Cf. H. T. Baker, PMLA, XXIII (1908), 100 ff.
19 S. Spiker, SP, XXX (1933), 551 ff.; P. Edwards, SS 5 (1952), 25 ff.
20 ES, XLIV (1963), 401 ff.
21 See n. 17 above.
22 op. cit., xviii–xix.
23 ibid., Appendix B.

34 CYMBELINE

1 *Dr. Johnson on Shakespeare*, ed. W. K. Wimsatt (1969), 136.
2 *Prefaces*, II (1930), 247.
3 R. W. Boodle, NQ (1887), 405; J. M. Nosworthy, New Arden ed., xxiv. I am greatly indebted to Professor Nosworthy's edition.
4 op. cit., xxv–xxvi.
5 Cf. E. Jones, 'Stuart *Cymbeline*', EC, XI (1961), 84–99; J. P. Brockbank, 'History and Histrionics in *Cymbeline*', SS 11 (1958), 42–9; G. Wickham, 'From Tragedy to Tragi-Comedy', SS 26 (1973), 33–48.
6 Wickham, op. cit., 44.
7 Brockbank, op. cit., 48.
8 Appendix to New Arden ed.
9 Spenser, *F.Q.*, II. x. 48.
10 Bullough, VIII. 11.
11 ibid., VIII. 62.
12 ibid., VIII. 403.
13 Arthur C. Kirsch, ELH, XXXIV (1967), 285–306.
14 A. H. Thorndike, *The Influence of Beaumont and Fletcher on Shakespeare* (1901), 152–60.
15 *W.T.*, IV. iv. 127 ff.; *Philaster*, IV. vi. 2 ff.
16 Similarly Auden's plays were influenced by Eliot's and vice-versa.
17 K. Muir and S. O'Loughlin, *The Voyage to Illyria* (1937), 216–17.
18 R. Warwick Bond, *Studia Otiosa* (1938), 69 ff.
19 E. M. W. Tillyard, *Shakespeare's Last Plays* (1938), 68 ff.

35 THE WINTER'S TALE

1 Recent discussions of Shakespeare's use of *Pandosto* are to be found in the following books and articles: New Arden, ed. J. H. P. Pafford (1963); *The Winter's Tale: A Commentary on the Structure* by F. Pyle (1969); Bullough, VIII, 115 ff.; John Lawlor, '*Pandosto* and the Nature of Dramatic Romance', PQ, XLI (1962), 96 ff.; Hallett Smith, *Shakespeare's Romances* (1972), 95 ff.
2 N. Coghill, 'Six Points of Stagecraft', SS 11 (1958), 31 ff.; W. Matchett, 'Some Dramatic Techniques in *W.T.*', SS 22 (1969), 93–107.

F. Pyle, op. cit., 16–17, denies that Hermione is visibly pregnant.

3 ibid., 39.

4 *Shaw on Shakespeare*, ed. E. Wilson (1969), 171.

5 Bullough, VIII. 163–8.

6 S. L. Bethell, *The Winter's Tale: A Study* (1947), 47 ff.

7 ibid., 65.

8 Thomas R. Price in *Shakespeariana* VII (1890); E. Schanzer, 'The Structural Pattern of *W.T.*' Both these and Coghill's article (n. 2 above) are reprinted in K. Muir's *Casebook* (1968).

9 VIII. xix.

10 Bullough, VIII. 203. He also includes a bear episode from *Mucedorus*.

11 E. Honigmann, PQ, XXIV (1955), 27–38.

12 Bullough, VIII. 173.

13 ibid., 176.

14 ibid., 219.

15 Barbara Melchiori, however, *Eng. Misc.* XI (1960), 59–74, discusses traces of incest in the last plays, apparent in *Pericles* and *Pandosto*, faintly in Leontes' admiration for Perdita, and vestigially in Prospero's sermons to Ferdinand about chastity.

16 Honigmann, op. cit.; Bullough, VIII. 133, 222.

17 Bullough, VIII, 229.

18 *Shakespeare's Dramatic Heritage* (1969), 264.

19 See n. 1 above.

20 K. Muir, 'The Ending of *W.T.*' in *The Morality of Art*, ed. D. W. Jefferson (1969), 87 ff.

21 Cf. Coghill, op. cit.

22 See *Casebook*, 32, 45 ff.

23 Bullough, VIII. 171.

24 ibid., VIII. 162.

25 ibid., VIII. 184.

26 E. Honigmann discusses a number of other parallels. Sabie, e.g., says that he wrote the poem to expel 'the acoustomed tediousnes of colde winters nightes'; he and Shakespeare, unlike Greene, have the oracle consulted before the exposure of the babe; and the name given to Fawnia in *Flora's Fortune*, Sabie's sequel, may have suggested the comparison of Perdita to 'Flora/Peering in April's front'.

27 *The Third Party of Conny-Catching* (1592). Bullough, VIII. 217.

28 *The Second Part of Conny-Catching* (1592). Bullough, VIII. 215.

29 ibid., Bullough, VIII. 214.

30 G. Wilson Knight, *The Crown of Life* (1947), 101.

31 IV. iv. 660 ff.

32 J. E. Bullard, W. M. Fox, TLS (1952), 189.

33 op. cit., 104 ff.

34 New Camb. ed., 168.

35 SAB, XVIII (1943), 114–20. Reprinted *Casebook*.

36 The last sentence of the quotation seems to be echoed in Florizel's description of Perdita, IV. iv. 143–6.

37 Ovid, v. 391 ff.; Golding, v. 491 ff.

38 REL, v (1964), 83 ff. Reprinted in *Casebook*. John Lawlor, op. cit., has a comment linking the discussion of art and nature with the final scene of the play: 'It is the actual truth of this play that art restores happiness by becoming nature: the statue moves . . . and descends. In a deeper sense, the truth of the romance-kind, in the theatre, turns directly upon the audience being given not a foresight of events to come – indeed, surprise must play the largest part in the final unfolding – but a foretaste of a happiness which will not finally be withheld . . . The crowning surprise of the romance play, if it is not to be mere *coup de théâtre*, must come as fulfilment of a happiness the audience has begun to hope for in despite of probability'.

36 THE TEMPEST

1 E. K. Chambers, *William Shakespeare*, I. 493.

2 Bullough, VIII. 316.

3 K. M. Lea, *Italian Popular Comedy* (1934), II. 443 ff.; Bullough, VIII. 259 ff.

4 F. Kermode, New Arden ed., lxv, lxix; Bullough, VIII. 245.

5 The suggestion that James Rosier's account of a ceremonial Virginian dance with the cry of 'Baugh, Waugh' influenced the burthen of Ariel's first song seems flimsy. It was not published until 1613. Cf. New Arden ed., xxxiii.

6 Bullough, VIII. 334. Possibly, as Nosworthy suggests, the storm in the *Aeneid* (I. 81 ff.) may have contributed, and also the shipwreck in Juvenal's 12th satire.

7 op. cit., 36.

8 SSt, I. 261 ff.

9 New Arden ed., 143.

10 Robert Graves, *Poetic Unreason* (1925), 208 ff.; Ann Pasternak Slater, SS 25 (1972), 125 ff.

11 J. M. Nosworthy, RES, XXIV (1948), 287 ff.; F. N. Lees, NQ (1954), 147–9.

12 2 Peter, iii. 11.

13 Ed. Kastner and Charlton (1921), 1553–62, 33, 1154–6, 2144–5.

14 Golding (1567), VII. 258 ff. Ovid, *Metam.*, VII. 192 ff.

15 Frances A. Yates, *Theatre of the World* (1969), 171, has argued that Prospero is in some sense a portrait of John Dee. Cf. her *Shakespeare's Last Plays, A New Approach* (1975), *passim*.

37 HENRY VIII

1 *Henslowe's Diary*, ed. R. A. Foakes and Rickert (1961), 318.
2 ibid., 171, 180, 184.
3 New Arden, ed. R. A. Foakes (1957), xxi–xxii.
4 Bullough, IV. 452 ff.
5 ed. cit., 120n.
6 Bullough, IV. 443; Foakes, ed. cit., xxxvi.
7 Holinshed, *Chronicles* (1587), 907; Bullough, IV. 467.
8 S. Schoenbaum, ed. *Henry VIII* (1967), xxxiii; Bullough, IV. 450.
9 DUJ (1948), 48 ff. Reprinted *Shakespeare's Histories*, ed. William A. Armstrong (1972).

INDEX

THE PLAYS (IN CHRONOLOGICAL ORDER)